LATVIA

MINERAL, MINING SECTOR INVESTMENT AND BUSINESS GUIDE

VOLUME 1

STRATEGIC INFORMATION AND REGULATIONS

International Business Publications, USA
Washington DC, USA - Latvia

LATVIA

MINERAL, MINING SECTOR INVESTMENT AND BUSINESS GUIDE

VOLUME 1 STRATEGIC INFORMATION AND REGULATIONS

UPDATED ANNUALLY

We express our sincere appreciation to all government agencies and international organizations which provided information and other materials for this guide

Cover Design: International Business Publications, USA

2015 Edition Updated Reprint International Business Publications, USA
ISBN 1-4330-2932-4

For customer service and information, please contact:

in the USA: **International Business Publications, USA**
P.O.Box 15343, Washington, DC 20003
Phone: (202) 546-2103, Fax: (202) 546-3275.
E-mail: rusric@erols.com

Printed in the USA

LATVIA

MINERAL, MINING SECTOR INVESTMENT AND BUSINESS GUIDE

VOLUME 1

STRATEGIC INFORMATION AND REGULATIONS

TABLE OF CONTENTS

STRATEGIC AND BUSINESS DEVELOPMENT PROFILES

Capital and largest city	Riga 56°57′N 24°6′E56.950°N 24.100°E
Official languages	Latvian[a]
Ethnic groups	62.1% Latvians 26.9% Russians 3.4% Belarusians 2.2% Ukrainians 2.2% Poles 1.2% Lithuanians 0.3% Jews 0.3% Roma 1.4% others / unspecified
Demonym	Latvian
Government	Parliamentary republic
- President	Andris Bērziņš
- Prime Minister	Laimdota Straujuma
- Saeima Speaker	Ināra Mūrniece
Legislature	Saeima
Independence from the Russian Empire	
- Declared[b]	18 November 1918
- Recognized	26 January 1921
- Soviet occupation	5 August 1940
- Nazi German occupation	10 July 1941
- Soviet re-occupation	1944
- Announced independence	4 May 1990
- Restored independence	21 August 1991
- Joined the European Union	1 May 2004
Area	
- Total	64,589 km^2 (124th) 24,938 sq mi
- Water (%)	1.57% (1,014 km^2)
Population	
- 2014 estimate	2,165,165 (148th)
- 2011 census	2,070,371
- Density	34.3/km^2 (166th) 88.9/sq mi
GDP (PPP)	2015 estimate
- Total	$51.058 billion
- Per capita	$25,195
GDP (nominal)	2015 estimate
- Total	$34.118 billion
- Per capita	$16,836
Gini (2013)	35.2 medium
HDI (2013)	0.810

	very high · 48th
Currency	Euro (€) (EUR)
Time zone	EET (UTC+2)
- Summer (DST)	EEST (UTC+3)
Drives on the	right
Calling code	+371
ISO 3166 code	LV
Internet TLD	.lv[c]

LATVIA: STRATEGIC PROFILE

Latvia officially the **Republic of Latvia** (Latvian: *Latvijas Republika*), is a country in the Baltic region of Northern Europe, one of the three Baltic states. It is bordered by Estonia, Lithuania, Russia, and Belarus, as well as a maritime border to the west with Sweden. Latvia has 2,070,371 inhabitants and a territory of 64,589 km^2 (24,938 sq mi). The country has a temperate seasonal climate.

Latvia is a democratic parliamentary republic established in 1918. The capital city is Riga, the European Capital of Culture 2014. Latvian is the official language. Latvia is a unitary state, divided into 118 administrative divisions, of which 109 are municipalities and 9 are cities.

Latvians and Livs are the indigenous people of Latvia. Latvian is an Indo-European language; it and Lithuanian are the only two surviving Baltic languages. Despite foreign rule from the 13th to 20th centuries, the Latvian nation maintained its identity throughout the generations via the language and musical traditions. Latvia and Estonia share a long common history. As a consequence of the Soviet occupation, both countries are home to a large number of ethnic Russians (26.9% in Latvia and 25.5% in Estonia), some of whom are non-citizens. Latvia is historically predominantly Protestant Lutheran, except for the Latgale region in the southeast, which has historically been predominantly Roman Catholic.

The Republic of Latvia was founded on 18 November 1918. However, its *de facto* independence was interrupted at the outset of World War II. In 1940, the country was forcibly incorporated into the Soviet Union, invaded and occupied by Nazi Germany in 1941, and re-occupied by the Soviets in 1944 to form the Latvian SSR for the next fifty years. The peaceful Singing Revolution, starting in 1987, called for Baltic emancipation of Soviet rule. It ended with the dissolution of the Soviet Union in 1991, and Latvia declared the restoration of its de facto independence on 21 August 1991.

Latvia is a member of NATO, the European Union, the United Nations, the Council of Europe, CBSS, the IMF, NB8, NIB, OSCE and WTO. It is currently in the accession process for joining the OECD. For 2013, Latvia is listed 48th on the Human Development Index and as a high income country until 1 July 2014. It used the Latvian lats as its currency until this was replaced by the euro on 1 January 2014

LATVIA: STRATEGIC AND BUSINESS INFORMATION

Background: Along with most of the other small nations of Europe, Latvia shares a history of invasion by a succession of expansionist nations, e.g., Sweden, Poland, Germany, and Russia. After a brief period of independence between the two World Wars, Latvia was annexed by the USSR in 1940 under the Molotov-Ribbentrop Pact. The USSR recaptured Latvia from its German occupiers in 1944. Latvia reestablished its independence in August 1991, a few months prior to the collapse of the Soviet Union; the last Russian troops left in 1994. The status of ethnic Russians, who make up 30% of the population, is an issue of concern to Moscow. Unemployment has become a growing problem and Latvia hopes to receive an invitation to begin EU accession talks by the end of 1999.

GEOGRAPHY

Location: Eastern Europe, bordering the Baltic Sea, between Estonia and Lithuania
Geographic coordinates: 57 00 N, 25 00 E
Map references: Europe

Area:
total: 64,589 sq km
land: 64,589 sq km
water: 0 sq km

Area—comparative: slightly larger than West Virginia
Land boundaries:
total: 1,150 km
border countries: Belarus 141 km, Estonia 339 km, Lithuania 453 km, Russia 217 km
Coastline: 531 km
Maritime claims:
continental shelf: 200-m depth or to the depth of exploitation
exclusive economic zone: 200 nm
territorial sea: 12 nm
Climate: maritime; wet, moderate winters
Terrain: low plain
Elevation extremes:
lowest point: Baltic Sea 0 m
highest point: Gaizinkalns 312 m
Natural resources: minimal; amber, peat, limestone, dolomite
Land use:
arable land: 27%
permanent crops: 0%
permanent pastures: 13%
forests and woodland: 46%
other: 14%
Irrigated land: 160 sq km
Natural hazards: NA

Environment—current issues: air and water pollution because of a lack of waste conversion equipment; Gulf of Riga and Daugava River heavily polluted; contamination of soil and groundwater with chemicals and petroleum products at military bases

Environment—international agreements:
party to: Air Pollution, Biodiversity, Climate Change, Endangered Species, Hazardous Wastes, Ozone Layer Protection, Ship Pollution, Wetlands
signed, but not ratified: Air Pollution-Persistent Organic Pollutants, Climate Change-Kyoto Protocol

PEOPLE

Population: 2,353,874

Age structure:
0-14 years: 18% (male 216,369; female 207,242)
15-64 years: 67% (male 749,396; female 825,988)
65 years and over: 15% (male 114,038; female 240,841)

Population growth rate: -1.25%
Birth rate: 8.1 births/1,000 population
Death rate: 15.82 deaths/1,000 population

Net migration rate: -4.75 migrant(s)/1,000 population

Sex ratio:
at birth: 1.05 male(s)/female
under 15 years: 1.04 male(s)/female
15-64 years: 0.91 male(s)/female
65 years and over: 0.47 male(s)/female *total population:* 0.85 male(s)/female

Infant mortality rate: 17.19 deaths/1,000 live births

Life expectancy at birth:
total population: 67.3 years
male: 61.24 years
female: 73.66 years

The Baltic Sea Area

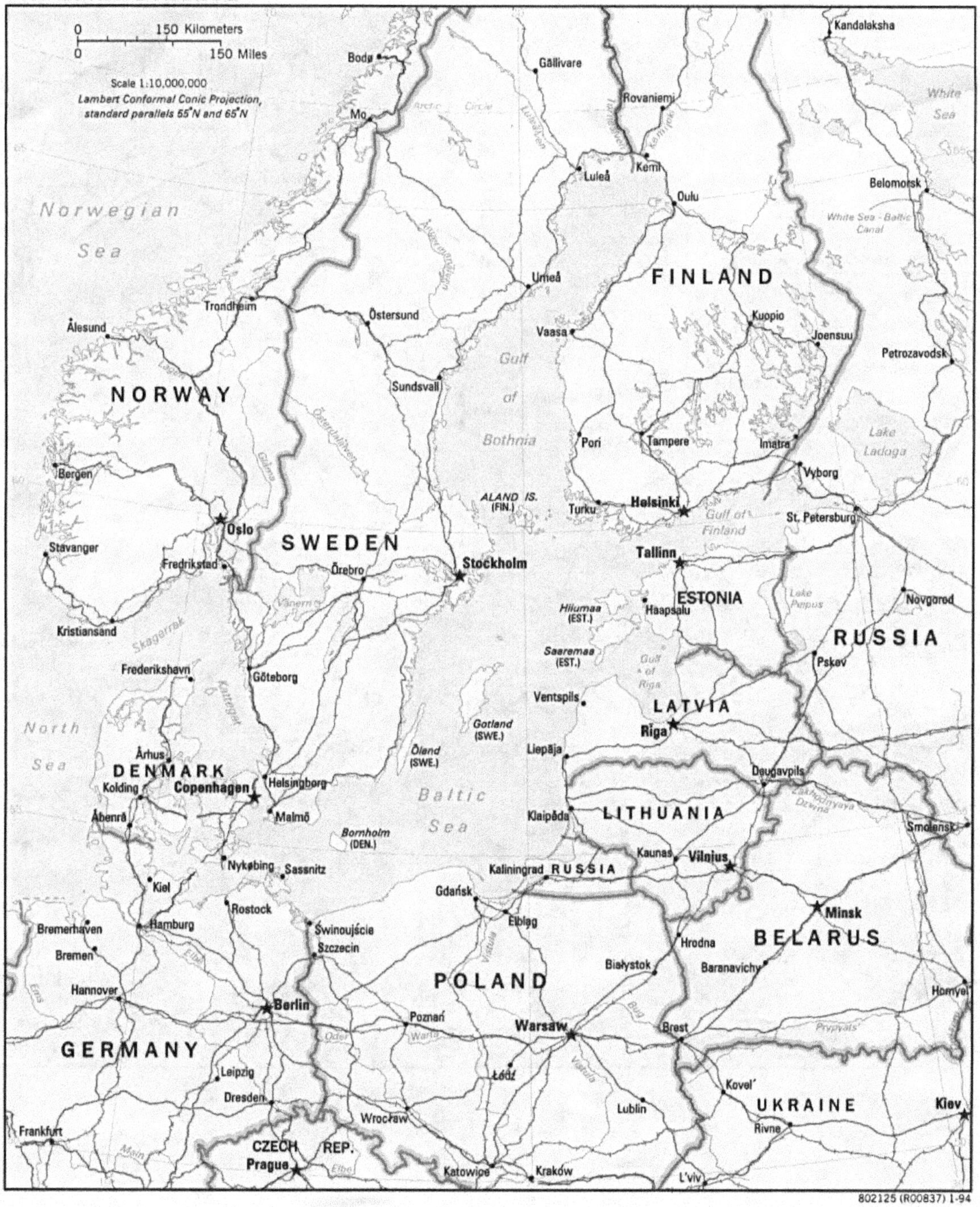

802125 (R00837) 1-94

Base 802618 (R01780) 12-98

Total fertility rate: 1.18 children born/woman

Nationality:
noun: Latvian(s)
adjective: Latvian

Ethnic groups: Latvian 56.5%, Russian 30.4%, Byelorussian 4.3%, Ukrainian 2.8%, Polish 2.6%, other 3.4%
Religions: Lutheran, Roman Catholic, Russian Orthodox
Languages: Lettish (official), Lithuanian, Russian, other

Literacy:
definition: age 15 and over can read and write
total population: 100%
male: 100%
female: 99% (1989 est.)

GOVERNMENT

ECONOMY

COMMUNICATIONS

TRANSPORTATION

MILITARY

TRANSNATIONAL ISSUES

IMPORTANT INFORMATION FOR UNDERSTANDING LATVIA

OFFICIAL NAME: Republic of Latvia

PROFILE

Geography
Area: 64,589 sq. km. (24,938 sq. mi.); slightly larger than West Virginia.
Cities (2009): *Capital*--Riga (713,016). *Other cities*--Daugavpils (104,857); Liepaja (84,747); Jelgava (65,419); Jurmala (55,870); Ventspils (42,963); Rezekne (35,526).
Terrain: Fertile low-lying plains predominate in central Latvia, highlands in Vidzeme and Latgale to the east, and hilly moraine in the western Kurzeme region. Forests cover one-third of the country, with over 3,000 small lakes and numerous bogs. Although there are more than 12,000

rivers in the country, the only major waterways are the Daugava (Dvina) River, which flows through the center of the country and empties into the Gulf of Rîga, and the Gauja River, which rises in the Vidzeme Upland.
Land use: 45.7% forest and woodland, 18.2% arable land, 10.2% meadows and pastures, 22.3% other.
Climate: Temperate, maritime, with four seasons of almost equal length. Average temperatures in January range from -3°C (26.6°F) in the western, coastal town of Liepaja, to -6.7°C (19.9°F) in the inland town of Daugavpils. Mean temperatures for July range from 16.4°C (61.52°F) in Liepaja to 17.0°C (62.6°F) in Daugavpils. Annual precipitation averages 57 centimeters (23 in.).

People
Nationality: *Noun and adjective*--Latvian(s).
Population (2010): 2,248,000
Annual population growth rate (2009): 0.57%. *Birth rate*--9.6/1,000. *Death rate*--13.3/1,000. *Migration rate* (2009)--2,688 immigrants; 7,388 emigrants.
Density (2008): 35.2/1 sq. km (this figure is far lower in the rural parts of Latvia). *Urban dwellers*--67.9%.
Major ethnic groups (2008): Latvians 59.2%, Russians 28.0%, Belarusians 3.7%, Ukrainians 2.5%, Poles 2.4%.
Religions (2003): Lutheran (23.8%), Roman Catholic (18.4%), Russian Orthodox (15.0%).
State language: Latvian. Russian also is spoken by most people.
Education: *Years compulsory*--9. *Enrollment* (2009/2010)--174,177 students in 1,548 schools (including pre-school establishments and vocational education institutions) and 112,555 university students. *Literacy*--99.8%.
Health: *Infant mortality rate*--7.8/1,000 (2009). *Life expectancy* (2009)--68.3 yrs. male, 78.1 yrs. female.
Work force (2009, 1.153 million): *Industry*--15.6%; *trade*--19.6%; *construction*--7.7%; *agriculture/forestry*--9.0%; *transport/communications*--9.9%; *public administration/defense*--7.9%; *education*--8.9%; *health care/social welfare*--5.4%.

Government
Type: Parliamentary democracy.
Constitution: The law "On the Republic of Latvia Status as a State," passed by Parliament on August 21, 1991, provided for the reinstatement of the 1922 constitution.
Branches: *Executive*--President (head of state), elected by Parliament every 4 years; Prime Minister (head of government). *Legislative*--Saeima (100-member parliament). *Judicial*--Supreme Court; Constitutional Court; civil law system.
Administrative regions: 109 districts and 9 cities.
Principal political parties: People's Party--17 seats, Alliance of Political Organizations (Harmony Center)--18 seats, Greens and Farmers--17 seats, New Era--15 Seats, Latvia's First Party and Latvia's Way Union--10 seats, Civic Union--7 seats, Fatherland and Freedom--5 seats, For Human Rights in United Latvia--5 seats, independent--6 seats.
Suffrage: universal adult (18 years of age).

Major sectors of the economy: Retail and wholesale trade (13.8% of GDP); real estate, renting, and business activities (18% of GDP); manufacturing (8.7% of GDP); transport, storage, and communication (10.3% of GDP); construction (5.8% of GDP); financial intermediation (6.1% of GDP).

Trade: *Exports*--$9.423 billion: base metals and articles of base metal 16.7%; wood and articles of wood 16.6%; machinery and mechanical appliances; electrical equipment 12.5%; products of the chemical or allied industries 8.4%; prepared foodstuffs; beverages, spirits and vinegar; tobacco 7.9%; textiles and textile articles 5.5%, vegetable products 5.1%. *Major markets*--

Lithuania 16.7%, Estonia 14%, Russia 10%, Germany 8.1%, Sweden 6.6%, Denmark 4.6%. *Imports*--$16.015 billion: machinery and mechanical appliances; electrical equipment 18.3%; mineral products 15.6%; vehicles, aircraft, vessels and associated transport equipment 10.7%; base metals and articles of base metal 10.3%; products of the chemical or allied industries 9.7%; prepared foodstuffs; beverages, spirits and vinegar; tobacco 6.8%; plastics and articles thereof; rubber and articles thereof 4.7%; textiles and textile articles 4.0%. *Partners*--Lithuania 16.5%, Germany 13%, Russia 10.6%, Poland 7.2%, Estonia 7.1%, Sweden 4.4%, Finland 4.4%.

PEOPLE

The behavior of most Latvians reflects the strong cultural and religious influences of centuries-long Germanic and Scandinavian colonization and settlement. They are viewed as self-reliant, independent, persistent, and reserved. Eastern Latvia (Latgale) retains a strong Polish and Russian cultural and linguistic influence. This highly literate society places strong emphasis upon education, which is free and compulsory until age 16. The majority of Latvians belong to the Evangelical Lutheran Church; a sizable minority is Russian Orthodox, and Eastern Latvia is predominantly Roman Catholic.

Historically, Latvia has always had fairly large Russian, Jewish, German, and Polish minorities, but traumatic wartime events, postwar emigration, deportations, and Soviet Russification policies from 1939 to 1989 reduced the percentage of ethnic Latvians in Latvia from 73% to 52%. In an attempt to preserve the Latvian language and prevent ethnic Latvians from becoming a minority in their own country, Latvia enacted language, education, and citizenship laws which require a working proficiency in the Latvian language in order to become a citizen. Such legislation has caused concern among many non-citizen resident Russians, despite Latvian legal guarantees of universal human and civil rights regardless of citizenship.

Written with the Latin alphabet, Latvian is the language of the Latvian people and the official language of the country. It is an inflective language with several analytical forms, three dialects, and German syntactical influence. The oldest known examples of written Latvian are from a 1585 catechism. Latvians and Lithuanians are the only surviving direct descendents of the Baltic peoples who speak languages of the Indo-European family. While Latvia was a member of the U.S.S.R., Russian was the official language, so many Latvians also speak Russian, and the resident Slavic populace generally speaks Russian as a first language.

HISTORY

By the 10th century, the area that is today Latvia was inhabited by several Baltic tribes who had formed their own local governments. In 1054, German sailors who shipwrecked on the Daugava River inhabited the area, which initiated a period of increasing Germanic influence. The Germans named the territory Livonia. In 1201, Riga, the current capital of Latvia, was founded by the Germanic Bishop Alberth of Livonia; the city joined the Hanseatic League in 1285 and began to form important cultural and economic relationships with the rest of Europe. However, the new German nobility enserfed the indigenous people and accorded them only limited trading and property rights.

Subsequent wars and treaties led to Livonia's partition and colonization for centuries. In 1721 Russia took control over the Latvian territories as a result of its victory over Sweden in the Great Northern War. During this time there was little sense of a Latvian national identity, as both serfdom and institutional controls to migration and social mobility limited the boundaries of the indigenous people's intellectual and social geography. However, in the 1860s, the Young Latvian Movement was formed in order to promote the indigenous language against Russification policies and to publicize and counteract the socioeconomic oppression of Latvians, 60% of whom belonged to the landless, urban class. This growing proletariat became fertile ground for the ideas of western European socialism and supported the creation in 1903 of the Latvian Social

Democratic Union (LSDU), which continued to champion national interests and Latvia's national self-determination, especially during the failed 1905 Revolution in Russia.

The onset of World War I brought German occupation of the western coastal province of Kurzeme, which Latvians heroically countered with several regiments of riflemen commanded by Czarist generals. The military campaign generally increased Latvian and LSDU support for the Bolsheviks' successful October Revolution in 1917, in the hopes of a "free Latvia within free Russia." These circumstances led to the formation of the Soviet "Iskolat Republic" in the unoccupied section of Latvia. In opposition to this government and to the landed barons' German sympathies stood the Latvian Provisional National Council and the Riga Democratic Bloc. These and other political parties formed the Latvian People's Council, which on November 18, 1918 declared Latvia's independence and formed an army. The new Latvian Army won a decisive battle over the German forces and consolidated that success against Red Army forces on the eastern Latgale front. These developments led to the dissolution of the Soviet Latvian government on January 13, 1920 and to a peace treaty between Latvia and Soviet Russia on August 11 later that year. On September 22, 1921, an independent Latvia was admitted to the League of Nations.

The government, headed by Prime Minister Ulmanis, declared a democratic, parliamentary republic. It recognized Latvian as the official language, granted cultural autonomy to the country's sizeable minorities, and introduced an electoral system into the Latvian constitution, which was adopted in 1922. The ensuing decade witnessed sweeping economic reform, as the war had devastated Latvian agriculture, and most Russian factories had been evacuated to Russia. However, economic depression heightened political turmoil, and, on May 15, 1934, the Prime Minister dismissed the Parliament, banned outspoken and left-wing political parties, and tightened authoritarian state control over Latvian social life and the economy.

The German-Soviet Nonaggression Pact of 1939 steadily forced Latvia under Soviet influence, culminating in Latvia's annexation by the Soviet Union on August 5, 1940. On June 14 of the following year, 15,000 Latvian citizens were forcibly deported and a large number of army officers shot. The subsequent German occupation witnessed the mobilization of many Latvians into Waffen SS legions, while some Latvians joined the Red Army and formed resistance groups, and others fled to the West and East.

An estimated 70,000, or 89.5%, of Latvian Jews were killed in Latvia under Nazi occupation. Up to one-third of Latvia's pre-war population (approximately 630,000 residents) was lost between 1940 and 1954 due to the Holocaust and the Soviet and Nazi occupations.

After World War II, the U.S.S.R. subjected the Latvian republic to a social and economic reorganization which rapidly changed the rural economy to one based on heavy industry, transformed the predominantly Latvian population into a more multiethnic populace, and converted the peasant class into a fully urbanized industrial worker class. As part of the goal to more fully integrate Latvia into the Soviet Union, Stalin deported another 42,000 Latvians and continued to promote the policy of encouraging Soviet immigration to Latvia.

In July 1989, following the dramatic events in East Germany, the Latvian Supreme Soviet adopted a "Declaration of Sovereignty" and amended the Constitution to assert the supremacy of its laws over those of the U.S.S.R. Candidates from the pro-independence party Latvian Popular Front gained a two-thirds majority in the Supreme Council in the March 1990 democratic elections. On May 4, the Council declared its intention to restore full Latvian independence after a "transitional" period; three days later, a Latvian was chosen Prime Minister. Soviet political and military forces tried unsuccessfully to overthrow the Latvian Government. On August 21, 1991, Latvia claimed de facto independence. International recognition, including that of the U.S.S.R., followed. The United States, which had never recognized Latvia's forcible annexation by the U.S.S.R. and continued to accredit a Latvian Ambassador in Washington, recognized Latvia's renewed independence on September 2. In 2007, the United States and Latvia celebrated 85 years of continuous diplomatic relations.

Since regaining its independence, Latvia has rapidly moved away from the political-economic structures and socio-cultural patterns which underlay the Soviet Union. Latvia has maintained and strengthened the democratic, parliamentary republic that it revived in 1990. Through a U.S. initiative, on April 30, 1994, Latvia and Russia signed a troop withdrawal agreement; Russia withdrew the bulk of its troops by August 31 of that year. Except for some large state-owned utilities, Latvia has privatized most sectors of its economy, which enjoyed years of rapid development before slowing down in 2007. By the end of 2008, the Latvian economy was facing a looming recession.

Internationally, Latvia has accomplished a great deal. It became a member of the United Nations (UN) on September 18, 1991, and is a signatory to a number of UN organizations and other international agreements, including the International Civil Aviation Organization (ICAO), the International Monetary Fund (IMF), and the World Bank. It is also a member of the Organization on Security and Cooperation in Europe (OSCE) and officially became a member of the North Atlantic Treaty Organization (NATO) on March 29, 2004. On May 1, 2004 Latvia joined the European Union (EU).

Since 2004, Latvia has emerged as a significant player in foreign affairs, standing out as a successful post-Soviet transition society. Strong memories of occupation and oppression motivate Latvia to reach out to countries struggling to move beyond authoritarian politics and state-controlled economies. It has worked closely with the U.S. and the EU to promote democracy in Ukraine, Belarus, Moldova, and Georgia. Latvia also supports pro-market, pro-free-trade policies in European and international organizations. It was the European Union's fastest-growing economy in 2004 through 2006.

Latvia has developed a policy of international security cooperation through participation in crisis management and peacekeeping operations. In 2006, Latvia deployed over 10% of its active duty military to support UN, NATO, and coalition military operations. That percentage is well above the European average in terms of per capita contributions. In 2008, Latvia increased its participation in the NATO International Security Assistance Force (ISAF) in Afghanistan to 170 soldiers and planned to maintain the number in 2009, despite its economic challenges. While Latvia was active in the Balkans, budget cuts forced the end of its operations there in 2009. Latvia supported the NATO mission in Kosovo with peacekeepers, and the European Union Force (EUFOR) mission in Bosnia with liaison officers. Latvia also contributed to the EU and OSCE missions to Georgia. In November 2006, Latvia hosted a NATO Summit in its capital, Riga, and in May 2010, it hosted a NATO Parliamentary Assembly.

GOVERNMENT AND POLITICAL CONDITIONS

The highest organ of state authority in Latvia is the Saeima, a unicameral legislative body of 100 members who are elected by direct popular vote to serve four-year terms. The Saeima initiates and approves legislation sponsored by the Prime Minister. The Prime Minister is the head of government and has full responsibility and control over the Cabinet. The President, who is elected by the Saeima every four years, holds a primarily ceremonial role as head of state, though the President must sign each law into force and has the power to return laws to the Saeima twice for review and revision. The President also has the power to call for a referendum on legislation that the Saeima refuses to change after twice being sent back.

In the autumn of 1991 Latvia re-implemented significant portions of its 1922 constitution, and in the spring of 1993 the government took a census to determine eligibility for citizenship. Latvia finalized a citizenship and naturalization law in the summer of 1994, which was further liberalized in 1998. By law, those who were Latvian citizens in 1940 and their descendants (regardless of ethnicity) could claim citizenship. Forty-one percent of Latvia's population is ethnically non-Latvian, yet almost three-fourths of all residents are citizens of Latvia. Requirements for naturalization include a conversational knowledge of Latvian, a loyalty oath, renunciation of former citizenship, 5 years of residency in Latvia, and a basic knowledge of Latvian history. Dual citizenship is allowed for those who were forced to leave Latvia during the Soviet occupation and adopted another citizenship. Convicted criminals, agents of Soviet intelligence services, and certain other groups are excluded from becoming citizens.

On March 19, 1991 the Supreme Council passed a law explicitly guaranteeing "equal rights to all nationalities and ethnic groups" and "to all permanent residents in the Republic regardless of their nationality, equal rights to work and wages." In addition, the law prohibits "any activity directed toward nationality discrimination or the promotion of national superiority or hatred."

In the June 5-6, 1993 elections, in which more than 90% of the electorate participated, eight of Latvia's 23 registered political parties passed the 5% threshold to enter parliament. The centrist party Latvia's Way received a 33% plurality of votes and joined the Farmer's Union to head a center-right-wing coalition government.

The September 30-October 1, 1995 elections resulted in a deeply fragmented parliament with nine parties represented and the largest party commanding only 18 of 100 seats. Attempts to form right-of-center and leftist governments failed; seven weeks after the election, a broad but fractious coalition government of six of the nine parties was voted into office under Prime Minister Andris Skele, a popular, nonpartisan businessman.

In the 1998 elections, the Latvian party structure began to consolidate, with only six parties obtaining seats in the Saeima. Andris Skele's newly formed People's Party garnered a plurality with 24 seats. Though the election represented a victory for the center-right, personality conflicts and scandals within the two largest right-of-center parties--Latvia's Way and the People's Party--prevented stable coalitions from forming. Two shaky governments quickly collapsed in less than a year. In May 2000, a compromise candidate was found in the Latvia's Way mayor of Riga, Andris Berzins. His four-party coalition lasted until parliamentary elections in October 2002. Those elections left Latvia's Way, for the first time since 1993, with no seats in parliament. The New Era Party, which ran on an anti-corruption platform, gained the most seats and formed a four-party coalition government until the abrupt resignation of the Prime Minister in February 2004 over issues relating to personalities and management of the ruling coalition.

In 1999, the Saeima elected Vaira Vike-Freiberga, a compromise candidate with no party affiliation, to the presidency. Though born in Riga in 1937, she settled in Canada during the years of the Soviet occupation, becoming a well-respected academic on the subject of Latvian culture and psychology. Following her election, she became one of the most popular political figures in Latvia. She was overwhelmingly re-elected by parliament for another four-year term in June 2003. She was also credited with bringing Latvia to the world's stage and serving as an important check on the ruling coalitions.

With the tacit support of leftist parties, a minority government led by Greens and Farmers Union leader Indulis Emsis took office on March 9, 2004. The new government focused on smoothing Latvia's entry into NATO and the European Union, which took place in the first half of 2004. The government collapsed on October 28, 2004 after parliament voted against the 2005 budget. A new coalition government, led by Prime Minister Aigars Kalvitis, took office on December 2, 2004 and was re-elected on October 7, 2006. Those election results marked the first time that an incumbent administration won re-election in the history of independent Latvia.

In July 2007, the Saeima elected Valdis Zatlers, another candidate with no political affiliation, to the presidency. An orthopedic surgeon by trade, Zatlers was the director of the Latvian Traumatology and Orthopedics Center until his election and had no prior political experience. His start was clouded by charges that he had accepted supplemental payments for medical services on which he did not pay taxes. Zatlers complied with investigations which in the end concluded he had committed no breaches of law.

In December 2007, Prime Minister Kalvitis resigned after his government came under intense criticism for attempting to dismiss the head of the anti-corruption bureau. President Zatlers nominated veteran politician Ivars Godmanis to form a new government. Godmanis' governing coalition consisted of the same four center-right parties that made up the previous government.

On December 23, 2008, the International Monetary Fund approved a $2.35 billion rescue loan for Latvia. The loan was part of a $10.5 billion bailout that included additional funding from the European Commission (EC), World Bank, and the Scandinavian countries. The IMF funds were intended to "stem the loss of bank deposits and international reserves and to take fiscal measures to limit the widening of the budget deficit." On January 13, 2009, the worsening economic crisis sparked an unprecedented riot when, after a political rally to protest government actions on the economy, hundreds of disgruntled citizens took to the streets of Riga, with a smaller group smashing police cars and windows. On February 20, Prime Minister Godmanis resigned amidst growing public distrust and tension over Latvia's economic decline.

On February 26, President Zatlers nominated European Parliament member and former Finance Minister Valdis Dombrovskis (New Era) to be Prime Minister. Dombrovskis took office on March 13, 2009, when the Saeima approved his cabinet. For the next year his coalition was made up of five center-right parties; three of the previous four coalition partners, plus New Era and Civic Union. After assuming office, Dombrovskis announced that the country was "on the verge of bankruptcy" and that major budget cuts would have to be made to secure financial stability. Accordingly, Latvia implemented $1 billion in budget cuts in 2009 and another $1 billion in cuts in 2010. In March 2010, the largest member of the coalition pulled out due to disputes over how to handle Latvia's economic crisis, leaving Latvia with a minority government.

The next parliamentary election is scheduled to take place in October 2010.

Latvia's flag consists of two horizontal, maroon bands of equal width, divided by a white stripe one-half the width. The national holiday is November 18, Independence Day, which marks Latvia's 1918 independence.

Principal Government Officials

Position	Name	Party	Dates
Prime Minister	Laimdota Straujuma	Unity	5 November 2014 – present day
Minister for Defence	Raimonds Vējonis	Union of Greens and Farmers	5 November 2014 – present day
Minister for Foreign Affairs	Edgars Rinkēvičs	Unity	5 November 2014 – present day
Minister for Economics	Dana Reizniece-Ozola	Union of Greens and Farmers	5 November 2014 – present day
Minister for Finance	Jānis Reirs	Unity	5 November 2014 –

			present day
Minister for the Interior	Rihards Kozlovskis	Unity	5 November 2014 – present day
Minister for Education and Science	Mārīte Seile	Independent	5 November 2014 – present day
Minister for Culture	Dace Melbārde	National Alliance	5 November 2014 – present day
Minister for Welfare	Uldis Augulis	Union of Greens and Farmers	5 November 2014 – present day
Minister for Environmental Protection and Regional Development	Kaspars Gerhards	National Alliance	5 November 2014 – present day
Minister for Transport	Anrijs Matīss	Unity	5 November 2014 – present day
Minister for Justice	Dzintars Rasnačs	National Alliance	5 November 2014 – present day
Minister for Health	Guntis Belēvičs	Union of Greens and Farmers	5 November 2014 – present day
Minister for Agriculture	Jānis Dūklavs	Union of Greens and Farmers	5 November 2014 – present day

Latvia maintains an embassy in the United States at 2306 Massachusetts Ave NW, Washington DC 20008 [tel: (202) 328-2840].

ECONOMY

Currency	€ 1 Euro (EUR) = 100 cent
Fiscal year	Calendar year
Trade organisations	EU, WTO, Nordic Investment Bank
	Statistics
GDP	▲$42,471 billion (PPP, 2014 est.)
GDP rank	52th (PPP, 2013 by IMF.)
GDP growth	▲4.6% (Real est.)
GDP per capita	▲$20,291 (PPP, 2014 est.)
GDP by sector	agriculture: 4.4%; industry: 26.3%; services: 69.3% (2012 est.)
Inflation (CPI)	▼0,6% (CPI, 2014)
Gini coefficient	35.2 (2013)
Labour force	884 600 employed (2014)
Labour force by occupation	agriculture: 8.8%; industry: 24.0%; services: 67.2% (2010 est.)
Unemployment	▲9.1% (February 2015)
Average gross salary	765 €, monthly (2014)
Average net salary	535 €, monthly (2014)
Main industries	processed foods, processed wood products, textiles, processed metals, pharmaceuticals, railroad cars, synthetic fibers, electronics
Ease-of-doing-business rank	25th[2]
	External
Exports	▲€ 10.2287 billion (2014)
Export goods	food products, wood and wood products, metals, machinery and equipment, textiles
Main export partners	Russia 18.3% Lithuania 15.0% Estonia 12.0%

	Germany 7.2% Poland 5.6% Sweden 4.8%
Imports	▲$15.92 billion (2012 est.)
Import goods	machinery and equipment, consumer goods, chemicals, fuels, vehicles
Main import partners	Lithuania 18.9% Germany 11.5% Russia 9.3% Poland 8.1% Estonia 7.5% Italy 4.6% Finland 4.4%
FDI stock	▲$13.38 billion
Gross external debt	▼$35.34 billion
Public finances	
Public debt	▼35.0% of GDP (2015 est.)
Revenues	€7 253 942 233 (2015 est.)
Expenses	€7 471 315 445 (2015 est.)
Economic aid	recipient: $96.2 million
Credit rating	Standard & Poor's: A- (Domestic) A- (Foreign) AAA (T&C Assessment) Outlook: Stable Moody's: Baa3 Outlook: Positive Fitch: BBB Outlook: Positive
Foreign reserves	US$8.961 billion

The **economy of Latvia** is an open economy in Northern Europe and is part of the European Union's (EU) single market. Latvia is a member of the World Trade Organization (WTO) since 1999, a member of the European Union since 2004, and of the Eurozone since 2014. Latvia is ranked the 21st in the world by the Ease of Doing Business Index prepared by the World Bank Group, According to the Human Development Report 2011, Latvia belongs to the group of very high human development countries. Due to its geographical location, transit services are highly developed, along with timber and wood-processing, agriculture and food products, and manufacturing of machinery and electronic devices.

Latvia's economy has had rapid GDP growth of more than 10% per year during 2006–07, but entered a severe recession in 2009 as a result of an unsustainable current account deficit, collapse of the real estate market, and large debt exposure amid the softening world economy. Triggered by the collapse of the second largest bank, GDP decreased by almost 18% in 2009, and the European Union, the International Monetary Fund, and other international donors provided substantial financial assistance to Latvia as part of an agreement to defend the currency's peg to the euro in exchange for the government's commitment to stringent austerity measures. In 2011 Latvia achieved GDP grew by 5.5% and thus Latvia again was among the fastest growing economies in the European Union. The IMF/EU program successfully concluded in December 2011.

Privatization is mostly complete, except for some of the large state-owned utilities. Export growth contributed to the economic recovery, however the bulk of the country's economic activity is in the services sector. In May 2013, the OECD decided to open accession negotiations with Latvia

For centuries under Hanseatic and German influence and then during its inter-war independence, Latvia used its geographic location as an important East-West commercial and trading center. Industry served local markets, while timber, paper, and agricultural products supplied Latvia's main exports. The years of Soviet occupation tended to integrate Latvia's economy into the U.S.S.R. in order to serve that empire's large internal industrial needs. Since reestablishing its independence, Latvia has proceeded with market-oriented reforms. Its freely traded currency, the Lat, was introduced in 1993 and has held steady or appreciated against major world currencies. Before late 2007, Latvia's economic performance was among the best of the EU accession countries. Real per capita GDP had more than doubled compared to its 1995 level; the economy was expanding rapidly, with GDP growth hitting 12.2% in 2006. In 2008, however, unwinding domestic imbalances combined with adverse external factors to bring a halt to Latvia's economic growth. Its GDP shrank by 4.6% in 2008 and by a staggering 18% (year on year) in 2009.

The recession is causing widespread unemployment, especially in Latvia's eastern regions. The harmonized unemployment rate in September 2009 reached 19.7%. Latvia registered some of the highest inflation rates in the EU in recent years, which delayed prospects of introducing the Euro currency. As of November 2009, Latvia was experiencing deflation as a result of rapidly falling demand. In response to the worsening macroeconomic situation, in late December 2008 Latvia signed a 27-month Stand-by Arrangement with the IMF, the EC, and several other partners for an assistance package totaling approximately EUR 7.5 billion ($10.5 billion). The program is centered on restoring competitiveness through economic adjustment, fiscal prudence, and factor price deflation. At the same time, Latvia's current account balance has improved markedly. From 2006 through 2008, it experienced a deficit ranging from 12.6% to 22.5% of GDP, but since early 2009 Latvia's exports have outnumbered its imports.

Independence forced Latvia into a precarious position regarding its energy supply. With the exception of peat and timber, Latvia had no significant domestic energy resources and received 93% of its imported energy from Soviet republics. Latvia has sought ways to diversify its energy sources and to increase energy conservation. In August 2001, the Kegums hydroelectric power plant was reopened, contributing to Latvia's ability to supply 25% of its energy that year. On May 6, 2009, state-owned energy utility Latvenergo opened the first reconstructed power unit of the Riga thermal power station No 2. The reconstructed power plant provides 600 megawatts (Mw) electrical and 1,123 Mw thermal capacity. The new power unit (420 Mw) has increased the power efficiency of the plant and is supposed to decrease Latvia's power supply dependency by 30%. The expectations are that the new power unit will reduce the import of electricity by 1,400 gigawatt hours per year on average. Latvia is also looking to regional cooperation arrangements to diversify its energy supplies. With the other Baltic states, it plans to create an electricity network able to operate independently of its Russian counterpart. It is planning major infrastructure projects to provide energy supplies via Scandinavia, and it is working with Estonia, Lithuania, and Poland to build a new nuclear power station in Lithuania.

All of Latvia's previously state-owned small and medium enterprises have been privatized, leaving in state hands the electric utility, the Latvian railway company, and the Latvian postal system, as well as state shares in several politically sensitive concerns. Despite the lack of transparency of the early stages of the privatization process and certain difficulties in privatization of some of the largest companies, Latvian privatization efforts have led to the development of a dynamic and prosperous private sector, which accounts for approximately 70% of the country's GDP.

In the last few years, Latvia has implemented many positive reforms in the business sphere (ranking 27th worldwide on the ease of doing business there, according to the World Bank Doing Business 2010 report). Most reforms deal with licensing, taxes, and business closures. In the 2005/2006 period, Latvia made it easier for businesses to comply with building requirements and reduced the number of licenses and permits required. In addition, Latvia launched an electronic tax filing system and improved the regulation of bankruptcy administrators in order to reduce corruption.

In response to the economic crisis, foreign direct investment (FDI) flows are drying up, but FDI stock remains relatively high as a result of a high level of Western and Eastern investment following Latvia's accession to the EU. Representing 4.2% of Latvia's total foreign direct investment, the U.S. FDI stock in Latvia stood at $461 million at the end of the second quarter of 2008, according to the Bank of Latvia's figures. In 2008, U.S. goods and services accounted for 1% of Latvia's total imports, while exports to the United States accounted for 1.6% of Latvia's total exports. Latvia has been a member of the World Trade Organization since 1999. Latvia and the United States have signed treaties on investment, trade, intellectual property protection, and avoidance of double taxation.

In the long term, Latvia's return to economic growth will depend on comprehensive structural reforms, economic adjustment and improvements to the business environment, particularly the drive to reduce corruption and strengthen the rule of law, and on Latvia's ability to use the opportunities presented by EU membership.

DEFENSE

Latvia's defense concept is based upon four basic pillars: collective defense as a member of NATO, professionalization of the armed forces, support and coordination with civil society, and international military cooperation. The armed forces consist of the regular forces, a home guard called "Zemessardze", and the Reserve. The regular forces are composed of the land forces, an air force focused on air surveillance and search and rescue, and naval forces focused on coastal surveillance, assertion of sovereignty, mine countermeasures, search and rescue, and environmental protection. Additionally, there are some other minor units adding to the total armed forces personnel of 5,000. Zemessardze is an autonomous 10,600-man-strong volunteer reserve organization which performs traditional national-guard duties such as crisis response and support for military operations. The Latvian National Armed Forces became fully professional in November 2006. Defense spending has risen in recent years, and the government has committed 2% of its GDP to defense spending through 2013. However, in view of current economic problems, spending in the military sector is unlikely to reach that goal.

FOREIGN RELATIONS

After regaining its independence, Latvia began to work at reintegrating into the West. In 1991, Latvia joined the Organization on Security and Cooperation in Europe (OSCE) and became a member of the United Nations (UN). It is party to a number of UN organizations as well as other international agreements including the International Civil Aviation Organization (ICAO), the International Monetary Fund (IMF), and the World Bank. Since 2004, Latvia has been an active member of the North Atlantic Treaty Organization (NATO) and the European Union (EU).

Latvia has emerged as a significant international player, courageously supporting peace and democracy world-wide. Per capita, it is one of the largest contributors to international military operations. It has deployed troops to Iraq, Afghanistan, Georgia, and the Balkans. It also works closely with the U.S. and the EU to support and promote democracy in the former Soviet Union states of Ukraine, Belarus, Moldova, and Georgia. A testament to the close relationship between the U.S. and Latvia is the fact that President George W. Bush visited the country twice, the second time to attend the NATO Summit held in Riga on November 28-29, 2006.

Russia has expressed concern over how Latvia's language and naturalization laws affect Latvia's Russian-speaking population. Russians comprised 28% of the population in 2008. In turn, Latvia is interested in the welfare of ethnic Latvians still residing in Russia. Latvia and Russia signed a border treaty agreement in March 2007. It was ratified by both sides and went into effect at the end of 2007.

Latvia maintains embassies in the United States, Austria, Azerbaijan, Belarus, Belgium, Canada, the People's Republic of China, the Czech Republic, Denmark, Egypt, Estonia, Finland, France, Germany, Georgia, Greece, Hungary, Ireland, Israel, Italy, Japan, Kazakhstan, Lithuania, the Netherlands, Norway, Poland, Portugal, Russia, Slovenia, Spain, Sweden, Turkey, Ukraine, the United Kingdom, and Uzbekistan. It also operates missions to the United Nations in New York City and Geneva, the European Council, the European Union, the Chemical Weapons Nonproliferation Organization, NATO, the Organization for Security and Cooperation in Europe, the World Trade Organization, UNESCO, and the UN Council on Food and Agriculture.

Latvia has a Consulate General in Russia; Consulates in Belarus and Russia; Honorary Consulates General in Brazil, Denmark, Italy, Cyprus, Lebanon, Norway, Sri Lanka, Turkey, and Venezuela; and Honorary Consulates in USA, Argentina, Armenia, Australia, Austria,, Belgium, Bulgaria, Canada, Chile, Columbia, Croatia, Cyprus, Denmark, Dominican Republic, Egypt, Finland, France, Georgia, Germany, Greece, Hong Kong, Iceland, India, Indonesia Ireland, Israel, Italy, Jamaica, Japan, Jordan, Kazakhstan, Kyrgyzstan, Luxembourg, Malta, Morocco, Macedonia, Mexico, Moldova, the Netherlands, New Zealand, Norway, Pakistan, Panama, Peru, Philippines, Poland, Portugal, San Marino, South Africa, South Korea, Spain, Syria, Sweden, Switzerland, Thailand, Tunisia, Turkey, Ukraine, and the United Kingdom.

U.S.-LATVIAN RELATIONS

The United States established diplomatic relations with Latvia on July 28, 1922. The U.S. Legation in Riga was officially established on November 13, 1922 and served as the headquarters for U.S. representation in the Baltics during the interwar era. The Soviet invasion forced the closure of the legation on September 5, 1940, but Latvian representation in the United States has continued uninterrupted since 1922. The United States never recognized the forcible incorporation of Latvia into the U.S.S.R. and views the present Government of Latvia as a legal continuation of the interwar republic.

Latvia and the United States have signed treaties on investment, trade, intellectual property protection, extradition, mutual legal assistance, and avoidance of double taxation. Latvia has enjoyed most-favored-nation treatment with the United States since December 1991. In 2008, Latvia joined the visa waiver program.

Principal U.S. Embassy Officials

Chargé d'Affaires a.i. Sharon Hudson-Dean

Sharon Hudson-Dean is a career American diplomat currently serving as Chargé d'Affaires, a.i. at the U.S. Embassy in Riga, Latvia. From 2010-2013, Ms. Hudson-Dean was the Counselor for Public Affairs at the U.S. Embassy in Harare, Zimbabwe,

Deputy Chief of Mission--Bruce Rogers
Political/Economic Counselor--Brian Phipps
Management Counselor--Eric Kettner
Consul--Timothy Buckley
Public Affairs Chief--Ryan Roberts

Defense Attaché--Lt. Col. Colin Smith

The U.S. Embassy in Latvia is located at Raina Boulevard 7, Riga [tel. (371) 6703-6200].

TRAVEL AND BUSINESS INFORMATION
The U.S. Department of State's Consular Information Program advises Americans traveling and residing abroad through Country Specific Information, Travel Alerts, and Travel Warnings. **Country Specific Information** exists for all countries and includes information on entry and exit requirements, currency regulations, health conditions, safety and security, crime, political disturbances, and the addresses of the U.S. embassies and consulates abroad. **Travel Alerts** are issued to disseminate information quickly about terrorist threats and other relatively short-term conditions overseas that pose significant risks to the security of American travelers. **Travel Warnings** are issued when the State Department recommends that Americans avoid travel to a certain country because the situation is dangerous or unstable.

For the latest security information, Americans living and traveling abroad should regularly monitor the Department's Bureau of Consular Affairs Internet web site at http://www.travel.state.gov, where the current Worldwide Caution, Travel Alerts, and Travel Warnings can be found. Consular Affairs Publications, which contain information on obtaining passports and planning a safe trip abroad, are also available at http://www.travel.state.gov. For additional information on international travel, see http://www.usa.gov/Citizen/Topics/Travel/International.shtml.

The Department of State encourages all U.S. citizens traveling or residing abroad to register via the State Department's travel registration website or at the nearest U.S. embassy or consulate abroad. Registration will make your presence and whereabouts known in case it is necessary to contact you in an emergency and will enable you to receive up-to-date information on security conditions.

Emergency information concerning Americans traveling abroad may be obtained by calling 1-888-407-4747 toll free in the U.S. and Canada or the regular toll line 1-202-501-4444 for callers outside the U.S. and Canada.

The National Passport Information Center (NPIC) is the U.S. Department of State's single, centralized public contact center for U.S. passport information. Telephone: 1-877-4-USA-PPT (1-877-487-2778); TDD/TTY: 1-888-874-7793. Passport information is available 24 hours, 7 days a week. You may speak with a representative Monday-Friday, 8 a.m. to 10 p.m., Eastern Time, excluding federal holidays.

LATVIA MINING SECTOR: STRATEGIC INFORMATION

GEOLOGICAL AND NATURAL RESOURCES

LATVIA

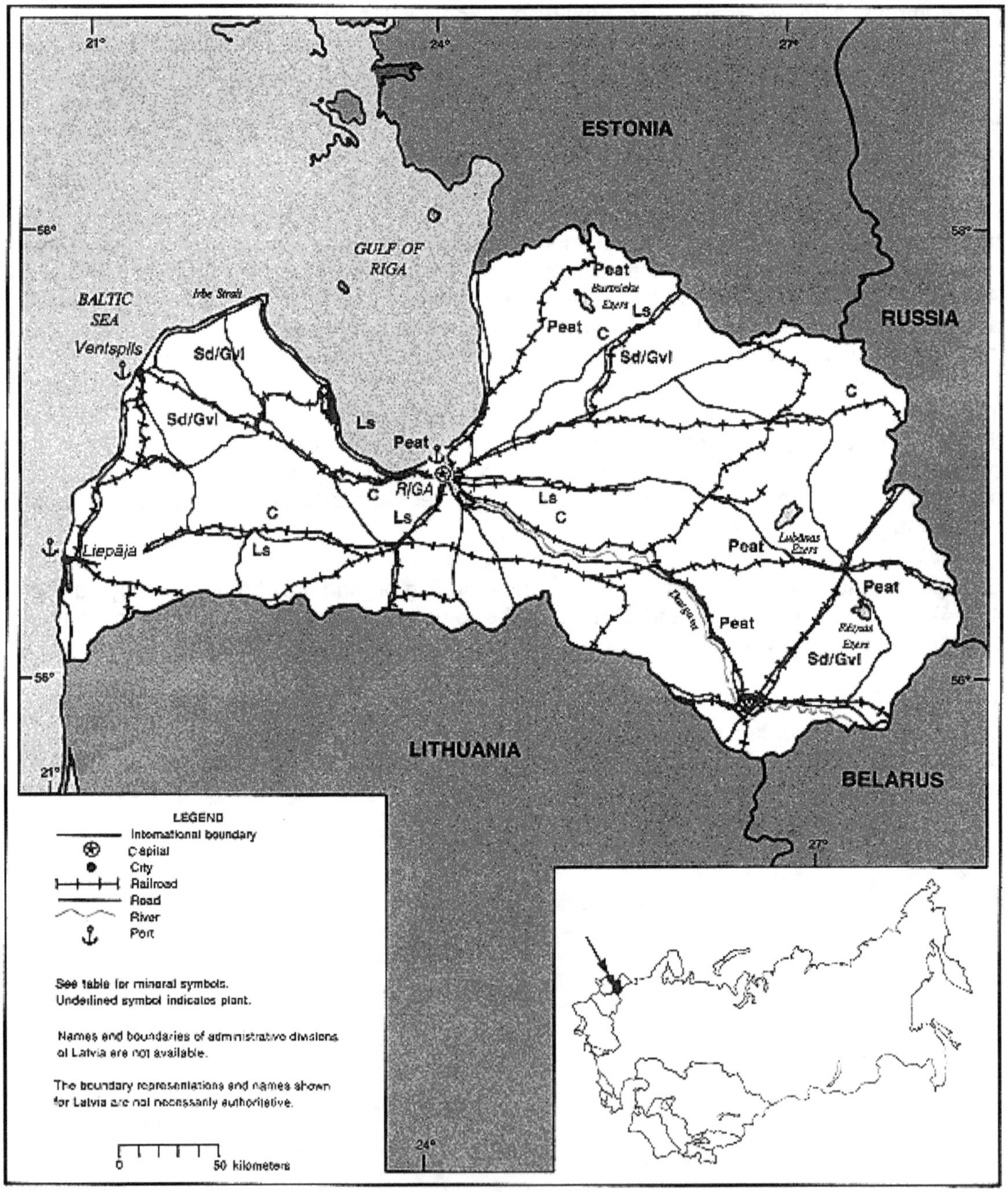

NATURAL CONDITIONS

Latvia is situated in a transitional area between northern coniferous forests and moderate zone broad-leaved forests - between the oceanic climate and the continental. Mixed forests are typical of this zone. The territory of Latvia contains many plant and animal distribution boundaries. Every change of natural conditions (climate, vegetation) over the last 13 000 years has left its marks - rare species, unique biotopes, relict nature monuments.

Table 1. Diversity of species and their protective status in Latvia

	Total species	In the Baltic Red Book	
		Number of species	% from the total
PLANTS			
Flowering plants	1600	256	16
Ferns	48	19	39.6
Mosses	485	203	41.9
Lichens	500	34	6.8
Algae	2680	-	-
Mushrooms	3600	38	1.1
ANIMALS			
Vertebrates			
Mammals	83	24	28.9
Birds	325	78	24
Reptiles	7	3	42.9
Amphibians	13	6	46.9
Fish	106	-	-
Cyclostomatia	3	-	-
	Total species	In the Latvian Red Book	
		Number of species	% from the total
Invertebrates			
Insects	20 000	9	0.045
Spiders	430	-	-
Mites	15 000	-	-
Crustaceans	250	2	0.8
Worms	3 000	1	0.3
Molluscs	185	1	0.5
Others	200	-	-

GEOLOGICAL RESOURCE EXTRACTION

With the decline of the national economy in Latvia, also the extraction of mineral resources fell sharply. Presently, extraction is stable, but considerably less than in the previous decade. The most extracted mineral resources in 1997 were sand-gravel, dolomite, limestone and peat.

Peat is one of the most important natural resources for the national economy in Latvia. The total extraction of peat in 1997 was 635,238 tonnes. In 1996, 21.2% of the peat extracted in Latvia was exported. The largest amounts of peat were exported to Germany, the Netherlands and France. Altogether, 128,267 tonnes of peat have been exported to 21 European countries.

In 1996, the extraction of sapropel was resumed, and 934 tonnes were extracted in 1997.

If peat and sapropel are used rationally, a balance between their renewal and extraction can be maintained. In 1997, the amount of the extracted peat was 63% of the yearly renewal of peat resources (around 1 million tonnes). However, in the 1980ies, the extraction of peat amounted to 3.5 million tonnes yearly, and exceeded the yearly renewal amount.

MINERAL DEPOSITS

Latvia has rich resources of quaternary sand and grit (approximately 43 billion m3). Dolomite resources are also abundant (26 billion m3). Clay is widely used in Latvia, especially in the production of bricks, regular roof, as well as pottery items. There are different rocks in Latvia – chalkstone, rock gypsum. One of the most widespread minerals is turf. There is also wide choice of mineral waters (in Kemeri, Baldone, Sigulda).

THE MINERAL INDUSTRY OF LATVIA

In 2012, Latvia's gross domestic product (GDP) increased by 5.6% compared with that of 2011. The services sector accounted for 69.6% of the GDP; the industrial sector, 25.2%; and the agricultural sector, 5.1%. Latvia's industrial growth rate in 2012 was 7.8%, and its main trade partners, in order of the volume of trade, were Lithuania, Russia, Germany, and Estonia (U.S. Central Intelligence Agency, 2013).

Latvia produced mainly industrial minerals and was not a significant world producer of any mineral commodities; it had, however, the Baltic States' only steel mill, JSC Liepājas Metalurgs. According to the company, 98% of the steel mill's production was for export, and this material accounted for 10% of total Latvian exports. The company invested in the construction of an electric arc furnace, and the first new production started in August 2011. By December 2012, the new furnace reached the designed production level and had a production capacity of 850,000 metric tons (JSC Liepājas Metalurgs, 2013a, b).

SIA CEMEX was the sole producer of cement in Latvia. In the summer of 2010, SIA CEMEX finished construction of a new cement plant with a capacity of 1.6 million metric tons per year at Broceni. SIA CEMEX planned to export its production to Belarus, Estonia, Finland, Lithuania, and Russia (CEMEX S.A.B. de C.V., 2013).

AMBER IN LATVIA

What is the significance of the Latvian word for amber – *dzintars*? Our choral music is brought to audiences abroad by the *Dzintars* Choir, and dance is presented by the children's dance ensemble *Dzintariņš*. The name of our main perfumery company is *Dzintars*; we love to put *Dzintars* cheese spread on our bread at breakfast. We all have somebody called Dzintars or Dzintra among our friends – the name is so common among us who live at the shore of *Dzintara jura*, the Amber Sea, and who have so many fine songs about amber and the sea that nurtures it. What is this sun-stone caressed by the currents of the Baltic Sea?

Amber has a special place among all the precious and semi-precious stones. Unlike other decorative materials, amber absorbs body heat and is comparatively easy to work. This is because amber consists primarily of organic compounds, instead of being formed through the action of inorganic substances. Amber is fossil resin. The chemical formula for amber is taken to be $C_{40}H_{64}O_4$, but in reality the chemical composition differs for each piece of amber.

How amber is formed

In the first stage, resin oozed from the trees. This took place intermittently and intensively, and often occurred repeatedly.

In the second stage, the amber ended up in the soil of the "amber forest". In the dry, well-aerated sandy soil physical and chemical changes took place in the resin, through the action of oxygen. The resin became harder and more durable.

In the third stage of amber formation, the amber-bearing deposits were washed out, transported and redeposited in a water-body. Amber was formed when the resin was washed by water rich in oxygen and alkaline sodium compounds. The action of these led to the formation of succinic acid and its salts. Amber that has been excavated or washed up changes under the influence of oxygen, so unlike the inorganic minerals, amber is unstable and changeable.

THE AGE OF AMBER

Amber is found in deposits of different ages. Well-known amber finds occur already in strata of the Mesozoic Era. However, the most important sources are deposits of the Tertiary Period. Baltic amber also belongs to this period, having been formed during the Eocene and Oligocene Epoch. Thus, our amber is about 30–40 million years old. Resin was also exuded by plants of the Palaeozoic Era, and some of this also fossilised, but since the fossilisation process has continued for a long time, the resin has carbonised and merged with coal. In the Quaternary Period too, in places with suitable climatic conditions, resin has been fossilised. However, this resin does not yet display all the characteristic properties of amber, and so is called copal, dammar or kauri.

FORMS OF AMBER AND THEIR WORLD DISTRIBUTION

Amber from the Mesozoic Era, most common in Cretaceous deposits, occurs in Japan, Taimir, Switzerland, Lebanon, Alaska, New Jersey and elsewhere. Amber that is earlier than the Tertiary Period is regarded as originating only from conifers. An example is New Jersey amber, exhibiting various shades of colour that are redder and darker than Baltic amber. Alaskan amber, on the other hand, is unusually transparent and intensely coloured, displaying a range of tones from honey-yellow to black. Japanese amber often has a pleasant caramel colour. It occurs together with marine fossils and is about 85 million years old. Located on Russia's Taimir Peninsula is possibly the world's largest Cretaceous amber deposit, while Lebanon has one of the oldest occurrences of amber, from about 120–130 million years ago.

Gemologists are only interested in a few forms of amber that have served as raw material for jewellery in different historical periods. These were all formed during the Tertiary: Baltic amber (succinite), Romanian amber (rumenite), Sicilian amber (simetite), Burmese amber (burmite), as well as amber from Mexico and the Dominican Republic. Succinite characteristically displays honey-coloured shades of yellow, and is unique in having a very high content of succinic acid: 2–8%. The term rumenite was introduced by Otto Helm in 1891 for the red-brown amber from the Buzeu Valley. It is not really correct to apply the term to the other forms of amber from Romania, since they are mostly pale yellow and exhibit marked internal cracking. The name simetite comes from the River Simeto, along whose banks Sicilian amber may be found. This amber, often fluorescent and showing an unusual range of colours, has nowadays become very rare. Burmite varies in colour from a rich brown to a watery yellowish tint (sherry-coloured), but intensive yellows and bone colours never occur. Most highly valued is cherry-red burmite. Often noted in the literature is the property of burmite of fluorescing in daylight with a blue-green or violet colour. Although Dominican amber is mentioned already by Columbus, it has become more widely known only during the past 20 years. The recently discovered sources are quite rich and provide comparatively large pieces. It is the softest form of amber, but in terms of other properties, Dominican amber resembles simetite.

Where is amber used?

The most widespread use of amber is in jewellery. Since ancient times, amber pendants, buttons and beads have been made, as well as more complex items. Amber has been widely used to make religious artefacts. Equally ancient is the use of amber for medicinal purposes. Amber is used to heal both internal and external disorders. Amber's curative properties are thought to be connected with its content of succinic acid, which is a unique biostimulant. Since it is practically Baltic amber alone that contains a significant amount of succinic acid, we may consider that only Baltic amber has these medicinal properties, and each piece has them to a different degree.

The chemical composition of succinite is the reason why a large proportion of this amber is chemically processed. Pure succinic acid is produced for making medicines and is used as a strategic material on nuclear submarines and in the engines of spacecraft. By-products include amber oil and amber varnish. These are used to make high quality paints and varnishes. Amber varnish is essential for restoring the gilded roofs of architectural monuments.

The optical properties of amber have been utilised for a long time. In the Middle Ages, spectacles were made from amber, and at the present day, several manufacturers of optical equipment use amber to improve the quality of lenses.

Amber, particularly pressed amber or amberoid, is used as an insulator in electrical equipment. Such amber cores were also used in the equipment that measured radiation levels after the Chernobyl nuclear disaster.

Amber in the world's ancient cultures

Egypt, Assyria, Greece and Rome figure prominently in all accounts of the history of civilisation, and among the archaeological finds from these cultures there also occur amber artefacts. Chemical analysis has shown this to be Baltic amber. Amber and tin were the goods that first aroused an interest in northern and western Europe among the people of the ancient world. Circulation of these materials stimulated the spread of civilisation. The Bronze Age world is symbolised by bronze weapons and amber religious ornaments – the secular and sacred providers of security.

Amber is mentioned in lists compiled by Assyrian jewellers around 1000 BC. In the Assyrian capitals Assur and Babylon amber beads have been recovered from temple and tower foundations. On the banks of the Tigris, at the site of the Assyrian city of Kalah, an amber figure has been found of Assyrian ruler Assurnasirpal (883–859 BC). Analysis has established that this is Baltic amber.

The ancient Greeks called amber *elektron*, which means "substance of the sun", and the capacity of amber to become charged and attract small particles later led to the name "electricity". Large numbers of amber beads have been found in the ruins of Mycenae. Amber also adorned the shoulders and hair of the ladies of Thebes, but it was most popular in ancient Rome. For example, the amber collections at the archaeological museum at L'Aquila in Italy include ladies' toiletry articles, mythological figures and groups, genre figurines, pieces in the shape of fruit, and rings. Particularly interesting is a collection of rings with female heads, accumulated during a comparatively short period, 60–160 AD. The value of amber in ancient Rome is indicated by the fact that a single piece of amber was equal in price to a strong slave. It was fashionable for ladies to carry a ball of amber in the palm of the hand, while amber-coloured hair was particularly favoured in the reign of Nero. There is reason to believe that amber was endowed with a special mystical, ritual or magical significance among the women of ancient Rome.

How did amber reach the cultures of the ancient world?

The amber routes

The earliest written evidence regarding Baltic amber may be found in the writings of Tacitus. He notes that the *Aesti* are the only people who collect this treasure from the Baltic Sea and sell it to others. Along the trade routes, amber passed through the hands of several intermediaries, so the Greek and Roman descriptions of the northern lands where amber originated are inaccurate and often mystical. Much clearer than the vague mentions in written sources are the hoards of amber that mark the routes by which Baltic amber was traded to the lands of the ancient world.

Apart from the route leading from Jutland, where amber sources were used up already in the centuries before Christ, all of the later routes come only from the Baltic: the Sambian Peninsula, the Couronian Spit and the coast of Kurzeme. The eastern route (mentioned by Herodotus) led through the Sea of Azov and the Black Sea and was also used by the Near Eastern states. The Vistula-Dniester route brought amber to the borders of the Roman Empire from the east, and the so-called Moravian Gate gave access to the heart of the empire. This depression connects the upper course of the Oder (and Vistula) with the upper reaches of the Morava, extending to the Danube at Bratislava. This is called the Great Amber Route, since it was very actively used during the reign of Emperor Nero, when amber was at the height of its fashion in Rome.

Amber gathering and use in the Baltic

Already in distant antiquity, the people living along the shore of the Baltic Sea not only collected amber for trade, but also made practical use of it as a decorative, curative and religious material. The oldest amber animal figurines date from the 8th–7th millennium BC. In the territory of present-day Latvia and Lithuania amber processing began in the 4th millennium BC. The most interesting finds of artefacts come from Sarnate, Lubana and Juodkrante, and recently also from Purciems (Gipka). Many of these finds have been obtained in work directed by Dr hab. hist. Ilze Loze, corresponding member of the Latvian Academy of Sciences, who is also a member of the Amber Committee of the International Union of Prehistoric and Protohistoric Sciences. Amber was widely used as a magical material with curative properties and as a component of religious rituals among the neighbouring ancient Slavic peoples in Kievan Rus and Poland.

Along with the conquest of the Baltic by the crusaders in the 13th century, the local amberworking traditions declined. In the coastal area around Danzig, the Dukes of Pomerania established for themselves a monopoly right to collect amber. The Teutonic Order, having taken control of Prussia, seized the right to all the amber that was obtained. The local people, if they did not give up amber, were punished by hanging. The coastal villages of Latvia too were "adorned" with gallows for amber-thieves. To prevent theft of unworked amber, workshops were established as far as possible from the sources: at Bruges in 1302, at Lübeck in 1310, at Danzig in 1477, at Elbing in 1539 and at Königsberg only in 1641. The craft corporations produced mainly rosary beads. Gradually, the technique of amberworking was perfected. Characteristic finds from the 17th and 18th centuries include amber mosaics, inlaid designs and various sculptures. This was one of the boom periods of amberworking, when a unique Amber Cabinet was made, and later an Amber Room as well. The 19th century saw a transition from amber collection to amber mining at the sources in Palmnicken (Jantarnij). Initially, mining was from shafts, but opencast mining later developed. These are the world's richest sources of amber. The source is on the seashore, and part of it is under the sea. The prevailing marine current still transports lumps of amber from these sources, to be washed up on the shore of Lithuania and Latvia. The source is worked by the Kaliningrad Amber Plant.

Amber in Latvian ethnography

Only in the 19th century, when the monopoly on amber gathering was lifted, could the coastal people re-establish the ethnographic tradition of amberworking that had been forbidden for centuries. The folk costumes in coastal areas preserve three typical ethnographic items made of amber. These are *kniepkeni*, brooches and beads. The *kniepkens* was used to fasten the opening of the woman's blouse at the neck, in a similar manner to modern-day men's cuff-links (see drawing), and were richly adorned with pendants. This motif is nowadays widely used in making a variety of pins. The brooches, used to fasten various items of clothing, were made of pure amber, with a traditional design engraved from the left-hand side. Usually they are round, but atypical examples, such as heart-shaped and leaf-shaped brooches, also occur. There are also metal brooches inset with amber. Beads include three forms: cylindrical, barrel-shaped and rounded. Amber crosses are often found too.

Forms of Baltic amber and amber processing

99.8% of Baltic amber is succinite. There are very rare finds of beckerite and stantienite. The predominant tones of our amber are the yellows, but these may extend to red, brown, blue and green. The transparency also changes – from clear and transparent to bone-white and opaque, with a great variety of transitional forms. Just try to find two identical lumps of amber! You never will. There is no end of colour tone and transparency combinations. These are a consequence of differences in chemical composition, impurities and density.

Nowadays, amber is worked by professional craftspeople and applied artists. Contemporary jewellery often continues ethnographic traditions, retained by the inhabitants of the coast of western Kurzeme, but modern trends also appear. There is a Riga school of amberworking, where metallic elements are also important, and a Liepaja school, where the unique character of the amber itself is highlighted. Professional craftspeople are nowadays trained at Liepaja. Right up to the early 20th century, whole families along the coast near Liepaja derived their main income from amber gathering.

The largest pieces of amber have been found in Prussia: one weighing 6750 g was found in 1803, and another weighing 9700 g came to light in 1860. Medieval sources mention even larger pieces – 12 kg and 16 kg lumps of amber, but there is no accurate information on these. The Amber Museum in Kaliningrad has a 4280 g amber piece, found in the 1950s. The largest modern-day find is from Sarawak in Malaysia, weighing over 50 kg and now kept in Stuttgart Museum of Natural History.

Inclusions in amber

Amber is a unique embalming agent, so inclusions in amber attract considerable attention. The largest proportion of the inclusions – 80% – are insects. The aromatic resin attracted the tiny inhabitants of the "amber forest" and preserved them through the centuries, trapped in its shining embrace as evidence of the insect fauna of the time. Spiders are also common among the inclusions, and there are unique finds such as an amber-encased lizard and a frog. Forgeries of inclusions in amber are also sold. The inclusions help to date the amber.

Plant remains are often found as inclusions in amber. These are much more difficult to identify. They are used to reconstruct the landscape of the "amber forest". For example, swamp cypress remains occur in amber from both Europe and America. This suggests that the resin of the swamp cypress could also have changed into amber.

Mineral matter and soil also occurs as inclusions.

Where can amber be seen and purchased?

The richest collection of Baltic amber is kept at Palanga Amber Museum. Unfortunately, since the border shifted in 1921, this is no longer the territory of Latvia. The Latvian Nature Museum also has a comparatively rich collection. The largest archaeological and ethnographic amber collections are held at the Liepaja Museum of Art and History, the Latvian History Museum and the Latvian Institute of History. These are exhibited only in part, so visitors with a special interest need to apply in advance.

Worked amber is sold at many souvenir and art shops in Riga and other cities, and, particularly during the tourist season, in squares and parks as well, mainly in the old town of Riga.

BUILDING MATERIALS INDUSTRY IN LATVIA

Latvia has been identified as a priority market for building materials. Not only is there major renovation of the country's infrastructure, including roads, railways and ports, but there is a demand for better housing. In Riga, this manifests itself in renovation of the 19th Century core of the city, redevelopment of high rise housing and development of new greenfield housing.

Latvia has good natural resources that can be used to produce building materials. Although there is a strong demand for all building materials, it is the luxury and DIY ends of the market that offer the greatest opportunities to overseas companies.

LATVIA GEOLOGICAL SERVICE

State agency
"Latvian Environment, geology and meteorology agency"
Maskavas Str. 165, Riga, LV-1019, Latvia
Secretariat: +371 703 26 00
Customer service: + 371 7032 620, 7 032 665
Fax: +371 714 51 54
E-mail lvgma@lvgma.gov.lv
Questions and proposals: webmaster@meteo.lv

Eksporta iela 5, Rīga LV-1010
Tālr: 7 320 379
Fakss: 7 333218
e-pasts: vgd@vgd.gov.lv
Reģ. Nr. 90000090840
Latvijas Banka, kods LACBLV2X
konts LV65TREL221018007000

The Latvian Hydrometeorological Agency(LHMA) is a national institution under the wing of the Ministry of the Environment that has been implementing the national policy in meteorology, climatology, hydrology, air quality and environmental impact of the long-range transfer of pollutants.

The ultimate task of the LHMA is responding to demands for weather services through the timely provision of adequate information to human activities dependent on the climate and weather conditions and the environmental quality.

With these in mind, particular emphasis is put on meeting the needs of our core customers – aviation, the energy and heat supply sectors, port authorities, traffic, agriculture, forestry, etc. General and specialized meteorological, hydrological and environmental quality information; weather forecasts; warnings of weather extremes and natural desasters are provided to governmental and local authorities, the media, and to physical and legal persons.

The LHMA is authorized to represent the Republic of Latvia with the World Meteorological Organization (WMO) and the International Civil Aviation Organization (ICAO). LHMA is the Executive Agency of Latvia for implementing international conventions related to meteorology, hydrology and environmental quality.

The LHMA provides for functioning the Global Telecommunication System in Latvia compliant with the international requirements.

The ultimate task of the LHMA is responding to demands for weather services through the timely provision of adequate information to human activities dependent on the climate and weather conditions and the environmental quality.

Meteorological current or forecast information and analysis allows planning of weather-dependent activities to be made.;this generates savings for customers or an increase in revenue. The international experience evidences that 85% of the national economy's branches depend upon the weather.

The implications of a drought, a flooding or a strong wind are bound to affect many aspects of human life and activities: adverse weather conditions cause a decrease in the sales' rate, failures in the operation of HPPs and power supply. The rainy and cold weather effects tourism; unforseen weather do not allow building of roads, their seasonal repairs and maintenance that would generate losses.

It is impossible to change the weather. However, it is predictable. The accurate weather forecast being available, current and long-term planning of activities is feasible.

CONTACTS

Amats	Vārds, Uzvārds	tālruņa nr.	e-pasta adrese
Vietnieks ģeoloģijas jautājumos	Māris Segliņš	7 770 000	Maris.Seglins@vgd.gov.lv

Zemes dzīļu resursu nodaļa			
Amats	Vārds, Uzvārds	tālruņa nr.	e-pasta adrese
Nodaļas vadītājs	Agris Lācis	7 770 003	Agris.Lacis@vgd.gov.lv
Hidroģeoloģijas daļa			
Daļas vadītāja	Natālija Levina	7 770 009	Natalija.Levina@vgd.gov.lv
Hidroģeologs	Rita Gaile	7 770 025	Rita.Gaile@vgd.gov.lv
Galvenais hidroģeologs	Igors Levins	7 770 012	Igors.Levins@vgd.gov.lv
Galvenais hidroģeologs	Askolds Cīrulis	7 770 026	Askolds.Cirulis@vgd.gov.lv
Vadošais ģeologs	Lidija Stiebriņa	7 770 048	Lidija.Stiebrina@vgd.gov.lv
Vadošais hidroģeologs	Gaļina Agarkova	7 770 028	Galina.Agarkova@vgd.gov.lv
	Tatjana Birgere	7 770 045	tanya@vgd.gov.lv
Ģeologs	I. Sevastjanova		
Reģionālās ģeoloģijas daļa			
Daļas vadītājs	Atis Mūrnieks	7 770 002	Atis.Murnieks@vgd.gov.lv
Galvenais ģeologs	Aivars Gilucis	7 770 010	Aivars.Gilucis@vgd.gov.lv
Galvenais seismologs	Valērijs Ņikuļins	7 770 011	Valerijs.Nikulins@vgd.gov.lv
Vadošais ģeologs	Jānis Misāns	7 770 062	
Vadošais ģeologs	Ludmila Guseva	7 770 061	
Vadošais ģeologs	Andris Karpovičs	7 770 058	Andris.Karpovic@vgd.gov.lv
Vadošais ģeologs	Zigurds Meirons	7 770 002	
Ģeologs	Jūlija Markova		
Perspektīvo zemes dzīļu resursu daļa			
Sektora vadītājs	Ināra Nulle	7 770 018	Inara.Nulle@vgd.gov.lv
Galvenais ģeologs	Raisa Pomeranceva	7 770 017	Raisa.Pomeranceva@vgd.gov.lv
Vadošais ģeologs	Olga Ivanova	7 770 031	
Vadošais ģeologs	Tatjana Šadrina	7 770 033	
Vadošais kartogrāfs	Aleksandra Jemeļjanova	7 770 035	
Ģeologs	Lidija Bēra	7 770 034	Lidija.Bera@vgd.gov.lv

Tulkotājs	Aleksejs Tukacinskis	7 770 021	Aleksejs.Tukacinskis@vgd.gov.lv
Būvmateriālu izejvielu daļa			
Sektora vadītājs	Sarmīte Kondratjeva	7 770 019	Sarmite.Kondratjeva@vgd.gov.lv
Vadošais ģeologs	Dace Rutka	7 770 030	
Ģeologs	Antra Kregžde	7 770 019	Antra.Kregzde@vgd.gov.lv

Ģeoloģijas informācijas nodaļa			
Amats	Vārds, Uzvārds	tālruņa nr.	e-pasta adrese
Latvijas Valsts ģeoloģijas fonds un urbumu un seržu etalonparaugu glabātava			
Fondi		7 320 379	
Daļas vadītāja	Alda Reuta	7 320 490	
Galvenais ģeologs	Georgijs Konšins	7 770 022	Georgijs.Konsins@vgd.gov.lv
Ģeologs	Mārīte Aizsalniece	7 770 057	
Vadošais ģeologs	Andrejs Visvaldis Pūriņš	7 620 605	
Ģeologs	Dzintra Berdņikova	7 770 032	Dzintra.Berdnikova@vgd.gov.lv
Vadošais ģeologs	Kristīne Šterna	7 770 059	kristine@vgd.gov.lv
Vadošais ģeologs	Daiga Buša	7 770 065	Daiga.Busa@vgd.gov.lv
Ģeologs	Zigurds Upmalis	7 620 605	
Informācijas tehnoloģiju daļa			
Daļas vadītājs	Eduards Takčidi	7 325 725	Eduards.Takcidi@vgd.gov.lv
Galvenais programmēšanas inženieris	Viktors Kuzņecovs	7 770 013	Viktors.Kuznecovs@vgd.gov.lv
Galvenais datu bāžu programmētājs	Juris Freimanis	7 770 015	Juris.Freimanis@vgd.gov.lv
Galvenais ģeofiziķis	Marta Cirša	7 770 039	
Vadošais ģeofiziķis	Jurijs Belozerovs	7 770 042	Jurijs.Belozerovs@vgd.gov.lv
Vadošais ģeofiziķis	Viktors Svitins	7 770 043	
Vadošais ģeofiziķis	Valentīna Pņova	7 770 040	
Vadošais ģeologs	Tatjana Krutofala	7 770 046	Tatjana.Krutofala@vgd.gov.lv
Vadošais ģeologs	Valentīna Vikulova	7 770 040	
Vadošais ģeologs	Natālija Nartiša	7 770 036	Natalija.Nartisa@vgd.gov.lv
Ģeologs	Eva Nulle	7 770 60	Eva.Nulle@vgd.gov.lv
Skaitļ./elektr. inženieris	Aleksandrs Zlatopoļskis	7 770 051	
Vadošais programmētājs	Dzintra Slavinska	7 770 044	

Tehniķis ģeologs	Andrejs Makarevičs	7 770 050	

Licencēšanas nodaļa			
Amats	Vārds, Uzvārds	tālruņa nr.	e-pasta adrese
Nodaļas vadītājs	Andris Graudiņš	7 770 005	Andris.Graudins@vgd.gov.lv
Licenču sagatavošanas un izsniegšanas daļa			
Sektora vadītājs	Vladimirs Krutofals	7 770 008	Vladimirs.Krutofals@vgd.gov.lv
Galvenais ģeologs	Vilma Venska	7 770 007	Vilma.Venska@vgd.gov.lv
Ģeologs	Vera Bauļina	7 770 053	
Ģeologs	Irēna Temščuka	7 770 054	
Ģeologs	Ārija Kampare	7 770 052	
Zemes dzīļu izmantošanas pārraudzības daļa			
Vadošais ģeologs	Regīna Muizniece	7 770 055	Regina.Muizniece@vgd.gov.lv
Ģeologs	Indra Zviedre	7 770 049	Indra.Zviedre@vgd.gov.lv

Upju baseinu vadības nodaļa tālr. 777 00 67			
Amats	Vārds, Uzvārds	tālruņa nr.	e-pasta adrese
Nodaļas vadītājs	Uldis Nulle	7 323 860	Uldis.Nulle@vgd.gov.lv
Hidroloģijas daļa			
Daļas vadītāja	Maija Purviņa		Maija.Purvina@vgd.gov.lv
Sektora vadītāja vietnieks	Baiba Brikmane	7 770 016	Baiba.Brikmane@vgd.gov.lv
Hidrologs	Katerīna Ivanova		Katerina.Ivanova@vgd.gov.lv
Hidrologs	Evija Zeiliša		
Hidrologs	Ainis Legzdiņš		
Stratēģijas daļa			
Daļas vadītāja	Sigita Šulca		Sigita.Sulca@vgd.gov.lv
Galvenais datu bāžu programmētājs	Nikolajs Farafonovs	7 770 014	
Vecākais ģeologs	Tatjana Krutofala	7 770 046	Tatjana.Krutofala@vgd.gov.lv
Ārējo sakaru daļa			
Sektora vadītāja	Ingrīda Cirmane		Ingrida.Cirmane@vgd.gov.lv
Vecākais Ārējo sakaru koordinators	Andris Tihomirovs		
Ekonomiskās analīzes daļa			
Ekonomists	Gundars Ancens		Gundars.Ancens@vgd.gov.lv
Ekonomists	Kristīna Fedorovīča		Kristina.Fedorovica@vgd.gov.lv

Tehniskā nodrošinājuma sektors			
Amats	Vārds, Uzvārds	tālruņa nr.	e-pasta adrese
Apsardze		7 770 024	
Autovadītājs	Edgars Ivanovskis		
Autovadītājs	Aija Bernāne		
Autovadītājs	Juris Silamednis		
Sakaru līniju montieris	Vladimirs Šitovs		
Ēkas elektriķis un santehniķis	Georgs Siļēvičs		

IMPORTANT ORGANIZATIONS

STATE INSTITUTIONS

Environment Data Centre
http://www.vdc.lv/

Land Cadaster Centre, State Land Service
http://www.lzkc.org.lv/

Ministry of Environmental Protection and Regional Development
http://www.varam.gov.lv/

Marine Environment Board
http://www.jvp.vdc.lv/eng/

National Environmental Health Centre
http://www.nvvc.org.lv/

Regional Environment Boards
http://www.varam.gov.lv/English/Structure/enforcin/reb.htm
http://www.varam.vdc.lv/eng/regioni.htm

State Environmental Inspectorate
http://www.varam.gov.lv/English/Structure/enforcin/envinsp.htm
http://www.varam.vdc.lv/eng/insp.htm

State Fishery Board
http://www.bzi.lv/English/board.htm

State Geological Survey
http://www.varam.gov.lv/English/Structure/sectoradm/geold_e.htm
http://www.vgd.gov.lv/

State Hydrometeorological Agency
http://www.varam.gov.lv/English/Structure/sectoradm/hidromet_e.htm
http://www.meteo.lv/

State Statistical Bureau
http://www.csb.lv/

State Scientific Production Enterprise "Raziba", Ministry of Agriculture
http://www.cs.llu.lv/ZemMin/index.html

MUNICIPALITIES

Riga City Council
http://www.rcc.lv/

Ventspils City Council
http://www.ventspils.lv/english/index.htm

INTERNATIONAL ORGANISATIONS

European Environment Agency
http://www.eea.eu.int/

IUCN - World Conservation Union
http://www.iucn.org/

Nordic Council of Ministers
http://www.norden.org/

Organisation for Economic Co-operation and Development
http://www.oecd.org/

United Nation Development Programme
http://www.undp.org/

UNIVERSITIES AND INSTITUTES

Fisheries Research Institute

Institute of Aquatic Ecology, University of Latvia
http://www.lza.lv/INST/IN22.HTM

Institute of Biology, University of Latvia
http://www.lza.lv/inst/in11.htm

Latvian University of Agriculture
http://www.cs.llu.lv/

NON-GOVERNMENTAL ORGANISATIONS

Fishery Foundation
http://www.bzi.lv/English/fund.htm

Fund for Nature
http://www.daba.lu.lv/LDF/

NATURAL RESOURCES AND ENVIRONMENT

THE LEGAL SYSTEM

Legislation is one of the most important instruments for implementation of environmental policy. As in any other field of law, environmental law may be divided into two parts:

umbrella laws that sanctify general policy goals;
subordinate legislation, rules, regulations, etc., that specify norms, codes and the functions of government agencies.

The Constitution (Satversme) has a higher legal standing than any other law. Unfortunately, since it was adopted quite some time ago (in 1922), it does not include any provisions directly pertaining to the environment. In the constitutional law of the Republic of Latvia on 'Human and civil rights and duties' (1991) there is the following provision: 'The protection of nature, cultural environments, landscapes, historical and architectural monuments and the environment shall be the duty of every individual, the general public and the State. Laws shall provide the general framework for environmental protection in Latvia, which shall then be further specified in other enactments (Cabinet decisions, regulations, orders etc., orders issued by the Prime Minister, other enactments issued by public administration institutions within the scope of their competency, local government enactments, etc.)'

As in the rest of the world, Latvian environmental law was initially closely connected with the regulation of the use of natural resources. Therefore many doctrines of environmental protection are found in laws/acts/regulations that regulate the use of natural resources. The most important of these are the following:

On the Use of Land and the Organisation of Land Use (1991)
Code on the Use of the Earth's Sub-surface Resources (1976) (a new law On the Use of the Earth's Sub-surface Resources is presently being drafted)
Water Code (1972)
On the Use and Managment of Forests (1994)
On the Use and Protection of Animals (1981)
On Protection of the Atmosphere (1981)

During the 1990s, work has been undertaken on drafting laws necessary for the solution of specific environmental problems. To date, the following laws have been adopted:

On Environmental Protection (1991)
On the State Ecological Expertise (1990)
On the Environmental Protection Committee (enacted in 1990, but revoked in 1993 due to the establishment of the Ministry for Environmental Protection and Regional Development)
On the Natural Resources Tax (1990)
On Hazardous Wastes (1993)
On the Particularly Protection Natural Territories (1993)
On Radiation and Nuclear Safety (1994)
Regulations on the Republic of Latvia's State Environmental Protection Inspection (1990)

A SHORT OVERVIEW OF THE LAWS ADOPTED FROM 1990-1994

The law 'On Environmental Protection' (1991): can be considered the base law for environmental protection. It includes basic provisions and programme guidelines on the rights of the population to a quality human environment, information about the condition of the environment, measures for the solution of many environmental problems, control of environmental protection, liability for environmental violations, international co-operation in environmental protection, the division of responsibilities in environmental protection, and other issues. This law first refers to several new instruments for environmental protection: mandatory ecological insurance and ecological certification. However, mechanisms for the implementation of these instruments has not yet been elaborated.

The law 'On the State Ecological Expertise' (1990): governs the procedures for the performance of ecological expertise by the State, its goals, objectives and other basic regulations. This law has helped the establishment of a very significant and powerful environmental policy implementation instrument. Now it is no longer possible to implement many plans, programmes, construction projects, etc. without the prior approval of the State Ecological Expertise.

The law 'On the Environmental Protection Committee of the Republic of Latvia' (passed in 1990, but revoked in 1993 due to the establishment of the Ministry for Environmental Protection and Regional Development) established the legal basis for many rights and instruments of environmental protection for State administration institutions (receiving information, the right to visit any site or object in the territory of Latvia for the purpose of ensuring adherence to environmental requirements, disallowing the operations of industrial and other entities, etc.) The law was revoked by the establishment of the Ministry for Environmental Protection and Regional Development, but many ideas included in the law did or still do influence the activities of environmental protection institutions until the adoption of new legislation.

The law 'On Natural Resources Tax' (1990): with the introduction of this law, a special tax for the involvement of natural resources in economic activity and environmental pollution was first established in Latvia. A natural resources tax is one of the most efficient economic instruments for environmental protection. At present, a new law 'On Natural Resources Tax' is being drafted, which will extend the types of natural resource use subject to taxation, as well as introduce a natural resources tax on the consumption of goods and products hazardous to the environment (for more details, see 4.3.).

The law 'On Hazardous Wastes' (1993): regulates the procedures for operations involving hazardous wastes. The provision of this law banning the import of hazardous wastes has turned out to be very important for Latvia.

The law 'On Particularly Protected Nature Territories' (1993): lists the categories of protected territories, the procedures for their establishment and protection etc. The law also governs the rights of land ownership and land use in protected territories, and is therefore the basis for protection of these territories during the present period of land reform which includes the re-establishment the private ownership on land.

The law 'On Radiation and Nuclear Safety' (1994): at present, this is the newest environmental law, as well as the first Latvian law in this field. The law regulates the procedures for operations involving sources of ionising radiation (licensing of entrepreneurial activity, procedure for receiving permits, as well as the performance of other operations involving sources of ionising radiation), as well as the performance of other associated activities that ensure the preservation of human life, health, property and the environment.

Regulations 'On Environmental Protection State Inspection' (1990); regulates the rights, duties, and level of competency required by the State's environmental protection inspectors. The regulations also partially govern the procedure for receiving permits for the use of many natural resources.

A very important group of laws are those which are not directly connected with environmental protection, but are necessary to administer the enforcement of other laws. These are:

Administrative Liability Code of Latvia (1984)
Criminal Code of Latvia (1961)
The Civil Law (1937) was restored in 1992. It specifies the fundamental principles of civil liability. In it, liability is apportioned as determined by other enactments, e.g. Cabinet regulations and decisions. However, sanctions, fines, rates of compensation, etc., for crimes against the environment are not mentioned and therefore the law needs to be amended.
Labour Code of Latvia (1972) and Cabinet regulations 'On Disciplinary Penalties for Public Servants' (1994).

In order to solve environmental issues more efficiently, the above listed laws are not enough. Inclusion of environmental requirements in other enactments has been performed in part. It is particularly necessary for laws governing entrepreneurial activity, for example, in the laws 'On Entrepreneurial Activity' (1990), 'On Procedures for Staying the Operation of Enterprises, Institutions and Organisations' (1991), as well as enactments governing privatisation, e.g. in the law 'On Land Reform'.
At present, many environmental issues are not regulated at all by legislation or the existing laws are outdated and in need of redrafting. Work has commenced on drafting the following laws:

On the Use of the Earth's Sub-surface Resources (draft concept approved by the Cabinet of Ministers)
On the Protection of Species and Biotopes
On Chemical Substances
On Air Protection
On Protection Belts (draft adopted by Cabinet is presently being discussed in Parliament (Saeima))
On Mandatory Liability Insurance for Damage to the Environment
On Household Waste

The following laws are very necessary, however work on their drafting has not yet been started:

On the Use and Protection of Water
On Industrial Waste
On the Rational Use and Protection of Land Resources
On the Protection and Maintenance of Landscapes etc.

Along with those laws pertaining directly to environmental protection, there are also a number of legal norms that touch upon the field indirectly, such as the law 'On Regional Development' (concept being drafted), 'On Tourism' (being drafted), 'On Food' (being drafted), 'Construction Regulations' (adopted by the Cabinet in 1995, currently being redrafted into a law).

Many specific environmental problems are tackled by enactments adopted in the past by the Council of Ministers or presently by the Cabinet of Ministers. They cover environmental protection, hunting, fishing, water protection, pollution, forest protection, hazardous sites/risk objects. Decision No 107. adopted by the Council of Ministers of the LSSR 'On particularly protected nature objects in the territory of the LSSR', dated April 10, 1987 in one example of this. This decision approves lists of territories and objects under special protection, lists of species under special protection, the fundamental provisions for the protection of the said territories, objects and species, and regimes of coastal protective zones along the Baltic Sea and the Gulf of Riga.

In the near future, it is planned to draft new Cabinet regulations on the issues of radiation and nuclear safety, on environmental monitoring, on nature objects and territories under special protection, and more.

It is important to note that until they are revoked or superseded, the legislation of the Latvian SSR still apply, provided they are not contrary to the Republic of Latvia Constitutional Law of 1991 'On the national status of the Republic of Latvia'. This is provided for by the Decision of the Supreme Council of the Republic of Latvia 'On the application of legislation of the Latvian SSR in the territory of the Republic of Latvia' dated August 29 1991, as well as by the Declaration of the Supreme Council of the Latvian SSR 'On the restoration of independence of the Republic of Latvia' dated May 4 1990.

Standards and norms of the Latvian SSR and the USSR are also applicable until new ones are drafted or the existing ones are explicitly revoked pursuant to Decision No 337 of the Council of Ministers of the Republic of Latvia 'On the application of norms and technical standards in the Republic of Latvia' dated August 14 1992. The drafting of new standards is time consuming and expensive, therefore change needs time.
In accordance with the political orientation of the Republic of Latvia towards the European Union, it is planned to co-ordinate enactments (including standards and norms) with EU directives. By 2005, the EU system of standards and normatives should be completely introduced in the Republic of Latvia. Thus, the necessary standards and norms need to be developed and existing ones improved. Where Latvian standards and norms are stricter than those applicable in the EU, it will be necessary to determine whether they should remain as they are or modified in line with EU standards.

Box 7.

Standards for the quality of sludge produced by waste water treatment facilities

The standards for sludge quality in wastewater treatment facilities are much stricter in Latvia than in the EU and Germany: Ni standards are 3 to 4 times stricter; Cr exceeds German standards by 4.5 times; Cu exceeds EU standards by 2 to 4 times; Cd exceeds EU standards by 1 to 3 times. The relaxation of these standards is not envisaged.

Latvian environmental legislation is influenced also by signing of international agreements. Latvia has become party to several conventions and several others are signed and prepared for ratification.

Convention requirements have also been included in Latvian laws. If an international agreement provides for different requirements than legislation of the Republic of Latvia, provisions of the international agreement apply unless Latvian laws provide for stricter requirements.

Latvia has also signed bilateral and multilateral international agreements on environmental co-operation. Such agreements have been signed with Germany, Sweden, Finland, Estonia and Belarus. Work in underway regarding bilateral agreements with Lithuania, Kazakhstan, Russia, Poland, as well as on a trilateral agreement between Estonia, Lithuania and Latvia.

While the system of environmental legislation has been established in part, some laws still require the development of supporting rules, regulations, standards, etc., in order to implement all the provisions within the law. Also, for the effective application and enforcement of laws, proper guarantees are necessary, such as a system of State environmental administration institutions, material and technical support (e.g. guaranteed budget funding), environmental education, State and other types of environmental control, etc. Therefore, while laws are without doubt a good foundation for the implementation of environmental policy, they cannot guarantee it. Therefore, other environmental policy instruments need to be applied together with legislation.

NATIONAL PROGRAMS

The Republic of Latvia's Cabinet of Ministers' Declaration of 1993 provides for the development and implementation of national programs for the country's gradual realization of its economic plans.

Also, the Republic of Latvia's Cabinet of Ministers' Declaration of 1994 refers to national programs as the main instrument for development promotion. Therefore, this policy instrument should be applied also in the future.
The concept of national programs elaborated by the Ministry of Economy provides that 'national programs are developed in order to achieve the most important goals of the government's economic policy'.

The following programmes are currently under elaboration:

National programme for the development of rural areas of Latvia, providing for the reduction of unemployment, and development of infrastructure and industries derived from production.
National environmental program for the Baltic Sea, with the aim to mobilize by the year 2000 local, national and international intellectual, financial and material resources to implement projects complying with recommendations and requirements of the Helsinki Commission and EU in at least ten point sources of pollution that present the greatest hazards to the environment and human health in the basin of the Baltic Sea.
Public investment program: At present, economic reform in Latvia is aimed at the development of the private sector, but this is impossible to achieve without well-developed infrastructure. In order to plan, co-ordinate and evaluate prospective allocations of public investment, taking into consideration resources available and the development priorities of the national and sectoral economies, the Public Investment Department at the Ministry of Economy, on the basis of sectoral strategies elaborated and projects submitted by sectoral ministries, has elaborated the Public Investment Programme.
National indicative programme: The aim of this programme is to gather information about the supply and demand for foreign technical (non-refundable) assistance, and to ensure its efficient and purposeful use in accordance with the priority development directions set by the government. The programme for 1995-1997 has been elaborated by the Ministry of Finance's Department for Foreign Economic Relations in co-operation with sectoral ministries, in accordance with the priorities set by the government.

In the future, programmes may develop into one of the main forms of environmental policy implementation, as it is in many countries, where a specific programme is developed for the implementation of every political goal or the solving of a priority problem, with a specific plan of activities, organizational structure, timetable and regular State budget funding.
In Latvia, such programmes might be the following:

environmental protection of watercourses in the Baltic Sea basin,
air protection,
waste management,
protection of biotopes,
promotion of clean technologies,
reduction of production risk,
abatement of transboundary pollution,
environmental education,
use of the Earth's sub-surface resources.

ECONOMIC INSTRUMENTS

Parallel to the application of legal and administrative instruments in environmental policy implementation, application of economic instruments is increasing. In many cases they are more efficient, since they have an immediate effect on a polluter's budget. The importance of economic instruments is increased by the growth of production and consumption, as well as the increase of pollution abatement costs.

The goal of economic instruments is to reduce pollution by ensuring that polluters and consumers make the best choices for the environment voluntarily. In fact, they establish financial feedback links between polluters and the public. Without economic instruments, it would be necessary to provide additional funding for the implementation of environmental projects.

The main principles for choosing economic instruments should be the following:

the polluter pays;
they should promote activities to abate pollution;
they should be simple and flexible;
they should be fair towards different polluters;
amounts collected for pollution should be used for environmental investment in regions that suffer due to a specific polluter;
amount of financial compensation to be paid by the polluter should be determined on the basis of measurements, not theoretical calculations.

The natural resources tax was introduced in 1990 to conserve natural resources and limit environmental pollution, as well as to accrue funds for financing environmental activities. The tax consists of two parts: a base rate for the use of natural resources and for permission to pollution within specified limits; and penalty rates for excessive pollution and use of resources.

To date, the tax has not promoted pollution abatement and resource conservation because the rates have devalued, even though revised several times. The tax revenues are also inadequate to compensate damage to the environment. It is cheaper for a polluter to pay a fine for excess pollution than to invest funds to avoid it.

At present, due to inadequate pollution monitoring technology, taxes and fines are based on calculations instead of measurements. These calculations often don't reflect the actual situation.

A new law on the natural resources tax has been drafted. In the new law, taxes will be paid for abstraction (use) of natural resources, emission of pollutants into the environment, environmental or resource degradation, and the sale or import of goods and products harmful to the environment.

The draft also provides for the application of several new economic instruments.

An expansion of the notion of use of natural resources, introducing the expression *goods or products harmful to environment*; use of such products and services is subject to excise tax. Such goods include fuels (coal, liquid fuel, gas, peat), gasoline, batteries and accumulators, ozone-depleting substances, fluorescent lamps, different types of packaging, etc.
The increase and better preparation of tax rates for the use of natural resources and environment pollution
The introduction of emission licences, investment tax credits and a CO2 tax to be collected as excise on fuel.

Apart from the natural resources tax, the following economic instruments are available and often used in Latvia:

Subsidies, e.g. budget subsidies, subsidies by the Environmental Fund or different foreign donors, soft loans.
State loan guarantees - the State extends guarantees for loans necessary to implement such projects that solve State priority environmental problems, provided the respective local government is capable of implementing the project (this is also supported by the environmental policy principles regarding projects that are nationally acceptable and locally practicable).
Tax relief for environmental investments not provided for by the present taxation system.
Administrative charges for issuing permits and licences.
The State Environmental Fund to make payments for environmental damage.
Compensation for environmental damage.

Besides the natural resources tax, compensation for environmental damage is one of the most widely applied economic instruments. It is also one of the forms of liability for environmental violations. Compensation for damage is usually set in accordance with specific calculation rates for losses that are determined taking into account the notional value of natural resources, costs for their renewal or clean-up, including a fine as a penalty for the element of violation. Rates for loss calculation are set by Cabinet decisions or decisions or orders of specific ministries. Compensation of losses is usually applied together with other forms of liability for environmental violations, but in the case of damage to the environment, losses have to be compensated irrespective of whether the person has been held liable in any other form. The guilty party may compensate losses voluntarily, otherwise they are collected by enforcement measures following a court order.
In the future, prices of goods and services should include environmental costs, which is not the case at present. Methods for determination (calculation) of environmental protection and remediation should be developed and elaborated. In general, the importance of economic instruments will continue to grow.
The main goal for Latvian environmental investment policy should be to promote environmentally-friendly investment, including public and private, domestic and foreign. The main focus should be on solving local problems, while keeping in mind regional and international problems.

TERRITORIAL PLANNING

Territorial planning, which is a part of development planning, involves the elaboration of a plan for a specific territory, taking into consideration forecasts based on social and economic development programmes. In a territorial plan drafted at a national, regional or local level, present land use, natural characteristics, economic characteristics, requirements for environmental protection, as well as environmental impact of every planned activity within the territory are subject to a balanced evaluation.

Thus, territorial planning is an instrument for implementing environmental policy, which attempts to regulate the interaction of the public and the environment, and set requirements and provisions for solving specific environmental problems. It is of particular significance in connection with such priority environmental problems as the reduction of biodiversity, landscape degradation and unsustainable use of natural resources. In this respect, territorial planning is closely related to EIAs for new projects (see "Environmental Impact Assessment"). Territorial planning performs preventive environmental protection functions.

Within existing capability, it is necessary to develop territorial plans for the territory of Latvia as a whole, for its separate regions, towns and pagasts (the smallest rural administrative unit). The procedures for territorial planning are provided by the Cabinet regulations 'On Territorial Planning' (1994).

STATE ENVIRONMENTAL CONTROL

State control over compliance of environmental protection and regional development requirements in the territory of the Republic of Latvia is performed by the State Environmental Inspection (SEI), the regional Environmental Protection Committees, as well as the administrations of nature reserves under special protection. SEI implements State control over the use of natural resources and construction in the territory of the Republic of Latvia, its continental shelf and the economic zone of the Republic of Latvia in the Baltic Sea. The main function of SEI is enforcement - to ensure that all legal entities and physical persons observe the environmental enactments of laws providing for the use of natural resources and construction requirements, as well as to ensure that legal entities and physical persons fulfil their commitments to public programmes, plans, projects, the use of natural resources and construction.

ENVIRONMENTAL IMPACT ASSESSMENT (EIA)

An EIA attempts to determine the potential impact of some economic activity upon the environment, biodiversity, human health and society. EIAs can be used to evaluate 'projects', such as new constructions or renovations, as well as proposed policy changes. The result of an EIA should be an impact assessment and comparison of alternative scenarios, leaving the decision making to local governments or the national government. A significant role in the EIA process is allocated to public participation in the course of design and assessment of the final project.

In the future, the government plans to establish an EIA institution, by licensed experts and designers, to perform EIAs, co-ordinate projects (i.e. current practice) and control compliance with EIA requirements and recommendations. Establishment of such an institution would be provided by a new 'Law on EIA' which should also provide that EIAs evaluate possible impacts on human health, the social consequences of projects, as well as the effects of any past and planned environmental protection activities.

HYDROCARBON RESOURCES

BALTIC SEA REGION

Although only minor energy producers and consumers, the Baltic states--including Estonia, Latvia, and Lithuania--occupy a strategic location as transit centers for Russia's northern oil exports.

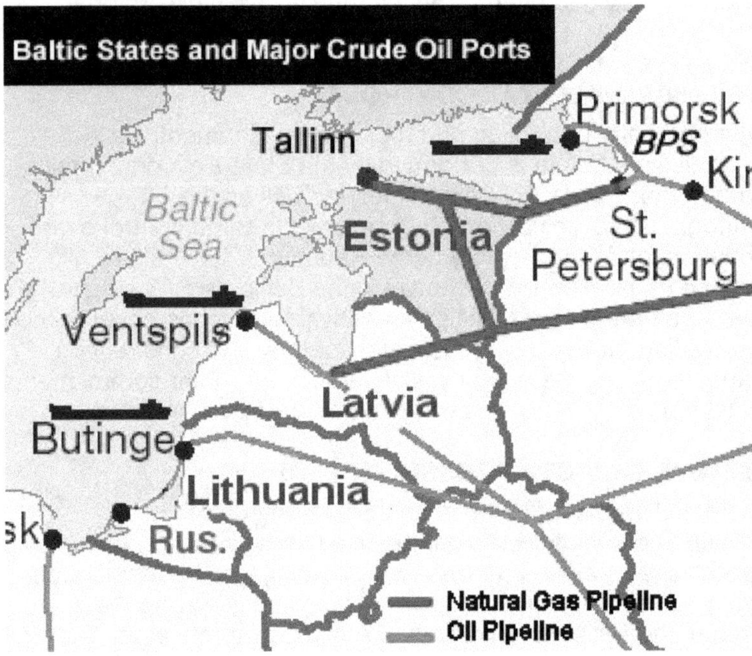

GENERAL BACKGROUND

Alone among the former Soviet republics, the Baltic Sea region states of Estonia, Latvia, and Lithuania were quick to adopt market economies and to implement democratic reforms. As a result, they largely have avoided the economic and political crises that have beset other regions in transition from a centrally planned economy, including the Balkan region and southeastern Europe. Privatization in the Baltics is nearly complete, and in 2003, despite the slowdown in the global economy, the three countries posted an average 6.6% increase in their real gross domestic product (GDP).

With a combined population of only 7.2 million people, Estonia, Latvia, and Lithuania have achieved greater presence in the international community by joining forces in a number of political and economic arenas. In 2004, after years of preparations, Estonia, Latvia, and Lithuania are expected to join the North Atlantic Treaty Organization (NATO) as well as the European Union (EU). Membership in NATO and the EU has been a stated foreign policy goal in each of the three countries since they became independent.

REGIONAL ENERGY ISSUES

Although the Baltic states are not important energy consumers or producers, together they occupy a key transit location for Russian oil exports. The Russian crude oil pipeline system is connected to three ports on the Baltic Sea: Latvia's port of Ventspils (completed in 1961); Lithuania's port of Butinge (completed in 1999); and the Russian port of Primorsk (completed in 2002). These three ports transited roughly 500,000 barrels per day of (bbl/d) of crude oil in 2002, or roughly 10% of Russia's net exports. Smaller quantities of crude oil are also distributed to other Baltic ports via rail as well as significant quantities of petroleum products.

With the completion and upgrades at Butinge and Primorsk, export capacity in the Baltic region has nearly doubled since 1999 (detailed below). Because virtually all of the oil exported through these ports comes from the Russian pipeline system, competition among the regional players has been fierce, and the distribution of market share has changed dramatically in recent years. As a result, Latvia and Lithuania have been compelled to compete with Russia's own export route at Primorsk.

BALTIC SEA REGION: MAJOR CRUDE OIL PORTS

Ventspils (Latvia)
Before the recent expansion of export capacity in the Baltic region --led by the construction of Russia's Primorsk facility (see below)-- Ventspils was the largest port in the Baltics and the second largest oil export terminal for Russian crude after the Black Sea port of Novorossiysk. In late 2002, the Russian pipeline monopoly, Transneft, stopped deliveries of crude oil to Ventspils following the completion of its own port of Primorsk. Having been left starved for oil, authorities at Ventspils undertook an effort to increase shipments of crude oil and petroleum products delivered by rail. Over the course of 2003, this effort has reportedly served to mitigate some of the losses owing to the absence of Russian crude oil, and in 2003 the port exported roughly 215,000 bbl/d of oil (total), roughly one-third less than pre-embargo averages. Ventspils has, however, lost significant market share, and has exposed its balance sheet to greater risk as petroleum products and rail-borne crude oil are more expensive than crude delivered via pipeline and carry slimmer profit margins.

The future of Ventspils is still uncertain. The two primary owners are the Latvian government and a private concern, Latvijas Naftas Tranzits. Several firms from around the world have expressed interest in acquiring a stake in the port's management, including Russia's Transneft and Rosneft, the Russian-UK joint venture TNK-BP, Kazakhstan's Kaztransoil, and the U.S. investment company BroadStreet Group. The ability of the Ventspils shareholders to secure a reasonable selling price and award a tender will be largely determined by the future of Russian pipeline deliveries to the port.

BUTINGE (LITHUANIA)

Although considerably smaller in terms of capacity, Lithuania's port of Butinge exported slightly more oil in 2003 than the port of Ventspils. This is because Butinge has enjoyed considerably better relations with its Russian suppliers than has Ventspils since 2002 when Russian oil major Yukos became the port's largest shareholder. In 2003, Butinge underwent significant expansion and exported roughly 230,000 bbl/d of crude oil. Port authorities plan to increase throughput to 260,000 bbl/d next year while also increasing storage capacity, thereby ensuring a stable supply of crude oil during inclement weather.

The port of Butinge is one part of a larger Lithuanian oil and gas complex controlled by the company Maizekeiku Nafta which operates the port, as well as Lithuania's only oil refinery, Mazeikiai, and a pipeline system connecting the complex to Russia and to Latvia. Maizekeiku Nafta's two main shareholders are the Russian oil major Yukos (53.7%) and the Lithuanian government (40.66%). Butinge was designed with both import and export capabilities, giving the Latvians the option to import oil should Russian supplies be disrupted.

PRIMORSK (RUSSIA)

The port of Primorsk came online in December 2001 along with Russia's Baltic Pipeline System (BPS), which carries oil from Russia's West Siberian and Timan-Pechora oil provinces westward to the Russian Gulf of Finland. Significant expansion took place over the course of 2003, and by the end of the year throughput had reached approximately 600,000 bbl/d, making Primorsk the Baltic region's busiest port.

Primorsk is wholly owned and operated by Transneft, Russia's state pipeline monopoly. Accordingly, Russian crude oil which traditionally moved through the Baltic states has been re-routed to Primorsk. Russian authorities have stated publicly that when allocating the country's exports, precedence will be given to sea ports in which Russia has a stake over foreign ones; in other words, Primorsk over other Baltic ports.

OIL: MARKET DYNAMICS

The countries of the Baltic region are net oil importers, depending on Russia for approximately 90% of their supply. In 2002, regional domestic production totaled roughly 10,000 bbl/d with Lithuania and Estonia each producing roughly 5,000 bbl/d. Most of Estonia's oil production comes from oil shale. Lativa produces no oil domestically and is entirely dependent on imports.

The Baltics region has only one oil refinery, Lithuania's 263,000-bbl/d Mazeikiai refinery, which sells its products in Lithuania and Estonia and is jointly owned by the Lithuanian government and Russia's Yukos oil company. The refinery underwent modernization in September 2003 enabling the refinery to produce higher grade gasoline compliant with EU standards. The region also imports petroleum products from Russia and is heavily populated by filling stations branded by Russian oil major LUKoil.

NATURAL GAS: MARKET DYNAMICS

The countries of the Baltic region are entirely dependent on natural gas imports to meet their domestic consumption needs. The Baltic countries produced no natural gas in 2001 while consuming a total of 202 billion cubic feet (bcf). Natural gas imports come mostly from Russia and are handled by Russia's natural gas monopoly Gazprom and its subsidiaries. Gazprom holds long-term supply agreements with each of the Baltic states.

Gazprom is also increasingly becoming an owner of natural gas utilities in the Baltic region. Gazprom holds a 25% stake in Latvia's Latvian Gaze and a 37% stake in Estonia's Eesti Gaas (along with other major foreign shareholders, Germany's Ruhrgas and Finland's Fortum). Most recently, in January 2004, Gazprom finalized its acquisition of a 34% stake in Lithuania's natural gas company, Lietuvos Dujos. With the three Baltic states scheduled to join the European Union in May 2004, Gazprom's growing influence in the Baltics could serve as a staging ground for greater exports to the countries of the European Union.

ELECTRICITY: MARKET DYNAMICS

Estonia and Lithuania are net electricity exporters, sending their surplus to neighboring Latvia and parts of northwest Russia. In 2001, Estonia generated 7.9 billion kilowatts (bkwh) of electricity, the preponderance of which came from the country's Narva oil shale-fired power plants. Lithuania generated 14.6 bkwh in 2001, of which 11.4 bkwh came from the country's Soviet-era Ignalina nuclear power plant which is to be closed in two stages beginning in 2005 and ending in 2009. While Lithuania has agreed to the shutdown of its nuclear facilities under strong safety concerns from the EU, the country has indicated its interest in developing a new nuclear facility. The proposal has received support from Estonia, which will see its environmentally hazardous oil shale-fired electricity generation decline over time under EU environmental policies. Importation of nuclear electricity from Lithuania would then serve as an alternative to imports of natural gas from Russia.

Latvia is the region's only net electricity importer, buying from other Baltic states as well as from Russia. The country has some hydroelectric facilities, but in a dry year is estimated to be only 60% self-sufficient. Latvia is working with Estonia and Finland to develop the "Estlink" project, a 315-megawatt underwater cable linking the Baltic states to the Scandinavian and Nordic power grids. The cable is designed to reduce regional dependency on Russia, and is expected to be completed in 2005.

LATVIAS REPORT ENERGY

PROGRESS SINCE THE LAST REGULAR REPORT

Latvia continued the alignment with the energy acquis and progress has been achieved, in particular as regards security of supply and the creation of the internal energy market. Steps have been taken to further improve the administrative capacity and to reinforce the legal base for the functioning of the Public Utilities Commission and the State Energy Inspectorate.

Concerning security of supply, in March 2002 a Regulation aiming at compliance with EC legislation on maintaining oil stocks was approved. Oil stocks will be held by the companies holding licenses for business operation with oil products and by the State itself. Oil stocks will be increased gradually to the required level, while the burden will be shared among the licence holding companies and the State.

Legislation concerning the energy information system was adopted in May 2002. It requires the Ministry of Economy to establish an energy database in order to ensure balanced energy consumption and demand, and to prepare for energy crisis management.
The Ministry of Finance and the Ministry of Economy have been nominated as the institutions responsible for the control of the formation and maintenance of oil stocks. In July 2002, the Ministry of Economy established the first monthly report on the level of oil stocks.

Regarding oil supply crisis management measures, progress has continued with the adoption of implementing legislation in March 2002 defining restrictions on energy consumption. A State Energy Crisis Centre has been established, which includes representatives of ministries and the largest enterprises. The Energy Department of the Ministry of Economy is the Secretariat of the Crisis Centre.

In the area of competitiveness and the internal energy market, a policy document on Energy Policy in the Electricity Sector, aiming at ensuring the reliability and quality of electricity supply and at creating competition in the electricity market, was approved in September 2001. In line with this document, implementing legislation was adopted in January 2002, concerning production of electricity from renewable sources and the purchase price for surplus electricity generated thereby.

Regarding the electricity market, the market is being opened gradually. In November 2001, instructions and criteria on electricity consumption for the status of eligible customer were approved. In 2001, there were 10 eligible customers representing together 13.8 % of the total consumption of electricity in Latvia. As the threshold was not changed for 2002, the number of qualified customers remains approximately the same. Currently the threshold is set at an annual consumption of 40 GWh. This threshold will be lowered to 20 GWh from January 2003, corresponding to a market opening of approximately 20 %. Full market opening is scheduled for 2006.

In the framework of the implementation of the Plan for restructuring the state-owned energy utility, Latvenergo Joint Stock Company (JSC), the Transmission System Operator was established and registered in December 2001. The new Transmission System Operator is a separate legal entity fully owned by Latvenergo JSC.

Further progress has been made for the creation of legal preconditions for the liberalisation of the gas market. In October 2001, the Concept on the Liberalisation of the Gas Market was adopted. The concept aims at introducing elements such as third party access, designation of eligible customers, regulation of transmission, distribution and storage tariffs, and abolition of regulated natural gas selling prices. In October 2001, an Action Plan for implementation of the Concept was adopted.

The privatisation of Latvijas Gze was completed in February 2002. The last 3% of the state-owned shares were sold through a public offering accepting privatisation vouchers.
The regulatory body for energy issues (responsible also for telecommunications, postal and railway transportation), the Public Utilities Commission (PUC), is financed through state-collected fees from regulated enterprises. The approved annual budget for the PUC in 2002 is LVL 1 million (EUR 1.8 million). As of April 2002, the PUC had 66 employees. Staff of the Public Utilities Commission benefited during the reporting period from extensive training.

Concerning energy efficiency and renewable energy, in accordance with the Energy Efficiency Strategy approved in November 2001, implementing legislation was adopted in January 2002 to promote the use of renewable energy sources and domestic production of heat and electricity in combined heat and power plants.
The State Energy Inspectorate, the institution responsible for energy efficiency control and supervision, has been operational since November 2001; its statute was approved in May 2002. In 2002, LVL 52 700 (EUR 94 100) were allocated for the Inspectorate, which had contracted 7 employees by the end of April 2002.

As regards nuclear energy, Latvia operates no nuclear power plant. In the field of nuclear safety, the decommissioning of the Salaspils nuclear reactor, a pool-type research reactor closed in 1998, is continuing. Tender procedures on the right to prepare tender documentation and to organise the tender procedures for decommissioning and dismantling of the reactor were completed in May 2002. Latvia has continued to make progress in finding solutions for managing spent fuel from the research reactor and radioactive waste. Implementing legislation dealing with the requirements for practices involving radioactive waste and related materials and with the criteria and principles for determining equivalence between low, intermediate and high level radioactive wastes, has been adopted in March and April 2002. To ensure operation of the Radiation Safety Centre, responsible for the supervision and control of radiation safety, LVL 184 439 (EUR 329 355) were allocated in the state budget for 2002. The Centre completed 179 working days of educational and training activities in 2001.

OVERALL ASSESSMENT

Concerning security of supplies, implementing legislation now has to be adopted to achieve alignment with the energy acquis. A continuous effort will be required to ensure the financing and build-up of the mandatory oil stocks. On the administrative side, the services in the Ministries of Economy and Finance responsible for the control of oil stocks should be strengthened.

On competitiveness and the internal energy market, the issue of energy price distortion remains to be addressed. The Public Utilities Commission has to be further strengthened and assure its full independence in order to be able to carry out the functions defined in the Electricity and Gas Directives.

Latvia is well advanced in implementing the internal energy market, but harmonisation with the Electricity and Gas Directives has not yet been fully accomplished. Concerning electricity, the market was opened, albeit to a limited extent, ahead of accession; the gradual opening of the market should continue in order to achieve at least the minimum requirements of the Electricity Directive upon accession. Reorganisation of the state electricity utility, Latvenergo, has to be completed with the establishment of separate and independent distribution, administration and power generation companies. Regarding gas, alignment with the Gas Directive should be completed, while the sector needs further restructuring. The Energy Law should be amended to provide the legal basis for third-party access and the establishment of eligible customers.

Concerning energy efficiency, harmonisation with the acquis on labelling appliances and minimum efficiency standards has to be completed. Additional efforts are required to improve further energy efficiency and to enhance the use of renewable energy. The State Energy Inspectorate should be strengthened.

In June 2001, the Council of the European Union took note of a Report on Nuclear Safety in the Context of Enlargement. Whereas Latvia does not operate commercial nuclear power stations, the Report contains recommendations of relevance to Latvia with regard to other nuclear installations, including the safe management of radioactive waste. During the first half of 2002, a special Peer Review on nuclear safety assessed the progress made by candidate countries in implementing all recommendations. This exercise under the auspices of the Council resulted in a Status Report published in June 2002, which concludes that Latvia has accepted and adequately addressed all the recommendations contained in the June 2001 Report on Nuclear Safety in the Context of Enlargement.
Longer-term solutions for spent fuel and nuclear waste will continue to need attention. On the administrative side, the capacity of the Radiation Safety Centre should be strengthened.
Latvia will need to ensure compliance with Euratom requirements and procedures. In this respect, due attention will need to be given to preparing the implementation of Euratom Safeguards procedures, in particular, direct reporting of nuclear material flows and inventories by the persons or undertakings operating nuclear installations, or storing nuclear material. This includes small holders like universities, hospitals and medical practices. It should be noted that Latvia has concluded a Full-Scope Safeguards Agreement with the IAEA.

CONCLUSIONS

In its 1997 Opinion, the Commission concluded that provided that Latvia`s efforts were intensified, no major problems were foreseen to approximate progressively to the then existing acquis in the medium term, adding that aspects such as the adjustment of monopolies, access to networks, energy pricing, emergency preparedness, including the building up of mandatory oil stocks, energy efficiency remained of specific importance. The Commission added that, while no major difficulties were foreseen for compliance with Euratom provisions, Latvia should become rapidly party to certain international nuclear regimes.

Since the Opinion, Latvia has made progress in aligning with the acquis in all areas, especially over the last two years. The implementation of the internal energy market is under way. The formation of oil product reserves has begun. Steps have been taken to improve the administrative capacity and the functioning of the Public Utilities Commission and of the State Energy Inspectorate. An overall reasonable level of legislative and administrative alignment with the EC requirements has been achieved.

Negotiations on this chapter have been provisionally closed. Latvia has been granted a transitional arrangement concerning the building up of oil stocks until 31 December 2009. Latvia is generally meeting the commitments it has made in the accession negotiations in this field.

In order to complete preparations for membership, Latvia`s efforts should now focus on ensuring full and timely implementation of legislation in this area, in particular with regard to implementing legislation on oil stocks, the internal energy market (gas and electricity), on ensuring finance to progressively build up oil stocks and on reinforcing the administrative capacity of the various bodies (independence of the energy regulator).

LATVIA WITHIN THE BALTIC PETROLIFEROUS PROVINCE

Latvia is a part of the so-called Baltic Syneclise and the Latvian Saddle, located on the northwestern edge of the East European Platform. The Latvian hydrocarbon prospects are associated with Western Latvia and the adjacent part of the Baltic Sea shelf, i.e. the northern part of the Baltic Syneclise.

The Baltic Syneclise is a sedimentary basin with thick succession of sedimentary rocks and is regarded as highly prospective, being part of a proven, Baltic petroliferous province, with oil production in several countries. In total about **35 hydrocarbon accumulations** have been discovered there. Most of them are oil accumulations, but offshore Poland gas pools were also found.

In the **Kaliningrad district,** oil production began in 1975. Currently they produce about 900,000 cu m per year (5.6 million bbl/year) from the onshore field. In the second half of 2004, production from the offshore D6 field started.

The **Lithuanian onshore** oil production started after the restoration of independence in 1991. It was very limited at the beginning, but increased quite fast and reached about 450,000 cu m (2.8 million bbl) in 2003.

In the **Polish sector of the Baltic Sea**, the B3 field is producing with the yearly production about 300 thousand cu m (1.9 million bbl/year). The project on development of offshore gas fields is under consideration.

Also, in the northern part of the basin, from time to time small-scale oil production takes place on the **Swedish island of Gotland**.

In Latvia, several small oil accumulations were discovered some time ago, and there was no exploration activity during the last 10 years. Only minor, short time oil production took place during the crisis time in 1990.

Now, the country has opened its offshore and onshore for further exploration and oil production.

LATVIA – PETROLEUM POTENTIAL AND EXPLORATION OPPORTUNITIES.

Mini-Atlas prepared through the cooperation between the State Geological Survey of Latvia and PGS Reservoir (Norway).
This mini-atlas offers to the oil industry an introduction to the region presenting condensed facts on the country itself and on the Baltic basin in general. The mini-atlas has nine chapters containing relevant information on the geological history of the area, updated stratigraphy and palaeogeography, together with information on reservoirs, source rocks and hydrocarbon habitat of the region.

Brangulis, A.P., Kanev, S.V., Margulis, L.S. & Pomerantseva, R.A. 1993: **Geology and hydrocarbon prospects of the Palaeozoic in the Baltic region**. In: Parker, J.R. (ed.)

Petroleum Geology of NW Europe . Proceedings of the 4th Conference, London , March-April 1992. Geol. Soc., 1993.

Freimanis, A., Margulis L.S., Brangulis, A., Kanev, S. and Pomerantseva, R. 1993: **Geology and hydrocarbon prospects of Latvia** . Oil & Gas Journal, Dec. 6, 1993 .

Kanev, S., Margulis, L., Bojesen-Koefoed, J.A., Weil, W.A., Merta, H. & Zdanaviciute, O. 1994: **Oil and hydrocarbon source rocks of the Baltic Syneclise.** Oil & Gas Journal, July 11, 1994 .

Kanev, S., Kushik E., Peregudov Y. 2000: **A Large Ordovician Carbonate Buildup offshore Latvia**. Latvijas Geologijas Vestis Journal, 8/00.

Kanev S., Lauritzen O., Schmitz U. 2001: **Latvia 's First Offshore Round – Its Potential and Perspectives**. OIL GAS European Magazine 3/2001.

Dobrova H., Kolly E., Schmitz U. 2003: **E&P Ventures in the Eastern-Central Europe. Transformation States after 1989 - a Review of Expectations and Results**. OIL GAS European Magazine 4/2003.

MAIN ACTIVITIES IN THE HYDROCARBON SPHERE

Since 1990s, when the Latvian state made the decision to start hydrocarbon licensing, the main tasks of the Latvian Environment, Geology and Meteorology Agency are as follows:

1. Prepare geological, geophysical and other information:
- Databases of well and seismic data for the oil-prospective area.
- Digitization of well logs. Now, all the logs are available not only in the paper format, as it was earlier, but also in the digital LAS format.
- Demultiplexing of seismic data to the international SEG-Y format.

2. Evaluation of the hydrocarbon potential, exploration and production possibilities:
- Interpretation of log diagrams, determining petrophysical properties of reservoirs, as well as effective thickness, oil saturation etc.
- Potential Latvian offshore prospects were evaluated, including calculations of potential oil resources, evaluations of the geological risk, field development concepts and economic calculations, etc.
- Seismic data reprocessing projects, in order to be able to better demonstrate seismic data from the future licensing areas;
- Different research projects to search for new oil prospective objects, increasing the oil potential.

3. Presentation of the oil potential to both foreign oil companies and local businessmen.

4. Preparation of petroleum geological information for oil companies and the regional development planning.

5. Dealing with geological aspects of the preparation and marketing of licensing rounds.

6. Development of licensing strategies together with the Ministry of Economics.
7. Participation in the Licensing Commission, evaluating licence applications.

GEOLOGICAL SETTING AND STRUCTURAL ELEMENTS

Western Latvia and the adjacent Baltic Sea shelf are situated within the northern part of a single sedimentary basin called the Baltic Syneclise.

The Baltic Syneclise is a large marginal depression within the East-European Platform, whose most important features in the Baltic Region (including Latvia) is subsidence of the top crystalline basement towards south and south-west; it is characterised by the maximum thickness of the sedimentary cover (it reaches 2 km in Latvia) and stratigraphically most complete section; its structure is faulted, in some places, block structure is observed.

The main structural components of the Baltic Syneclise in Latvia are: the *Liepaja-Saldus Ridge*, *Gdansk-Kura* and *Liepaja depressions*, as well as the *Latvian-Estonian* and *Lithuanian Border Zones.*

The Liepaja-Saldus Ridge is a regional faulted zone with a complex structure, oriented SW-NE. It transverses from the central part of the Baltic Sea onshore to central Latvia over a distance of more than 300 km. The Liepaja-Saldus Ridge is bounded by major faults, with displacement of Caledonian sediments up to 600 m. The high incorporates several structures of lesser rank, with which most Latvian oil prospects are associated.

The Gdansk-Kura Depression is a large regional structure, continuing as far as Poland. Only its northern part reaches Latvia, incorporating the southern part of Western Latvia and the adjacent part of the Baltic Sea. Several oil discoveries were made there in Lithuania and Kaliningrad District; several oil prospective local highs were discovered in Latvia as well.

The Liepaja Depression is located, predominantly, in the Baltic offshore area, also occupying a small area in onshore. It is an important relatively simple structure that is considered as a possible oil generation zone.

The *Latvian-Estonian* and the *Lithuanian Border Zones* are situated in the border zones of the Baltic Syneclise and are characterised my monoclinal layering and relatively shallow basement where small anticline and reefoid structures were discovered.

The Latvian area is a part of an old platform, the geological section of which displays two components characteristic of palaeoplatforms: the crystalline basement and sedimentary cover. The sedimentary cover, unconformably overlying the heavily eroded surface of the crystalline basement, consists of the terrigenous, carbonate and sulphate rocks of U. Proterozoic (Vendian Complex) and Phanerozoic – Cambrian through Jurassic. The Cambrian, Ordovician, Silurian and Devonian rocks are the most abundant, while Carboniferous, Permian, Triassic and Jurassic deposits were observed in SW Latvia alone. The major depositional stages are separated by periods of non-deposition and erosion; these unconformities within the sedimentary succession reflect the major tectonic events.

SOURCE ROCKS

In the Baltic Region three prominent source rock intervals are found within the Lower Palaeozoic succession within Upper Cambrian to Tremadocian, Ordovician (Caradocian) and Lower Silurian (Llandoverian) succession. The table (see fig.) illustrates identified and potential source rock intervals for Latvia and the entire Baltic Region.

Upper Cambrian to Tremadocian deposits constitute excellent source rocks, being time equivalent to the Alum Shale of Bornholm and Scania. These organic rich shales have been eroded in the eastern parts of the Baltic Syneclise, including Latvian area. At the same time, the southwestern part of Latvia's offshore area is geographically close to the Leba High offshore Poland, where Alum Shales are identified in all wells. Therefore potential source rocks could occur in this region. In the southern part of Latvia, organic rich shales are found within the Late Tremadocian succession.

Caradocian black shales, referred to as the Fjäcka and Mossen Formations, constitute excellent source rocks, TOC values up to 16% and pyrolysis yields of 65-75 kg/ton. A total thickness is about 5-10 m.

A prolific source rock interval occurs within the **Llandoverian** deposits (Dobele Formation). These shales display excellent source rock properties in Latvia; TOC values may reach 15-17% with pyrolysis yields of up to 70 kg HC/ton rock. A thickness is about 5-25 m.

The type of organic matter in these source rocks is similar, irrespective of geologic age. The kerogen type, which dominates, is typically marine Type II; the variations observed being ascribed to original richness and thermal maturity variations only.

THERMAL MATURITY

In the Polish, Kalinigrad district and Lithuania areas these shales are thermally mature, being immature to very early mature in Latvia. Therefore, hydrocarbon occurrence in Latvia is dependent on migration pathways and distances from the main kitchen areas.
In addition, it is forecast that a possible oil generation zone (local kitchen) is located in the Liepaja Depression.

LATVIAN OILS CHARACTERISTICS

The properties of oils are shown in the table.
As regards physical and chemical parameters, Latvian onshore oils are heavier than Lithuanian and Kaliningrad oils and contain somewhat more sulphur and asphaltene-tar components. The oil from offshore E6 well is lighter and practically the same as oils from other pars of the Baltic basin.

HYDROCARBON LICENSING

In **1995**, an oil exploration and production licence was issued to AMOCO/OPAB for operations in the SW Latvian offshore area, but that licence still has not come into force due to the offshore border dispute between Latvia and Lithuania. OPAB is the present Licensee.

In 1997, the Cabinet of Ministers has approved the concept "The establishment of the industry of development of oil resources and establishment of oil industry in the Republic of Latvia", which envisages the licensing of oil prospecting, exploration and production in

WELL / AREA	Reservoir age	Test interval (m)	Density g/cm³ (20°C)	Viscosity cp (20°C)	Sulphur (%)	Asphaltene & Tar (%)	Wax (%)	Fraction boiling up to 300 °C
OFFSHORE								
E 6	U. Ordovician	729-739	0.836	6.3	0.21	3.7		61.0
KULDIGA AREA								
Adze 6	U. Ordovician	827-834	0.886		0.37	16.7	3.9	32.0
Adze 6D	M. Cambrian	992-994	0.909		0.60	16.4	1.3	
P 2	M. Cambrian	983-986	0.891		0.40	13.4	1.0	50.0
Riekstini 15	L. Ordovician	910-975	0.900	10.7	0.40	11.2	2.5	50.0
BERNATI AREA								
Bernati 53	U. Ordovician	1015-1019	0.876	8.5			0.8	
Bernati 2	U. Ordovician	994-1004	0.870	20.0	0.30	1.0	0.9	45.6
Bernati 24	U. Ordovician	1031-1041	0.864					
Bernati 6	U. Ordovician	993-995	0.854	23.7	0.54			41.7
DURBE AREA								
Durbe 36	U. Ordovician	923-930	0.855	18.6	0.58	2.4		46.6
Aistere 15	L. Ordovician	1066-1069	0.852	16.5		3.2		

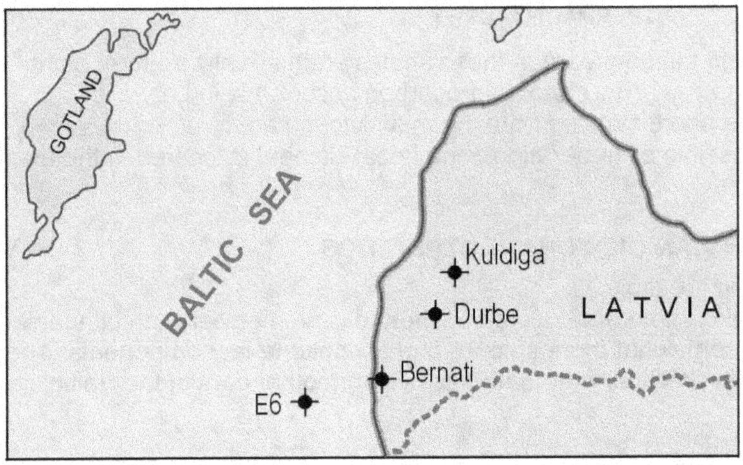

Latvian oil characteristics

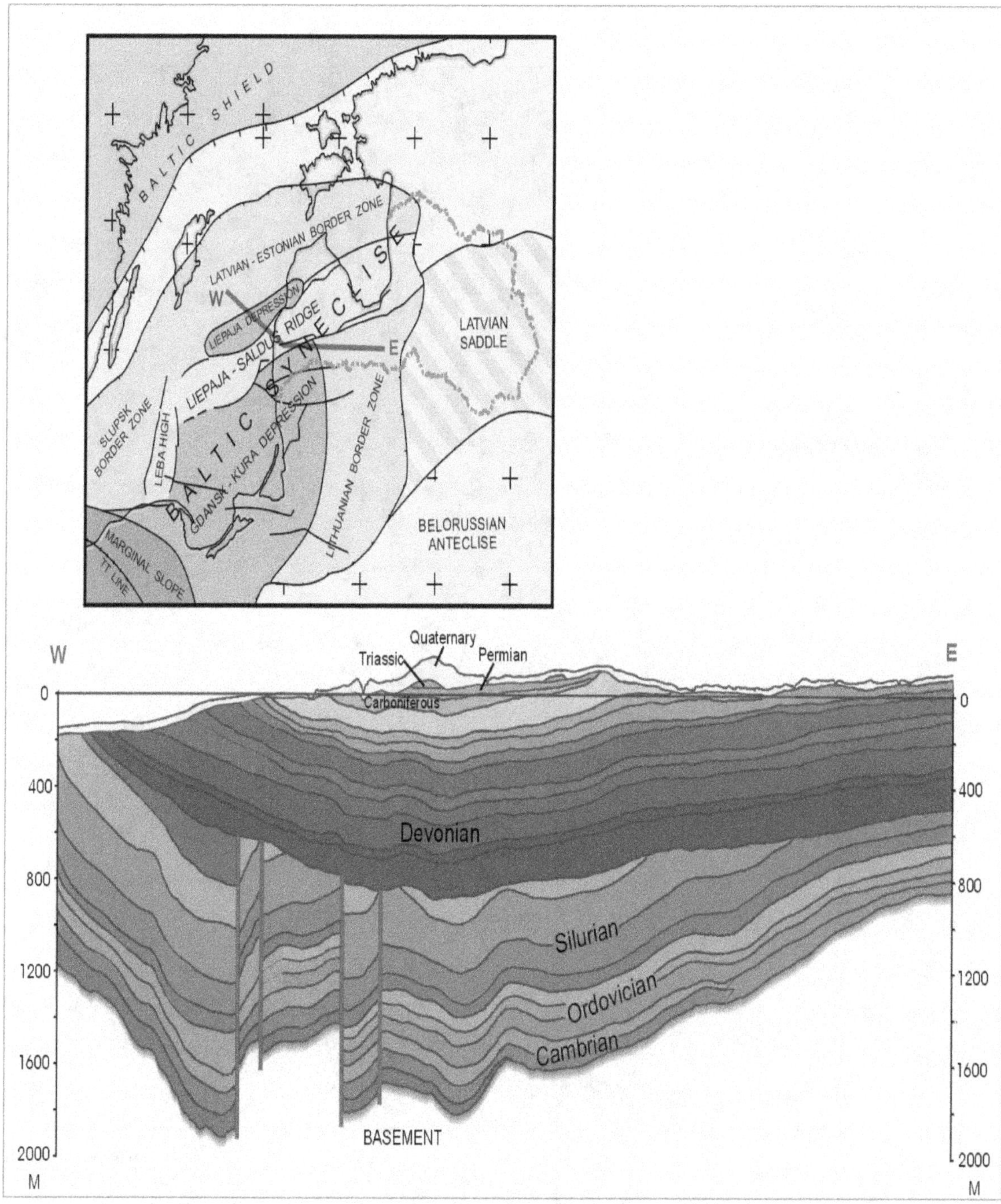

Major structural elements of the Baltic region and Geological cross-section of Baltic Syneclise in Latvia

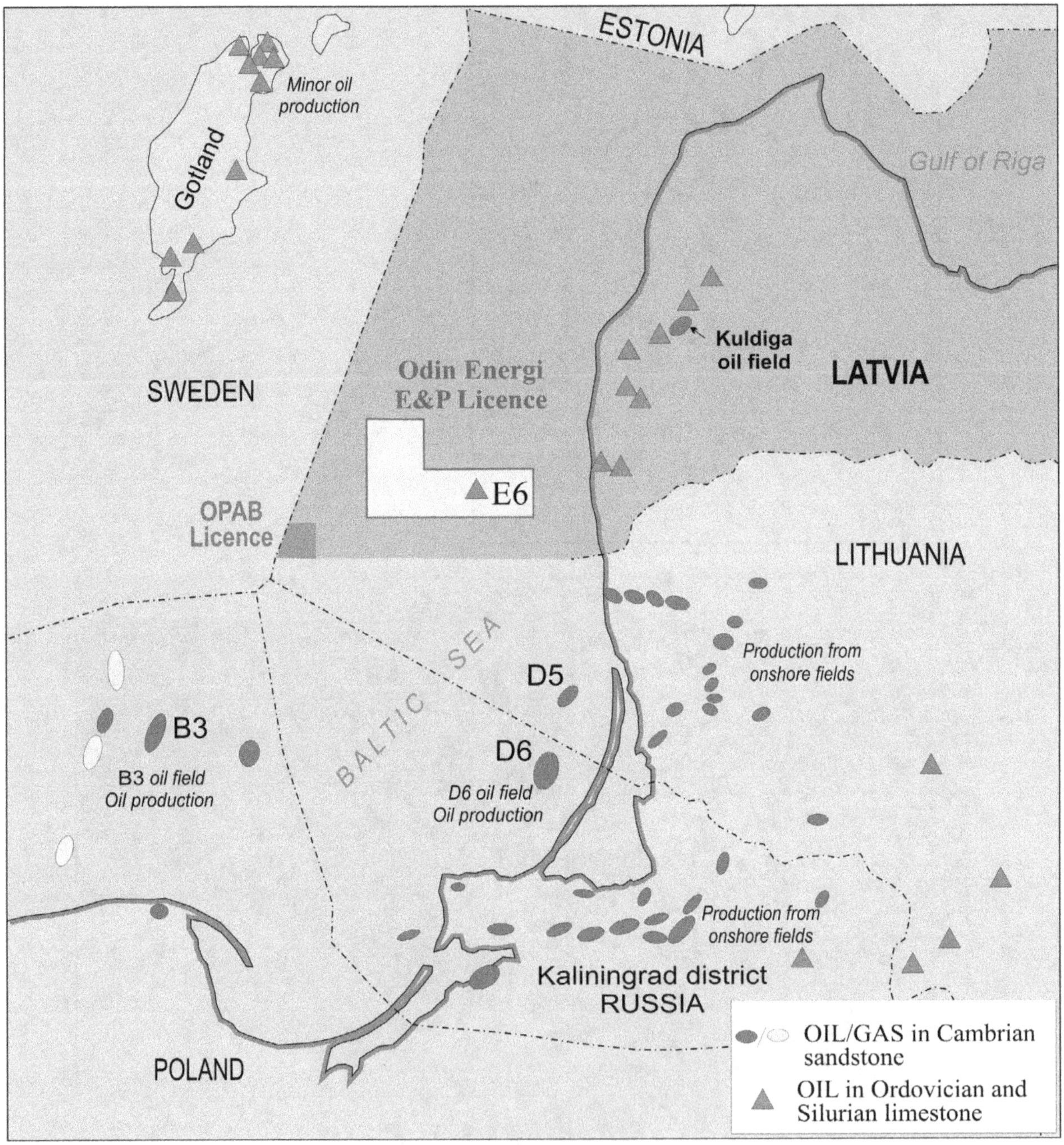

HC accumulations and oil production in Baltic Region

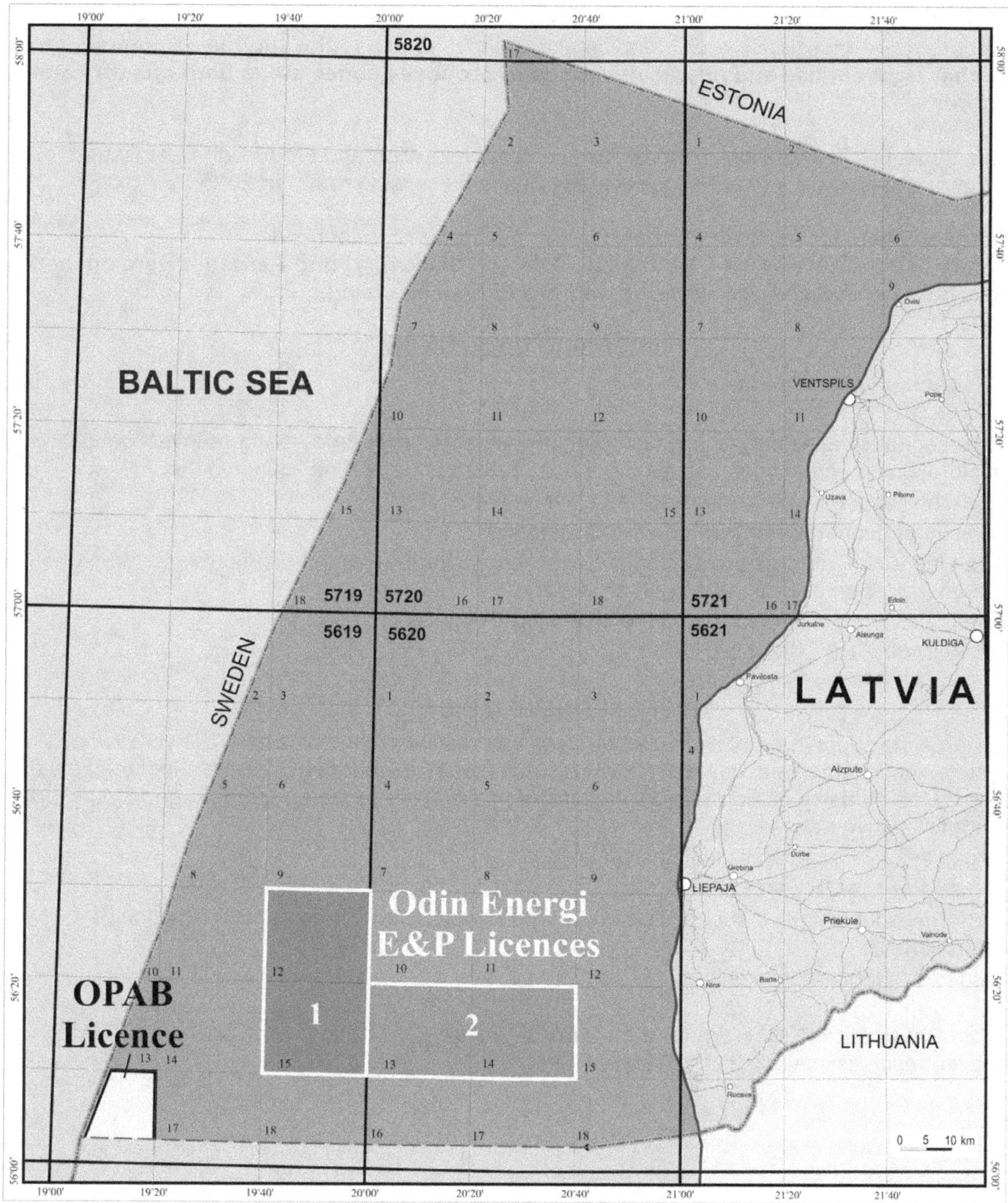

Latvia, thus providing possibilities to participate in such operations for both foreign and Latvian entrepreneurs.

Hydrocarbon licensing in Latvia was initiated **in 2001** by announcing the **1st offshore licensing round.**

In **April 2003**, the Cabinet of Ministers accepted Amendments to all Regulations regarding Hydrocarbon Pre-Investigation, Exploration and Production, **thus allowing the oil companies or any other legal entities and physical persons to propose licence areas both offshore and onshore**.

In **July 2004**, two licences for offshore hydrocarbon exploration and production were issued. It is planned to prepare and announce the 2nd offshore licensing round **in 2005**.

In October 2004, the first onshore licensing competition was announced.
Recently two onshore areas – Kuldiga (Kuldiga oil discovery) and Bernati - were opened for onshore hydrocarbon exploration and production licensing.

LICENSING PROCEDURE

The licensing procedure is as follows:

- A person (any legal entity or physical person) interested in hydrocarbon pre-investigation, exploration and production can initiate the procedure to determine licence areas.
- The Cabinet of Ministers approves the Licence area.
- Ministry of Economics announces the Competition.
- The Licensing Commission reviews the applications for the Permit (Licence) for hydrocarbon pre-investigation or exploration and production.
- The positive/negative decision of the Licensing Commission.
- AWARD OF THE LICENCE.

THE RESPONSIBLE INSTITUTION

As regards the supervision of hydrocarbon use, irrespective of the ownership of hydrocarbons (the state, local authorities, any legal or physical persons), is conducted, on behalf of the Latvian State , by the **Ministry of Economics**, in compliance with the procedures envisaged by the legal and administrative acts:

- Organises hydrocarbon licensing rounds;
- Issues Permits (Licences);
- Performs administrative supervision of pre-investigation, exploration and production of hydrocarbons;
- Controls hydrocarbon activities.

Latvian Environment, Geology and Meteorology Agency function - see section **LEGMA function;** main task see section **LEGMA main task**

Attachment to
the Regulations of the Cabinet of Ministers
No. 52 of February 8, 2000

HYDROCARBON RELATED INFRASTRUCTURE

Current hydrocarbon related infrastructure in Latvia comprises pipelines for oil, oil products and gas. A large amount of Russian oil/oil products is exported through the ports of Latvia. An oil pipeline crosses over from Russia to Latvia, terminating in Ventspils, from where Russian oil is exported. The present capacity of the oil terminal in Ventspils (see www.Ventspils.lv) is more than 30 million tons per year. Russian oil is also exported through the port of Riga.

Gas storage is important in the country's gas supply sector, and Incukalns is a big underground gas storage established within the Cambrian sandstone reservoir, with a capacity of 4 billion m³. Gas transportation facilities incorporate a network of gas pipelines, connecting the Incukalns gas storage with Russia, Estonia and Lithuania.

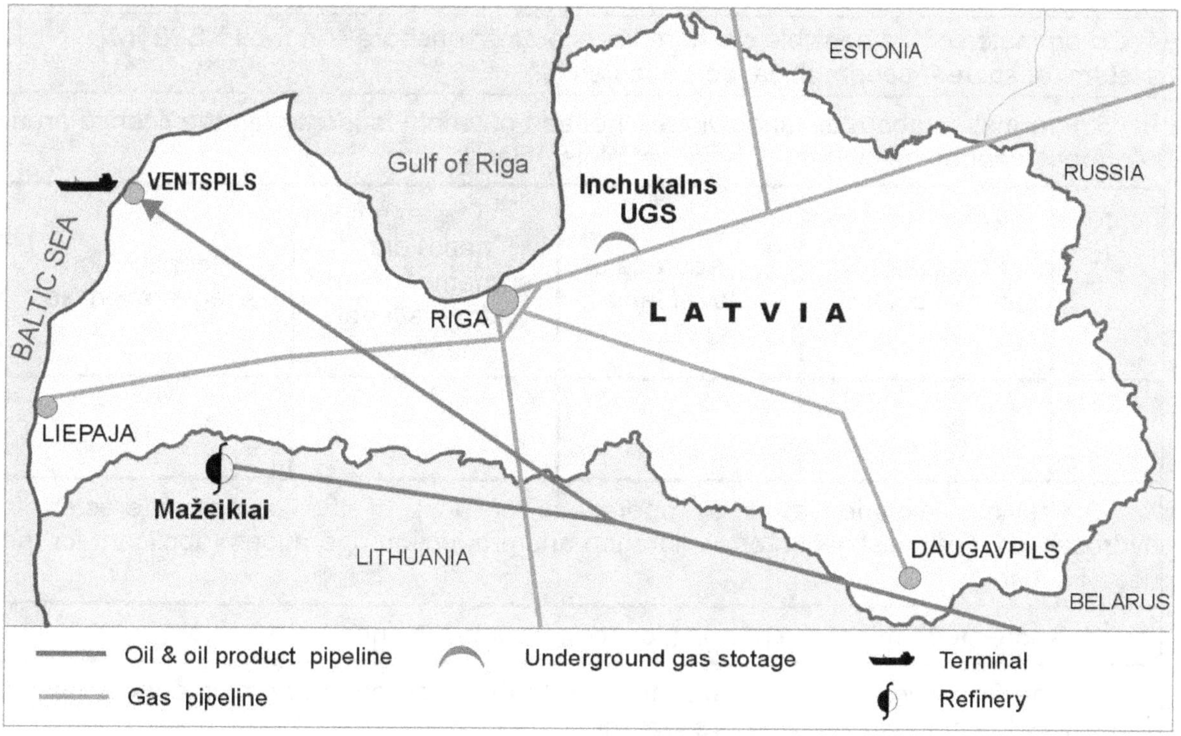

Current infrastructure for the oil and gas industry in Latvia

APPLICATION FOR THE DETERMINATION OF A LICENCE AREA FOR HYDROCARBON PROSPECTING (PRE-INVESTIGATION),

EXPLORATION AND PRODUCTION

1. Information about the Applicant	
1.1. First name, surname/name	
1.2. Identity No./Registration No., date and place	
1.3. Place of residence/legal address	
1.4. Telephone No.	
1.5. Fax No.	
1.6. E-mail address	
1.7. Internet home page address	
2. Purpose of the use of subsoil	
3. Location of the possible onshore licence area – administrative area	
4. Co-ordinates of the possible onshore licence area: onshore – in the LKS92TM system, offshore – geographical co-ordinates	

5. Information about all landowners, the land of whom is located in the licence area, information about the owners of adjacent plots of land:

No.	Cadastre No. of plot of land	Address of plot of land	Owner's first name and surname/ name; address/legal address	Identity No. /Registration No.

6. Previous experience in oil operations (if any) of the person interested in hydrocarbon pre-investigation or exploration and production operations (applicant for the use of subsoil)

7. Requested term of the permit (licence), if such is planned

8. The following documents are attached to the application (if document copies are submitted, the originals must be presented):

	Type of document		Number of pages
8.1.	Copy of businessman's registration certificate/copy of passport of physical person		

8.2.	The landowner's requirements to the licensee, which will be included in the Statute of Competition for hydrocarbon exploration and production operations	î	
8.3.	General substantiation of geological prospectivity of the licence area	î	
8.4.	Map of land boundaries (certified copy), if the possible licence area is located onshore	î	
8.5.	Document confirming land ownership (certified copy)	î	
8.6.	Map of the possible licence area issued by the State Land Survey, with co-ordinates (two originals) and certificate regarding plots of land existing in the licence area, with landowners and land cadastre numbers indicated	î	
8.7.	Notarised Power of Attorney for the person making transactions on behalf of the landowner, landholder or businessman	î	

(Applicant's signature and name) (date)

HYDROCARBON LICENSING. OFFSHORE.

In **1995**, an oil exploration and production licence was issued to AMOCO/OPAB for operations in the SW Latvian offshore area, but that licence still has not come into force due to the offshore border dispute between Latvia and Lithuania. OPAB is the present Licensee.

In **April 2001**, the **1st offshore licensing round** was announced for hydrocarbon prospecting, exploration and production offshore Latvia.

In **April 2002**, a repeated licensing round was announced for hydrocarbon exploration and production offshore Latvia, as well as the **2nd round** for offshore prospecting.

In **2002**, two hydrocarbon prospecting licences were issued to TGS-NOPEC. The licence area incorporates almost the whole Latvian shelf, comprising about 20,000 sq. km. These licences are not valid any longer.

In **July 2004**, two hydrocarbon exploration and production licences were issued to Odin Energi A/S. The licence areas are located in the southern part of the Latvian offshore area (see map), comprising 1,532 km^2.

In 2005, The Latvian Government prepares to announce the 2nd licensing round for hydrocarbon exploration and production in the southwest and nothern part of the Latvian offshore in the Baltic Sea.

ONSHORE HYDROCARBON LICENSING

Since April 2003, it is possible to obtain a permit (licence) for onshore hydrocarbon prospecting, exploration and production.
The Cabinet of Ministers has announced several licence areas in Liepaja and Kuldiga districts, where competitions for hydrocarbon exploration and production were announced.

One of them resulted in an application (Liepaja area), which is considered by the Licensing Commission at the moment.
Applications are being submitted in two more competitions (Kuldiga and Bernati areas).

KULDIGA AREA

On April 5, 2005, the Ministry of Economics has announced a licensing competition for exploration and production at the Kuldiga oil deposit. The licence area is located in Gudenieki Parish, Kuldiga District, and Lazha Parish, Liepaja District (see map). **Application for the competition must be submitted until August 25, 2005, 12:00 hours.** The applications must be submitted to the Ministry of Economics, Office 315, 55 Brivibas Street, LV-1519, Latvia; the contact person is Maija Vimba.

The Statute of the Licensing Competition is obtainable from the Ministry of Economics (Office 315). The price of the Statute is 300.00 LVL .

More detailed information about the competition can be obtained by e-mail: Maija.Vimba@em.gov.lv ; telephone: + 371 7013173 ; fax: + 371 7013177.

The **Kuldiga oil discovery** is located within the licence area, discovered in 1963, it is the very first oil discovery within the Cambrian succession of the Baltic Region. It is associated with the Kuldiga High, and is an asymmetrical north-northeast trending anticlinal structure (see map). The size of this fold is about 45 km^2 with a vertical closure of 60 m, its eastern flank is steep and fault controlled. Based on the drilling data, the identified oil occurs within a 7 m (based on seismic data -15? m) thick sandstone layer of the Deimena Formation, which is 55 m thick there. The sandstone is poorly cemented, and the porosity exceeds 20%, permeability might exceed 1D. The oil-bearing bed is sealed by 8-11 m of Early Ordovician mudstone. The Kuldiga oil-water contact is horizontal at depth of 962 (961?) m. The driving mechanism in the structure is predominantly by water; reservoir temperature is 22ºC and initial pressure was 102 atmospheres. In the well Kuldiga R-2 (Kuldiga-2) the oil flow reached 3.3 m3 per day on test.
Besides, at the Kuldiga deposit, oil was observed in the Ordovician deposits as well.

AVAILABLE GEOPHYSICAL AND GEOLOGICAL DATA

Small-scale CDP seismic investigations were carried out in the area of the Kuldiga oil deposit; several wells were drilled.

Well and seismic data are available to the oil industry for purchase and inspection:

BERNATI AREA

On June 22, 2005, the Ministry of Economics has announced a competition for hydrocarbon exploration and production in two licence areas, which are located in Otanki Parish and Nica Parish, Liepaja District (see map).

Applications for **the competition for hydrocarbon exploration and production operations in the licence area located in Otanki Parish and Nica Parish, Liepaja District must be submitted** to the Ministry of Economics of the Republic of Latvia, Contact Person Maija Vimba, Office 315, 55 Brivibas St. (Structure 2), Riga, LV-1519, Latvia, **before October 24,12:00 hours.** The Statute of the Licensing Competition is obtainable at the Ministry of Economics, Office 315, from June 23, 2005. The price of the Statute is 300 LVL.

Two wells are located within the licence area or in the vicinity - Bernati-24 and Nica, where oil shows were observed in the Top Ordovician (Saldus Formation) limestone.

During 1986-1987 and 1990-1992 CDP seismic investigations were carried out in the Bernati area. Several wells were drilled thee, mostly during 1960-70s. Well locations and seismic grid – see the map.

Well Bernati-24 general data, well summary sheet and logging, Well and seismic data are available to the oil industry for purchase and inspection:

LIEPAJA AREA

June 13, 2005 was the deadline for applications for the licensing competition for hydrocarbon exploration operations in the licence area (see map), located in the Dunalka Parish and Durbe Territory, Liepaja District. One application was received, which is under consideration by the Licensing Commission at the moment.

The Ministry of Economics is going to announce a competition for hydrocarbon exploration operations in "Kaleji", Dunalka Parish, Liepaja District (see map).

Both areas are within the Liepaja Structure. Several wells were drilled there in 1960s, small-scale CDP seismic investigations were carried out there (in 1992-1993).

From the well Aistere (Durbe)-15, a small oil flow (0.1-0.15 m^3/day) was obtained from the Top Ordovician (Saldus Formation) limestone and Lower Ordovician siltstone (Kriukai Formation). From the well Durbe-36, there was a small oil flow from the Top Ordovician (Saldus Formation) limestone, oil shows were observed in the cores from the Lower Ordovician siltstone (Kriukai Formation) and Middle Ordovician deposits (Taurupe and Dreimani Formations).

Well and seismic data are available to the oil industry for purchase and inspection:

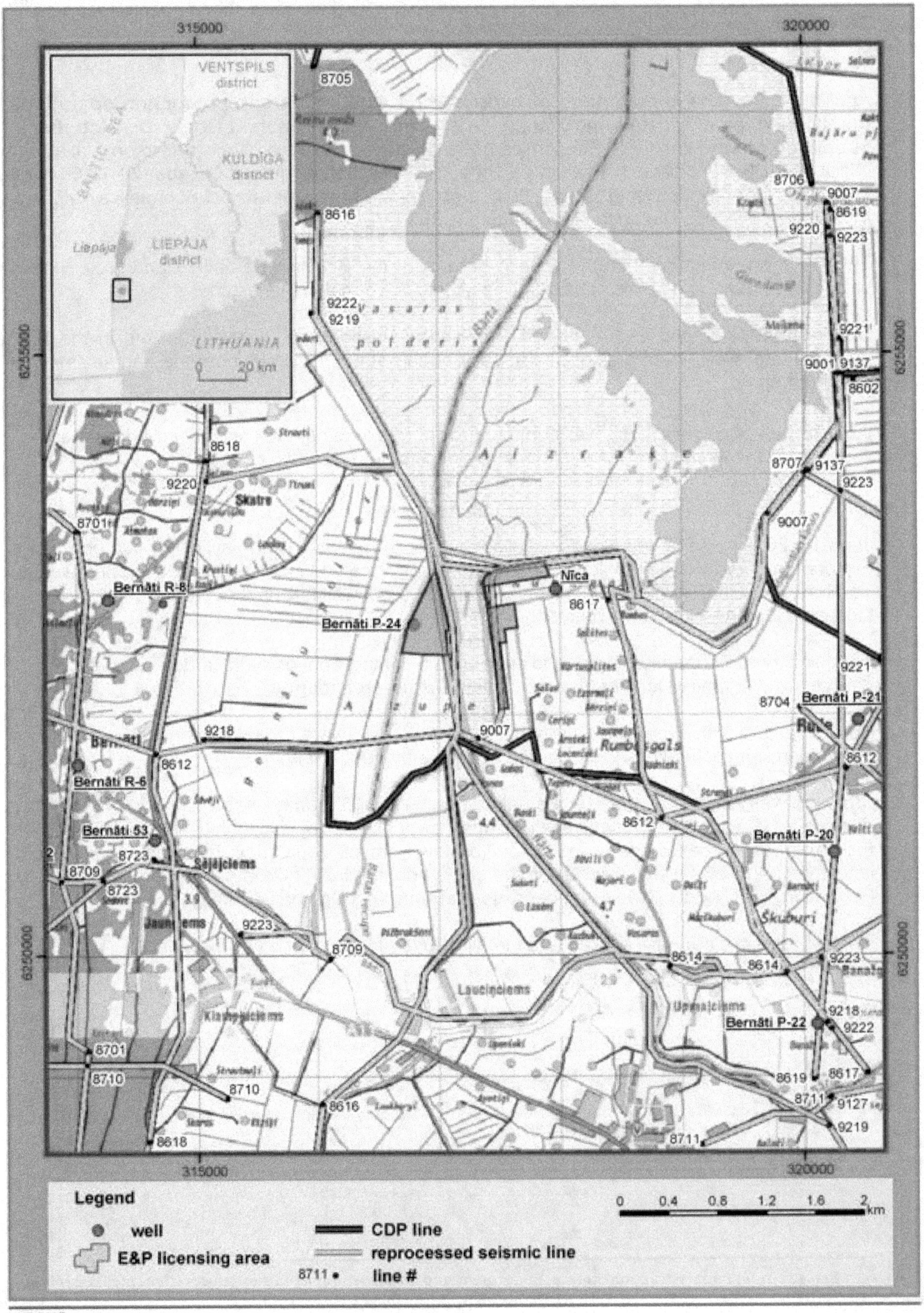
315000
320000
6255000
6250000
VENTSPILS district
KULDĪGA district
LIEPĀJA district
Liepāja
BALTIC SEA
LITHUANIA
0 20 km
Nīca
Bernāti R-8
Bernāti P-24
Bernāti R-6
Bernāti 53
Bernāti P-21
Bernāti P-20
Bernāti P-22
Skatre
Sājājciems
Jaunciems
Lauciniciems
Rumbasgals
Škuburi
Upmalciems
Legend
well
E&P licensing area
CDP line
reprocessed seismic line
8711 • line #
0 0.4 0.8 1.2 1.6 2 km

IMPORTANT LAWS AND REGULATIONS FOR MINING, OIL AND GAS EXPLORATION

Law of the Republic of Latvia on Subsoil

Regulations for Pre-investigation, Exploration and Production of Hydrocarbons

Regulations of the Competition for Award of the Licenses for Pre-investigation, Exploration and Production of Hydrocarbons

Regulations on the State Fee for the Oil Production

Regulations regarding the Protection of the Environment during Exploration and Production of Hydrocarbons in the Sea

LAW ON THE SUBSOIL

SECTION I GENERAL PROVISIONS

Terms used in the text of the Law
The following terms are used in the text of the Law:
topsoil – the upper porous layer of the earth crust formed under the influence of atmospheric and biological factors and where natural vegetation occurs;
common mineral resources – mineral resources, commonly occurring in Latvia, with sufficient reserves;

mineral resources – formations of inorganic or organic origin (including groundwater), the use of which is practical and economically feasible;
a deposit of mineral resources – a natural accumulation of mineral resources, the amount, quality and conditions of production of which have been evaluated and which can be practically used;

Cadastre of deposits of mineral resources – a set of data pertaining to the reserves and quality of such deposits;

production of mineral resources – a set of operations at a commercial deposit, aimed at the production of minerals;

exploration for mineral resources – geological, geophysical geochemical and technical operations in the licence area, aimed at the determination of the quality and reserves of minerals in the deposit, and to evaluate the commerciality of mineral resources;
balance of reserves of mineral resources – a set of data collected during a certain period of time, pertaining to the volumes of production, depletion of reserves and remaining reserves of mineral resources;

prospecting for mineral resources – purposeful geological studies aimed at finding deposits of minerals prospective for the subsequent exploration;
cased well – a cased well aimed at the intake of groundwater;
geological information – data pertaining to the structure, properties and resources of the subsoil;
geological investigations – all types of geological operations aimed at determining the structure, composition, properties, condition of the subsoil, as well as the regularities of occurrence and distribution of mineral resources and useful properties of the subsoil;
driven or drilled well – a strengthened well with pipes aimed at the intake of groundwater;

licence area – a subsoil area (block) or a combination of several areas (blocks) or their parts aimed at a concrete type of the use of the subsoil, within the limits of which a permit (licence) for a certain use of the subsoil or a permit for the production of common minerals is valid;

hydrocarbons – untreated oil (crude oil), natural gas and condensate;
easement – the right to use the subsoil when property rights regarding the use of the subsoil are limited in favour of a certain entity;

mineral resources of State importance – hydrocarbons [untreated oil (crude oil), natural gas] and groundwater (freshwater, mineral water, water for the use by the industry);
deposit of mineral resources of State importance – a deposit determined as such by the Cabinet of Ministers, located within the Latvian territory or the Exclusive Economic Zone (EEZ), and the reserves of which satisfy the needs of the State or its several regions in a mineral resource;

subsoil area of State importance – subsoil areas determined as such by the Cabinet of Ministers, located within the Latvian territory or EEZ, possessing certain subsoil properties, and the use of which may be of a particular importance in the State economy, defence and other fields;

subsoil – a part of the earth crust below topsoil and surface water as deep as it is economically and technologically possible to carry out geological investigations, production of mineral resources or to use the subsoil;
use of the subsoil – geological investigations, production of mineral resources and the use of the properties of the subsoil;
permit (licence) for the use of the subsoil – a document confirming the right of its holder to use the subsoil within stated limits, for stated purposes, in the stated manner and during a certain period of time, complying with the stated requirements and regulations;
the Earth crust – the external hard layer of the Earth, its thickness in Latvia being 40-64 km;

the subsoil fund – all the usable or non-usable subsoil, notwithstanding the type of property (owner) within the Latvian territory or EEZ;
subsoil monitoring – a system of the subsoil observations, control, analyses and forecasting;

State geological supervision of the subsoil fund – a system of measures in compliance with the administrative acts, aimed at the supervision of the procedures of the use of the subsoil, the target of which is to supervise the compliance with the procedures of the use of the subsoil as determined by the legal acts, administrative documents and permits or licences (the compliance of geological investigations with the programme and evaluation of achieved results, accept and accounting of reserves of mineral resources).

(As amended by the law "Amendments to the law "On the Subsoil" of February 11, 1999, coming into force on March 10, 1999).

1. The implementation of the Law

This Law determines the procedures for comprehensive, rational and environmentally safe use of the subsoil as well as the requirements for the use and protection of the subsoil.

Property rights
The subsoil and all mineral resources therein belong to the landowner.
The landowner may use the subsoil, insofar as this Law and other legal acts do not limit his rights.

SECTION II SUPERVISION OF THE SUBSOIL FUND OF THE REPUBLIC OF LATVIA

Institutions supervising the use of the subsoil fund

The supervision of the use of the subsoil fund is carried out, on behalf of the State, notwithstanding the type of property (owner), in compliance with procedures contained in the administrative acts, by:
the Ministry of Environmental Protection and Regional Development (MEPRD) and institutions within its structure, under its administration and supervision;
the Ministry of Economy (ME);
the local authorities of parishes and towns (cities).
(2) The competence of the above institutions is defined by this and other laws, as well as the Statutes of the above Ministries and the State Geological Survey (SGS), and other administrative acts.
(3) SGS is a State administrative institution under the administration of MEPRD which, within the limits of its competence, safeguards the rational use of the subsoil and carries out the geological supervision of the state subsoil fund. The activities of SGS are governed by this Law and the Statutes approved by the Cabinet of Ministers.
(4) ME organises competitions for hydrocarbon prospecting, exploration and production (permits) licences for the areas and in compliance with the procedures determined by the Cabinet of Ministers and issues such permits (licences), and carries out administrative supervision of hydrocarbon prospecting, exploration and production.
(5) The local authorities of parishes and towns (cities), within the territories under their administration:
in accordance with the procedures approved by the Cabinet of Ministers and the limits determined by MEPRD issue permits (licences) for the use of common mineral resources within the yearly quotas and limitations, excluding the cases mentioned in 4(7) and 10(2);
control the remediation of sites of deposits of mineral resources.
(6) The expenses of the local authorities necessary to carry out the functions delegated to them are covered from the fees received for the permits (licences) for the use of the subsoil.
(7) If a deposit of mineral resources occurs within the territories administered by several parishes and towns (cities), or the local authorities use the right of easement, the permits (licences) for the use of subsoil are issued by SGS.

(As amended by the law "Amendments to the law "On the Subsoil" of February 11, 1999, coming into force on March 10, 1999).

The forms of supervision of the use of the subsoil

(1) MEPRD, on behalf of the State and in compliance with the procedures set forward in this Law and other legal acts, while supervising the subsoil:

1) carries out the accounting of the reserves of mineral resources;

2) compiles the cadastre of the deposits of minerals and the balance of the reserves of minerals;

3) determines the volumes of production of minerals (except hydrocarbons);

4) prepares standards (norms, regulations) for the geological exploration of the subsoil, the use and the protection thereof, the safety regulations in the operations in conjunction with the use of the subsoil.

The Cabinet of Ministers, in the interests of the State, has the right to limit the rights of legal and physical entities regarding the land and the subsoil belonging to them, in cases stated by the legal acts, by imposing the limitations of the right to use the property.
In the interests of the national security, protection of the environment and the subsoil, the use of mineral resources and deposits of State importance, the use of subsoil areas of State importance, the construction and use of the structures of State importance, the land may be alienated from the landowners in compliance with the Law "On the Compulsory Alienation of Real Estate for State and Society Needs".

(As amended by the law "Amendments to the law "On the Subsoil" of February 11, 1999, coming into force on March 10, 1999).

SECTION III THE USE OF THE SUBSOIL

Basic principles of the use of the subsoil

(1) The subsoil is a non-renewable asset to be used, simultaneously, in the interests of landowners, the State and society.

(2) The cost of the subsoil is not included in the property cadastre cost; no property tax is payable for the subsoil. The use of the subsoil under the land belonging to or permanently used by entities for personal needs is free of charge. The commercial use of the subsoil is allowed if a pertinent permit (licence) is obtained in compliance with the provisions of Item 10 of this Law.

(3) During the use of the subsoil, it is obligatory to comply with the regulations dealing with the protection and use of specially protected areas and objects, the regulations for the protection of cultural monuments and other regulating limiting the use of the subsoil.

(4) In order to secure rational use and protection of the subsoil, the State and local authorities have the right to limit, interrupt or discontinue any physical or judicial entities' activities in conjunction with the use of the subsoil, in cases and based on conditions contained in this Law and other legal acts.

Purposes of the use of the subsoil

The purposes of the use of the subsoil are as follows:

1) to carry out geological exploration, scientific research, professional training and subsoil monitoring;

2) the production (mining) of mineral resources;

3) the construction and use of underground structures not related to the production of mineral resources;

4) the establishment of specially protected natural areas and objects;

5) the promotion of recreation, tourism and health-related measures;

6) the collection of samples for mineralogical, palaeontological and other geological collections;

Users of the subsoil

The subsoil is used by:

1) the landowner;

2) the entity to whom land has been granted for permanent use;

3) legal or physical entity, including foreign legal and physical entities, who have signed an agreement with the landowner.

Types and duration of the use of the subsoil

(1) The types of the use of the subsoil are as follows:

1) for an unlimited time period;

2) for a limited time period.

(2) For an unlimited time period, the subsoil may be allocated for the construction of subsoil objects not related to the production of mineral resources and for other State and society needs (specially protected geological objects, scientific and training sites, the establishment of natural monuments and other subsoil and above-ground formations).

(3) For a limited time period, the subsoil may be allocated:

1) for geological exploration purposes - for up to 5 years;

2) for the production of minerals - for up to 25 years;

3) for geological exploration and subsequent production of minerals - for up to 30 years.

The terms and the types of the use of the subsoil shall be stated in the permit (licence) for the use of the subsoil.

(As amended by the law "Amendments to the law "On the Subsoil" of February 11, 1999, coming into force on March 10, 1999).

The procedures of the use of the subsoil
The use of the subsoil may be initiated only after a permit (licence) has been obtained in compliance with the procedures set forward by the Cabinet of Ministers (except cases mentioned in Item 11). The permits (licences) for the use of the subsoil are issued by:
by the local authorities of a parish or town (city) – in cases mentioned in 4(5);
ME – in cases mentioned in 4(4);
SGS – in all other cases.
The procedures of the use of minerals, mineral deposits and subsoil areas of State importance, those of hydrocarbon prospecting, exploration and production, as well as those regarding environmental protection during offshore hydrocarbon exploration and production operations are determined by the Cabinet of Ministers. Regulations of the Cabinet of Ministers also govern the use of mineral resources of State importance in cases when the landowner and the owner of the equipment for production of minerals of State importance are not one and the same person. Groundwater may be used only if a permit for water use has been obtained (except cases mentioned in Item 11). Permits for water use are issued by Regional Environmental Boards.

Permits (licences) for the use of the subsoil are issued for a fee. The size of the fees and the procedures of their payment are determined by the Cabinet of Ministers.
Permits (licences) for the use of the subsoil are issued to the local authorities of parishes and towns (cities) free of charge for the lands belonging to them, or the lands belonging to the State or the local authorities allocated to them for permanent use, based on applications of such local authorities and the stated volume of production, if as a result of the use of the subsoil, the produced minerals are to be used for the road maintenance, the development of the area and for the maintenance of buildings belonging to the local authorities.

It is prohibited to sell, give away, use as collateral, exchange or otherwise alienate permits (licences) for the use of the subsoil. If the user of the subsoil changes, the existing permit (licence) is cancelled, and the new user shall obtain a new permit (licence) in accordance with the procedures contained in this Law. In case the user of the subsoil, the holder of a permit (licence) or property rights for the enterprise are changed, the earlier issued permit (licence) is cancelled, and, in such a case, the new owner of the enterprise, accepting the obligations contained in the existing permit (licence), may receive a new permit (licence) without competition (sale). The change of ownership of a permit (licence) for hydrocarbon exploration and production may occur if endorsed by the Cabinet of Ministers.

The permits (licences) for the use of the subsoil under the lands belonging to the State or the local authorities are issued based on competition or sale. Any legal or physical or legal, including foreign legal and physical entities, can participate in competitions or sales.

Permits (licences) for the use of the subsoil are issued to landowners (excluding the State and the local authorities) for the lands belonging to them based on applications and within certain production limits. This procedure is not applicable to the cases when mineral resources and deposits of State importance or subsoil areas of State importance are used. The landowner (except the State and the local authorities) may transfer the rights to use the subsoil to other legal and physical entities, by concluding an agreement, which is a necessary precondition for the issuance of permit (licence) for the use of the subsoil.

The landowner (excluding the State and the local authorities) has the right to arrange a competition or sale for the right to use the subsoil under the land he owns. Such a competition or sale and its conditions must be endorsed by SGS and the pertinent local authorities.

The general procedures for competitions or sales concerning the issuance of permits (licences) for the use of the subsoil and the procedures of competitions for hydrocarbon prospecting, exploration and production licensing are determined by the Cabinet of Ministers.

(As amended by the law "Amendments to the law "On the Subsoil" of February 11, 1999, coming into force on March 10, 1999 and the law "Amendments to the law "On the Subsoil" of September 07,2000, coming into force on September 28, 2000).

11. The use of the subsoil without permits (licences) for the use of the subsoil

The landowners (physical entities) and the physical entities to whom lands have been allocated for permanent use may use the subsoil within the limits of lands belonging to them without the permit (licence) for the use of the subsoil, complying with the provisions of Item 6(3) of this Law, and free of charge in the following cases:

1) the production of common mineral resources mentioned in the Appendix to this Law, excluding the cases when such activities are commercial;
2) To drill and use cased, driven and drilled water wells to the maximum depth of 20 metres and different structures (cellars, reservoirs, etc.) to the depth down to 5 metres for personal needs as well as water drains for land reclamation purposes to transport surface water.

Easement rights in the use of the subsoil

1) The State Road Service and the State Forestry Service have the easement rights to use mineral resources under occupied lands if such mineral resources are necessary for the construction, repair and maintenance of roads.
2) The local authorities of townships and towns have the easement rights to use mineral resources under occupied lands if such mineral resources are necessary for the construction, repair and maintenance of roads, area development or for the maintenance of structures belonging to the local authorities.
3) The imposition of easement under Items 12(1) and 12(2) is decided, in each and every case, by the Cabinet of Ministers.
4) The compensation to the landowner for the aforementioned easement is determined based on mutual agreement. If such an agreement cannot be reached, the size of the compensation is determined by the court.
5) After the expiry of easement, the user of easement shall be responsible for land remediation.

The rights of the users of the subsoil

The users of the subsoil have the following rights:
1) to use the subsoil for commercial or entrepreneurial activities mentioned in the permit (licence);
2) to make use of the products obtained as a result of the use of the subsoil in compliance with the issued permit (licence) and the existing legal acts;
3) to make use of the by-products obtained during the production and processing of mineral resources if the permit (licence) does not contain limitations;
4) to ask the permit (licence) issuing authority to change the conditions contained in the permit (licence) if, during the use of the subsoil, circumstances have been encountered which considerably differ from those mentioned in the permit (licence);

5) to obtain prolongation of the term of the permit (licence) for the use of the subsoil or to obtain a new permit (licence) if the conditions of the previous one have been properly fulfilled and if such is permitted by the agreement with the landowner.

The obligations of the users of the subsoil

The obligations of the users of the subsoil are as follows:

1) to comply with legal requirements, standards, norms, permit (licence) requirements and other regulations in conjunction with the activities aimed at the use of the subsoil;

2) to comply with the regulations for the production of mineral resources and occupational safety regulations;

3) during geological exploration of the subsoil, to produce geological documentation and to safeguard its safe storage;

4) to transfer to SGS geological information and data in compliance with the terms and deadlines contained in the permit (licence) as well as the data about the reserves of mineral resources and their components;

5) to submit necessary reports about the use of the subsoil in compliance with the procedures contained in legal acts;

6) to comply with standards, norms and regulations safeguarding the protection of the environment and cultural monuments, land transformation, the protection of structures and other objects and prevent adverse effects on them as a result of the use of the subsoil; the users of the subsoil shall not be responsible for the violations of pertinent standards, norms and regulations by previous users;

7) to remove and preserve the fertile part of the soil for remediation;

8) at his own expense, to liquidate the damage to the land as a result of the use of the subsoil during the term stated in the licence;

9) to compensate all the damages occurring as a result of their use of the subsoil to the owners and users of the subsoil, the environment, cultural monuments;

10) to interrupt the use of the subsoil if geological formations important for science, culture, environmental protection, meteorites, archaeological and other objects are discovered, immediately informing about the discovery the permit (licence) issuing authority, the regional environmental protection institution or State inspection for the protection of cultural monuments as well as SGS. If continued use of the subsoil endanger or damage such objects, the use of the subsoil shall be interrupted. The damages as a result of the interruption of the use of the subsoil shall be compensated to the user of the subsoil in compliance with the procedures contained in the Law "About the Land Use and Land Management".

SECTION IV PROTECTION OF THE SUBSOIL

Principal requirements for the protection of the subsoil

The principal requirements for the protection of the subsoil are as follows:

1) complete and comprehensive exploration of the subsoil;

2) rational production of mineral resources and use of by-products found in the deposits;

3) the use of the subsoil which does not lead to adverse effects on the reserves of mineral resources and useful properties of the subsoil;

4) the use of the subsoil which does not lead to the pollution by ecologically dangerous substances and sewage from underground and above-ground structures and storages;

5) the regulation and the control of the use of the subsoil.

16. Limitation, interruption and termination of the use of the subsoil

(1) The use of the subsoil by the holder of the permit (licence) may be limited if newly discovered circumstances prevent full implementation of the rights contained in the permit (licence).

(2) The use of the subsoil may be interrupted if:

1) during the use of the subsoil, there are violations of the requirements contained in the permit (licence) or legal acts regulating the use of the subsoil;

2) as a result of the use of the subsoil, there is danger to human health, life, the environment and property;

3) as a result of the use of the subsoil or in the area where such use takes place, there are force majeure situations (flood, fire etc.);

4) there is a new user of the subsoil (the interruption lasts until a new permit (licence) for the use of the subsoil is obtained);

5) as a result of the use of the subsoil, cultural monuments are endangered.

(3) The use of the subsoil is terminated if:

1) the permit (licence) has expired;

2) the user of the subsoil refuses to continue the use of the subsoil of his own free will or terminates his entrepreneurial activity;

3) within a year from obtaining a permit (licence), the use of the subsoil has not been initiated;

4) the subsoil has been used for purposes not mentioned in the permit (licence) or Item 11 of this Law has been violated;

5) the land is to be alienated for the State or society needs;

6) there are systematic violations of regulations for the use and protection of the subsoil.

(4) The use of the subsoil (except hydrocarbon prospecting, exploration and production) is limited in compliance with Item 16(1), interrupted in compliance with Items 16(2) 1)-4) and terminated in compliance with Items 16(3)1)-3) by the order of SGS, a regional environmental protection boards or State environmental inspectorate, according to Item 16(3)5) - in compliance with the contract or the existing law, the interruption in compliance with Item 16(2)5) - by the order of the State inspectorate for the protection of cultural monuments of the Ministry of Culture, the interruption in compliance with Items 16(3)4), 16(3)6) - by court order. The regional environmental protection authorities or the State environmental inspectorate may interrupt the use of the subsoil in cases mentioned in Item 16(2). The local authorities may interrupt the use of the subsoil in cases mentioned in Items 16(2)1),3),4).

The use of the subsoil for hydrocarbon prospecting, exploration and production is limited in the case mentioned in 16(1), interrupted in the cases mentioned in 16(2)1)2)3)4) and terminated in the cases mentioned in 16(3)1)2)3) by the licence-issuing authority based on the applications by the competent state institutions in compliance with the procedures stated in the administrative acts. Entities whose rights are involved may request limitation, interruption or termination of the subsoil by court action in other cases when the provisions of this Law are violated during the use of the subsoil.

(As amended by the law "Amendments to the law "On the Subsoil" of February 11, 1999, coming into force on March 10, 1999).

Conditions for new construction in the areas of occurrence of mineral resources

(1) While investigating projects to build residential, industrial or recreational structures or other construction projects, environmental protection institutions must evaluate whether there are deposits of mineral resources of State importance in the subsoil under the area where the new construction is to take place.

(2) The construction in the areas of occurrence of mineral resources or subsoil areas of State importance as well as design and construction of underground structures are allowed only after permission from SGS has been obtained.

Control of the use and protection of the subsoil

(1) The control of the use of the subsoil and its protection, in accordance with the procedures stipulated by this Law and other legal acts regulating the use of the subsoil, is carried out by the authority issuing permits (licences) for the use of the subsoil, MEPRD, State environmental inspectorate and regional environmental protection boards.

(2) The local authorities of regions, towns and townships, after obtaining an endorsement from MEPRD and in compliance with the procedures prescribed by MEPRD, may carry out measures of local importance aimed at the protection and the control of the use of the subsoil within the framework of this Law.

SECTION V RESPONSIBILITY FOR VIOLATIONS DURING THE USE OF THE SUBSOIL AND COMPENSATION OF DAMAGES

19. Responsibility for violations during the use of the subsoil

The persons who, while using the subsoil, have violated the requirements contained in this Law and other administrative acts, as well as the officials who, against the stipulations of this Law and other administrative acts, have issued permits (licences) for the use of the subsoil, are liable to responsibility in accordance with the legislation.

(As amended by the law "Amendments to the law "On the Subsoil" of February 11, 1999, coming into force on March 10, 1999).

20. Compensation of damages

(1) Irrespective of being or not being liable to administrative or criminal responsibility, the guilty party shall compensate the damage suffered by the subsoil.

(2) The methods and rates (tariffs) for compensations for damage to the subsoil are determined by the Cabinet of Ministers.

Irrespective of being (or not being) liable to a kind of liability, the guilty party shall take measures to minimise or liquidate the damage suffered by the subsoil.

(As amended by the law "Amendments to the law "On the Subsoil" of February 11, 1999, coming into force on March 10, 1999).

21. The responsibility for the damages inflicted by previous landowners and users of the subsoil

(1) The landowner, whose land property rights have been restored or land property rights have been granted anew in compliance with the Laws "About the Land Reform in the Towns of the Republic of Latvia" and "About Land Privatisation in the Countryside", are not responsible for the damage to the land and the subsoil inflicted by previous landowners or users of the subsoil.

(2) The owner or the user of the subsoil may liquidate, at his own expense, the damage inflicted on the land and the subsoil by other entities before his obtaining land ownership rights, carrying out remediation and cleaning. If this is the case, it shall be mentioned in the permit (licence) for the use of the subsoil, and the fee for obtaining this permit (licence) shall be correspondingly diminished.

(3) During the land reform, the landowners are freed from paying court expenses if they apply to the court for the compensation of damages from an institution issuing an illegal permit for the use of the subsoil or against the persons illegally using the subsoil belonging to the landowner.

22. The information base of the use and the protection of the subsoil

(1) The information (data) base of the use and protection of the subsoil is established based on the results of geological exploration, scientific research, subsoil monitoring, the data obtained during the production of mineral resources and other types of the use of the properties of the subsoil.

(2) Geological exploration, scientific research and subsoil monitoring are conducted based on orders from the State, the local authorities, users or owners of the subsoil.

(3) On lands belonging to the State and the local authorities, geological exploration and scientific research are carried out according to the programmes of geological investigations and scientific research or orders obtained from the State and the local authorities. On lands belonging to physical and legal entities, such operations are carried out according to scientific research programmes or orders obtained from the State, the local authorities, the users of the subsoil or the landowners and during the period of time or before the deadlines endorsed by the landowners or the users of the subsoil.

(4) The entities carrying out geological exploration, scientific research of the subsoil and subsoil monitoring shall arrange for the protection of the environment and the property belonging to the landowners and the users of the subsoil.

(5) The damages as a result of geological exploration, scientific research and subsoil monitoring shall be compensated in compliance with the provisions of the Law "About the Land Use and Land Management".

23. The basic principles of the use of geological information

(1) The information obtained during geological exploration, scientific research, as a result of subsoil monitoring and other types of the use of the subsoil belongs to the State if such work was carried out using the funds from the State budget or the budgets of the local authorities. If such information is obtained based on orders from legal or physical entities and funded by them, it belongs to these legal or physical entities.

The local authorities, all legal and physical entities shall transfer all the information obtained as a result of the use of the subsoil, irrespective of the funding of operations, to the State, represented by SGS, concluding an agreement concerning its use. SGS shall also submit to ME information obtained as a result of geological investigations in conjunction with hydrocarbons, as well as that obtained during hydrocarbon prospecting, exploration and production.

(3) The owner of geological information does not have the right to forbid the use of information if, as a result of failing to use it, potential ecologically dangerous or ecologically dangerous situations or ecological disasters may occur.

(4) The Cabinet of Ministers determines the general conditions for the use of geological information.

(As amended by the law “Amendments to the law “On the Subsoil” of February 11, 1999, coming into force on March 10, 1999).

REGULATIONS FOR PRE-INVESTIGATION, EXPLORATION AND PRODUCTION OF HYDROCARBONS

Amendments: Regulations of the Cabinet of Ministers No. 98 of 06.03.2001 (Latvijas Vestnesis, 08.03.2001, No. 38; Regulations of the Cabinet of Ministers No. 155 of 08.04.2003 (Latvijas Vestnesis, 15.04.2003, No. 58); Regulations of the Cabinet of Ministers No. 476 of May 6, 2004 (Latvijas Vestnesis, 11.05.2004, No. 73); Regulations of the Cabinet of Ministers No. 1009 of December 14, 2004 (Latvijas Vestnesis, 17.12.2004, No. 201).
(minutes No.7, Paragraph 11)

Issued in compliance with the law 'On the Subsoil',
Item 4, Part 4 and Item 10, Parts 2 and 4
(as amended by the Regulations of the Cabinet of Ministers
No. 155 of 08.04.2003, which came into force on 16.04.2003).

I. GENERAL ISSUES

Terms used in these regulations:
permit (licence) – document which entitles to carry out correspondingly either pre-investigation or exploration and production activities of hydrocarbons within a License area;

1.2. ***discovery*** - a new hydrocarbon deposit, found as a result of the exploration of hydrocarbons;
block – territory, defined in the contest regulations for petroleum activities and in the Permit (licence), situated within the offshore territories, continental shelf and the exclusive economic zone of the Republic of Latvia, and bounded by meridians and parallels with definite coordinates of geographical latitude and longitude, as well as by borders of states, their economic zones and coast lines;

Operator – a person designated as a manager of the joint activities of petroleum, considering proposals of the physical persons and legal entities to whom a Joint permit (license) has been awarded;

deposit - spatially bounded accumulation of hydrocarbons in the subsoil;
Joint Operating Agreement – contract concluded for organizing a mutual collaboration between the legal entities or physical persons to whom a common Permit (licence) for the exploration and production of hydrocarbons has been awarded;

Licensee - physical person or legal entity or several such persons or entities to whom a Permit (licence) has been awarded according to the procedure established by law;
measurement point - a point of a hydrocarbon production equipment where petroleum or natural gas reaches the measuring device (meter) connected to the outlet flange of a drilling-well;
petroleum – crude oil and gas condensate;

1.10.***petroleum activities*** - pre-investigation, exploration or production operations of hydrocarbons or other combinations of the aforementioned operations;
1.11. ***hydrocarbon field*** (commercial deposit) a natural deposit of hydrocarbons or a group of such deposits, discovered as a result of exploration activities and suitable for practical use;
1.12. ***production of hydrocarbons*** - activities performed for the purpose of extracting hydrocarbons from a Licence area, including the drilling of wells, pumping of petroleum, injection of gas or water, any gathering, preliminary processing and storage of hydrocarbons for transportation by ship, any transport of the same to the shipment point, as well as the placing or constructing and operating of installations for the purposes of hydrocarbon production;

1.13.***exploration for hydrocarbons*** - geological, geophysical, geochemical and technical activities, carried out in order to discover a hydrocarbon field, evaluate its extent and value, the type of the natural reservoir and its reaction to the hydrocarbon production. These operations may also include the drilling of exploration wells, the documenting of wells, and processing and evaluating the data obtained;
1.14.***pre-investigation (prospecting) for hydrocarbons*** - geological, geophysical and geochemical activities, as well as processing and evaluating the data obtained during the aforementioned activities.

These Regulations define provisions for hydrocarbon pre-investigation, exploration and production within the territory and exclusive economic zone of the Republic of Latvia, as well as the fee for a permit (licence) for the use of subsoil and procedures of its payment.

(As amended by the Regulations of the Cabinet of Ministers No. 155 of 08.04.2003, which came into force on 16.04.2003).
2^1. A licence area is defined:
2^1.1. onshore – over one or several adjacent subsoil areas;
2^1.2. offshore – over one or several adjacent blocks.
(As amended by the Regulations of the Cabinet of Ministers No. 1009 of December 14, 2004).
2^2. An onshore licence area is defined:
2^2.1. for hydrocarbon pre-investigation – with an area at least 1,000 ha;
2^2.2. for hydrocarbon exploration and production – with an area at least 15 ha.
(As amended by the Regulations of the Cabinet of Ministers No. 1009 of December 14, 2004).
2^3. If a hydrocarbon deposit is a field, the licence area is defined over the whole hydrocarbon field area.
(As amended by the Regulations of the Cabinet of Ministers No. 1009 of December 14, 2004).

Petroleum operations shall be commenced and carried out exclusively when a permit (licence) has been obtained according to the procedure under these regulations.
4. Permits (licences) of the following types may be issued for petroleum activities:
4.1. Permit (licence) for hydrocarbon pre-investigation;
4.2. Permit (licence) for the exploration and production of hydrocarbons.
5. Prior to receiving the Permit (licence), an applicant shall submit to the Ministry of Economics the evidence to prove the applicant's capability to cover the possible damages which may be unlawfully caused to the environment, people and to the financial interests of third persons as a result of petroleum activities, or that a third party, providing a guarantee (warranty), has assumed the liability risk.
6. Compensation guarantees against losses may be as follows:
6.1. insurance providing a reasonable indemnity, taking into consideration a risk exposure, which pertains to the activity of a Licensee, and premium costs;
6.2. evidence submitted by the Licensee that the Licensee has a sufficient financial resources to indemnify for the possible damage (self-security);
6.3. guarantee (warranty) given by a parent company, a recognized bank or other third party ensuring compensation for the possible damage.

II. General procedures for awarding the Permits (licences) for areas within the territorial waters and the exclusive economic zone of the Republic of Latvia

Permits (licences) are issued based on a competition.
(As amended by the Regulations of the Cabinet of Ministers No. 155 of 08.04.2003, which came into force on 16.04.2003).

8. The announcement and process of the competition are regulated by the legal and administrative acts regarding the competitions for licensing hydrocarbon activities of pre-investigation, exploration and production.

8[1]. *Deleted by the Regulations of the Cabinet of Ministers No. 476 of 06.05.2004, which came into force on 12.05.2004).*

If a Latvian state share is envisaged in the permit (licence), the Cabinet of Ministers, in order to manage that state share, by its decision, designates a company (commercial enterprise), where 100% of the capital belongs to the Latvian state. In that case, the applicants for the permit (licence) informs about their consent to co-operate with the above-mentioned enterprise. If the Cabinet of Ministers has not designated the respective company (commercial enterprise), the Latvian state share is managed by the Latvian Investment and Development Agency.
(As amended by the Regulations of the Cabinet of Ministers No. 476 of 06.05.2004).

Both a consolidated petition of several applicants and an individual application including a notification of willingness to co-operate with other applicants, are admissible.
(As amended by the Regulations of the Cabinet of Ministers No. 476 of 06.05.2004).

11. If a joint permit (licence) is granted to several applicants, a licenser shall appoint the operator according to the proposals of such applicants.
12. The permits (licences) may be awarded without a contest in case a licensee applies for a supplementary territory situated next to the license area, and for which no permit (licence) has been issued to any licensee, and the award of such an additional territory is based on the location of the petroleum deposit specified later in the previously granted permit (licence). If another licensee applies for the aforementioned supplementary territory with a similar reason, the Ministry of Economics shall decide on awarding the permit (licence) for utilising the supplementary territory subsequent to negotiations with both interested licensees.

13. If a joint permit (licence) is issued to several physical persons or legal entities, they shall sign a Joint Operating Agreement within 180 days after the approval of the Work Supervisor (Operator), pursuant to the provisions of Section XIV of these Regulations.
(As amended by the Regulations of the Cabinet of Ministers No. 1009 of December 14, 2004).

III. PERMIT (LICENCE) FOR PRE-INVESTIGATION OF HYDROCARBONS

14. The permit (licence) for pre-investigation of hydrocarbons is non-exclusive. Several permits (licences) for the same licence area may be awarded simultaneously.
15. The permit (licence) for hydrocarbon pre-investigation entitles the licensee to pre-investigate hydrocarbons within the licence area. A special permit should be obtained from the Ministry of Economy for drilling.
(As amended by the Regulations of the Cabinet of Ministers No. 155 of 08.04.2003, which came into force on 16.04.2003).

16. While performing offshore seismic investigations, the licensee shall be authorized to continue the seismic measurements in the contiguous area but not exceeding 2000 meters in depth. The time period of these operations should be co-ordinated with the licensee of the respective territory.
(As amended by the Regulations of the Cabinet of Ministers No. 155 of 08.04.2003, which came into force on 16.04.2003).
16[1]. While performing onshore seismic investigations, the licensee has the right to continue the seismic measurements in the contiguous area but not exceeding 500 m, if a written agreement is

concluded with the respective landowner for conducting the above operations and their schedule. A copy of the agreement between the landowner and the licensee is submitted to the Ministry of Economics within 14 days from the date of its signing (presenting the original).
(As amended by the Regulations of the Cabinet of Ministers No. 1009 of December 14, 2004).

17. A permit (licence) for the exploration of other natural resources within the same license area may be issued, besides the permit (licence) for pre-investigation of hydrocarbons. In such cases the licensees should mutually coordinate the activities to be carried out within the license areas.
18. The award of the permit (licence) for pre-investigation of hydrocarbons gives no preference to the receipt of the permit (licence) for hydrocarbon exploration and production.
19. The permit (licence) for pre-investigation of hydrocarbons shall be granted for a period of two years. This validity period may be extended but not exceeding five years.

IV. PROCEDURE FOR PRE-INVESTIGATION OF HYDROCARBONS

20. The licensee shall submit to the Ministry of Economics a schedule for the execution of pre-investigation activities not later than 30 days before the start of the relevant operations.
(As amended by the Regulations of the Cabinet of Ministers No. 1009 of December 14, 2004).

21. The Ministry of Economics shall consider the submitted schedule within 30 days.
22. If the Ministry of Economics considers the schedule as inadequate it shall, within 30 days of receiving the schedule, provide the Licensee with a written notice by indicating due grounds thereof. The Licensee shall make the required alterations to the schedule within 60 days following the receipt of that notice.
23. In case the activities of hydrocarbon pre-investigation envisaged in the schedule are related to the navigation of aircraft, helicopters and ships, the Licensee shall, not later than 30 days before the commencement of these operations, submit to the Ministry of Economics the following information:
23.1. investigation area, grid references thereof;
23.2. planned commencement and completion dates of pre-investigation activities;
23.3. reference to the helicopters, ships, aircraft and other large-size mobile objects to be used in pre-investigation, indicating their registration state, place of stationing, ships' name and speed.
24. The Ministry of Economics shall communicate the information provided in Paragraph 23 to the competent authorities of the Republic of Latvia, shipping and fishing services, as well as to the mass media.
25. During the pre-investigation activities, the Licensee shall furnish the Ministry of Economics and the State Geological Survey with a report on the course of activities according to the approved schedule and the procedure for submission of the information and samples obtained during petroleum activities.

V. PERMIT (LICENCE) FOR EXPLORATION AND PRODUCTION OF HYDROCARBONS

26. The permit (licence) for the exploration and production of hydrocarbons confers upon the Licensee exclusive rights to explore for and to produce hydrocarbons within the License area.

27. The permit (licence) for the exploration and production of hydrocarbons shall be granted for a period up to 30 years, inclusive of up to five years for exploration. If the permit (licence) for hydrocarbon exploration and production is awarded for a shorter period of time, the Ministry of Economics is empowered to prolong the term of the permit (license) for a period up to 30 years, inclusive of the period previously determined. Hydrocarbon exploration may be subdivided into several stages of operations, if it is envisaged by the provisions of the permit (licence).
(As amended by the Regulations of the Cabinet of Ministers No. 1009 of December 14, 2004).

28. A request for extension of the term of the permit (licence) for exploration and production of hydrocarbons shall be submitted not later than 180 days prior to the expiry date of the permit (licence).

29. During the validity period of the permit (licence) for exploration and production of hydrocarbons, the licensee may relinquish a license area or its part by giving a 90 days' written notice thereof. The Ministry of Economics may require that removal of installations and other duties connected with the cessation of operations are performed, a Geological Report on the accomplished operations is submitted, as well as other liabilities under the permit (licence) are discharged prior to the abandonment of the licence area.

29[1]. The Licensee may submit to the Cabinet of Ministers an application aimed at making changes in the subdivision of the licence partners' shares between the existing or newly invited partners in the licence. The Ministry of Economics considers the application within 30 days. If the Licensee's application is approved, the Ministry of Economics submits to the Cabinet of Ministers a draft Order regarding the change in the subdivision of the licence partners' shares.
(As amended by the Regulations of the Cabinet of Ministers No. 476 of May 6, 2004).

30. The award of the permit (licence) for exploration and production of hydrocarbons to the licensee shall not exclude the granting of rights to third persons to explore for and produce other natural resources within the same license area, as well as to carry out the pre-investigation of hydrocarbons therein on condition that such operations do not cause unsubstantiated inconvenience to the respective licensee at the performance of petroleum activities. The licensees shall agree on the nature, sequence and duration of the activities to be performed and coordinate the aforementioned issues with the Ministry of Economy within 90 days of awarding the permit (licence) to the third party.

31. If a discovery is made of any other natural resources within the area covered by the permit (licence) for exploration and production of hydrocarbons, and further operations aimed at their development cannot be performed without interrupting oil exploration and production operations, carried out by the licensee pursuant to the permit (licence), the Ministry of Economics in collaboration with the interested state authorities and the landowner shall decide, which operations are to be suspended or postponed to a later time and, if necessary, to what extent. Making such a decision the following should be taken into consideration: the nature of the new discovery, investments hitherto made, stage of activities, duration and volume of operations, their economic and social impact, impact on the activities carried under the permit (licence) for exploration and production of hydrocarbons, as well as damages to be paid to the licensee.
(As amended by the Regulations of the Cabinet of Ministers No. 155 of 08.04.2003, which came into force on 16.04.2003).

32. If, as a result of exploration activities, it is discovered that the prospective oil deposit extends beyond the licence area, the licensees should enter into an Unitisation agreement (providing for united exploitation of the deposit in case the borders of a licence area divide the deposit into several parts). In case the licensees of all the portions of that deposit fail to enter into the aforementioned agreement within 180 days, the Ministry of Economics has the right to require the licensees to sign the agreement on unitised exploitation of the common deposit on terms proposed by the Ministry of Economics after consultations with all the respective licensees.

32[1]. If, as a result of onshore exploration, it is discovered that the prospective oil deposit is larger than the determined licence area, and there is no other licensee in the respective part of the oil deposit, the licensee concludes a subsoil use agreement with the landowner regarding the extra part of the oil deposit. In order to increase the licence area, the licensee submits to the Ministry of Economics a substantiated written application about the extension of the licence area,

corresponding to the area of the relevant part of the oil deposit. The following is attached to the application:
32^1.1. an agreement with the landowner (except the State) for the use of subsoil or lease of land (notarised or certified copies) for the additional part of the oil deposit;
32^1.2. a map of the licence area issued by the State Land Survey, with co-ordinates in the LKS92TM system and certificate regarding plots of land existing in the licence area, with landowners and land cadastre numbers indicated;
32^1.3. a document confirming land ownership (certified copy);
32^1.4. substantiation of geological prospectivity of the additional licence area.
(As amended by the Regulations of the Cabinet of Ministers No. 1009 of December 14, 2004).
32^2. If, as a result of exploration, it is discovered that the prospective oil deposit is smaller than the determined licence area, the area may be reduced as necessary, but it cannot be smaller than 15 ha. In order to reduce the licence area, the licensee submits to the Ministry of Economics a substantiated written application about the reduction of the licence area. The following is attached to the application:
32^2.1. geological and technical substantiation for the reduction of the licence area;
32^2.2. a map of the licence area issued by the State Land Survey, with co-ordinates in the LKS92TM system and certificate regarding plots of land existing in the licence area, with landowners and land cadastre numbers indicated.
(As amended by the Regulations of the Cabinet of Ministers No. 1009 of December 14, 2004).

33. The licensee, whose action is suspended in a licence area due to the conditions indicated in Paragraph 31 of these Regulations, may request to extend the validity period of the permit (licence) for the duration of such delay. If the activity which may be carried out pursuant to the permit (licence) is suspended regarding only a part of its territory, the Ministry of Economics may prolong the permit (licence) for a shorter period of time, not prolong it at all or prolong it only in a part of the territory covered by the permit (licence).
34. The third person to which rights have been given to perform operations in the licence area should cover the losses arising out of the suspension or reduction of operations to the licensee.

VI. PROCEDURES FOR EXPLORATION AND PRODUCTION OF HYDROCARBONS

35. In order to commence exploration of a specific oil deposit, the licensee shall submit a Plan for the exploration of the oil deposit to the Ministry of Economics. The Plan must include the programme of additional investigations, and dates and deadlines for such operations.
(As amended by the Regulations of the Cabinet of Ministers No. 1009 of December 14, 2004).

36. Such a Plan should contain technical, safety, as well as environmental impact assessments of exploration activities pursuant to the law 'On the environmental impact assessment'. In the event of some installation to be placed in an offshore or onshore territory outside the license area in the course of exploration, additional suggestions should be furnished in the Plan thereof.
37. On working out the Plan for exploration of the petroleum deposit, the licensee shall be subject to the Minimum Work Programme for exploration, which has been submitted together with the applicant's application for the contest and is an inalienable part of the permit (licence). If any part of the aforementioned Work Programme has not been fulfilled, the licensee shall, within 60 days following the expiry of a due date of the operations fixed in the Programme, pay in cash in the State Budget an amount equal to the costs of the operations he/it failed to perform.

38. The Ministry of Economics shall approve the Plan for hydrocarbon exploration within 30 days of the submission thereof. According to the law 'On the environmental impact assessment', the Ministry of Environment is authorised to require the licensee to submit information relevant to the exploration and production of hydrocarbons.
(As amended by the Regulations of the Cabinet of Ministers No. 155 of 08.04.2003 and the Regulations of the Cabinet of Ministers No. 476 of 06.05.2004).

39. If the Ministry of Economics considers the Plan submitted by the licensee as unsatisfactory, the licensee should make the necessary amendments to the Plan within a period of 120 days following the receipt of the notice thereof.
40. Subsequent to the fulfilment of the Plan for exploration, the licensee submits to the Ministry of Economics, within sixty 60 days, a Report on the discovery together with a preliminary evaluation of the discovery, indicating whether the licensee considers feasible further appraisal of the discovery.

41. Should the licensee consider the deposit worthy of commencing the appraisal, he shall submit an Appraisal plan for the discovery to the Ministry of Economics within 60 days after the submission of the report under Paragraph 40 of these Regulations. The Ministry shall approve the aforementioned plan within 30 days of receiving that plan.

42. The licensee shall, within 60 days after the completion of the Appraisal plan for the discovery, furnish the Ministry of Economics with a Report on whether the discovery should be deemed a hydrocarbon field or not.

43. If the licensee states in the Report on the evaluation of the discovery that the discovery is not considered a hydrocarbon field, he should submit a Report on the future activity to the Ministry of Economics within 60 days.
44. If the licensee states in the Report on the evaluation of the discovery that the discovery is a hydrocarbon field, he shall submit a Plan for Hydrocarbon Field Development and Petroleum Production to the Ministry of Economics within 200 days.

45. The Work Programme for Field Development and Petroleum Production should contain the following:
the territory of field development and production;
45.1[1] a calculation of reserves and their parts within the limits of properties, which belong to each landowner, endorsed by the landowners, if it is discovered during the exploration operations that the potential oil find transcends the boundaries of property of a single landowner.
preliminary activities: wells to be drilled for hydrocarbon production and gas or water injection, installation of gathering lines, installation of platforms and equipment; installation of separators, cisterns, pumps and other production and injection equipment, installation of the necessary devices and pipelines for the initial processing and transportation of hydrocarbons, other activities necessary for the preparation and implementation of hydrocarbon production according to generally accepted international petroleum industry practices. This part of the programme shall incorporate information regarding the planned number of wells, methods of quantitative and qualitative measurements of oil and gas, measurement instruments and locations, as well as regarding production and storage and other equipment;
Suggestions about the organizing of hydrocarbon transportation:
conclusion of the necessity to construct pipelines from the place of oil production to the shipment point of petroleum,

Plan for the construction of pipelines comprising a special part on the environmental safety issues,

Plan for the extension of the pipeline system,
Plan for the abandonment or removal of pipelines,
conditions concerning the access of third parties to pipeline exploitation;
order for transportation of hydrocarbons to the shipment point;

the estimated amount of petroleum and gas production and the prospective duration of exploitation of the hydrocarbon deposit;
the amount of capital investments and other expenditures;
safety measures to be taken in the course of preliminary (development) and production activities, including emergency measures;
Report on the environmental impact assessment, Plan for the environment protection,

Plan for ecological monitoring;
circumstances which can influence negatively the licensee's capability to complete a plan for development (preliminary) activities;

Schedule for the field development and petroleum production, deadlines;
Plan for the cessation of activities and the abandonment of the hydrocarbon field.
(As amended by the Regulations of the Cabinet of Ministers No. 155 of 08.04.2003, which came into force on 16.04.2003).

The Ministry of Economics shall consider the Plan for Field Development and Petroleum Production within 30 days and request from the competent state authorities (the Ministries of Interior, Finance, Welfare, Transport and Environment) opinions regarding the submitted Plan for Field Development and Petroleum Production. After the endorsement and approval of the Plan, the Ministry of Economics permits to commence the relevant operations.

(According to the text of the Regulations of the Cabinet of Ministers No. 98 of 09.03.2001, amended by the Regulations of the Cabinet of Ministers No. 155 of 08.04.2003 and the Regulations of the Cabinet of Ministers No. 476 of 06.05.2004).

The licensee shall measure the volume and determine the composition of the extracted hydrocarbons according to practice accepted within the oil industry of Western Europe. The Ministry of Economics and the licensee shall agree upon the suitability of measuring devices and measuring methods. The Ministry or its designated institution has the right to test the operation of measuring devices and the accuracy of measurement readings.
(As amended by the Regulations of the Cabinet of Ministers No. 155 of 08.04.2003, which came into force on 16.04.2003).

During these activities the licensee shall submit to the Ministry of Economics and the State Geological Survey with a report on the process of activities according to the approved schedule and the procedure for submission of the information and samples obtained during petroleum activities.

The licensee is entitled to use for technological purposes, free of charge, the amount of hydrocarbons extracted from the area covered by the permit (licence), which is necessary for implementing petroleum activities.
The licensee, at least 30 days prior to the planned commencement of the commercial petroleum production, shall inform the Ministry of Economics and the Ministry of Environment thereof.

(As amended by the Regulations of the Cabinet of Ministers No. 155 of 08.04.2003, which came into force on 16.04.2003).

During a war or in the case of a real threat of war, the Cabinet of Ministers may establish that the licensee should sell petroleum produced to the Republic of Latvia in whole or in part at a price not lower than world market prices for petroleum.

VII. PROPRIETARY RIGHTS TO HYDROCARBONS AND THE GEOLOGICAL DATA

Petroleum and gas produced pursuant to the permit (licence) become the licensee's property from the moment the petroleum or gas cross the measurement point.
The licensee is an owner of the data obtained during pre-investigation, exploration and production activities of petroleum, and authorized to dispose of such data according to Paragraph 65 herein.

VIII. INVOLVEMENT OF LATVIAN COMPANIES (COMMERCIAL ENTERPRISES) IN THE ACTIVITIES. AND TRAINING OF THE LOCAL PERSONNEL

(The title of this section is as amended by the Regulations of the Cabinet of Ministers No. 476 of 06.05.2004).

The licensee should provide the Latvian companies and (commercial enterprises) with equal opportunities in competition with other enterprises and companies (commercial enterprises) to enter into turnkey, purchasing, vendor and other contracts for participating in the fulfilment of the program under the Permit (licence).
(As amended by the Regulations of the Cabinet of Ministers No. 476 of 06.05.2004).

The Ministry of Economics is empowered to require the licensee to furnish data on the announcement of tenders for supplies, works and services, on the results of such tenders, and the contracting partners nominated.

Taking into consideration the proposals of the applicants, the permit (licence) may include conditions on the amount of the licensee's funds to be assigned for the training of Latvian residents in various issues of petroleum industry, for working out and implementing a training program, and financing scientific research. The Ministry of Economics shall, within 90 days following the end of each permit (licence) year, provide the licensee with a report on the use of these funds.

(As amended by the Regulations of the Cabinet of Ministers No. 155 of 08.04.2003, which came into force on 16.04.2003).

IX. CONTROL AND INSPECTION

The Ministry of Economics shall perform the administrative supervision of pre-Investigation, Exploration and Production of hydrocarbons and control petroleum activities (approving a Work Programme and Budget for the succeeding year, approving the Exploration Plan, coordination of exploration wells, receipt of the Report on the discovered petroleum field, approving the Plan for Development and Production and alterations in the Production Plan, coordination of activities of the final phase of petroleum production, coordination of production cessation operations and abandonment of the licence area).

57[1]. The State Geological Survey carries out geological supervision of hydrocarbon pre-investigation, exploration and production operations (geological expert evaluations of work programmes, geological control during the implementation of projects and preparation of expert conclusions).

(As amended by the Regulations of the Cabinet of Ministers No. 98 of 06.03.2001, which came into force on 09.03.2001).

Institutions, which, according to the law, are authorised to control and inspect activities relevant to the pre-investigation, exploration and production of hydrocarbons, shall submit a Plan for control and inspections for the following year to the Ministry of Economics before October 20 each year. The Ministry of Economics shall prepare a united plan for control and inspections by taking into account the plans submitted, and coordinate that Plan with the licensee.

The licensee should cooperate with persons executing the control and inspection and provide transportation of the respective persons to the oil rigs and arrange their stay there during the planned inspections.

(As amended by the Regulations of the Cabinet of Ministers No. 155 of 08.04.2003, which came into force on 16.04.2003).

When conducting the control and inspection, the state authorities have no right to interrupt unreasonably the licensee's operations. The Ministry of Economics shall inform the licensee on the planned inspection at least 48 hours in advance. Officials of the Ministry of Economics may also participate in the inspections.

X. PROCEDURES FOR THE USE OF INFORMATION

60. The information obtained during pre-investigation, exploration and production activities of hydrocarbons should be classified into:
60.1. information of limited access (business secret);
60.2 information of public access.

61. Information of limited access (business secret) is the data disclosure or loss of which may cause an economic harm to the lawful interests of the owner of that information. The licensee (applicant for the permit (licence) may disclose the information of limited access *(business secret) exclusively to the competent authorities of the Republic of Latvia by indicating its confidential status, but the State authorities may disclose the information of limited access exclusively to the licensee [applicant for a permit (licence)].*

62. State bodies may disclose the information of limited access (business secret) received from the applicant for the permit (licence) or the licensee to their employees and other State bodies to such an extent only that is necessary for the purposes of licensing, supervision and control of petroleum activities. The institution, which has received the information from the applicant for the permit (licence) or the licensee, shall be responsible for maintaining the respective information (business secret) confidential.

63. The information of limited access (business secret) received from the government by the licensee may be divulged to the licensee's employees and affiliated companies (parent or subsidiary enterprises), particular contractors and subcontractors to the extent such information is necessary for implementing petroleum activities, or credit institutions to the extent such information is required to settle financial matters.

64. Divulgence of information to the extent prescribed by the laws and regulations of the state authorities binding upon the licensee shall not be deemed disclosure of the information of limited access (business secret). The licensee shall be responsible for maintaining the respective information of limited use (business secret) confidential.

65. The licensee shall have exclusive rights to petroleum exploration data throughout five years after obtaining thereof. The licensee should submit the geological data obtained during petroleum activities to the State Geological Survey and sign an agreement on the use of that information in compliance with legislation and resolutions.

66. The information of limited access (business secret) must be kept confidential for 5 years of its obtainment unless there is another agreement reached thereof.

XI. CESSATION OF PETROLEUM ACTIVITIES

67. In case the licensee relinquishes the permit (licence), the permit (licence) expires or the use of some installation should be terminated partly or in whole, the licensee shall submit a Plan for cessation of activities to the Ministry of Economics. The plan should contain assessment of the equipment and information on the prospective utilization of the equipment, which is necessary for making decision pursuant to Paragraphs 69 and 73 thereinafter.

68. The plan for cessation of activities should be submitted not later than 1 year prior to the expiry of the permit (licence), observing item 45.3.4. herein. In case the licensee relinquishes the permit (licence) or anticipates terminating the use of installation due to unforeseen circumstances, the plan should be submitted at least 180 days before the aforementioned activities.

69. Upon the consideration of the plan for cessation of operations, the Ministry of Economics shall decide, within 60 days, upon the further exploitation (utilisation) or removal of the stationary installed equipment by taking into account technical, safety, environmental and economic aspects, as well as the interests of landowners and other users of the subsoil.

(As amended by the Regulations of the Cabinet of Ministers No. 155 of 08.04.2003, which came into force on 16.04.2003).

70. If the Ministry of Economics makes a decision on further exploitation (utilization) of the installation it shall determine the next user and a date and procedure for assigning the installation, as well as acquit the licensee from every obligation and responsibility in connection with the further utilization of such an installation.

71. These Regulations do not apply to a complete or partial removal or abandonment of a private offshore or onshore installation provided for the purposes other than specific petroleum operations.

72. The State or landowner has the right to take over the licensee's stationary installed equipment (provided the licensee agree with) in the following cases:

72.1. the expiry of the permit (licence);

72.2. the licensee relinquishes the permit (licence);

72.3. the use of the subsoil is interrupted pursuant to Item 16 of the law 'On the Subsoil';

72.4. the exploitation of the installation is terminated.

(As amended by the Regulations of the Cabinet of Ministers No. 155 of 08.04.2003, which came into force on 16.04.2003).

73. Based on proposals by the Minister of Economics, the Cabinet of Ministers shall make a decision on granting the licensee compensation for the equipment alienated by the state.

(As amended by the Regulations of the Cabinet of Ministers No. 155 of 08.04.2003, which came into force on 16.04.2003).

74. If the Ministry of Economics decides to take over the stationary installed equipment on behalf of the State, the alienation should be performed within 180 days after the occurrence of the circumstances under Paragraph 72 of these Regulations.

75. In case the landowner or the state does not use his/its rights to take possession of the equipment the licensee shall have a duty to dismantle them in compliance with the safety and environmental standards and good practice within the oil industry in Western Europe, pursuant to the respective normative documents issued by the Ministry of Environment and the Ministry of Welfare.

(As amended by the Regulations of the Cabinet of Ministers No. 155 of 08.04.2003, which came into force on 16.04.2003).

XII. FEE FOR THE PERMIT (LICENCE)

(This section - as amended by the Regulations of the Cabinet of Ministers No. 155 of 08.04.2003, which came into force on 16.04.2003).

76. The fee for the permit (licence) for pre-investigation of hydrocarbons is 2000 Lats. The fee must be paid prior to receiving the permit (licence); it is transferred to the principal state budget.

77. The fee for the permit (licence) for offshore exploration and production of hydrocarbons is 75000 Lats. The fee for the permit (licence) for onshore exploration and production of hydrocarbons is 1000 Lats for 1 square kilometre, but at least 2000 Lats for one licence. In case of a change of the subsoil user (joint holder of the permit (licence), the fee for the issue of a new permit (licence) is 250 Lats. The fee for the permit (licence), as well as the fee for the new permit (licence) in case of a change of the subsoil user (joint holder of the permit (licence), must be paid prior to receiving the permit (licence); it is transferred to the principal state budget.

(As amended by the Regulations of the Cabinet of Ministers No. 476 of 06.05.2004).

XIII. FORCE MAJEURE

78. The licensee is not responsible for the failure to fulfil the obligations determined in the permit (licence) or for the delay of the fulfilment insofar as the failure or the delay arises from Force Majeure.

79. Force Majeure as used herein shall include conditions that are extreme and uncontrollable by the licensee and impede the implementation of the obligations stated within the permit (licence). The following should be regarded as Force Majeure: acts of God, storms, floods, fires that have not been caused by the licensee, as well as war, civil disturbances, strikes, restrictions acts of governmental authorities and other calamities that prevent or delay the licensee to perform petroleum activities or access to the territory covered by the permit (licence).

80. The Licensee should immediately inform the Ministry of Economics about the Force Majeure and attach all the information at his disposal about the nature and the consequences caused by these circumstances, and should take all the possible actions in order to reduce the consequences.

81. If Force Majeure interrupts, delays or makes the petroleum activities impossible, the expiry date of the permit (licence) and the due date for particular activities stated within the permit (licence) must be extended for a time period equal to the period of the Force Majeure and the time required for resuming the activities.

82. If the objectives of the permit (licence) cannot be achieved due to Force Majeure, the Ministry of Economics together with the licensee should decide upon the modifications in the terms and conditions of the permit (licence) or the interruption of the activities under the permit (licence).

XIV. BASIC PRINCIPLES OF CO-OPERATION OF THE LICENSEES

83. If a joint permit (licence) for hydrocarbon exploration and production is granted to several legal entities or physical persons, their mutual collaboration should be organized by signing a Joint Operating Agreement.

84. The following issues are to be adjusted by the Parties (participants) in the Joint Operating Agreement:

84.1. management institution of collaboration, procedures of its meetings, powers, voting rules;

84.2. the functions, rights and duties of a Work Supervisor (Operator);

84.3. the working-out of Work Programmes and Budget;

84.4. ensuring consolidated accounting and payments according to the legislation of the Republic of Latvia;

84.5. mutual obligations and responsibility of participants and liability in relations with third persons, sole risk activities.

85. A stipulation should be provided for in the Joint Operating Agreement that each Party casting its vote for the cooperation issues has the number of votes corresponding to the Participating Interest of a Party. The Agreement may provide for the issues which require more than fifty (50%) percent of votes of the participants and for the issues requiring a qualified majority of votes or unanimous decision.

86. The Joint Operating Agreement should be submitted to the Ministry of Economics within 14 days of its signing.

XV. FINAL PROVISIONS

87. (Deleted according to the Regulations of the Cabinet of Ministers No. 98 of 09.03.2001, which came into force on 09.03.2001).

88. Prior to making the final decision in accordance with Paragraphs 19, 35, 38, 39, 40 and 69 of these Regulations, the Ministry of Economics shall co-ordinate the issues in connection with the rational use of subsoil and geological supervision of the activities with the State Geological Survey.

Information reference to the European Union Directive

(The reference - as amended by the Regulations of the Cabinet of Ministers No. 1009 of December 14, 2004).

These Regulations contain legal provisions, which comply with the 94/22/EC Directive of the European Parliament and Council of May 30, 1994 as regards the provisions for the issue and use of permits for hydrocarbon pre-investigation, exploration and production.

SECTION VI FINAL CONDITIONS

24. Resolution of disputes

Disputes arising during the use of the subsoil are resolved in accordance with the existing legal and administrative acts.

CONDITIONS OF TRANSITION

1. In conjunction with the approval of this Law, the Law "About the Approval of the Latvian Subsoil Code" and the Latvian Subsoil Code (see Official Publications of the Supreme Council and the Council of Ministers of the Latvian SSR, 1976, No. 23; 1980, No. 9; 1982, No. 52, 1985, No. 1; 1988, No. 1) are declared nullified.

2. The Cabinet of Ministers, within 6 months after this Law coming into force, shall approve the list of deposits of mineral resources of State importance.

3. Before the approval of the list of deposits of mineral resources of State importance, these deposits shall be considered as such in accordance with the list of commercial deposits of mineral resources contained in the Decree of the Council of Ministers of the Republic of Latvia No. 316 of 13 November 1991 "About the Approval of the List of Commercial Deposits of Mineral Resources and Peat".

4. The Cabinet of Ministers shall, within 6 months after this Law coming into force, prepare the regulations for the use of mineral resources of State importance and their deposits as well as the regulations for the use of subsoil areas of State importance.

APPENDIX LIST OF COMMON MINERALS

1. Clay.

2. Sand, gravel.

3. Loose freshwater limestone.

4. Peat deposits with an area up to 5 hectares within the limits of a property belonging to a single owner.

This Law was passed by the Saeima (Parliament) on May 2, 1996

REGULATIONS 597 REGARDING PROSPECTING, EXPLORATION AND PRODUCTION OF HYDROCARBONS AND PROCEDURES FOR PAYMENT AND AMOUNT OF STATE FEE

I. GENERAL PROVISIONS

1. These Regulations prescribe the procedures for the licensing of hydrocarbon prospecting and hydrocarbon exploration and production activities, the procedures for the prospecting of hydrocarbons and the exploration and production of hydrocarbons in the territory of the Republic of Latvia on dry land and sea, as well as the fee amount for an authorisation for the utilisation of subsoil and the payment procedures.

2. The following terms are used in these Regulations:

2.1. experimental production of hydrocarbons – production of hydrocarbons from an exploration well;

2.2. deposit – spatially bounded accumulation of hydrocarbons in the subsoil;

2.3. licensee – a merchant to whom a licence has been issued in accordance with the procedures specified in these Regulations;

2.4. offshore licence area – an area specified by the Cabinet for the prospecting, exploration and production of hydrocarbons in the territorial sea or exclusive economic zone of the Republic of Latvia (hereinafter – sea), which is limited by lines with specified co-ordinates of latitude and longitude, as well as state borders and borders of economic zones and the coastlines thereof, in which the licensee has the right to perform hydrocarbon prospecting or exploration and production activities;

2.5. onshore licence area – an area on dry land in the territory of the Republic of Latvia specified by the Cabinet, in which a licensee has the right to perform hydrocarbon prospecting or hydrocarbon exploration and production activities;

2.6. operator – a manager of hydrocarbon exploration and production activities.

II. GENERAL LICENSING PROCEDURES

3. A merchant may commence the prospecting of hydrocarbons, as well as the exploration and production of hydrocarbons only after such merchant has received a licence in accordance with the procedures specified by these Regulations.

4. The Ministry of Economics shall issue and register the following licences:

4.1. a licence for the prospecting of hydrocarbons – without competition;

4.2. a licence for the exploration and production of hydrocarbons:

4.2.1. for the exploration and production of hydrocarbons offshore or onshore on land owned by the State – through a competition procedure, except for the case specified in Paragraph 66 of these Regulations; and

4.2.2. for the exploration and production of hydrocarbons on land not owned by the State – without competition to a merchant selected by the owner of the land or his or her authorised representative if it complies with the requirements specified in Paragraphs 69 and 74 of these Regulations.

5. The determination of a licence area offshore may be initiated by the Ministry of Economics or a merchant who wants to perform hydrocarbon prospecting or hydrocarbon exploration and production offshore.

6. The determination of an onshore licence area may be initiated by the owner (owners) of the relevant plot of land or his or her (their) authorised person.

7. Landowners or their authorised person may unite their land properties into one licence area if such land properties have common borders. Landowners or their authorised person in the referred to case shall submit to the Ministry of Economics a joint submission regarding the proposal to determine a licence area.

8. The Ministry of Economics shall prepare a proposal regarding a licence area for the prospecting of hydrocarbons, as well as the exploration and production of hydrocarbons on the basis of the submission of an initiator.

9. The initiator of the hydrocarbon prospecting or hydrocarbon exploration and production activities shall submit to the Ministry of Economics a submission regarding the proposal to determine a licence area (Annex 1), except the case when the initiator is the Ministry of Economics.

10. The Ministry of Economics shall examine the submission within a time period of 30 days.

11. If the initiator has not submitted all the information and documents specified in Annex 1 of these Regulations, the Ministry of Economics shall request they be submitted within a time period of 30 days. If the initiator has not submitted the requested information within the specified period of time, the Ministry of Economics shall take a decision to reject the submission and shall inform the initiator thereof by returning the submission.

12. The initiator may re-submit the submission.

13. If the submission, information attached thereto and the documents comply with the requirements of these Regulations, the Ministry of Economics shall prepare a draft Cabinet Order regarding the determination of a licence area.

14. The landowner (owners) or his or her (their) authorised person, in accordance with Paragraph 89 of these Regulations, may propose to expand a licence area of prospecting of hydrocarbons or

the exploration and production of hydrocarbons to plots of land that are located nearby if the owners of the relevant plots of land agree on such a proposal. In such case the landowners or their authorised person shall submit to the Ministry of Economics a submission regarding the making of amendments to the licence area (Annex 2).

15. In the case referred to in Paragraph 88 of these Regulations a licensee may propose to expand a licence area for the prospecting of hydrocarbons or the exploration and production of hydrocarbons offshore or onshore that belongs to the State. In order to propose making amendments to the licence area, the licensee shall submit to the Ministry of Economics a submission regarding the making of amendments to the licence area (Annex 2).

16. The Ministry of Economics shall examine the submission regarding the making of amendments to a licence area and prepare a relevant draft Cabinet Order in accordance with the procedures specified in Paragraphs 10, 11, 12 and 13 of these Regulations.

17. A licensee shall be the owner of the geological and geophysical data obtained in hydrocarbon prospecting or hydrocarbon exploration and production activities.

18. If hydrocarbon prospecting or hydrocarbon exploration and production activities are related to ship traffic or the use of aircraft, a licensee shall have to receive a relevant permit for these activities and shall have to comply with the regulatory enactments regarding the procedures for the issuance of permits to foreign research vessels, as well as special aviation activities.

19. The Ministry of Economics and the Latvian Environment, Geology and Meteorology Agency (hereinafter – Agency) shall operate with geological and geophysical data and information obtained in hydrocarbon prospecting or hydrocarbon exploration and production activities in accordance with Section 5, Paragraph two and Section 7 of the Freedom of Information Law.

III. PROCEDURES FOR THE LICENSING OF HYDROCARBON PROSPECTING

20. The following shall be indicated in a licence for the prospecting of hydrocarbons:

20.1. justification for the issuance of the licence;

20.2. information regarding the licensee (firm name of the merchant, registration number, place of registration and legal address thereof);

20.3. time of operation of the licence;

20.4. the licence area plane co-ordinates on dry land in the Latvian co-ordinate system LKS92TM or ellipsoidal (geographic) co-ordinates on the sea in the WGS 84 system;

20.5. the programme of hydrocarbon prospecting activities; and

20.6. the procedures for the submission of information, data, reports and samples that are obtained during hydrocarbon prospecting activities.

21. A licence for the prospecting of hydrocarbons shall not be exclusive. Several licences may be issued for one licence area of prospecting of hydrocarbons.

22. If the licensee has a licence for the prospecting of hydrocarbons, such a licence shall not provide a privilege for the receipt of a licence for exploration and production of hydrocarbons.

23. The licence for prospecting of hydrocarbons shall be issued for a time period of up to five years.

24. After the issuance of the Cabinet Order regarding the determination of a licence area for hydrocarbon prospecting or refusal of such draft Order, the Ministry of Economics shall, within 15 days, inform the initiator thereof (except the case when the initiator is the Ministry of Economics).

25. After the issuance of the Cabinet Order regarding the determination of a licence area for the prospecting of hydrocarbons on the dry land that does not belong to the State, the land owner or his or her authorised person shall choose a merchant (hereinafter – applicant) who will apply for the receipt of a licence for the prospecting of hydrocarbons.

26. After issuance of the Cabinet Order regarding the determination of a licence area for the prospecting of hydrocarbons offshore or onshore that belongs to the State, the Ministry of Economics shall publish an invitation for applicants to apply for the receipt of a licence for hydrocarbon prospecting in the newspaper *Latvijas Vēstnesis* [the official Gazette of the Government of Latvia], as well as in the Official Journal of the European Union.

27. In order to receive a licence for the prospecting of hydrocarbons in the licence area specified by the Cabinet, the applicant shall submit to the Ministry of Economics a submission regarding the receipt of a licence for the prospecting of hydrocarbons (Annex 3). The documents indicated in Annex 3 shall be attached to the submission.

28. The Ministry of Economics shall, within 30 days, evaluate the compliance of the submission of the applicant with the requirements specified in Annex 3 to these Regulations. If the information and documents submitted comply with the referred to requirements, the Ministry of Economics shall issue a licence for hydrocarbon prospecting.

29. If the applicant has not submitted all the information and documents specified in Annex 3 to these Regulations, the Ministry of Economics shall request that they be submitted within 30 days. If the applicant has not submitted the requested information within the specified period of time, the Ministry of Economics shall take a decision to reject the submission and shall inform the applicant regarding such decision by returning the submission.

30. The applicant may re-submit the submission.

IV. PROCEDURES FOR PROSPECTING OF HYDROCARBONS

31. The licensee shall, not less than 30 days before the commencement of the relevant activities, submit to the Ministry of Economics a schedule for the performance of the hydrocarbon prospecting activities in two copies. The time periods planned for the commencement and termination of prospecting activities provided in the programme of activities specified in the licence shall be indicated in the schedule for the performance of activities. The Ministry of Economics shall send one copy of the schedule for the performance of the hydrocarbon prospecting activities to the Agency.

32. The licensee has the duty, in accordance with the procedures specified in the licence, to submit to the Agency the data, samples and information that is obtained during the hydrocarbon prospecting activities

33. In performing seismic prospecting on the sea, the licensee has the right to continue seismic measurements in the territory located adjacent to the licence area, not exceeding a distance of 2000 metres from the border of the licence area. The licensee shall inform the Ministry of Economics regarding the referred to activities and the time of performance thereof and enter into a written agreement regarding the performance of seismic activities (hereinafter – agreement)

with the licensee of the neighbouring licence area, if appropriate. The licensee shall submit the written agreement to the Ministry of Economics within five days after signing thereof and initiate the activities.

34. In performing seismic prospecting on dry land, the licensee has the right to continue seismic measurements in the territory located adjacent to the licence area, not exceeding a distance of 500 metres from the border of the licence area. The licensee shall enter into a written agreement with the landowner of the relevant territory regarding the seismic prospecting activities and the time of performance thereof. The licensee shall submit the written agreement to the Ministry of Economics within five days after signing thereof and initiate the activities.

V. GENERAL LICENSING PROCEDURES FOR HYDROCARBON EXPLORATION AND PRODUCTION

35. The following shall be indicated in a licence for the exploration and production of hydrocarbons:

35.1. justification for the issuance of the licence;

35.2. the information regarding the licensee (firm name of the merchant, registration number, place of registration and legal address thereof);

35.3. the time of operation of the licence;

35.4. the licence area plane co-ordinates on dry land in the Latvian co-ordinate system LKS92TM or ellipsoidal (geographic) co-ordinates on the sea in the WGS 84 system;

35.5. the division of hydrocarbon exploration activities broken down by years;

35.6. the minimum programme of exploration activities and costs thereof; and

35.7. the procedures for the submission of the information, data, reports and samples that are obtained during hydrocarbon exploration and production activities.

36. The licence for the exploration and production of hydrocarbons shall be issued for a period of up to 30 years, including for exploration phase – up to five years. If the licence for hydrocarbon exploration and production is issued for a shorter period, the Ministry of Economics may extend the term of the licence for hydrocarbon exploration and production for a period not exceeding 30 years, including the period previously specified.

37. The licence for the exploration and production of hydrocarbons shall provide exclusive rights to extend the validity period of the licence for the exploration for hydrocarbons up to 30 years.

38. A licence area, not smaller than 15 hectares, shall be provided for in the Cabinet Order for the exploration and production of hydrocarbons on dry land.

39. If several merchants wish to perform hydrocarbon exploration and production activities jointly, they shall establish a partnership that shall apply for the receipt of a licence.

40. If a licence is issued to a partnership, the merchants that compose the partnership shall be indicated in the licence.

41. The Ministry of Economics shall issue a licence for the exploration and production of hydrocarbons on the basis of a decision of the Hydrocarbon Exploration and Production Licensing Commission (hereinafter – Commission).

42. The Cabinet shall approve the Commission composed of seven members upon the proposal of the Minister for Economics. The Commission shall include the delegated representatives of the

Ministry of Economics, the Ministry of Finance, the Ministry of Justice and the Ministry of the Environment.

43. The Commission shall have a quorum if more than a half of the Commission members are present at the meeting. Minutes shall be taken at the Commission meetings.

44. The work of the Commission shall be technically provided for by the Ministry of Economics.

VI. Procedures for the Licensing of Hydrocarbon Exploration and Production Offshore or Onshore Land that Belongs to the State

45. The Ministry of Economics, within 280 days after taking of the Cabinet Order regarding the determination of a licence area, shall announce a licensing competition regarding exploration and production of hydrocarbons offshore or onshore that belongs to the State (hereinafter – competition).

46. An invitation to participate in the competition (hereinafter – invitation) shall be published in the newspaper *Latvijas Vēstnesis* and the Official Journal of the European Union.

47. The following information shall be indicated in the invitation:

47.1. the validator of the competition (the Ministry of Economics);

47.2. the licence type;

47.3. the place, time for the receipt of the competition regulations and the contact person;

47.4. the fee for the receipt of the competition regulations – LVL 350;

47.5. the deadline for the submission of the application; and

47.6. other information that may be necessary to the participants in order to prepare a good quality application for the competition.

48. The time period for the submission of applications shall not be less than 90 calendar days from publishing of the invitation in the newspaper *Latvijas Vēstnesis* and the Official Journal of the European Union.

49. The Ministry of Economics shall develop and approve the competition regulations.

50. The following shall be indicated in the competition regulations:

50.1. the information regarding the subject of the competition;

50.2. the procedures for the drawing up, submission and registration of the application;

50.3. the content of the application and qualification requirements for the participants of the competition in accordance with Paragraph 51 of these Regulations;

50.4. the validity period of applications;

50.5. the procedures for explanation of competition regulations;

50.6. the procedures for the amending, supplementing and repealing of application;

50.7. the procedures for the opening of applications;

50.8. the procedures and evaluation criteria of applications in accordance with Paragraph 52 of these Regulations;

50.9. the rights and obligations of the commission;

50.10. the amount of the non-repayable competition participation fee – LVL 1500 – and the procedures for the payment thereof;

50.11. a sample of the drawing up of the application; and

50.12. other information necessary for the procedures of the competition.

51. A participant shall be qualified for a licensing competition. The following documents and information shall confirm the qualification of a participant in accordance with the sample specified in competition regulations:

51.1. application form of the participant;

51.2. information regarding the participant;

51.3. information regarding the experience of the participant describing the capability thereof to perform hydrocarbon exploration and production activities in the licence area;

51.4. the minimum programme of hydrocarbon exploration activities which includes amounts, terms and costs of the exploration activities;

51.5. a document confirming that the participant has introduced a quality management system in accordance with LVS EN ISO 9001:2000, *Quality Management Systems – Requirements* or a similar standard;

51.6. a document confirming that the participant has introduced Regulation (EC) No. 761/2001 of the European Parliament and of the Council of 19 March 2001 allowing voluntary participation by an organisation in a Community eco-management and audit scheme (EMAS) or LVS EN ISO 14001:2005, *Environmental Management System – Requirements with Guidance for Use*, or an environmental management standard that is equivalent thereto;

51.7. the annual accounts of the participant regarding the last two financial years;

51.8. a copy of the merchant's registration certificate;

51.9. a bank guarantee or equivalent document which confirms that the participant is able to financially ensure the implementation of the minimum programme of hydrocarbon exploration activities; and

51.10. a document which confirms that the participant has paid the participation fee.

52. The following criteria shall be included in the competition regulations:

52.1. the financial parameters of the participant;

52.2. the manner in which the participant offers to perform the exploration for hydrocarbons and to initiate production thereof (the minimum programme of activities); and

52.3. work experience in the exploration and production of hydrocarbons.

53. The Commission shall evaluate the compliance of the competition participants with the qualification requirements.

54. The Commission shall examine the applications of the participants and evaluate only such applications that comply with Paragraph 51 of these Regulations and the requirements specified in the competition regulations.

55. The Commission shall evaluate the applications of the participants, granting them points in accordance with the criteria specified in Paragraph 52 of these Regulations.

56. The procedures for the granting of points for each criterion shall be specified in the competition regulations.

57. The meetings of the Commission shall be closed, except the meeting in which applications are opened.

58. The participant, to whose application the largest score has been granted, but not less than specified in the competition regulations, shall be recognised as the winner of the competition.

59. If the application does not comply with these Regulations or competition regulations, the Commission shall not evaluate such application, but draw up a relevant protocol regarding such application and inform the applicant in writing within 15 days after the Commission meeting.

60. If applications of several participants receive an identical score, the participant whose application receives the highest score for the minimum programme of activities and experience of the participant in hydrocarbon exploration and production activities shall be recognised as the winner.

61. If only one application has been received for the competition and it complies with the requirements specified in these Regulations and competition regulations, the Commission has the right to decide that the relevant applicant is the winner of the competition.

62. The Commission shall decide on issuance of a licence for hydrocarbon exploration and production to the winner of the competition.

63. The results of the competition, within 15 days after taking the decision of the Commission, shall be published in the newspaper *Latvijas Vēstnesis*, sent for publishing in the Official Journal of the European Union and notified in writing to all the participants of the competition.

64. The competition for the exploration and production of hydrocarbons shall be recognised as not having taken place if:

64.1. no application has been received;

64.2. all the applications submitted have been rejected by a decision of the Commission; or

64.3. the winner of the competition has declined the licence.

65. If the competition, in accordance with Paragraph 64 of these Regulations, has been recognised as not having taken place, the Ministry of Economics shall, within 180 days, announce a new competition notifying such decision in the newspaper *Latvijas Vēstnesis* and the Official Journal of the European Union.

66. A licensing competition shall not be organised if the licence area is being expanded in the case specified in Paragraph 88 of these Regulations.

VII. Procedures for the Licensing of Hydrocarbon Exploration and Production on Land that Does Not Belong to the State

67. After the taking of the Cabinet Order regarding the determination of the licence area for hydrocarbon exploration and production or refusal of such draft Order, the Ministry of Economics shall, within 15 days, inform the initiator thereof (except the case when the initiator is the Ministry of Economics).

68. After the taking of the Cabinet Order regarding the determination of the licence area for the hydrocarbon exploration and production, the landowner or his or her authorised person shall choose an applicant who will apply for the receipt of a licence for the hydrocarbon exploration and production.

69. In order to receive a licence for the exploration and production of hydrocarbons in the licence area specified by the Cabinet, the applicant shall submit a submission to the Ministry of Economics (Annex 4). The documents referred to in Annex 4 shall be attached to the submission.

70. The Commission shall evaluate the submission.

71. The Commission, within 30 days after receipt of the submission, shall evaluate whether the submission and the information submitted by the applicant complies with the requirements specified in Annex 4.

72. If the applicant has not submitted all the documents and information specified in Annex 4 of these Regulations, the Commission shall request that information and documents be submitted within a time period of 30 days. If the applicant has not submitted the necessary documents within the specified period of time, the Commission shall take a decision to reject the submission and shall inform the applicant regarding such decision by returning the submission.

73. If the submission complies with the requirements specified in Annex 4, the commission shall evaluate such submission, granting points in accordance with the evaluation criteria specified in Annex 5.

74. The minimum score that must be acquired so that the commission might take a decision regarding the granting of the authorisation, shall be 21 points.

75. If the submission complies with the evaluation criteria specified in Annex 5 and the evaluation thereof is not less than the minimum score specified in Paragraph 74 of these Regulations, the commission shall decide on the issuance of a licence for the hydrocarbon exploration and production.

76. If the submission does not comply with the evaluation criteria specified in Annex 5 or evaluation thereof is less than the minimum score specified in Paragraph 74 of these Regulations, the commission shall take a decision to reject the submission and shall return the submission to the applicant.

77. The applicant may re-submit the submission.

78. The Ministry of Economics shall issue a licence for the exploration and production of hydrocarbons on the basis of the decision of the commission.

VIII. PROCEDURES FOR THE EXPLORATION AND PRODUCTION OF HYDROCARBONS

79. A licensee may perform the functions of an operator himself or herself or transfer the performance thereof to another merchant. Regardless of who performs the functions of the operator, the licensee shall be responsible for the process of hydrocarbon exploration and production activities in the licence area and the compliance thereof with the requirements specified in regulatory enactments.

80. In order to commence any hydrocarbon exploration activities, the licensee shall, not less than 30 days before the commencement of the relevant activities, submit to the Ministry of Economics the following documents:

80.1. a schedule for the performance of the minimum programme of activities in two copies. The schedule shall include the time limits of commencement and cessation of the hydrocarbon exploration activities provided for in the performance of the minimum programme of activities specified in a licence, as well as a construction licence number, date of issue and issuing authority. If activities will be performed with an existing well or a new well will be drilled, the location of this well and the name and number thereof shall be indicated. The Ministry of Economics shall send one copy of the schedule for the performance of the minimum programme of activities to the Agency; and

80.2. the work safety plan.

81. The Ministry of Economics, within 30 days after the submission of documents, may request the licensee to supplement, amend or re-submit the documents referred to in Paragraph 80 of these Regulations if such documents do not comply with the requirements specified.

82. The licensee may commence the hydrocarbon exploration activities if, within 30 days after submission of the documents, supplementation or amendment thereof, it has not received the request referred to in Paragraph 81 of these Regulations from the Ministry of Economics.

83. The licensee has the duty to fulfil the minimum programme of activities specified in the licence within the time limits specified in the schedule for the performance of the activities referred to in Paragraph 80 of these Regulations.

84. If the licensee, who has received a licence for exploration and production of hydrocarbons offshore or onshore on land that belongs to the State, fails to fulfil any part of the minimum programme of exploration activities to the full extent, he or she, within 60 days after the end of the time limit specified in the schedule for the performance of activities, shall pay into the State basic budget a sum of money which complies with the costs of the activities that were not carried out and which is indicated in the licence for the exploration and production of hydrocarbons.

85. If the licensee wishes to perform additional hydrocarbon exploration activities that are not indicated in the minimum programme of activities specified in the licence, he or she, within 30 days before the commencement of additional activities, shall submit to the Ministry of Economics a programme of the activities to be performed additionally and a schedule of the performance thereof. The licensee shall submit to the Ministry of Economics all additional data regarding hydrocarbon exploration, samples (submit only to the Agency) and a summary of results in two copies within 30 days after the completion of activities. The Ministry of Economics shall send to the Agency one copy of the additional data regarding hydrocarbon exploration activities and a summary of results.

86. If the licensee wishes to perform experimental production of hydrocarbons, he or she, within 15 days before the commencement of the experimental hydrocarbon production activities, shall submit to the Ministry of Economics a schedule for the performance of activities in two copies. The co-ordinates of each well, name or number, number of wells, as well as the planned amount and debit of production, installations used, terms for commencement and termination shall be indicated in the schedule. A licensee shall submit to the Ministry of Economics a report within 30 days after the completion of experimental production. The co-ordinates of each well, name or number, number of wells, actual amount of hydrocarbons produced in each well in total and by months, the debit observed (expressed in barrels per day), actual terms for performance of activities, a description of the production technology shall be indicated in the report. The Ministry of Economics shall send one copy of the schedule for the performance of activities to the Agency.

87. The licensee may perform the experimental production of hydrocarbons for not longer than 180 days after the submission of the notification to the Ministry of Economics.

88. If the licensee during hydrocarbon exploration discovers that the deposit of hydrocarbons exceeds the borders of the licence area, he or she shall notify thereof:

88.1. the Ministry of Economics, if the deposit of hydrocarbons outside the licence area continues into the sea or land that belongs to the State; or

88.2. the landowner, if the deposit of hydrocarbons outside the licence area continues into land that does not belong to the State.

89. The extension of the licence area shall take place in accordance with the procedures specified in Paragraphs 14, 15 and 16 of these Regulations.

90. The licensee, within 30 days after the fulfilment of a minimum and additional (if appropriate) programme of hydrocarbon exploration activities, shall submit to the Ministry of Economics a report in two copies. The report shall contain a geological description of the deposit and the economic evaluation thereof, including total and obtainable stock of hydrocarbons, as well as indicate whether production of hydrocarbons from the evaluated deposit of hydrocarbons will be initiated. The Ministry of Economics shall send one copy of the report to the Agency.

91. If, in the report regarding the evaluation of the deposit, the licensee announces that he or she will commence hydrocarbon production activities, he or she shall submit the following to the Ministry of Economics before the commencement of the referred to activities:

91.1. a plan of the hydrocarbon deposit preparation activities and hydrocarbon production in two copies. The Ministry of Economics shall send one copy of this plan to the Agency; and

91.2. the work safety plan.

92. The licensee shall indicate the following information in the plan of the hydrocarbon deposit preparation activities and hydrocarbon production:

92.1. the planned amounts of hydrocarbon production in total and the expected average debit (expressed in barrels per day) by years, duration of the use of the deposit, the number of wells planned for the exploration and production of hydrocarbons and wells planned for the pumping of gas or water, as well as the location thereof;

92.2. a scheme of technical projects (in the draft stage) and the location of technological buildings and installations;

92.3. a description of the hydrocarbon production, transporting, storage and reloading technologies; and

92.4. total and obtainable stock of hydrocarbons and the description of the method for calculation thereof.

93. The Ministry of Economics, within 30 days after receipt of the documents, may request the licensee to supplement, amend or re-submit the documents referred to in Paragraph 91 of these Regulations if such documents do not comply with the requirements specified in Paragraphs 91 or 92 of these Regulations.

94. The licensee may commence the activities if, within 30 days after submission of the documents, supplementation or amendments thereof, he or she has not received from the Ministry of Economics the request referred to in Paragraph 93 of these Regulations.

95. By 1 April of each year the licensee shall submit to the Ministry of Economics a report in two copies regarding the performed activities and the amounts of the produced hydrocarbons for each month in the previous calendar year in accordance with the submitted plan of activities for the preparation of use of the hydrocarbon deposit and hydrocarbon production, as well as indicate the balance of total and obtainable stock and losses as of 31 December of the reporting year. The Ministry of Economics shall send one copy of the report to the Agency.

96. The hydrocarbons offshore or onshore on land that belongs to the State shall become the property of the licensee the moment when they cross the place of measurements. The place of measurements shall be a point of the hydrocarbon production installation where petroleum or natural gas reaches the measurement device (meter) linked with the flange of the well.

IX. STATE LICENCE FEE

97. The State licence fee for the prospecting of hydrocarbons shall be LVL 500.

98. The State licence fee for the exploration and production of hydrocarbons on dry land shall be LVL 2000.

99. The State licence fee for the exploration and production of hydrocarbons offshore shall be LVL 75 000.

100. The State licence fee shall be paid prior to receipt of the licence, and a copy of the document attesting the payment shall be submitted. The State fee shall be paid into the State basic budget.

101. If the licensee changes, the fee for issuance of a new licence shall be LVL 250. The State licence fee shall be paid prior to receipt of the licence. The State fee shall be paid into the State basic budget. If the licence is lost, stolen, destroyed or damaged, a duplicate licence shall be issued to a licensee on the basis of a submission with an explanation of the licensee. A duplicate licence shall be issued free of charge.

X. PARTICIPATION OF THE STATE IN THE EXPLORATION AND PRODUCTION OF HYDROCARBONS OFFSHORE OR ONSHORE ON LAND THAT BELONGS TO THE STATE

102. The State may participate in the production of hydrocarbons onshore or offshore on land that belongs to the State.

103. The State shall carry out the participation thereof in the production of hydrocarbons through a capital company in which all the capital shares belong to the State (hereinafter – State capital company).

104. The State capital company may participate in the production of hydrocarbons by paying a specified share (hereinafter – State participation share) of the hydrocarbon production expenditures and receiving the income share proportional thereto.

105. The State capital company shall be established within six months after the licensee has submitted the plan specified in Sub-paragraph 91.1 of these Regulations.

106. The Ministry of Economics shall be the holder of the capital shares of the State capital company.

107. In determining an offshore licence area or onshore licence area on land that belongs to the State, a part of the State participation in the amount of 10 % in each licence area or from 0 to 50%, if there is a specific justification for it, shall be provided for in the draft Cabinet Order.

108. If the State participates in the production of hydrocarbons, the following stipulations shall be included in the competition regulations and authorisation:

108.1. a State participation share as a percentage;

108.2. the capital company shall only pay for the share of hydrocarbon production expenditures corresponding to the State participation share;

108.3. the licensee who is not the manager of the State participation share shall cover the hydrocarbon extraction expenditures complying with the State participation share until the time when the licensee submits to the Ministry of Economics the plan of activities for the preparation of the hydrocarbon deposit and hydrocarbon production;

108.4. the capital company shall receive revenue from the hydrocarbon production proportionate to the State participation share, including revenue from the experimental production; and

108.5. the licensee shall enter into a collaboration contract with the State capital company. The stipulations for co-operation of the participants of the licence shall be specified in the contract. A draft collaboration contract shall be attached to the regulations of the licensing competition.

109. The collaboration contract shall be entered into within 15 months after the issuance of a licence.

110. The following shall be stipulated in a collaboration contract:

110.1. the governing body of collaboration and the competence thereof;

110.2. mutual obligations and the responsibility of the licensee and the State capital company;

110.3. the responsibility of the licensee and the State capital company as regards the third persons;

110.4. the procedures for preparation of the programme and budget of the hydrocarbon production activities;

110.5. the procedures for selection of the operator, the functions, rights, duties and responsibility thereof;

110.6. in deciding on collaboration issues, the State capital company and the licensee shall have a number of votes corresponding to the share of participation thereof;

110.7. the voting procedures in the governing body of collaboration; and

110.8. other stipulations which the parties consider as important.

111. The collaboration contract shall be submitted to the Ministry of Economics within a period of 14 days after signing thereof.

112. Within 40 months after issuance of the licence the Ministry of Economics shall submit to the Cabinet a draft concept regarding the financing of the State participation share for examination, providing the following options therein:

112.1. the State participation share shall be financed from the State budget;

112.2. the State capital company shall borrow the necessary financing in the financial market, using a State guarantee; or

112.3. the State participation share shall not be financed.

113. If the Cabinet takes a decision not to finance the participation share, the State shall sell the participation share thereof in an auction or give such share up in favour of the licensee and inform the licensee thereof within a time period of 30 days.

XI. Supervision of Hydrocarbon Prospecting and Hydrocarbon Exploration and Production Activities

114. The Agency shall carry out geological supervision of hydrocarbon prospecting and hydrocarbon exploration and production activities:

114.1. geological expert examination of the plan of activities;

114.2. geological control during the implementation of projects; and

114.3. preparation of expert examination reports.

115. State administrative institutions, in performing the control of hydrocarbon prospecting and hydrocarbon exploration and production activities at the sites of hydrocarbon production located offshore, shall notify the Ministry of Economics and the licensee regarding the planned inspection 48 hours prior to such inspection. The officials of the Ministry of Economics may also participate in the inspection.

XII. Termination of Hydrocarbon Prospecting and Hydrocarbon Exploration and Production Activities

116. The licensee shall, not later than 180 days before the termination of the hydrocarbon production activities, submit to the Ministry of Economics a plan for the termination of activities, if:

116.1. the licensee relinquishes the licence;

116.2. the validity period of the licence expires; or

116.3. the licensee wishes to terminate the utilisation of one or several installations of the hydrocarbon exploration or production.

117. The procedures for the dismantling of installations and transportation of the dismantled installations or the possible further exploitation of such installations, plugging of the well, recovering of soil after the dismantling of installations and other activities related to the completion of the hydrocarbon production shall be provided in the plan for the termination of activities.

118. If the licensee relinquishes the licence or intends to terminate the use of installations due to unplanned circumstances, he or she shall immediately notify the Ministry of Economics thereof. The information shall be included in the notification in accordance with Paragraph 116 of these Regulations and the reason why the use of the installations is being terminated shall be indicated therein.

119. The licence shall be suspended or cancelled in accordance with Section 16 of the Law On Subsoil.

120. The licensee has the duty to ensure that prior to leaving the licence area onshore or offshore on land that belongs to the State all the activities related to the dismantling of installations, plugging of the well, land reclamation, as well as other activities related to the completion of activities are carried out and the obligations of the licensee specified in the licence are fulfilled.

XII. FORCE MAJEURE CIRCUMSTANCES

121. Within the meaning of these Regulations, force majeure circumstances are exceptional circumstances which do not depend on the licensee, are not under his or her control and hinder the performance of the duties specified in the licence. Natural disasters, fires that have not been caused by the licensee, as well as warfare, terrorism, civil disturbances, strikes, restrictions or decisions of the Supreme State power and State administrative institutions and other exceptional circumstances that prevent or hinder the licensee to perform the production of hydrocarbons or prevent access to the territory covered by the licence shall be considered as force majeure circumstances.

122. The licensee shall not be responsible for the failure to fulfil the obligations specified in the licence or for the delay of the fulfilment if the failure to fulfil or the delay is related to the force majeure circumstances.

123. The licensee shall without delay notify the Ministry of Economics regarding the force majeure circumstances, adding the information at his or her disposal regarding the nature of the relevant circumstances and the effects caused thereby, and carry out actions to reduce the consequences.

124. If force majeure circumstances interrupt, impede the hydrocarbon exploration and production activities or make them impossible, the period of validity of the licence, as well as the due date for particular duties arising from the licence shall be extended for the time period equal to the length of the force majeure circumstances and the time period which is necessary for the resumption of the activities.

125. If due to force majeure circumstances it is impossible to reach the aims referred to in the licence, the Ministry of Economics shall, together with the licensee, decide on amendments to the provisions of the licence or the termination of validity of the licence.

XIV. CLOSING PROVISIONS

126. The competitions for the prospecting, exploration and production of hydrocarbons, which were announced prior to coming into force of these Regulations, are in effect, and applications submitted to these competitions shall be examined and evaluated, as well as licences for the prospecting, exploration and production of hydrocarbons shall be issued in accordance with the norms that were in effect prior to coming into force of these Regulations.

127. The licences issued prior to coming into force of these Regulations shall be valid until the period of time specified in the licence. The licensee shall have to comply with the stipulations of the licence and these Regulations.

128. The Commission referred to in Paragraph 42 of these Regulations shall be established within a time period of three months after coming into force of these Regulations. The evaluation of the submissions in order to receive a licence for the exploration and production of hydrocarbons shall be initiated after the establishment of the referred to Commission.

129. Until the establishment of the State capital company for the carrying out of the participation of the State in the production of hydrocarbons, the Latvian Investment and Development Agency shall manage the State participation share of Latvia provided for in the licence.

Informative Reference to European Union Directive

These Regulations contain legal norms arising from Directive 94/22/EEC of the European Parliament and of the Council of 30 May 1994 on the conditions for granting and using authorisations for the prospecting, exploration and production of hydrocarbons.

Acting for the Prime Minister –
Minister for Defence A. Slakteris

Minister for Economics J. Strods

Annex 1
Cabinet Regulation No. 597
4 September 2007

SUBMISSION FOR THE DETERMINATION OF THE LICENCE AREA FOR THE PROSPECTING OF HYDROCARBONS OR EXPLORATION AND PRODUCTION OF HYDROCARBONS

On the basis of Paragraph 9 of Cabinet Regulation No. 597 of 4 September 2007, Regulations Regarding Prospecting, Exploration and Production of Hydrocarbons and Procedures for Payment and Amount of State Fee, I (we) submit a proposal for the initiation of determination of a licence area, as well as a relevant information.

1. Information regarding the submitter:

1.1. given name, surname/firm name ______________________

1.2. personal identity number/merchant registration number, date and place ______________________

____

1.3. declared place of residence/legal address ______________________

1.4. telephone number ______________________

1.5. fax number (if applicable) ______________________

1.6. e-mail address (if applicable) ______________________

1.7. Internet homepage address (if applicable) ______________________

2. The purpose of utilisation of the sub-soil is the proposal of the licence area for hydrocarbons. ______________________
(prospecting/exploration and production)

3. Location of the proposed licence area on dry land:

______________, ______________, ______________
(district) (parish) (county)

4. Authorisation area:

4.1. plane co-ordinates on dry land in the Latvian co-ordinate system LKS92TM ______________________

4.2. ellipsoidal (geographic) co-ordinates on the sea in the WGS 84 system ______________________

5. The following documents have been attached to the submission (in submitting copies of documents, originals thereof shall be presented):

5.1. justification for the proposal to determine a licence area (in free form) p.__

5.2. copy of the merchant's registration certificate/copy of the passport of a natural person submitted by a non-resident p.__

5.3. written information regarding immovable properties which are located on the licence area specified in Paragraph 4 to this Annex*: p.__

5.3.1. location of the immovable property (district, parish, county);

5.3.2. name of the immovable property;

5.3.3. cadastre number of the immovable property;

* The document shall be submitted if the licence area is proposed on dry land.

5.3.4. given name, surname and personal identity number of the owner of the immovable property or the firm name and registration number of a merchant;

5.4. plan of the licence area (original in two copies) (not larger than in A3 format) issued by a licensed surveyor, the scale of which is determined by the initiator and which has been co-ordinated with the relevant regional department of the State Land Service*. p.__

The following shall be indicated in the plan:

5.4.1. plane co-ordinates on dry land in the Latvian co-ordinate system LKS92TM

5.4.2. boundaries of the immovable property included in the licence area;

5.4.3. name and cadastre number of the immovable property included in the licence area;

5.4.4. area and scale of the licence area;

5.4.5. a licence area location scheme;

5.5. notarially certified authorisation of the person who submits the submission regarding the proposal to determine a licence area on behalf of the landowner p.__

** ______________________________
(signature and full name of the submitter)

____
(date)

Minister for Economics J. Strods

** If a submission is submitted in electronic form, the signature area shall not be completed.

Annex 2
Cabinet Regulation Nr. 597
4 September 2007

SUBMISSION REGARDING MAKING AMENDMENTS TO THE LICENCE AREA FOR THE PROSPECTING OF HYDROCARBONS OR EXPLORATION AND PRODUCTION OF HYDROCARBONS

On the basis of Paragraph 14 of Cabinet Regulation No. 597 of 4 September 2007, Regulations Regarding Prospecting, Exploration and Production of Hydrocarbons and Procedures for Payment and Amount of State Fee, I (we) submit a proposal for making an amendment to the licence area that has been determined by the Cabinet Order of ___ _________ _____ No.___ "________________________________",

(title of the Cabinet Order)
as well as a relevant information.

1. Information regarding the submitter:
1.1. given name, surname/firm name ______________________________
1.2. personal identity number/merchant registration number, date and place ______________________________
____
1.3. declared place of residence/legal address ______________________________
1.4. telephone number ______________________________
1.5. fax number (if applicable) ______________________________
1.6. e-mail address (if applicable) ______________________________
1.7. Internet homepage address (if applicable) ______________________________

2. The purpose is to make amendments to the licence area for hydrocarbon ______________________________
(prospecting/exploration and production)

3. Location of the licence area to be amended on dry land:
______________, ______________, ______________
(district) (parish) (county)

4. Licence area:
4.1. plane co-ordinates on dry land in the Latvian co-ordinate system LKS92TM ____________
4.2. ellipsoidal (geographic) co-ordinates on the sea in the WGS 84 system ____________

5. The following documents have been appended to the submission (in submitting copies of documents, originals thereof shall be presented):

5.1. justification for the amendments to the licence area (to be submitted in free form) p.__
5.2. copy of the merchant's registration certificate/copy of the passport of a natural person p.__

submitted by a non-resident

5.3. written information regarding immovable properties which are located on the licence area specified in Paragraph 4 to this Annex*:

5.3.1. location of the immovable property (district, parish, county);

5.3.2. name of the immovable property;

5.3.3. cadastre number of the immovable property;

5.3.4. given name, surname and personal identity number of the owner of the immovable property or the firm name and registration number of a merchant; p.__

5.4. plan of the licence area (original in two copies) (not larger than A3 format) issued by a licensed surveyor, the scale of which is determined by the initiator and which has been co-ordinated with the relevant regional department of the State Land Service*. p.__

The following shall be indicated on the plan:

5.4.1. plane co-ordinates on dry land in the Latvian coordinate system LKS92TM

5.4.2. boundaries of the immovable property included in the licence area;

5.4.3. name and cadastre number of the immovable property included in the licence area;

5.4.4. area and scale of the licence area;

5.4.5. a licence area location scheme;

5.5. notarially certified authorisation to the person who submits the submission regarding making amendments to the licence area on behalf of the landowner. p.__

**

____
(signature and full name of the submitter)

____
(date)

Minister for Economics J. Strods

* The document shall be submitted if the licence area is located on dry land.

** If a submission is submitted in electronic form, the signature area shall not be completed.

Annex 3
Cabinet Regulation No. 597
4 September 2007

SUBMISSION FOR THE RECEIPT OF A LICENCE FOR THE PROSPECTING OF HYDROCARBONS

On the basis of Paragraph 27 of Cabinet Regulation No. 597 of 4 September 2007, Regulations Regarding Prospecting, Exploration and Production of Hydrocarbons and Procedures for Payment and Amount of State Fee, and the Cabinet Order of ___ _________ _____ No.___
"____",
(title of the Cabinet Order)

I submit the following information and documents for the receipt of a licence for the prospecting of hydrocarbons

____.
(district, parish, county)

1. Information regarding the submitter:

1.1. given name, surname/firm name ______________________

1.2. personal identity number/merchant registration number, date and place ______________________

____

1.3. declared place of residence/legal address ______________________

1.4. telephone number ______________________

1.5. fax number (if applicable) ______________________

1.6. e-mail address (if applicable) ______________________

1.7. Internet homepage address (if applicable) ______________________

2. Authorisation area:

2.1. plane co-ordinates on dry land in the Latvian co-ordinate system LKS92TM ____________

2.2. ellipsoidal (geographic) co-ordinates on the sea in the WGS 84 system ____________

3. The programme of activities for the prospecting of hydrocarbons. The following information shall be included in the programme of the activities:

3.1. division of the activities by years proposed by the merchant;

3.2. the amount of seismic activities to be performed (km, km^2);

3.3. the method how the seismic activities are performed technically (use of 2D (two-dimensional), 3D (three-dimensional) or 4D (four-dimensional) method);

3.4. the re-processing of seismic data, processing of seismic activities, acquisition of gravimetric, geochemical and other possible data.

4. The following documents have been appended to the submission (in submitting copies of

documents, originals thereof shall be presented):

4.1. a copy of the registration certificate of the merchant submitted by a non-resident p.__

4.2. a document confirming that all the landowners that are in the territory of the licence area (except the State) have chosen the applicant* p.__

**

(signature and full name of the submitter)

(date)

Minister for Economics J. Strods

* The document shall be submitted if the licence area is located on dry land.
** If a submission is submitted in electronic form, the signature area shall not be completed.

Annex 4
Cabinet Regulation No.597
4 September 2007

SUBMISSION FOR THE RECEIPT OF A LICENCE FOR THE EXPLORATION AND PRODUCTION OF HYDROCARBONS ON LAND THAT DOES NOT BELONG TO THE STATE

On the basis of Paragraph 69 of Cabinet Regulation No. 597 of 4 September 2007, Regulations Regarding Prospecting, Exploration and Production of Hydrocarbons and Procedures for Payment and Amount of State Fee, and the Cabinet Order of ___ _________ _____ No.___
"____",
(title of the Cabinet Order)

I submit the following information and documents for the receipt of a licence for the exploration and production of hydrocarbons

____.
(district, parish, county)

1. Information regarding the submitter:

1.1. given name, surname/firm name ________________________

1.2. personal identity number/merchant registration number, date and place ________________________

____

1.3. declared place of residence/legal address ________________________

1.4. telephone number ________________________

1.5. fax number (if applicable) ________________________

1.6. e-mail address (if applicable) ________________________

1.7. Internet homepage address (if applicable) ________________________

2. The desired time of operation of the licence (in years) ________________________

3. Information regarding the experience of the applicant describing the capability thereof to perform hydrocarbon exploration and production activities in the licence area:
3.1. projects in which the applicant has participated:

Location where hydrocarbon exploration and production activities were performed	Time when hydrocarbon exploration and production activities were performed	Title of the project	Issuer of the hydrocarbon exploration and production licence	Address of the issuer of the licence

3.2. complete curriculum vitae (CV) of those executive employees of the applicant whose employment relations with the merchant are longer than six months:

Given name, surname of employee	Position	Education

3.3. amount of hydrocarbons produced by the applicant:

Amount of hydrocarbons produced by the applicant during the last five years (bbl)				
year ____	year ____	year ____	year ____	year ____

4. The following documents have been attached to the submission (in submitting copies of officially registered documents, originals thereof shall be presented):

4.1. a copy of the merchant's registration certificate submitted by a non-resident ... p.

4.2. document confirming that all the landowners that are in the territory of the licence area have chosen the applicant ... p.

4.3. annual accounts regarding the last two financial years ... p.

4.4. minimum programme of activities in the exploration and production of hydrocarbons. The following information shall be included in the minimum programme of activities according to the offer of the merchant:

4.4.1. division of activities by years in the exploration stage of hydrocarbon production;

4.4.2. the method how seismic activities are performed technically (use of 2D (two-dimensional), 3D (three-dimensional) or 4D (four-dimensional) method);

4.4.3. processing and interpretation of seismic data;

4.4.4. the acquisition method for gravimetric and geochemical or other data;

4.4.5. exploration well (or wells) activities if such is planned;

4.4.6. programme for the evaluation of the technical condition of an existing well in order to clarify further possibilities of the utilisation thereof in exploration and production of hydrocarbons if the applicant has the intention to use the existing well, or programme for liquidation (closing) of the existing well in accordance with the requirements of environmental protection;

4.4.7. amount and costs of the exploration activities by separate types of activities;

4.5. document confirming that the participant has introduced a quality management system in accordance with LVS EN ISO 9001:2000, Quality Management Systems – Requirements, or an equivalent standard;

4.6. a document confirming that the participant has introduced Regulation (EC) No. 761/2001 of the European Parliament and of the Council of 19 March 2001 allowing voluntary participation by an organisation in a Community eco-management and audit scheme (EMAS) or LVS EN ISO 14001:2005, Environmental Management System – Requirements with Guidance for Use, or an environmental management standard that is equivalent thereto;

*

____
(signature and full name of the applicant)

____
(date)

Minister for Economics J. Strods

* If a submission is submitted in electronic form, the signature area shall not be completed.

Annex 5
Cabinet Regulation No. 597
4 September 2007

EVALUATION CRITERIA IN ORDER TO RECEIVE A LICENCE FOR EXPLORATION AND PRODUCTION OF HYDROCARBONS ON LAND THAT DOES NOT BELONG TO THE STATE

1. Financial indicators of the applicant. Maximum score 6 (six):
1.1. Equity capital:

1.1.1. up to LVL 70 000	-0.5 points
1.1.2. from LVL 70 001 – LVL 210 000	-1 point
1.1.3. from LVL 210 001 – LVL 350 000	-2 points
1.1.4. from LVL 350 001 – LVL 490 000	-2.5 points
1.1.5. from LVL 490 001 – LVL 630 000	-3 points
1.1.6. from LVL 630 001 – LVL 750 000	-3.5 points
1.1.7. from LVL 750 001 – LVL 850 000	-4 points
1.1.8. from LVL 850 001 – LVL 950 000	-4.5 points
1.1.9. from LVL 950 001 – LVL 1 050 000	-5 points
1.1.10. above LVL 1 050 001	-6 points

1.2. income. Maximum score 6 (six):

1.2.1. up to LVL 140 000	-0.5 points
1.2.2. from LVL 140 001 – LVL 280 000	-1 point
1.2.3. from LVL 280 001 – 420 000	-1.5 points
1.2.4. from LVL 420 001 – LVL 560 000	-2.5 points
1.2.5. from LVL 560 001 – LVL 700 000	-3 points
1.2.6. from LVL 700 001 – LVL 2 100 000	-3.5 points
1.2.7. from LVL 2 100 001 – LVL 4 200 000	-4 points
1.2.8. from LVL 4 200 001 – LVL 6 300 000	-4.5 points
1.2.9. from LVL 6 300 001 – LVL 7 700 000	-5 points
1.2.10. above LVL 7 700 001	-6 points

2. The method by which the submitter offers to perform the exploration for hydrocarbons (minimum programme of activities) and to initiate production thereof:

2.1. seismic prospecting 2D	-4 points
2.2. seismic prospecting 3D or 4D	-7 points
2.3. exploration wells:	
2.3.1. for each well drilled down to bedrock,	-10 points
2.3.2. for each well that reaches Ordovician sediment,	-6 points
2.4. other exploration methods	-2 points
2.5. for use of each well installed before determination of the licence area (inspection of technical condition, exploration, production, closing)	-4 points.

3. The applicant's experience in the production of hydrocarbons:
3.1. amount of hydrocarbons produced per year (on average during the last five years):

3.1.1. for each 1 mill. bbl	-1.5 points
3.1.2. no production	minus 4 points

3.2. practical work experience of the merchant in hydrocarbon exploration and production activities. Maximum score 6 (six):

3.2.1. experience is more than 21 years	-6 points
3.2.2. experience is from 16-20 years	-4 points
3.2.3. experience is from 11-15 years	-3 points

3.2.4. experience is from 5-10 years - 2 points
3.2.5. experience is from 1-4 years - 1 point
3.2.6. experience is less than 1 year -0.3 points
3.2.7. no experience minus 6 points
3.3. practical work experience of those executive employees (in years) in exploration and production of hydrocarbons, the applicant has working relations with for more than six months.

4. Altogether 0.5 points shall be granted for each year which the executive employee (whose complete curriculum vitae (CV) has been attached to the submission) has worked in hydrocarbon exploration and production activities.

COMPETITION PROCEDURES FOR THE AWARD OF PERMITS (LICENCES) FOR HYDROCARBON PRE-INVESTIGATION, EXPLORATION AND PRODUCTION ACTIVITIES

Amendments: Regulations of the Cabinet of Ministers No. 268 of 25.06.2002 (Latvijas Vestnesis, 28.06.2002, No. 97; Regulations of the Cabinet of Ministers No. 153 of 08.04.2003 (Latvijas Vestnesis, 15.04.2003, No. 58; Regulations of the Cabinet of Ministers No. 1010 of 14.12.2004 (Latvijas Vestnesis, 17.12.2004, No. 201).
(Minutes No.7, Paragraph 12)

Issued in compliance with the law 'On the Subsoil',Item 4, Part 4 and Item 10, Part 10

General Issues

These Regulations establish the competition procedure for the award of permits (licences) for the hydrocarbon pre-investigation (prospecting), exploration and production activities (hereinafter referred to as the 'Competition').

(As amended by the Regulations of the Cabinet of Ministers No. 153 of 08.04.2003, which came into force on 16.04.2003).

A competition shall be announced and organised by the Ministry of Economics on the basis of the order of the Cabinet of Ministers on a respective competition for a particular licence are within the territory or exclusive economic zone of the Republic of Latvia.

(As amended by the Regulations of the Cabinet of Ministers No. 153 of 08.04.2003, which came into force on 16.04.2003).

(Deleted by the Regulations of the Cabinet of Ministers No. 1010 of 14.12.2004).

The competition for a permit (licence) for hydrocarbon pre-investigation may be announced simultaneously with the competition for a permit (licence) for exclusive exploration and production of hydrocarbons (hereinafter referred to as the 'Permit (Licence) for exploration and production of hydrocarbons').

II. Preparation and announcement of the Competition

(This section - as amended by the Regulations of the Cabinet of Ministers No. 153 of 08.04.2003, which came into force on 16.04.2003).

1. A person, wishing to carry out hydrocarbon pre-investigation or exploration and production in a certain area, submits an application (see Attachment) to the Ministry of Economics.

(As amended by the Regulations of the Cabinet of Ministers No. 1010 of 14.12.2004).

5[1]. The Ministry of Economics considers the Application within 90 days and, if necessary, requests additional information from the relevant persons.

5[2]. *(Deleted by the Regulations of the Cabinet of Ministers No. 1010 of 14.12.2004).*

6. A Competition Invitation (hereinafter referred to as the 'Invitation') shall be published in the newspaper 'Latvijas Vestnesis' and in the Official Journal of the European Union.

(As amended by the Regulations of the Cabinet of Ministers No. 1010 of 14.12.2004).

7. The Invitation shall include the following information:

7.1. reference to the Ministry of Economics as the entity announcing the Competition;

7.2. the type of the permit (licence);
7.3. place, where the Competition Statute can be obtained and the contact person;
7.4. payment for the Competition Statute, if any;
7.5. other information necessary for the announcement of the competition.

8. The period for the submission of the competition applications (hereinafter referred to as Applications) shall be at least 90 calendar days from publishing the Invitation in the newspaper 'Latvijas Vestnesis' and in the Official Journal of the European Union.

(As amended by the Regulations of the Cabinet of Ministers No. 1010 of 14.12.2004).

8[1]. The Competition Statute is approved by the Minister of Economics.

8[2]. The requirements included in the Competition Statute cannot be changed until the end of the competition.

(As amended by the Regulations of the Cabinet of Ministers No. 1010 of 14.12.2004).

9. The Invitation shall include the following information:
9.1. reference to the Ministry of Economics as the entity announcing the Competition on behalf of the Republic of Latvia;
9.2. place (address) for the submission of applications;
9.3. data on the official entitled to provide information to applicants – first name, surname, position, telephone and fax numbers, address;

9.4. the type of the permit (licence) for which the competition is announced (the Permit

(Licence) for hydrocarbon pre-investigation or the Permit (Licence) for exploration and production of hydrocarbons);

9.5. reference to the Latvian state share provided in the Permit (Licence), if appropriate;

9.6. criteria for the determination of the competition results;

9.7. the co-ordinates of the licence area;

9.8. the procedure for and the place (address) of receipt of the necessary legal and administrative acts of the Republic of Latvia;

9.9. the commencement date of the respective activities after the award of the Permit (Licence);

9.10. submission date of applications;

9.11. competition participation fee;

9.12. if a competition for permits (licences) for onshore hydrocarbon exploration and production is announced, landowners' requirements towards the licence applicant in connection with the transfer of rights of the use of subsoil.

9.13. other information at the discretion of the Competition announcer.

III. Procedures for the submission of applications

10. An applicant may submit an application for one or several Permits (Licences), as well as a joint application of several applicants for one or several Permits (Licences)
11. The persons, wishing to obtain a Permit (Licence), may familiarise themselves with the legal and administrative acts and other documents concerning hydrocarbon pre-investigation, exploration and production including these Regulations and detailed documentation on the co-ordinates and location of the licence area at the place indicated in the Competition Regulation. The applicants shall be able to purchase geological data packages from the State Geological Survey. On receiving such packages, the applicant shall sign a Confidentiality Agreement (on the non-disclosure of business secret) with the State Geological Survey pursuant to the procedure for the use of information determined in the Regulations of the Cabinet of Ministers on Pre-investigation, Exploration and Production of Hydrocarbons.

(As amended by the Regulations of the Cabinet of Ministers No. 153 of 08.04.2003, which came into force on 16.04.2003).

12. During the submission period of applications, a representative of the Ministry of Economics shall provide consultations to the applicants with regard to drawing up applications. The information acquired while advising other applicants must not be divulged during these consultations.
13. The volume of the application (apart from appendices) should not exceed ten pages of A4 format.
14. Depending on the type of competition, the respective Appendices should be attached to the application:

14.1. Appendix 1 - an application summary in the form of a table;

14.2.Appendix 2 - in case of a legal entity: the applicant's name, address and state affiliation, notarised copies of documents or duplicates confirming the type of entrepreneurial activities, equity capital of the company, its registration place and the address of its main institution, main management institution of the company, its permanent address and its authorised person in Latvia (if any), as well as the company's annual reports for the last two years; if the applicant is a physical person: first name, surname, identity No.(if any) and address;

14.3. Appendix 3 – an assessment of economic prospects of the licence area applied for;

14.4. Appendix 4 – information on the applicant's experience proving his/its capability to carry out activities in the licence area

14.5. Appendix 5 – information on the applicant's experience concerning the recovery of oil production waste and regeneration of petroleum spills, which contaminate the environment;

14.6. Appendix 6 – documents, confirming the applicant's significant experience in managing hydrocarbon activities of pre-investigation, exploration and production in one's capacity as an Operator [should be provided by the applicant applying or being nominated for the position of Work Supervisor (Operator)].

14.7. Appendix 7 – the offer on the utilisation of Latvian goods in hydrocarbon pre-investigation, exploration and production within the scope of the permit (licence);

14.8. Appendix 8 – proposal to contribute to the training of the Latvian personnel;
14.9. Appendix 9 – guarantee (warranty) issued by a parent company, bank or other third person (if any);
14.10. the minimum Work Programme;
14.11. information on the applicant's experience in and capability of using environment-friendly technology;
14.12. *(Deleted by the Regulations of the Cabinet of Ministers No. 1010 of 14.12.2004).*

(As amended by the Regulations of the Cabinet of Ministers No. 153 of 08.04.2003, which came into force on 16.04.2003).

15. The following information should be included within the contest application for the Permit (Licence) for exploration and production of hydrocarbons:

15.1. name (or first name, surname), address and state affiliation of the applicant;

15.2. the licence area applied for, the corresponding designations and co-ordinates in accordance with the invitation. If several licence areas are mentioned in the application, areas with a higher of priority should also be indicated. If applicants submit a joint application, they should indicate the applicant nominated as the Work Supervisor (Operator);

15.3. reference to the consent to co-operate with an enterprise designated by the State if the Invitation prescribes Latvian state share.

16. The following information is included in the competition application for the Permit (Licence) for hydrocarbon pre-investigation:

16.1. name (first name, surname), address and state affiliation of the applicant;

16.2. the licence area applied for, the corresponding designations and co-ordinates in accordance with the invitation;

16.3. information on the applicant's technical experience in hydrocarbon pre-investigation,

16.4. the proposed Work Programme.

(As amended by the Regulations of the Cabinet of Ministers No. 268 of 25.06.2002, which came into force on 29.06.2002).

17. On submitting the application for the Permit (Licence) for Exploration and Production of Hydrocarbons, the applicant shall attach all the appendices mentioned in Paragraph 14 of these Regulations, but in case of the Permit (Licence) for Hydrocarbon Pre-investigation - the appendices mentioned in Sub-paragraphs 14.2, 14.4 and 14.11 of these Regulations.
18. The applicant shall submit the application and its appendices in a sealed envelope, indicating on the envelope for which competition the application has been submitted for.
19. Applications sent by post shall be deemed to be submitted before the deadline if received by the deadline for the submission of applications according to the Latvian time.
20. If the application does not contain all of the necessary information or documents, the applicant shall be entitled to submit amendments by the deadline for the submission of applications, without a special invitation or request.
21. The executive of the Competition Commission makes a note on the date of receipt on the envelopes of applications and their amendments and signs it.
22. The envelopes of applications and their amendments shall be opened only subsequent to the deadline for the submission of applications at the meeting of the Competition Commission, and the respective minutes shall be drawn up thereof.
23. The Competition Commission shall not examine the application which do not comply with the requirements of these Regulations or the competition terms and conditions; a protocol is made regarding this and the applicant is informed in writing about it within fifteen days of the meeting of the Competition Commission as indicated in Paragraph 22 of these Regulations.
24. The Ministry of Economics may prolong the term for the submission of applications within 30 days, in compliance with Paragraph 8 of these Regulations, making announcements about it in the "Latvijas Vestnesis" newspaper and relevant foreign publications, if:

24.1. no applications were submitted for a concrete licence area;

24.2. if, based on the decision by the Competition Commission, all the submitted applications for concrete licence area(s) are rejected.

(As amended by the Regulations of the Cabinet of Ministers No. 268 of 25.06.2002, which came into force on 29.06.2002).

24^1. if the term for the submission of applications is not prolonged, the competition for that licence area shall be regarded as non-existent.

(As amended by the Regulations of the Cabinet of Ministers No. 268 of 25.06.2002, which came into force on 29.06.2002).

24^2. the licence area, for which no applications were submitted, may be included in the next licensing round.

(As amended by the Regulations of the Cabinet of Ministers No. 268 of 25.06.2002, which came into force on 29.06.2002).

25. In case a single application for a certain licence area has been received, the Competition Commission, after evaluating the offer in the Application, shall be entitled to decide on awarding the Permit (Licence) to the applicant. The only grounds for a negative decision may be a discrepancy between the offer and the established criteria.

IV. The Competition Commission

26. The Competition Commission shall be approved by the Cabinet of Ministers according to proposals of the Minister of Economics, and shall consist of five to eleven members. Authorised representatives of the Ministry of Economics, the Ministry of Environment, the Ministry of Finance and the Ministry of Justice, as well as other competent officials shall be included in the commission.

(As amended by the Regulations of the Cabinet of Ministers No. 153 of 08.04.2003, which came into force on 16.04.2003).

27. For the purposes of evaluating the technical, financial, economic and ecological substantiation of applications and giving recommendations, the Competition Commission may form respective expert groups. The composition of such groups shall be approved by the Minister of Economics prior to the deadline for submitting applications.
28. **The Competition Commission shall have the power of decision if more than one half of its members are present at the meeting. Minutes of the meetings of the commission shall be taken.**
29. **Open voting shall take place at the commission's meetings. In case the number of affirmative and negative votes is equal, the chairman shall have the casting vote.**
30. **The Ministry of Economics shall technically support the work of the Contest commission.**

V. The evaluation criteria

The following criteria during competitions for permits (licences) for exploration and production of hydrocarbons shall be taken into consideration:

31.1. the applicant's technical resources and previous experience;

31.2. the applicant's financial capability to cover expenses related to the activities under the Permit (Licence);

31.3. the way of performing the hydrocarbon exploration (the minimum work programme) and commencing their production proposed by the applicant;

31.4. funds available for the minimum Work Programme and for the supplementary activities proposed by the applicant;

31.5. *(Deleted by the Regulations of the Cabinet of Ministers No. 1010 of 14.12.2004).*

31.6. the applicant's proposal to contribute to the training of the Latvian personnel;

31.7. the applicant's experience in and capability of using environment-friendly technology and protecting the environment.

(As amended by the Regulations of the Cabinet of Ministers No. 268 of 25.06.2002 and the Regulations of the Cabinet of Ministers No. 1010 of 14.12.2004).

The following criteria during competitions for permits (licences) for hydrocarbon pre-investigation shall be taken into consideration:

32.1. the applicant's technical capability;

32.2. the applicant's experience in and capability of using environment-friendly technology and protecting the environment.

Prior to making a decision, the Competition Commission shall be authorised to require more detailed supplementary information or the affirmation of the facts pursuant to the competition criteria. The additionally submitted information must not change the essence of the offer included in the application.

Subsequent to evaluating the applications pursuant to the criteria under Paragraphs 31 and 32 herein, if several applications have equal results, the Competition Commission shall use other objective and non-discriminatory criteria to make the final decision.

The Competition Commission shall have the right to take into account the applicant's work efficiency and quality during the validity period of the previous Permit (Licence) if such a Permit (Licence) has been formerly issued to the applicant in Latvia.

VI. DETERMINATION OF THE COMPETITION RESULTS

The competition applications shall be opened at the Competition Commission's meeting having a quorum, according to Paragraph 28 hereof, at a date at least five days later than the deadline for submitting the applications.

The Competition Commission shall consider the applications for the Permit (Licence) for

hydrocarbon pre-investigation and arrive at a decision on the results thereof within 60 days following the deadline for submitting the applications; in the case of a competition for the Permit (Licence) for hydrocarbon exploration and production - the results shall be decided within 120 days following the deadline for submitting the applications.

38. In the event that the Competition Commission considers it necessary to require additional information or to check the existing information, the decision-making period may be prolonged, but not to exceed 60 days. All the applicants should be informed thereof.

39. The meetings of the Competition Commission are closed ones. The information thereof should be provided in compliance with Paragraphs 41, 42 and 43 of these Regulations.

40. The competition results are published in the newspaper 'Latvijas Vestnesis' within ten days after making the final decision.

41. The competition results are communicated in writing to all the participants by sending notifications within 10 days after making the final decision.

VII. Documentation of the Competition process and information about it

42. Subsequent to the conclusion of the Competition, the Competition Commission shall keep and commit to the care of the archives of the Ministry of Economics the documents relevant to the Competition, which comprise the following information:

42.1. the competition announcer and the licence areas proposed;

42.2. composition of the Competition Commission, reference to the document under which this commission has been formed;

42.3. the competition Invitation;

42.4. first name and surname of the commission's members being present at the Competition Commission's meeting;

42.5. deadline and place for the submission of applications;

42.6. place and date for opening the application envelopes and the number of the applications submitted;

42.7. the applicants whose applications have been regarded valid;

42.8. minutes and resolutions of the Competition Commission meetings;

42.9. the applicants to whom the rights have been granted to receive the Permit (Licence);

42.10. minutes reflecting the inadequacy of documents;

42.11. the applicant, which has the right to receive the Permit (Licence), in case the applicant mentioned in subparagraph 42.9 of these Regulations, does not collect his/its Permit (Licence) within the appointed time, cancels his/its application, fails to sign a Joint Operating Agreement or to prepare other necessary documents;

42.12. name of each applicant;

42.13. description of the main points of each applicant's application;

42.14. a note on the applicant compliance with the requirements of the competition or on the rejection of the offer as inadequate, and the respective motivation;

42.15. a summary report on comparing and evaluating the offers and proposals by the Competition Commission, main arguments presented during the evaluation;

42.16. conclusions and recommendations of the expert groups, if such groups have been established;

42.17. motivation in case any of the applications or applicants have been rejected as non-complying with the requirements of the competition;

42.18. a note on correcting arithmetical errors (if any) within the applications submitted, as well as on the applicant's acceptance or refusal thereof;

42.19. information indicated by the applicant as strictly confidential.

43. There is no need to duplicate the information, indicated in Paragraph 42 of these Regulations being reflected in separate documents to be submitted for safe keeping, in the minutes of the Competition Commission's meeting, except the data on the applicants and applications.

44. The registration and recording of the Permits (Licences) issued in compliance with these Regulations shall be carried out by the Ministry of Economics. The Ministry of Economics shall transfer to the State Geological Survey the information on the awarded Permits (Licences). The registration and recording of the Permits (Licences), as well as the procedures for submitting the information to the State Geological Survey shall be subject to instructions approved by the Minister of Economics.

INFORMATION REFERENCE TO THE EUROPEAN UNION DIRECTIVE

(As amended by the Regulations of the Cabinet of Ministers No. 1010 of 14.12.2004).

These Regulations contain legal provisions, which comply with the 94/22/EC Directive of the European Parliament and Council of May 30, 1994 as regards the provisions for the issue and use of permits for hydrocarbon pre-investigation, exploration and production.

Prime Minister A. Skele

For the Minister of Economics - Minister of Finance E. Krastins

1. Information about the Applicant

1.1. First name, surname/name

1.2. Identity No./Registration No., date and place

1.3. Place of residence/legal address

1.4. Telephone No.

1.5. Fax No.

1.6. E-mail address

1.7. Internet home page address

2. Purpose of the use of subsoil

3. Location of the possible onshore licence area – administrative area

4. Co-ordinates of the possible onshore licence area: onshore – in the LKS92TM system, offshore – geographical co-ordinates

5. Information about all landowners, the land of whom is located in the licence area, information about the owners of adjacent plots of land:

No.

Cadastre No. of plot of land

Address of plot of land

Owner's first name and surname/ name; address/legal address

Identity No. /Registration No.

6. Previous experience in oil operations (if any) of the person interested in hydrocarbon pre-investigation or exploration and production operations (applicant for the use of subsoil)

7. Requested term of the permit (licence), if such is planned

8. The following documents are attached to the application (if document copies are submitted, the originals must be presented):

Type of document

Number of pages

8.1.

Copy of businessman's registration certificate/copy of passport of physical person

î

8.2.

The landowner's requirements to the licensee, which will be included in the Statute of Competition for hydrocarbon exploration and production operations

î

8.3.

General substantiation of geological prospectivity of the licence area

8.4.

Map of land boundaries (certified copy), if the possible licence area is located onshore

8.5.

Document confirming land ownership (certified copy)

ĩ

8.6.

Map of the possible licence area issued by the State Land Survey, with co-ordinates (two originals) and certificate regarding plots of land existing in the licence area, with landowners and land cadastre numbers indicated

ĩ

8.7.

Notarised Power of Attorney for the person making transactions on behalf of the landowner, landholder or businessman

REGULATIONS ON THE STATE FEE FOR THE OIL PRODUCTION

Issued in compliance with the law
'On taxes and duties', Article 10, Part 2.
(As amended by the Regulations of the
Cabinet of Ministers No. 154 of 08.04.2003,
which came into force on 16.04.2003).

I. GENERAL ISSUES

These Regulations determine the procedure for calculating and paying the state fee for the oil production (hereinafter referred to as Royalty).

The Royalty is a payment for the oil produced in the territory or the exclusive economic zone of Latvia.

The Royalty shall be paid by companies (enterprises), which have obtained a permit (licence) for the exploration and production of hydrocarbons (hereinafter - permit (licence) and produce oil in the territory or the exclusive economic zone of Latvia (hereinafter- licensee).

Companies (enterprises) shall calculate and pay the Royalty in Lats (LVL) for the amount of oil extracted from each separate deposit.

The amount of the oil produced shall be supervised by the Ministry of Economics.

II. PROCEDURE FOR CALCULATING THE ROYALTY

The Royalty rate shall be determined as a percentage from the amount of oil produced in the territory or the exclusive economic zone of Latvia.

The Royalty rate shall be applied depending on the daily amount of oil extracted from each separate oil deposit:

as regards oil produced in the territorial sea, as well in the territories, which are not state property:

Amount of oil production (Barrels of oil per day -'BOPD')	ROYALTY RATE
Up to 10.000 BOPD	2%
10.001- 20.000 BOPD	4%
20.001- 30.000 BOPD	6%
30.001- 40.000 BOPD	8%
40.001- 50.000 BOPD	9%
50.001- 80.000 BOPD	10%
Over 80.001 BOPD	12%

as regards oil produced in the territories, which are state property: 10%.

(As amended by the Regulations of the Cabinet of Ministers No. 154 of 08.04.2003, which came into force on 16.04.2003).

The amount of oil produced shall be fixed at the measurement point and at the time specified in the permit (licence).

The daily amount of the oil produced, calculated to the precision of one decimal place, shall be determined by means of dividing the total amount of oil in barrels, extracted during the accounting week, by the number of production days in a week.

The procedure for assessing the grade of the oil extracted shall be specified in the permit (licence).

The specific amount of the Royalty shall be calculated by multiplying the respective royalty rate under Paragraph 7 of these Regulations and the market value for the daily produced oil, determined pursuant to Paragraph 12 hereof.

The market value for the oil produced in the territory or the exclusive economic zone of Latvia shall be assessed every calendar week (from Monday at 00.00 to Sunday at 24.00) on the basis of the price for the Reference Petroleum 'Dated Brent' extracted in the North Sea and indicated in the price-list 'Argus Crude Report' (published on the next Monday following an accounting week after closing London International Oil Exchange) of the journal 'Argus Petroleum'. The market value for oil is calculated by taking into consideration the quality of the oil extracted:

W= Vx (P + Delta) where:

W- market value for oil,

V- volume of the oil extracted (in barrels),

P- price for the Reference Petroleum 'Dated Brent' in United States dollars per bbl,

Delta- an adjustment coefficient, which depends on the quality of the produced oil in API grades, on the sulphur content and the market demand for oil of such a quality.

III. Procedure for paying the Royalty

The Licensee shall submit to the State Income Service and the Ministry of Economics a report on oil production from each separate deposit and on the Royalty (Appendix) to be paid for each calendar month not later than on day 10 of the month following the respective reporting month.

Royalty payments shall be recalculated in the monetary units of the Republic of Latvia - Lats. Recalculation shall be made by applying the exchange rate stated by the Bank of Latvia on the specified date.

Royalty payments shall be commenced for the quarter when the first barrel of oil is produced and subsequently paid once a quarter, not later than on day 20 of the first month following that quarter.

If the Ministry of Economics and the Licensee have agreed upon interruption or termination of the oil production the Royalty shall not be paid for the quarter when oil is not extracted.

Revenues from the Royalty payments shall be transferred into the principal state budget.

IV. Final Issue

By April 1st, 2000, after obtaining an endorsement by the Ministry of Finance, the Ministry of Economics shall work out and the Minister of Economics shall approve the procedure for adjusting the price of the oil produced.

Information reference to the European Union Directive

(According to the Regulations of the Cabinet of Ministers No. 154 of 08.04.2003, which came into force on 16.04.2003).

These Regulations contain legal provisions, which comply with the 94/22/EC *Directive.*

Prime Minister A. Skele

For the Minister of Economics -

Minister of Finance E.Krastins

APPENDIX

to Regulations

of the Cabinet of Ministers No.53

of February 8, 2000

REPORT ON THE OIL EXTRACTED FROM THE DEPOSIT AND *ON THE PAYABLE ROYALTY*

COMPANY (ENTERPRISE)____

(name,

____

–

legal address and registration No.)

PERMIT (LICENCE)____

(number and date of issue)

DEPOSIT____

–

(name and location)

ACCOUNTING MONTH____

Date	Amount of the extracted oil (thousand bbl)	Royalty rate (per cent)	Market value of the produced oil (in USD)	Exchange rate stated by the Bank of Latvia	Royalty (in lats) (6=2·3·4·5)
1	*2*	*3*	*4*	*5*	*6*
1					
2					
Total					

Regulations regarding the Protection of the Environment during Exploration and Production of Hydrocarbons in the Sea

Issued pursuant to

Section 9, Clause 9

of the Law On Environmental Protection and

Section 10, Paragraph two

of the Law On Subterranean Depths

I. General Provisions

1. These Regulations prescribe environmental protection requirements during exploration and production of hydrocarbons in the sea, in order to eliminate or reduce environmental pollution, which may arise because of the exploration and production of hydrocarbons.

2. A person performing exploration or production of hydrocarbons has the duty to use the best available techniques, taking into account the principles of transparency, complexity, scientific justification, planning, precautions, the environment and the national economy.

II. Environmental Impact Assessment and Monitoring

3. Before the approval of exploration and production of hydrocarbons in the Cabinet, the Ministry of Environmental Protection and Regional Development shall submit the information regarding the state of the environment in these blocks to the Cabinet.

4. A manager of exploration and production of hydrocarbons (hereinafter – operator) shall, prior to commencing the exploration and production of hydrocarbons in the earliest possible stage of technical planning, design or taking of a decision regarding the intended operation, propose the performance of an environmental impact assessment in accordance with the requirements specified in the 1992 Helsinki Convention on the Protection of the Marine Environment of the Baltic Sea Area (hereinafter – the Helsinki Convention) and in the 25 February 1991, ESPO Convention On Environmental Impact Assessment in a Transboundary Context.

5. An operator shall ensure monitoring at the place of exploration and production of hydrocarbons, taking into account the opinion of the previously completed environmental impact assessment. A monitoring programme shall be approved by the Marine Environment Administration of the Ministry of Environmental Protection and Regional Development (hereinafter - Marine Environment Administration) prior to the receipt of authorisation for exploration and production of hydrocarbons.

6. Monitoring surveys shall be carried out in accordance with the requirements of ICES (International Council for the Exploration of the Sea) and HELCOM (Helsinki Commission), using standardised methods.

7. The monitoring data, obtained with the funds of legal or natural persons, is the property of the relevant legal or natural persons and shall be available to the State administrative bodies free of

charge. An operator shall submit the monitoring reports and copies of data to the Marine Environment Administration in accordance with the approved monitoring programme.

8. State monitoring, in accordance with the sea monitoring programme, shall be carried out notwithstanding monitoring being performed by the operator.

III. Discharge during Exploration and Production of Hydrocarbons

9. It is prohibited to discharge diesel oil drilling mud and waste thereof into the Baltic sea, but it shall be purified and reused on site or shall be conveyed to the shore for purification and utilisation, co-ordinating these operations with Marine Environment Administration.

10. The use of drilling mud produced from a diesel oil base shall only be permitted in exceptional cases, if it is necessary due to geological, technical or safety reasons and it has previously been co-ordinated with the Marine Environment Administration, ensuring compliance with the requirements referred to in Paragraph 9 of these Regulations.

11. It is prohibited to discharge water based drilling mud and waste thereof into the Baltic Sea, prior to the toxicity thereof being controlled in accordance with the Annex to these Regulations in a laboratory accredited for this purpose. Toxicity control shall be ensured by the operator who shall inform the Marine Environment Administration regarding the results.

12. If the results of the toxicity control referred to in Paragraph 11 of these Regulations verify the harmlessness of the drilling mud and drilling waste to the environment (none of the substances referred to in Paragraph 1.2, Annex I of Helsinki Convention have been added to the mud as components thereof and the concentration of mercury (Hg) or cadmium (Cd) does not exceed 1 mg/kg in the mud), after co-ordination with the Marine Environment Administration, the utilisation of the water based drilling mud and discharge of drilling waste into the sea shall be permitted.

13. It is prohibited to discharge chemical substances included in the list of harmful substances referred to in Paragraph 1.2, Annex I of the Helsinki Convention and materials containing such substances.

14. It is prohibited to discharge impure economic waste water and waste into the sea.

15. It is prohibited to discharge production waste water and replacement water into the sea, if the oil content therein, determined with analyses and sampling methods recognised by HELCOM (Helsinki Commission), exceeds 15 mg/l.

16. If, using the best available methods, it is not possible to fit within the limit referred to in Paragraph 15 of these Regulations (up to 15 mg/l), the Marine Environment Administration has the right to increase the discharge limit up to 40 mg/l and to request the execution of relevant additional measures in order to eliminate environmental pollution. The Marine Environment Administration shall review discharge limits at regular intervals taking into account developments in waste water production and purification technology.

17. The management plan for all types of waste water, waste and by-products (hereinafter – waste management plan) shall be approved by the Marine Environment Administration before obtaining an authorisation for exploration and production of hydrocarbons.

18. The authorisation for the use of water and for the release of polluting substances into the atmosphere in accordance with regulatory enactments and recommendations of HELCOM (Helsinki Commission), as well as taking into account the environmental impact assessment, shall be issued by the Marine Environment Administration.

19. Injection of gas and water into the oil-bearing bed for the promotion of production, as well as the re-injection of produced liquids into the oil-bearing bed in the course of proceeding with the production of hydrocarbons shall not be considered as pollution of subterranean depths. The operator shall co-ordinate the referred to operations with the Marine Environment Administration.

20. This Chapter does not apply to cases when human life or objects related to the production of hydrocarbons are under the threat of complete destruction and discharge is the only possibility of eliminating these threats and if there is the certainty, that the injury caused by the discharge will be less than that injury if the discharge has not happened. Such discharge shall be done so that possible injury to human life and the marine environment shall be reduced to a minimum.

21. Discharge performed in accordance with Paragraph 20 of these Regulations shall be notified to the Marine Environment Administration within 24 hours, beginning with the commencement of the discharge, indicating the content of the substances discharged, possible amount, place and time.

IV. ELIMINATION OF THE CONSEQUENCES OF DISASTERS AND THE OPERATIONAL PLAN IN THE EVENT OF UNEXPECTED POLLUTION

22. In accordance with Paragraph 472 of Cabinet Regulation No. 168 of 16 August 1994, Latvian Maritime Regulations (Maritime Code), an operator shall draw up an operational plan in the case of unexpected pollution for every object involved in the exploration or production of hydrocarbons (hereinafter – operational plan), which shall be approved by the Marine Environment Administration before obtaining the permit for exploration or production of hydrocarbons.

23. The location (storage) of equipment for the elimination of consequences of disasters shall be indicated precisely in the operational plan.

24. Equipment for the elimination of consequences of disasters shall be stored and maintained so that the pollution elimination measures may be commenced immediately. An operator shall ensure the immediate commencement of elimination measures of consequences of disasters, but that the commencement of additional measures provided in the operational plan – shall not be later than eight hours after the disaster.

25. Utilisation of dispersants during elimination measures of oil pollution shall be limited as much as possible and each case of utilisation thereof shall be previously co-ordinated with the Marine Environment Administration. It is prohibited to use oil sinking substances for the elimination of pollution.

26. Equipment for the elimination of consequences of disasters shall meet the following conditions:

26.1. the quantity of equipment shall comply in order to eliminate the possible consequences, if the leakage of oil has occurred from drillings, platforms or pipelines of exploration or production of hydrocarbons, taking into account the geological location of the drilling, evaporation and emulsification of oil;

26.2. oil collection systems, booms and transport materials shall be designed so they can be used and they are effective in the current conditions and the height of waves that prevail in the relevant region (a height of waves up to 2 meters and a current of up to 1 knot), and the equipment shall be capable of being operated in the prevailing temperature in the relevant region;

26.3. the capability of the equipment to be used in the conditions of ice for the elimination of consequences of disasters shall have been examined in conditions of low temperature, ice and under the ice;

26.4. the equipment intended for the elimination of pollution of harmful substances other than oil, used in a substantial amount, shall comply with the following conditions:

26.4.1. the quantity and type of equipment shall be such, so that the user may determine and inform about the amount of pollution and location thereof, avoid or reduce the release of substances and eliminate the pollution; and

26.4.2. if the pollution is floating and insoluble in water, the user may restrict, collect and transport it in the circumstances referred to in Sub-paragraph 26.2 of these Regulations.

27. The duties of an operator in the case of unexpected environmental pollution are the following:

27.1. immediately identify the source of the pollution;

27.2. carry out the necessary operations in order to liquidate pollution in accordance with the operational plan;

27.3. to provide the following information to the Marine Environment administration:

27.3.1. the type of pollution and amount;

27.3.2. the time and place of the determination of the pollution;

27.3.3. the source of the pollution;

27.3.4. the operations begun for the elimination of pollution and the causes thereof; and

27.3.5. the wind and sea conditions at the place of pollution.

V. CONTROL

28. Officials of the Marine Environment Administration shall carry out the State inspection of the observation of environmental protection requirements in exploration and production of hydrocarbons in the Economic Area of the Republic of Latvia and in the territorial waters pursuant to the following conditions:

28.1. The Marine Environmental Administration shall submit to the Ministry of Economics the control schedule for the following year by 20 October of each year, providing that the inspections are executed at least once in every half year;

28.2. Officials of the Marine Environment Administration have the right (with prior co-ordination with an operator) in accordance with the inspection schedule and in cases, when a cause for suspicion of environmental pollution from an object related to the exploration or production of hydrocarbons arises, to inspect observation of the environmental protection regulations and the conditions of authorisation, the implementation of the environmental protection and waste management plan, as well as the readiness for elimination of pollution and compliance of the operational plan with an actual situation, to be provided with accommodation free of charge at the object related to exploration or production of hydrocarbons, to receive information necessary for the performance of functions thereof and copies of documents; and

28.3. The Marine Environment Administration shall inform the Ministry of Economics and the operator regarding the results of the inspections.

29. Operators shall ensure:

29.1. transport of the Marine Environment Administration official to the object related to exploration and production of hydrocarbons, as well as the provide the relevant working conditions for performance of the inspection in the cases referred to in Sub-paragraph 28.2 of these Regulations;

29.2. the provision of all necessary information to the Marine Environment Administration;

29.3. automated control and registration of emissions, as well as the provision of regular reports to the Marine Environment Administration regarding substances discharged into the environment in accordance with the conditions referred to in the authorisations; and

29.4. the permanent inspection of the environment protection measures plan, the waste management plan and the operational plan once in every half year.

THE DETERMINATION OF TOXICITY OF DRILLING MUD AND CONDITIONS FOR UTILISATION

1. The toxicity of water based drilling mud shall be determined by testing – a test of how the water-soluble fraction, obtained by stirring the dregs for 20 hours in a closed system, then allowed to settle (forming a sediment) for two hours and taking a sample from the middle of the mass obtained, impacts:
   1.1. on the photosynthesis of seaweed (*Skeletonema costatum*);
   1.2. on the growth of sea mussel worms (*Mytilus edulis*);
   1.3. on the reproduction of marine crustaceans (*Acartia tonsa*); and
   1.4. on sea fish worms(*Clupea harengus*).

2. EC_{50}96h (a concentration, which causes functional changes in 50 % of test organisms within 96 hours) in the tests referred to in Paragraph 1 of these Regulations shall be at least 10 000 mg/kg.

3. The following additional tests may be carried out:

3.1. a test of biological degradation (in accordance with guidelines of Organisation for Economic Co-operation and Development (OECD)); and

3.2. a bio-accumulation test (for determination of lipophilic substances by the method of chromatography).

4. The content of petroleum products in emissions shall be determined by using the standardised method of infrared rays in three absorption regions (approximately 2925, 2960 and 3025 cm^{-1}).

TERMS OF HYDROCARBON PRODUCTION STAMP DUTY

I. General Provisions

1st These Regulations prescribe the procedure for calculating the hydrocarbon production fee (hereinafter - the fee), the amount of fees and payment arrangements.

2nd The fee is the charge of the Latvian Republic of the exclusive economic zone or the Latvian territory the lands owned by the hydrocarbons obtained.

3rd Fees paid by businesses (commercial), which received a license for hydrocarbon exploration and production (hereinafter - license) and the Latvian Republic of hydrocarbons obtained the exclusive economic zone or the territory of Latvian state-owned Lands (hereinafter - the licensee).

II. A complex quantity and the control

4th The resulting amount of hydrocarbons provides the licensee the license specified in the measurement space and time.

5th Monthly amount of extracted oil barrels down to the nearest barrel.

6th Month, resulting in cubic meters of natural gas shall be determined with an accuracy of up to one thousand cubic meters.

7th The resulting hydrocarbon volume records and the hole exhaust flange connected measuring devices (meter) readings are controlled by the Ministry of Economy.

III. Procedure for calculating fees

8th The Licensee fee shall be calculated separately for each hydrocarbon exploration and production license area resulting amount of hydrocarbons.

9th Levy rate is determined as a percentage of the Latvian Republic of the exclusive economic zone or the territory of Latvian public lands that belong to the quantitative value of the extracted hydrocarbons.

IV. Fees

10th The duty rate for oil is 15% of the monthly volume of oil extracted values for each hydrocarbon exploration and production license area.

11th The duty rate for natural gas is 10% of the monthly quantity of natural gas values obtained for each hydrocarbon exploration and production license area.

V. Toll of

12th The fee is calculated on the lats:

12.1. monthly oil production, using the following formula:

Onn = Wn x 0.15, where

Onn - the fee for petroleum hydrocarbons in lats;

Wn - oil lats value as determined in accordance with the provisions of Paragraph 13;

0.15 - decimal number expressed as a hydrocarbon oil duty;

12.2. monthly natural gas obtained using the following formula:

Ong = Wg x 0.10, where

Ong - hydrocarbon charge for natural gas in lats;

Wg - natural gas value in Lats, determined in accordance with the provisions of Paragraph 14;

0.10 - decimal number expressed as a hydrocarbon duty natural gas.

13th Oil extracted value is determined on a monthly basis for the calculation of oil etalonšķirnes "Dated Brent" the average monthly price. Calculations based on the agencies 'Platts' monthly working days of the publication of oil etalonšķirnes "Dated Brent" on the average daily price. Extracted oil is determined by the following formula:

Wn = Vn x Pvid x r, where

Wn - oil value in Lats;

Vn - month acquired amount of oil in barrels;

r - Latvian Bank of the United States dollar against the lats on the last working day;

Pvid - oil etalonšķirnes "Dated Brent" The average monthly price of United States dollars per barrel, which is calculated using the following formula:

Pvid = (P1 + P2 + P3 + ... + Pn) / n, where

P1, P2, P3, ... Pn - the average oil price of U.S. dollars per barrel for each working day of the month;

n - Number of working days in that month.

14th Acquired the natural gas value is determined every month, according to the energy equivalent of natural gas by equating the quantity of oil to the amount and calculation of oil etalonšķirnes "Dated Brent" the average monthly price. Calculations based on the agencies 'Platts' monthly working days of the publication of oil etalonšķirnes "Dated Brent" on the average daily price. Extracted natural gas is determined by the following formula:

Wg = Vg Pvid x x r x 5, where

Wg - natural gas value in Lats;

Vg - month acquired quantity of natural gas (thousand cubic meters);

r - Latvian Bank of the United States dollar against the lats on the last working day;

Pvid - oil etalonšķirnes "Dated Brent" The average monthly price of United States dollars per barrel, which is calculated using the following formula:

Pvid = (P1 + P2 + P3 + ... + Pn) / n, where

P1, P2, P3, ... Pn - the average oil price of U.S. dollars per barrel for each working day of the month;

n - Number of working days in that month.

VI. Fees Payment Procedure

15th Fees are being paid for the month, which produced the first barrel of oil or cubic meter of natural gas, and continue to be paid once a month until the fifteenth day of the previous month.

16th The Licensee fee shall be paid in Lats separately for each hydrocarbon exploration and production license area of the resulting amount of hydrocarbons.

17th Revenues from fee payments into the State budget.

VII. Closing

18th Be declared null and void Cabinet 8 February 2000 the provisions of No. 53 "Regulations on the oil stamp duty" (Latvian Herald, 2000, 44./46.nr., 2003, 58.nr.).

Informative Reference to European Union Directives

These Regulations contain legal norms arising from the European Parliament and Council Directive 94/22/EC of 30 May 2004 for granting and using authorizations for the prospection, exploration and production.

THE MINING WASTE MANAGEMENT PROCEDURES

I. GENERAL PROVISIONS

1st These Regulations prescribe the mining waste (hereinafter - the mining waste) management procedures.

2nd Terms used:

2.1. manager - this rule within the meaning of a natural or legal person who is responsible for mining waste management, including temporary storage of mining waste, mining waste facility, the management of its operations during and after the closure of the facility;

2.2. treatment - mechanical, biological, thermal or chemical process or a complex process carried out with the minerals in order to obtain the appropriate minerals, such as resizing, sorting, separation and leaching, and mining waste and the burning of limestone (other than smelting, thermal manufacturing processes and metallurgical processes);

2.3. caravans - sift the subject of solid mining waste storage on the ground;

2.4. fundamental change - a change in the mining waste facility, structure or management, under the competent authority and may have a significant adverse effect on human health or the environment;

2.5. Dam - Waterworks engineering structure of water or liquid extraction to retain or confine a pond;

2.6. mining industry - its provisions, all businesses engaged in mining or processing;

2.7. mining waste - soil, rock and sharps surpluses generated by prospecting, mining, processing and storage;

2.8. pond - its provisions formed naturally or built land the depth of fine-grained mining waste (tailings usually) storage along with varying amounts of free water, resulting from mineral processing and process water cleaning and recovery;

2.9. mining the site - all the land in a specific geographical location, under the supervision and control of an operator;

2.10. infiltration - the meaning of this provision, any liquid that is formed through sūcoties mining waste facility held by mining waste, mining waste is stored at a facility or removed from it, including polluted drainage, which may adversely affect the environment if they are under treatment;

2.11. structural integrity - these Regulations, the ability to hold mining waste mining waste facility in the way it was intended. Loss of structural integrity covers all possible incidents relating to the mining waste facility construction;

2.12. accident - an event collection on site during an operation in the management of mining waste in the company, if the accident caused a serious threat to human health or the environment, either immediately or over time, mining waste facility or outside it;

2.13. unpolluted soil - soil that when mining is removed and no contamination (corresponding laws and regulations on soil and soil quality of the standards);

2.14. excavation voids - mining process created a cavity in the earth beneath;

2.15. rehabilitation - the Regulations within the meaning of extractive waste facility affected by land clearing and the recovery at least to the extent that, in future not to impair the quality of soil, wild plants and animals, habitats, water bodies and landscape, and the area it would be possible to use a particular economic activity;

2.16. Slag - mining waste solids or slurries that occur after the minerals have been treated in separation processes (eg crushing, grinding, sieving, flotation and other physical and chemical techniques) to remove minerals from the less valuable rock;

2.17. weak acid dissociable cyanide - Cyanide and cyanide compounds, which decompose in a weak acid with a specific response to environmental acidity (pH).

3rd These provisions shall not apply to:

3.1. waste resulting from prospecting, extraction of mineral resources in accordance with the laws of the depths of the earth and their treatment, but that this activity does not directly;

3.2. waste resulting from prospecting, extraction of mineral resources in accordance with the laws of the subsoil and the processing of the coast (sea and seabed, which stretches into the sea from the normal or average low tide low water);

3.3. groundwater input, draining or pumping in accordance with laws and regulations on water use permit;

3.4. groundwater abstraction.

4th These rules (except for 12th, 13th and 14 of those requirements) shall not apply to the collection of waste for storage:

4.1. wastes that are not dangerous and there are mineral resources (except hydrocarbons and evaporītus but not gypsum and anhydrite) prospecting and extraction;

4.2. unpolluted soil;

4.3. wastes, yielding, after processing or storage of peat.

5th These rules apply to a mining waste management, from prospecting, extraction of mineral resources in accordance with the laws of the depths of the earth, mineral processing and storage, where mining waste deposited in a category of mining waste facility (in accordance with the provisions of Clause 16).

6th Mining waste facility is an area (including mining waste disposal sites), as irrespective of whether the mining waste is solid or liquid form, dissolved or suspended, accumulated or stored waste collection, if the site is stored:

6.1. of occurrence - A category of mining waste facilities and facilities for mining waste, mining waste management plan as dangerous;

6.2. more than six months from the time of - unplanned hazardous waste;

6.3. more than one year of occurrence - of mining waste, which is not dangerous and is not inert;

6.4. more than three years of occurrence:

6.4.1. unpolluted soil management facilities;

6.4.2. of prospecting, as well as peat extraction, processing and storage of mining waste, which is not dangerous;

6.4.3. inert waste.

7th Mining waste as inert waste if it meets the following criteria:

7.1. with them does not undergo any significant physical, chemical or biological transformations;

7.2. they are insoluble, or otherwise physically or chemically react, biodegrade or affect other matter with which it comes into contact and thus does not cause environmental pollution or harm to human health;

7.3. they do not burn and there is no risk of spontaneous combustion;

7.4. sulfur content of the sulphide mining waste does not exceed 0.1% sulfur or sulphide mining waste does not exceed 1% or neutralization potential ratio, calculated as the ratio of neutralization potential and acid potential and determined by the static test prEN 15875, is greater than 3;

7.5. environment and human health, potentially harmful substances, particularly arsenic, cadmium, cobalt, chromium, copper, mercury, molybdenum, nickel, lead, vanadium and zinc content of mining waste, and separate collection of waste smalkajās particles are so insignificant that neither short-nor long term could cause significant risk to human health and the environment. Matter is deemed a minor (such as not to cause significant risk to human health and the environment), if it does not exceed prescribed national soil and soil quality standards;

7.6. mining wastes no extraction or processing of products used, which could harm the environment or human health.

8th In assessing the geochemical state of mining waste, take into account the criteria referred to in paragraph 7. If, on the basis of the criteria referred to in paragraph 7, mining wastes are found to be inert waste, they are tested in accordance with the provisions of paragraph 5 of Appendix 1.

9th This provision in Paragraph 6 of the mining waste facilities are also considered a dam or other structure designed to retain, confine or otherwise support the provisions of Clause 6 of the items. This provision in Paragraph 6 of the object does not mine the site, the rehabilitation or construction purposes in a mining waste.

10th Management of prospecting, mining, processing and storage of the resulting inert waste and uncontaminated soil, this provision does not apply to Chapters IV and V, 74th, 75th and 81.punktā, as well as VIII, IX and Chapter X of this requirement if the waste in a category of waste collection facility.

11th Management of mining waste, which is inert and not dangerous, does not apply to these Regulations 74th, 75th, 81st, 85th, 86th and 88.punktā, and Chapters IX and X of that requirement, if these wastes in a category of waste collection facility.

12th Mining waste is managed:

12.1. without risk to human life and health;

12.2. without risk of surface and groundwater, air, soil, and flora and fauna;

12.3. up legislation on noise and odor prevention and control limits,

12.4. without adversely affecting the landscape and special areas of conservation;

12.5. without contaminating the environment.

13th It is forbidden to leave, dumping and uncontrolled disposal of mining waste.

14th To prevent or mitigate adverse effects on the environment and human health, the operator, using the best available techniques, provides:

14.1. mining waste management facility in operation;

14.2. mining waste management facility after closure;

14.3. accident prevention and limiting of their consequences, taking into account mining waste facility, the technical characteristics, its location and environmental conditions.

15th Filling the excavation voids with waste other than waste collection, the laws and regulations for landfill management requirements.

II. CRITERIA FOR MINING WASTE FACILITIES IN DETERMINING THE CLASSIFICATION OF

16th State Environmental Service mining waste facilities are recognized as category A if:

16.1. the expected consequences of an accident caused by mining waste facility structural integrity loss, or incorrect operation, short or long term, may threaten human life or the environment;

16.2. at the mining waste classified as hazardous according to the laws regarding waste classification and characteristics, which render the waste hazardous, if this provision in Paragraph 18 of the ratio of 5% or more;

16.3. it contains chemical substances or mixtures classified as hazardous according to laws and regulations on chemicals and chemical products, labeling and packaging.

17th This provision in Paragraph 16 of the criteria in the extractive waste facility hazard assessment takes into account all mining waste facility life cycle, including the period after its closure.

18th This provision paragraph 16.2 above the threshold is defined as the weight ratio (based on mining waste dry matter) among all the mining wastes, which are classified as hazardous according to the laws regarding waste classification and characteristics of hazardous waste makes it and who will be mining waste facility planned period of operation At the end, and mining waste, which will be located in the extractive waste facility planned operating period.

19th State Environmental Service shall evaluate whether this provision 16.3.apakšpunktā this criterion is met in accordance with the provisions of the 30th, 31st and Paragraph 32 of the observations.

20th The assessment of structural integrity loss of the consequences of the accident as a result of mining waste facility, got out of the immediate impact of the material, as well as an accident caused by the impact of short and long term.

21st This provision within the meaning of extractive waste facility in incorrect operation of any activity which may cause serious accidents, and improper environmental protection measures and faulty construction or design flaws.

22nd The evaluation of the improper operation caused by pollutants released include information on the impact of pollutant release the effects of short and long term. This assessment relates to the extraction of the waste facility operating period, as well as long-term period after closure. It shall include an assessment of the potential hazards posed by mining waste facilities, which are reactive mining waste, regardless of whether the mining waste in accordance with laws and regulations on waste classification and characteristics are classified as hazardous or non-hazardous.

23rd Under this provision the 24th and 25 of the State Environmental Service shall evaluate the mining waste facilities in the loss of structural integrity or improper operation caused the accident consequences.

24th Potential threat to human life or health are not considered meaningful or significant, if persons who could be endangered, except for mining waste facility workers, there is no permanent or long-term must be sensitive territory. A serious threat to human health be considered bodily injury, resulting in disability or cause long-term illness.

25th Potential threat to the environment is not considered substantial if:

25.1. potential contaminant source intensity short-term effects are substantially reduced;

25.2. accident does not cause permanent or long-term damage to the environment;

25.3. the affected environment can be restored by small-scale purification and recovery measures.

26th Tailings dam structural integrity in case of loss of human life considered to be endangered if the water or liquid mass level has risen at least 0.7 m above ground level, or if water or liquid mass flow rate is greater than 0.5 m / s.

27th The assessment of the threat to human life or health of the tailings dam structural integrity involves a loss of at least the following factors:

27.1. mining waste facility, the size and nature of its construction;

27.2. mining waste facility placed in the extraction of waste quantity and characteristics, including their physical and chemical properties;

27.3. mining waste facility, the location of the topography, and water permeability characteristics;

4.27. a possible flood wave arrival time to the areas where the people;

5.27. flood wave propagation speed;

27.6. water or liquid mass predicted levels;

7.27. water or liquid mass-level rise rate;

8.27. any relevant site-specific factors that may affect human life or health.

28th Formation of a prolapse of the caravans, any quantity of a moving mass to be considered dangerous to human life if people are staying in motion the mass of the waste collection area.

29th The assessment of the threat to human life or health of the formation of a prolapse of the caravans include at least the following factors:

29.1. extractive waste facility size and characteristics of its structure;

29.2. mining waste facility placed in the extraction of waste quantity and characteristics, including their physical and chemical properties;

29.3. caravans inclination angle;

29.4. groundwater formation probability of caravans;

5.29. ground stability;

6.29. topography;

7.29. distance from water bodies, structures and buildings;

8.29. mine site operations;

9.29. other site specific factors that may significantly affect the design risks.

30th Planned tailings ponds, the following methods:

30.1. carry out the inventory of substances and mixtures that are used in processes and are then combined with a mixture of pollutants into the tailings pond;

30.2. mining waste facility operating each year is calculated for each technological processes consumed the quantity of the substance or mixture;

30.3. each substance and mixture in accordance with laws and regulations on chemicals and chemical products, labeling and packaging to determine whether it is a hazardous substance or mixture;

30.4. using the formula specified in Annex 2, calculate the tailings pond discharged water volume increase per year (ΔQi) in stable conditions every year, the planned operation;

5.30. using the formula specified in Annex 2, is calculated for each hazardous substance or mixture (identified in accordance with these Regulations 30.3.apakšpunktu) the maximum concentration in the aqueous phase (C max) of the year. Mining waste facilities classified as category A, if, based on the maximum concentration (C max) in the calculation of the water phase is considered dangerous according to laws and regulations on chemicals and chemical products, labeling and packaging.

31st Service of existing tailings ponds, mining waste facilities classified in accordance with the provisions of Paragraph 30, or based on data obtained by chemical analysis of mining waste facility to the stored water and solids. Mining waste facilities classified as category A, where, under the laws of chemicals and chemical products, labeling and packaging of the water phase and its content is considered a dangerous mixture.

32nd Caravans washing facilities at which metals are extracted from ore bērtnēm by filtering the washing liquid mining waste facility closure of the State Environmental Service shall determine the presence of hazardous substances, based on flushing the chemical inventory and rinse chemical residues in the concentration of runoff after the completion of lavage. Mining waste facilities classified as category A, where, under the laws of chemicals and chemical products, labeling and packaging of the runoff water is considered a dangerous mixture.

33rd Paragraph 16.2 of these Regulations and the 18th, 19th, 30th, 31st and Paragraph 32 of these conditions do not apply to mining waste sites that contain only inert waste or contaminate the soil.

34th Extractive waste facility classification review of the State Environmental Service, if substantial changes are made in the authorization or significant change in operating conditions. Said classification shall be reviewed, mining waste facility operating at the end.

III. MINING WASTE MANAGEMENT PLANS

35th To treatment, recovery and storing mining waste, as well as reducing the amount of the operator draws up mining waste management plan, taking into account the principles of sustainable development, as well as the municipal land use plan.

36th Mining waste management plan has the following objectives:

36.1. prevent or reduce mining waste and its harmfulness, taking into account:

36.1.1. mining waste management in mining project development framework and used for mineral extraction and processing methods;

36.1.2. changes that may occur with mining waste, expanding the surface area of caravans and mining waste reaching the external environmental factors;

36.1.3. possibility of mining placing extractive waste back into the excavation void in accordance with environmental laws and regulations if it is technically and economically feasible;

36.1.4. possibility of mining waste facility closure put back in the topsoil, or use it elsewhere;

36.1.5. to mineral processing using less dangerous chemicals;

36.2. promote the collection of waste recovery options, re-use or recycling of such waste, if it complies with environmental quality standards and these Regulations as it applies to the case;

36.3. to ensure the safe collection of waste short-term and long-term storage, already at the design stage taking into account the planned management measures extractive waste facility operating during and after the closing, choosing projects that:

36.3.1. minimizes any closed mining waste facility monitoring, control and management;

36.3.2. prevents or minimizes a negative impact on the environment (such as pollutants from mining waste facility by air or water);

36.3.3. ensure that all dams caravans or long-term geotechnical stability.

37th Mining waste management plan shall include:

37.1. information about the proposed mining waste facility classification under the provisions of Chapter II:

37.1.1. if you need a Category object - information on accident prevention measures and security systems for their implementation;

37.1.2. if the operator considers that a Category A waste collection facility is not necessary - sufficient information to justify it, including possible accident hazards;

37.2. mining waste characterization in accordance with the provisions of Paragraph 38;

37.3. Information on the expected total mining waste to be stored in a mining waste facility operation;

37.4. description of the activity that poses a mining waste;

37.5. information on mining waste management as they arose;

37.6. information on mining waste deposited in the potential negative impact on the environment (including the landscape, especially in protected areas and human health) and measures to be taken to reduce mining waste facility, the environmental impact during its operation and after closure, in accordance with the provisions of 72.1. , 72.2., 72.4. and 72.5.apakšpunktam;

37.7. control and monitoring measures in accordance with the provisions of Paragraph 71 and 72.3.apakšpunktam;

37.8. measures for mining waste facility closure (including rehabilitation) and mining waste facility monitoring after closure in accordance with the provisions of Chapter VIII;

37.9. measures to be taken to prevent surface water and groundwater deterioration, as well as prevent or reduce air and soil pollution, in accordance with the provisions of the 76th, 77th, 78th, 79th, 80th 81.punktā and above;

37.10. the soil evaluation in accordance with laws and regulations on soil and soil quality standards that will be affected by mining waste facility.

38th Intermediary mining waste facility stored waste collection performance prepared in accordance with the provisions of Annex 1, taking into account the object structure of long-term physical and chemical stability to prevent accidents. This characterization is an integral part of mining waste management plan.

39th The operator shall ensure that mining waste characterization of the necessary information and data in accordance with the following procedures:

39.1. using existing research, studies and permits or licenses data, prospecting results, information on similar mining waste storage sites for inert waste lists, or applicable standards of similar materials, as they meet the requirements given in Annex 1 of mining waste characterization;

39.2. assess the quality and relevance and provides a possible missing information;

39.3. the absence of mining waste characterization information required in accordance with standard EN 14899:2006 "Characterization of waste. Waste materials sampling. The basic sampling plan for the development and use of" develop a sampling plan and sampling in accordance with this plan. The sampling plan shall be developed based on identified information it deems necessary, including the plan include:

39.3.1. purpose of collection;

39.3.2. testing program and requirements for sampling;

39.3.3. sampling points, and sampling of drill core, surface mining, conveyor belt, caravans, pond or other appropriate place;

39.3.4. procedures and guidelines for a model number, size, weight, description and operation of the samples;

39.4. evaluate the extraction process of waste characterization results, as well as the sampling results accuracy and quality. If necessary, obtain additional information. The final results of the mining waste management plan.

40th Intermediary developed by mining waste management plans submitted for approval by the State Environmental Service. Mining waste management plans may also be submitted electronically in accordance with the laws on electronic document development, presentation, storage and circulation.

41st State Environmental Service shall evaluate the submitted mining waste management plan compliance with the provisions of the 36th and Paragraph 37 of the above requirements and be approved within one month of mining waste management plan or, if the plan is not included in these Regulations 36th and Paragraph 37 of the information, request the necessary supplementary information, specifying a reasonable time information. The operator shall provide additional information to the State Environmental Service within the prescribed period.

42nd State Environmental Service shall control the mining waste management plan in accordance with mining waste storage permit (hereinafter - permit) conditions.

43rd Mining waste management plan manager shall be reviewed every five years and make the changes, if substantial changes in the management of extractive waste facility or waste stored therein. Within 14 days after the amendment of the plan manager shall notify in writing the State Environmental Service.

IV. MINING WASTE DISPOSAL PERMITS

44th Prior to mining waste facility start-up or 60 days before the expiry of the operator shall submit to the State Environmental Service in accordance with their registered office in the application of extractive waste storage permit (Annex 3) (hereinafter - application).

45th If the information indicated is incomplete, the State Environmental Department within five working days of receiving the application shall inform in writing the application and specify additional information to be submitted. That information may be communicated and also submit electronically, if the manager stated in the application.

46th State Environmental Service shall transmit the application and the attached copy of the local authority in whose administrative territory the planned mining waste storage. If the municipality is justified objections to the issuance of a permit or special permit requirements for content, so within 14 days after application and the documents attached to a copy of the receipt of proposals submitted to the State Environmental Service.

47th State Environmental Service shall issue a permit if:

47.1. authorization application, the information meets the requirements;

47.2. mining waste management plan conforming to the 36th and Paragraph 37 of the above requirements and the relevant regional waste management plans.

48th Permit shall state:

48.1. requirements of the environmental pollution that arises mining waste facility operation;

48.2. requirements for mining waste facility operation;

48.3. measures to prevent the risk of accidents or if it is not possible, avoid accidents, but in case of emergency - to reduce its effects;

48.4. requirements for mining waste control measures and environmental monitoring (Annex 4);

48.5. the condition of the obligation to provide information on the permit the collection of waste management operations in accordance with environmental protection authorities, other public institutions, municipalities and public demand.

49th State Environment Department within one month of receiving the application issue a permit for an electronic document format (Annex 5), or take a decision on refusal to issue a permit and notify the applicant of service on the website, as well as by mail or electronically.

50th State Environment Department within five working days after the permit or license revocation on its website publishes information on the issued and canceled permits.

51st Permit is issued for five years or a shorter period, if any, indicated in the application.

52nd State Environmental Service shall review and change the conditions of the permit:

52.1. if the permitted mining waste from permanent human health problems or impair environmental quality;

52.2. any significant change in the extractive waste facility or waste deposited;

52.3. based on the operator's monitoring results or the State Environmental Service of extractive waste facility inspection results;

52.4. taking into account the latest information on significant changes in best available methods.

53rd State Environmental Service shall cancel the permit in the following cases:

53.1. if an operator fails to comply with the requirements of the permit and the laws governing the mining waste;

53.2. if the operator has provided false or misleading information;

53.3. if the operator has submitted information on the business closure.

54th Permits the information for statistical purposes, the State Environmental Service shall provide the relevant authorities a written request, without disclosing the trade secrets and information on mining stocks.

V. PUBLIC PARTICIPATION

55th Within seven days after the State Environmental Service submitted the application to continue operations or of material changes in the operation, the operator provides information to the public in this way:

55.1. public - allowing the operator to receive information office or local government;

55.2. an individual basis - sending notices to owners (holders) of properties adjacent to proposed mining waste facility or in the direct area of impact;

55.3. the operator's website;

55.4. local newspaper.

56th The operator shall be informed in writing of the State Environmental Service of the way under the provisions of Paragraph 55 of the informed public.

57th State Environmental Service on their website placed this provision in Paragraph 58 of that information.

58th Intermediary this provision in Paragraph 55 of the procedures specified in the public informed of:

58.1. application and accompanying documents, as well as mining waste management plan;

58.2. extractive waste facility for cross-border impact and cooperation with other countries in accordance with the provisions of Chapter X;

58.3. State Environmental Service address and nature of possible decisions;

58.4. permit conditions (with details);

58.5. other public information activities performed by the operator;

58.6. operator's address.

59th In providing these provisions in Paragraph 58 of this information, the operator shall state the date by which, in accordance with the provisions of Paragraph 61 of the public may submit to the State Environmental Service written proposals on the provisions of Paragraph 58 of this information, as well as the website where the public can get acquainted with the this provision in Paragraph 58 of that information.

60th In addition to the information referred to in Paragraph 58 of the State Environmental Service company is also available, which can be used for decision making, but which become available only after informing the public in accordance with the provisions of Paragraph 56, or after a public consultation, as well as information about the public consultation period received the recommendations and reports.

61st Company within 30 days of this provision in Paragraph 58 of the disclosure may be in writing to the State Environmental Service proposals or opinions on the issuance of a permit or its conditions.

62nd State Environmental Service shall inform the operator of the proposals received and the views and indicate the date by which the operator submitted an explanation for them.

63rd State Environmental Service, when issuing a permit or a decision refusing to issue the permit, the public calls for proposals and opinions. On the decision of the State Environmental Service shall provide information to the public this provision 55.4.apakšpunktā procedures specified, indicating the content of the decision, the reasons and considerations on which decisions are based, as well as adding a copy.

VI. ACCIDENT PREVENTION AND INFORMATION

64th Mining waste management Category A facility providing accident hazards inventory, as well as mining waste facility design, installation, operation, closure and after the mining waste facility closure shall take the necessary measures to prevent accidents and mitigate their adverse effects on human health and the environment (including transboundary effects).

65th Intermediary prior to the class A mining waste facility start-up (if the object in accordance with the Civil Protection Act deemed to sensitive sites) developed and approved by the civil protection plan in accordance with the laws of the civil protection plan for the development and validation, as well as in accordance with the laws of the civil defense post officials responsible for civil protection plan implementation and periodic review.

66th Keeper of these Regulations 65 of these Regulations in the civil protection plan shall set out the following objectives:

66.1. reduce and control accidents and other incidents to minimize their effects, especially damage to human health and the environment;

66.2. implement measures to prevent accidents and other incidents, as well as the potential consequences of the accident on human health and the environment;

66.3. provide public access to information and relevant services of the local authority or authorities in whose administrative territory the mining waste facility;

66.4. ensure environmental rehabilitation, restoration and cleaning up after an accident.

67th The operator shall notify the natural and legal persons, which these Regulations III, V or Chapter VI of the decision or may be affected or who have an interest in the decision-making (hereinafter - the interested company), as developed by the civil protection plan, including information on the right to participate in decision-making process and opportunities to submit comments or questions. The operator shall evaluate the comments and questions and take the utmost account when approving the civil protection plan.

68th Interested public the following information:

68.1. operator (for natural person - name, merchant - a firm) and mining waste facility address;

68.2. information provider's name and title;

68.3. laws and regulations pertaining to mining waste facilities;

68.4. mining waste authorization date and number;

68.5. civil protection plan development and approval process;

68.6. clear and easy to set out an explanation as to what activity or activities undertaken in the mining waste storage facility;

68.7. household users of substances and compounds the names or terms (including the substance and connection properties), which is mining the waste facility, as well as mining waste, which can cause accidents and threats to humans and the environment;

68.8. potential accident hazards of nature, and their potential impact on the population and the environment;

68.9. procedures for alerting citizens about the incident and inform the extractive waste facility;

68.10. the people what to do when the accident occurred;

68.11 relates. the manager made for accident prevention and mitigation measures for mining waste storage site in cooperation with the emergency services;

68.12. on cooperation with the emergency services and the services of guidance and requirements in the event of an accident;

68.13. for additional sources of information under the Freedom of Information Act requirements.

69th Intermediary this provision in Paragraph 68 of the information is provided free of charge and restrictions. Every three years, review the information and make necessary changes. Information manager is placed on its website.

70th If an accident, the operator shall immediately inform the State Environmental Service, National Fire and Rescue Service and local authorities in whose administrative territory the mining waste facility, and provide all necessary information about the incident.

VII. EXTRACTIVE WASTE FACILITY INSTALLATION AND MANAGEMENT

71st If the mining waste is placed back into excavation voids for rehabilitation or construction manager:

71.1. ensure that mining waste facility compliance with the provisions of the 72nd 73.punktā and above;

71.2. ensure that the soil, surface water or groundwater pollution under the provisions of the 76th, 78th and Paragraph 80;

71.3. the mining waste and the excavation void in accordance monitoring in accordance with the provisions of the 84th and 85.punktam.

72nd State Environmental Service shall ensure that the operator, installing new mining waste facility or modifying an existing extractive waste facilities:

72.1. ensure that mining waste facility placement in a suitable place in accordance with the land use plan:

72.1.1. take into account the special area of conservation status, geological, hydrological, hydrogeological, seismic and geotechnical factors;

72.1.2. designs and installs mining waste facilities so that in accordance with the laws of surface and ground water quality and other laws and regulations to prevent short and long term soil, air, surface water or groundwater pollution;

72.1.3. the contaminated water and leachate collection in accordance with permit conditions;

72.1.4. reduces water or wind, to the extent permitted by the technical feasibility and economic justification;

72.2. ensure that mining waste facility installation, operation and maintenance, according to its stability, as well as removing the soil, air, surface water or groundwater pollution and causing damage to the landscape;

72.3. ensure that the operator's designated responsible person (a person who has technical knowledge and experience in waste management) regularly supervise and inspect the mining waste facilities and shall act in accordance with the requirements of these Regulations, if the monitoring and checking the results of a mining waste facility instability or water or soil pollution;

72.4. take measures to rehabilitation of the land and mining waste facility closure;

72.5. take action extractive waste facility management after closure;

72.6. ensure that the operator's designated responsible person is technically competent (the competence of supporting documents), and provides mining waste facility workers training mining waste issues.

73rd This provision 72.3.apakšpunktā the monitoring and inspection documentation and permits operator to keep records long enough period to ensure the transfer of information, a change of operator.

74th After an accident, the operator shall immediately inform the State Environmental Service, National Fire and Rescue Service and local authorities in whose administrative territory the mining waste facility for all events and conditions that may affect the mining waste facility stability and its impact on the environment, taking of mining waste facility control and monitoring procedures of the weaknesses identified. The operator shall implement civil protection plan of the measures comply with the instructions of services for disaster recovery measures, as well as cover the activities related costs.

75th Intermediary annually by March 1, submit to the State Environmental Service report on the monitoring results of the previous calendar year.

76th In order to prevent surface water and groundwater deterioration, the operator shall take the following steps:

76.1. evaluate the possibility of mining waste, mining waste stored in the facility, during its operation and after closure may occur in leachate (the pollution content of the leachate);

76.2. eliminate or minimize leachate generation and surface water or groundwater and soil contaminated by mining waste;

76.3. collect and process the mining waste site contaminated water and leachate in accordance with laws and regulations on water use, to their discharge.

77th The operator shall take measures to prevent or reduce dust and gas emissions.

78th This rule 76.2. and 76.3.apakšpunktā these requirements do not apply if it is found that the mining waste facility poses risks to soil and surface water or groundwater, and the State Environmental Service decides that the leachate is collected and processed.

79th Mining waste, regardless of whether they are solid, slurry or liquid form, water can be stored in a facility not built mining waste storage, if the operator complies with the requirements laid down in laws and regulations on water management.

80th By placing extractive waste back into excavation voids, the operator shall take measures to prevent or reduce water and soil pollution in accordance with laws and regulations on water protection, and 14 days after the measures notified in writing to the State Environmental Service.

81st Operator, taking into account the circumstances of collection on site and using the best available techniques, ensure that the weak acid dissociable cyanide concentrations of less than 10 mg / kg. After the State Environmental Service request manager, using a risk assessment that takes into account the specific mining-site conditions, showing that the concentration limits need not be further lowered.

VIII. MINING WASTE FACILITY CLOSURE AND AFTER-CLOSURE

82nd The operator shall enter into the object, if at one of the following conditions:

82.1. provided for mining waste management permit conditions;

82.2. State Environmental Service has taken a decision based on the operator's written request;

82.3. State Environmental Service has decided on its own initiative.

83rd Mining waste facilities considered to be closed after the State Environmental Service has taken the last inspection in a closed facility, the operator examined the reports and information on the remediation of land affected, as well as the entry into force of the State Environmental Service decision on mining waste facility closure.

84th After the acquisition phase of a facility manager shall ensure extractive waste facility maintenance, monitoring, inspection and corrective measures to the State Environmental Service decision to the deadline, taking into account mining waste facility posed a threat to the environment and human health and the duration, unless the State Environmental Service shall take a decision to take over the obligations of the operator.

85th Intermediary for mining waste facility closure examine the object of physical and chemical stability and reduce the adverse impact on the environment (especially for surface and underground waters), provided that:

85.1. mining waste facility to the existing building is monitored and maintained, and control and measuring equipment is always ready for use;

85.2. overflow channels and spillways are clean and there is no dike.

86th After the acquisition phase of a facility operator shall immediately inform the State Environmental Service, National Fire and Rescue Service and local authorities in whose administrative territory the object of all the events or incidents affecting the closed mining waste facility, its stability and any adverse effects on the environment based on mining waste management facilities to control and monitoring measures. The operator shall implement civil protection plan of the measures, and follow any staff instructions on how to carry out the measures cover all related costs.

87th State Environmental Service decision in the cases and time the operator shall notify the State Environmental Service of the monitoring results of the mining waste facility closure.

88th At least once a year, the State Environmental Service shall examine the extractive waste facility (including a closed mining waste facility) is complying with the provisions of Chapter IV of the above requirements and the conditions of the permit, as well as to examine whether the operator to keep these rules 73.punktā these documents.

89th State Environmental Service shall inform the public limited liability company "Latvian Environment, Geology and Meteorology Agency" (hereinafter - Centre) of the decisions taken in respect of the mining waste facilities (including abandoned mining waste facilities) closure, which cause significant environmental impacts or may pose a threat to human health or the environment. Centre prepared and up to 1 May 2012 in a center's website, as well as regularly updated collection of closed waste facilities (including abandoned mining waste sites) list a significant impact on the environment or may pose a threat to human health or the environment .

IX. FINANCIAL GUARANTEES

90th Before starting the activities related to mining waste accumulation or deposit of extractive waste facility, the operator shall submit to the State Environmental Service of copies (the original document presented by the State Environmental Service request), which proves the existence of the financial guarantee financial security, security, performance security policy or a credit guarantee form.

91st This rule Paragraph 90 of the financial guarantee shall ensure:

91.1. compliance with the requirements laid down in accordance with these rules permit (including requirements on mining waste management facility after closure);

91.2. at any time, access to financing for mining waste facility in accordance with the remediation of land affected by mining waste management plan and procedures prescribed in these Regulations permit issued.

92nd Decision on Paragraph 90 of these Regulations that the financial guarantee amount determined by the State Environmental Service, taking into account:

92.1. mining waste facility, the expected impact on the environment and human health, the category of mining waste types and characteristics of the rehabilitated land and mining waste facility in future applications;

92.2. carried out rehabilitation work with the laws and regulations on prevention and rehabilitation measures and procedures, which assessed the environmental damage and to calculate preventive, emergency and decontamination measures;

92.3. laws and regulations on environmental protection, and mining waste facility, the physical stability of the minimum soil and water quality standards, as well as pollutants in the maximum rate of evolution;

92.4. measures that focus on mining waste facility, stability, limiting damage to the environment;

92.5. measures necessary to achieve the extraction of waste management plan of mining waste facility closure during and after the closure of the land remediation, if necessary, treatment and monitoring after the facility closure, as well as measures to restore biodiversity;

92.6. estimates of the harmful effects of the duration and the necessary mitigation measures;

92.7. assessment of the costs associated with remediation of mining waste facility closure and measures after the closure of the facility, including the potential for monitoring after site closure or removal of pollutants.

93rd An independent expert with appropriate qualifications by the rules 92.7.apakšpunktā that evaluation, taking into account the unintended or premature mining waste facility closure probability.

94th State Environmental Service shall periodically review the financial guarantee amount, taking into account the planned mining waste facility in the land affected by rehabilitation work in accordance with mining waste management plan and permit conditions, as well as the event of a change in permit conditions.

95th If the State Environmental Service agrees with the mining waste facility closure in accordance with the provisions of Paragraph 83, the manager issued a written statement, the operator shall be exempt from the provisions of Paragraph 90 of the guarantee obligation (except for the 84.punktā the post-closure liabilities).

X CROSS BORDER IMPACT

96th If the Latvian territory of an existing category of extractive waste facility may have a significant adverse effect on the environment of another European Union Member States and thus pose a threat to human health, as well as other European Union Member State of the written request of the State Environmental Service latter (and at the same time the Latvian population) gives VI of these Regulations Chapter information. Preparation of the information provided in the language manager. That information can serve as the basis for any consultations necessary for the bilateral relations on a reciprocal and equivalent basis.

97th This provision in Paragraph 96, the State Environmental Service shall ensure that the permit application in accordance with the provisions of Chapter V is available in sufficient time to the European Union Member State concerned company, which could affect the mining waste facility could express their views on the subject before State Environmental Service shall take a decision.

98th If the accident took place this provision in Paragraph 96 of the extractive waste facility, the State Environmental Service shall immediately forward the provisions 70.punktā the information with the relevant EU Member State.

XI. CLOSING

99th If a mining waste facility operating from May 1, 2008, its compliance with the requirements of these Regulations (except for those provisions of Chapter IX) secured by May 1, 2012. Chapter IX of these Regulations shall enter into force on May 1, 2014.

100th These rules do not apply to mining waste facilities closed by May 1, 2008.

One hundred and first This rule III, and IV, the 65th, 67th and 70.punktā, Chapter V, Paragraph 82, and Chapter IX of the above conditions shall not apply to mining waste facilities, which also meet the following requirements:

101.1. they have stopped accepting waste before collection, 2006 May 1;

101.2. 1 May 2008 completed the closure and rehabilitation activities;

101.3. they were closed until 31 December 2010.

102nd This provision in Paragraph 101 of the mining waste facilities operated under these rules and laws on water protection requirements.

103rd The following are repealed by the Cabinet of 19 May 2008 No 354 "Mining waste management procedures" (Latvian Herald, 2008 90.nr., 2009 184.nr.).

Informative Reference to European Union Directives

These Regulations contain legal norms arising from the European Parliament and Council Directive 2006/21/EC of 15 March 2006 on mining waste and amending Directive 2004/35/EC.

Annex 1

MINING WASTE CHARACTERIZATION

I. General Information

1st General information on mining activities and the objectives of:

1.1. information on prospecting, mining or processing;

1.2. mining method description;

1.3. the planned nature of the product.

II. Used for finding geological report

2nd Determined by the extraction and treatment of atsedzamās mining waste unit, providing the appropriate information:

2.1. the surrounding rock types, their chemical and mineralogical composition of the digested rock and a blank rock hydrothermal changes;

2.2. mineral deposits of the characteristics of the digested rock or mineral-containing rock characteristics;

2.3. of mineral types, their chemical and mineralogical composition, as well as their physical characteristics such as density, porosity, fraction division, water content of the minerals, mineral impurities, minerals, hydrothermal transformed influences;

2.4. the deposit shape and size;

2.5. of weathering and supergēnajām changes of geochemical and mineralogical point of view.

III. Mining waste and planned activities

3rd Provide a description of all the mining wastes, arising in any prospecting, mining and processing stages, including Harvested overburden, waste rock and contamination by providing information on the following elements:

3.1. collection of waste at source and origin of the process of generating the waste, such as geological exploration, mining, milling and enrichment;

3.2. mining waste;

3.3. mining waste transportation systems;

3.4. treatment chemicals and description;

3.5. mining waste classification in accordance with the laws and regulations on waste classification and characteristics which make waste hazardous;

3.6. planned mining waste facility type, exposure to mining waste collection and final type of waste disposal technique mining waste facility.

IV. Geotechnical mining waste status

4th In view of the mining waste facility type, determine the appropriate parameters to assess mining waste inherent physical properties. The relevant parameters to be taken into account are as follows: texture, plasticity, density and water content, degree of compaction, shear strength and friction angle, permeability and porosity ratio, compressibility and consolidation.

V. Mining waste geochemical characteristics and status

5th Specifies the collection of waste chemical and mineralogical characteristics, as well as any mining waste remaining additives or residues. Runoff chemistry in the collection for each type of waste, taking into account the planned activities, in particular:

5.1. metals, oxygen-containing anions and salts leachability assessment period, as determined by one or more of the following methods:

5.1.1. leaching test, depending on the pH;

5.1.2. transmission capacity test;

5.1.3. time-critical release;

5.1.4. other suitable test method;

5.2. sulphides containing mining waste by static or kinetic tests to determine acid rock drainage and metal leaching during the

Environmental Protection and Regional Development Minister - Minister of Transport, U. Augulis

Annex 2

Calculate the average formula was discharged tailings pond water volume increases and the maximum concentration for calculating the water phase

1st On average, the tailings pond water abstracted increase in the quantity ΔQ is calculated using the following formula:

$\Delta Qi = (\Delta Mi / D) \times P$, where

ΔQi - pollutants discharged into the pond water volume increase (m3/year) "i" during the year;

ΔMi - channeled into the pond tailings mass (tonnes dry matter / year) "i" during the year;

D - deposited tailings dry mass density (t/m3);

P - deposited tailings in the medium porosity (m3/m3), defined as the pore volume ratio of the total volume of deposited tailings.

If there is no precise data are available, dry bulk density of the default for 1.4 t/m3 and porosity 0.5 m3/m3.

2nd The maximum concentration in the aqueous phase (C max) is calculated using the following formula:

$C_{max} = S_i / \Delta Q_i$ where

Si - each identified substance in the preparation and mass per year, which drained into the pond "i" during the year.

LATVIAN PROPERTY AND COLLATERAL LAW AND PROTECTION OF FOREIGN INVESTMENTS[1]

1. SOURCES OF LAW AND ABSOLUTE RIGHTS OF THE PROPRIETOR

Main sources are the Constitution of the Republic of Latvia, the Latvian Civil Law Act, and the Commercial Pledge Act. The Latvian Civil Law Act as a code of institutional system, which is similar to the French code, was restored in Latvia in its structure of 1937.

Part III of the Latvian Civil Law Act, which specifically deals with property and collateral rights, was introduced by the Act on the Time and Procedure by which the Part of Introduction, Inheritance Rights and Rights on Things of the Renewed Republic of Latvia 1937 Civil Law Act Takes Effect as of 7 July 1992.

Initially, the Constitution of Latvia did not deal with any property rights at all. Amendments of such kind were passed only in 1998, when the additional chapter 8 on fundamental human rights was introduced, which included section 105 stating that everyone has the right to property. This important amendment introduced a new understanding of property rights compared to a more conservative view reflected in the Latvian Civil Law Act.

The Latvian Civil Law Act states in section 927 that property means having total power over a thing, *i.e.* the right to possess and use it, receive all possible benefit from it, handle it and demand the return of it from any third person by claiming ownership. In addition to this general principle, section 928 declares that although property may be restricted according to private will or by the law, any of such restrictions shall be interpreted in its narrow meaning, and in case of doubt it shall always be assumed that the property is without restriction.

According to section 1038 an owner may be in possession of a thing, which belongs to him or her, receive its fruits, use it at will to increase his or her assets, and in general, use it in any way, even though it may cause a loss to another person.

Contrary to these provisions, section 105 of the Constitution states that property may not be used against the interests of society.

2. CLASSIFICATION OF THINGS AS OBJECTS OF PROPERTY RIGHTS

The Latvian Civil Law Act uses common classification of things as tangible and intangible (section 841). However, in dealing with a difficult question, what could be a subject of property rights, the Latvian Civil Law Act is nearly as narrow as the early Roman law. This approach is causing difficulties each time when one is confronted with the problem of rights regarding intangible things.

Although the Latvian Civil Law Act declares that a subject of property may be anything that has not been taken out of circulation by law (section 929), this general declaration is not supported by any other norm. Even further, in dealing with particular elements of the property rights, the authors of the Latvian Civil Law Act carefully avoided using the term "property" in relation to

---

[1] Jānis Rozenfelds

intangibles. Thus, regarding the claim of ownership, section 1050 expressly states that the subject of a claim of ownership may be a separate item as well as an aggregate of things consisting only of tangible things, but not a thing, which is composed of both — tangible and intangible things.

There is no doubt that in light of such clearly stated limits, a claim for intangible things is out of the question — it is hardly surprising that the same narrow approach also prevails in practice. The Latvian Constitutional Court found in favour of this more narrow approach. It was a particular case of interpreting section 105 in the meaning that a person's right to property does not include his or her right to certain claims. *1

2.1. Movable and immovable things, and buildings in particular

As provided for by section 842, tangible things are either movable or immovable, "depending on whether or not they can be moved without exterior damage from one place to another". This general principle apparently includes not only land, but, by extension, buildings as well as other permanent structures. In the Latvian legal environment this fullest sense of the word "immovable" was not only extensively used with regard to buildings, but somehow led to a phenomenon, which could be defined as separation of buildings from the land in a way which is not clearly defined by the Latvian law and is regarded in the Latvian practice as an exclusion from the common principles the Civil Law Act is based on.

It must be pointed out that the 7 July 1992 Act on the Time and Procedure by Which the Part of Introduction, Inheritance Rights and Rights on Things of the Renewed Republic of Latvia 1937 Civil Law Act Takes Effect has established a very important principle as compared with the original meaning of the Latvian Civil Law Act.

As section 968 of the Latvian Civil Law Act states, a building, constructed on and firmly attached to a piece of land, shall be considered a part of same. According to section 973 trees and other plants, which have been replanted on another person's land, belong to its owner from the time they have become rooted in this land.

Section 14 of the 7 July 1992 Act stated otherwise — that the provisions of sections 968 and 973 of the Civil Law Act shall not be applicable in cases when a building has been built (legally acquired in another way) or the orchard (trees) has been planted on the land allocated for this purpose in accordance with the laws in effect at that time, but the ownership rights to the land have been renewed to the previous owner or his or her heirs (assignee). It soon becomes clear that this important amendment, which was initially designed as just a temporarily introduced exclusion from general principles, is here to stay permanently.

Once Pandora's box was open, this notorious section 14 started to accumulate more and more so-called exclusions from the general principle. Soon it was discovered that the rule on buildings as separate items was also applicable to the unfinished ones, and sometimes even to the tiny remains, which laid covered deeply in the ground and, like an accident waiting to happen, were threatening the previous owners whose rights were restored by a special law. These remains and their consequences were as unpredictable and at the same time as inevitable as natural forces. It sometimes seems that the more desperately legislators are trying to extinguish these so-called exclusions, the more difficult is the life they deliver both to the owners of the land and to the owners of the buildings separated from each other and deeply divided by this controversy.

During the denationalisation and privatisation period this controversy provided countless litigation cases and hundreds — if not thousands — of them are still waiting to be resolved.

Separation of the buildings from the land is a clear example of difficulties, which arise when an old act is taken as an orchard and planted in an adverse environment, which is fertilised by a different way of thinking. When the Act on the Time and Procedure by which the Part of Introduction Inheritance Rights and Rights on Things of the Renewed Republic of Latvia 1937 Civil Law Act Takes Effect was drafted, the authors of this bill had to take into account the fact that the land reform and denationalisation was still continuing. Therefore the reintroduction of the Civil Law Act of 1937 had a purpose to facilitate this process and not to become an obstacle in its way. The authors of this bill had also to consider that separation of the building from the land was at the time a matter of fact, which could not be averted.

As it is well known, in 1940, nationalisation was also carried out in several separate steps. Land was seized first, buildings and enterprises were seized afterwards. Denationalisation was reflecting the same order of steps, but taken the other way around. *2 First, the rural land reform Decree on Land Reform in the Republic of Latvia rural regions was passed in 1990. The city land reform Decree on Land Reform in the Republic of Latvia Cities was passed in 1991. The rural land privatisation Decree on Land Privatisation in Rural Regions was passed in 1992 (the rural land reform completion Decree on Completion of Land Reform in Rural Regions was passed in 1997, but the city land reform completion Decree on the Completion of Land Reform in Cities — in 1999). Decrees on privatisation of buildings always followed land reform decrees. For instance, the agriculture and fisheries privatisation Decree on Privatisation of Agricultural Enterprises and Collective Fisheries was passed in the same year of 1991.

It has to be underlined as well that the whole privatisation process — in which Latvia is notoriously behind most of the other East European countries — was in a permanent process of legislative changes, which continued from the early nineties up to 1994, when the public property privatisation Decree on the Privatisation of Objects of State and Municipal Property as well as a package of necessary supplementary laws were finally passed, under which, at long last, the privatisation of countless enterprises could take place.

The Denationalisation of Buildings in the Republic of Latvia Act was passed in 1991 and is in force from 1 January 1992. Thus, when the Civil Law Act was introduced, separation of the buildings from the land was already there. The great failure of dealing with this problem in 1992 was the fact that the legislation facing this problem did not provide a theoretical solution, but chose a shaky mode of exclusions instead. The result was that by trying to avert, not solve the problem, and by intending to sweep it under the carpet, the legislator in fact deepened the problem and, as time passed by, made it into one more and more difficult to solve.

One can only guess which way this contradiction between the law of 1937 and its contemporary legal environment could be resolved.

In general there are two extremes in proposed ways for solving this problem. One extreme is to extinguish this separation altogether and return to classical principles of the Civil Law Act of 1937. Another extreme is to re-establish emphiteuzis — a situation when a person who is not the owner of a piece of land is entitled to use it as his or her own in perpetuity, as he or she is an owner of the building, which was already there before the Civil Law Act of 1937 was originally introduced. Today, the difficult relationship between the owner of the building and the owner of the land under this building is solved through the so-called mandatory rental agreement between them.

To my own understanding, emphiteuzis is the only way to solve this problem, and it is already present in our real legal environment except for one feature; in today's situation, a person who is not the owner of a piece of land, but who is entitled to use it as his or her own in perpetuity as a building owner, is not subject to forfeiture for non-payment of a fixed rent.

This is nearly the only feature, which distinguishes the Latvian situation from the Roman or, if you like, the Feudal ownership of the Middle Ages. We can learn from history, which gives us a lesson in the form of a similar situation, which the Latvian state had already faced when the Civil Law Act was introduced in 1937. A specific procedure of buying out landlords' rights for the land was established. The owners of the buildings were reluctant to follow this procedure, and when the Latvian legal system was extinguished altogether in 1940 and 1941, the former relationship was still there.

2.2. Vessels

Another problem of the classification of things, which has led to far-reaching consequences in practice, could be found in a very short appendix to section 842. This appendix says that the railway with all its accessories shall be considered an immovable thing, but ships with all their accessories — movable things. This principle makes the implementation of the maritime lien or seizure of the vessel, as it is provided for by section 60 of the Latvian Maritime Code Act of 1994, highly unlikely due to procedural difficulties connected with the above principle which states that ships must be considered as movable things.

In practice it leads to fairly serious consequences, especially in the area of protecting rights of foreign companies and individuals who happen to deal with Latvia in the maritime area.

Let us suppose that a foreign company has a claim towards another foreign company, none of them is registered in Latvia, but the defendant is a ship owner, and the ship happens to be in the Latvian harbour.

Under the Latvian maritime law and the Latvian civil process law, the claimant is entitled to impose the lien on this ship unless the defendant pays his debt.

However the problem is that the same Latvian Civil Procedure Code does not entitle one for a claim, which could be submitted to a Latvian court towards a foreign company or an individual unless he or she has some kind of a legal entity representative or some immovable property inside the Latvian territory.

The watershed lies between the personal property and the immovable one. You cannot sue a foreigner in Latvia on the basis that he or she has some kind of assets here unless you prove that he or she owns land or other immovable property in Latvia.

It would be easy to handle such cases if only the Latvian Civil code regarded a ship as immovable. Unfortunately this is not the case. For this reason such cases, while initiated in Latvian Courts, usually fail, and such ships, after the claims to seize them are heard and rejected by Latvian Courts, quickly disappear from Latvian harbours.

I see no other possible solution of this problem but to change the principle stated in section 842 of the Latvian Civil Law Act and to declare that ships shall be considered as immovable things.

3. PLEDGE

The Civil Law Act states that a pledge right is a right to another person's thing (section 1278). It is a kind of purely Roman view on the pledge, contrary to the more contemporary view on this institute as a tool increasing commitment rights.

Pledge in the Civil Law Act is regulated in part III as one of the chapters devoted to property in general, or — as it is defined in the Latvian Civil Code — to the rights on things. On the other hand, commercial pledge law was from the very beginning considered as a part of the Commercial Act and initially was even included as part VII of the drafted Commercial Code of Latvia. However, later on, it was adapted as an independent law and now is not even included in the latest version of the Commercial code. The Latvian Civil Law Act distinguishes three different modifications of pledge: -the so-called hand pledge, which is in fact a deposit of personal property as security for a debt;
-mortgage, which is related to the pledged real property;
-usage pledge of an immobile fruit bearing item, which is pledged so that the creditor has possession of it, and obtains the fruits of it.

Due to these definitions by the Civil Law Act, the authors of the Commercial Pledge Act were faced with the need to distinguish the commercial pledge from both the so-called hand pledge and mortgage.

On the one hand, commercial pledge as an institute dealing mainly with items of personal property has some similarity with the pledge as such (hand pledge). On the other hand, commercial pledge was designed to avoid handing over of the item by the grantor of a pledge (pledgor) to the person who accepts a pledge (pledgee), which inevitably makes commercial pledge similar to mortgage.

It was absolutely necessary to resolve this problem also because the implementation of the principles introduced by the Civil Law Act faced extreme difficulties in practice, especially in connection with the stated necessity to deliver the object of the pledge in actual possession of the pledgee. Interpretation of the above principles of the Civil Law Act caused hard times for the judges, especially because the Civil Law Act gives a very wide interpretation of what would be regarded as an actual possession of the item of personal property.

In practice it led to the situations that sometimes it was extremely difficult to find out who actually held the pledged item, especially if a pledgee allowed the thing to remain with the pledgor who then could be regarded as an agent of the pledgee. This, unfortunately, from time to time led to intolerable situations. For instance, one who already had granted his personal property as a pledge to another person and with a consent of the pledgee kept this property in his custody as an agent of his own pledgee, soon stepped into the pledge agreement with another person by granting the same property as a pledge again. In court practice of the early nineties it was found that sometimes all belongings of companies served as a pledge to different banks, even on as many as four consecutive occasions. No wonder that in the given situation banks were the main subsidiaries in promoting the Commercial Pledge Act.

The Commercial Pledge Act was adopted on 21 October 1998. The Act modified the principles of the pledge right under the guidelines set by the Civil Law Act.

According to section 2 of this Act, a commercial guarantee is a pledge, which, following the procedure determined by the Act, is registered in the commercial guarantees register. The Act also stated that the general provisions of the pledge right as set forth in the Civil Law Act should be applied to commercial guarantees insofar as the Act did not provide otherwise.

The new Act stated that the subject of a commercial guarantee could be any movable object and even an intangible object, which belongs to an enterprise, as well as the aggregation of the objects including all the property of an enterprise (entrepreneurial association).

This was a big step forwards as compared with the Latvian Civil Law Act, which in fact covered only tangible things but intangible things could become a subject of a pledge right only if actual possession of the thing by a pledgee was possible. Thus, although intangibles could become a subject of a pledge right in principle, necessity to prove that the intangible thing in question was in the possession of a pledgee, made implementation of this principle extremely difficult and caused a lot of disputes in practice.

However, substantial assets still could not be a subject of a commercial guarantee, a vessel or securities in public circulation as well as the claim arising from a check or a promissory note could not be a subject of a commercial guarantee.

Even if all the property of an enterprise is pledged or an obligation of objects is pledged, the above- mentioned items shall be considered as excluded from the pledged property.

It is not a very big surprise as well that we find very tough restrictions on imposing commercial pledge under this law. Being a reaction to the horrors of the early nineties, these restrictions could also be treated as an over-reaction. Given that commercial pledge like mortgage has to be duly registered in the Centralised Commercial Guarantees Register, one could see no danger in registering several consecutive commercial pledges in the same item of personal property if it is valuable enough. And a consecutive pledgee has to be aware about the status of the item, which is already registered in a publicly available register as an item of somebody else's pledge right.

However, the Latvian Commercial Pledge Act prohibits such repeated granting of an item as a second pledge. A special amendment to the Latvian Criminal Code, which was introduced as a package of amendments in current Latvian laws when the Commercial Pledge Act was passed, qualifies such action as a crime.

It must be pointed out that, notwithstanding the above shortcomings, the Commercial Guarantees Act was a big step forwards, covered a lot of unsolved problems, and it is working in practice. A lot of subjects, however, are not covered by this law and are still regulated only by the Civil Law Act. This relates first of all to immovables, given that restoration of the Land Register Act and the Recording Real Estate with Land Registers Act was adopted shortly after the Civil Law Act came into force. Mortgage rights can be registered easily, and this institution is functioning relatively well.

Some difficulties in court practice arose only in connection with immovables which, at the time when they were used as a security, were still unregistered in the land books. This caused some confusion in practice, which sometimes led to curious situations where a land unit was treated as a movable thing. However, the inherent contradictions, such as dual attitude towards land and buildings (see chapter 2.1), and proposed ways of solution of these difficulties have had a huge impact on mortgage rights. For instance, both owners — the one of the land and the one of the building have the right of refusal if the other party decides to alienate its right in the immovable. It is unclear how and when such right of refusal can be implemented, if the immovable is pledged and the pledgee faces the necessity to sell the property.

Another problem is that mortgage rights stated by the Civil Law Act do not fit very well with the procedure of the auction of real estate as stated in the Civil Procedure Act, which sometimes in practice leads to situations when the mortgagee finds himself circumvented by other claimants, who had either weaker or later claims but were smart enough to use shortcomings of the Latvian Civil Procedure Code in their favour.

4. PROTECTION OF FOREIGN INVESTMENTS

The Latvian Foreign Investment Act defines foreign investment as a long-term investment in the basic capital, separated by foreign investors for performing entrepreneurial activity in the Republic of Latvia.

According to section 8 of the Act, the Republic of Latvia ensures the protection of foreign investments. The compulsory alienation of foreign investments by the Republic of Latvia may only be carried out in accordance with a specific law, adopted pursuant to the Republic of Latvia 15 September 1992 Eminent Domain Act.

It has to be underlined that bilateral agreements, which are concluded between Latvia and nearly all economically developed countries of the world, define investment differently than the above-mentioned Foreign Investments Act. These bilateral agreements usually state that the term "investment" shall mean any kind of property invested by a natural or legal person of a contracting party in the territory of the other contracting party.

Such wider definition of the investment is also approved by Latvian practice of implementation of the law, as well as in international disputes. *3

According to this principle the only condition, which must be met by a foreign investor, is that investment must be carried out in the territory of Latvia. For this reason expenditure by foreign investors, which was carried out abroad, like payments for drawings, design, patenting, *etc.* are not accepted as investments unless they are turned into real construction or industrial works on the territory of Latvia.

Such kind of disputes from time to time arise in connection with the privatisation process, sorting out *4 whether subjects of privatisation, which frequently happen to be of foreign origin, meet the conditions stipulated by the purchase agreement of the Latvian enterprise.

Notes:

*1 20 April 1999 Judgement of the Republic of Latvia Constitutional Court. C. Case No. 04-01 (99). Available at: http://www.satv.tiesa.gov.lv/Eng/Spriedumi/04-01(99).htm.

*2 J. Rozenfelds. Problems of legislation on privatization in Latvia. Wirtschafts- und Gesellschaftsrecht Osteuropas im Zeichen des Übergangs zur Marktwirtschaft. Redaktion W. Seiffert. München: C. H. Beck'sche, 1992, pp. 355–358; Latvia: Legislation and denationalization of land. – The Law Institute Journal, 1993, May, pp. 258–259.

*3 See Arbitration Award in the matter of an arbitration under article 7 (2) of the Agreement between the Government of the Kingdom of Sweden and the Government of the Republic of Latvia on the Promotion and Reciprocal Protection of Investments between Swembalt AB, Sweden, and the Republic of Latvia, dated 23 October 2000. Available at: http://bnsnews.bns.lv/1234.

THE LAND REGISTER DEPARTMENT

The Land Register Department is directed by **I. Kalniņa** (722-4847), the Land Register Information Dissemination and Statistics Division is directed by **E. Balševics** (777-0888), the

Land Register Registration System Maintenance Division is directed by **S. Bogdanova** (777-0887), and the Land Register Operations Division is directed by **I. Bērzkalne** (722-4902).

The Land Register Department of the Court Administration provides for the organisational administration of the Land Register, and for the maintenance of the Computerised National Land Book.

The Computerised National Land Book (CNLB)

Primary functions: The Computerised National Land Book, in accordance with the law on the Land Register, brings together the databases of all 28 Land Registers. Thus the CNLB can be seen as the central database of information about all properties in Latvia that are registered in the Land Register. The primary function for the CNLB is to maintain data that are submitted to the Land Register, ensuring that the data are secure and are not changed.

Services: The Computerised National Land Book ensures the accessibility of data from the Land Register – information about the legal status of all real estate that is recorded in the Land Register is available from a single source.
The Computerised National Land Book offers information about all of the real estate that is recorded in the Land Register of the Republic of Latvia.

The Land Register Department disseminates data in the following ways:

It provides information from the Computerised National Land Book in spoken or electronic form, issuing unconfirmed data printouts (Article 133 of the law on the Land Register);

Once a day, it submits electronic information about each transfer of real estate ownership and each instance of events identified in Article 62 of the law on the Land Register to the State Land Service and to local governments;

It processes data at the motivated request of government institutions and officials and submits the resulting data to institutions and officials for their official needs;

In accordance with procedures defined by the Cabinet of Ministers, it provides information from the corroboration journal, real estate cases and indicator of personnel to government institutions and officials.

Contact information: The Land Register Department of the Court Administration
Mārstaļu iela 19, Rīga LV-1050, Latvia
Telephone +371-722-2072
Fax +371-722-1628
E-mail: info@zemgram.lv
www.zemesgramata.lv

Working hours:
Mo.-Thu. – 8:30 AM-12:30 PM, 1:00-5:15 PM
Fri. – 8:30 AM-12:30 PM, 1:00-4:00 PM

Visiting hours to receive computer printouts from the Computerised National Land Book:
Mo.-Thu. – 9:00 AM-Noon, 1:00-5:00 PM
Fri. – 8:30 AM-12:30 PM, 1:00-4:00 PM

The Land Register maintains electronic versions of Land Register sections, the confirmation journal, real estate cases, alphabetical indicators, as well as other information as defined by law.

CIVIL LAW OF THE LATVIAN REPUBLIC

According to existing legislation foreigners can buy land in Latvia except territories in Latvia's border area, dune areas of the Baltic Sea and Riga gulf and other protected territories, land of state reserves, land usable for agriculture and forestry in accordance with the general plan of the region. Buyer have to receive a permission from a local authority in whose territory the land is situated. The lot must be registered in a Land Book where rights on property in Latvia are fixed. Land is subject to a real estate tax at a rate of 1.5%, charged to its assessed value.

1. **Civil Law of the Latvian Republic.**

In territory of the Latvian Republic all bargains with the immovable property are cocluded according the Civil Law . The given law defines, that real estate can be got in property, and also be alienated, concluding agreements, inheriting etc. In Civil law are reflected general norms of legal regulation of the property. The civil Law concerns all subjects of the bargains, and also all kinds of immovable property in the Latvian Republic.

2. **About privatization of state objects of the property and objects of the property of self-managements**.

According to the given law private persons (both physical, and legal), in the Latvian Republic, have the right to get in the property for a payment state objects of real estate, and also objects of the real estate of self-managements.

The citizens of the Latvian Republic, and also persons having privatization and/or the compensatory certificates, serving as a means of payment for object, got in the property, have the rights to get in the property real estate, using as a means of payment both certificates, and money.

The persons, which meet the requirements of the given law, but are not the proprietors of the privatization / compensatory certificates, can get objects of state real estate, and also real estate of self-managements in the property for money, participating in auction.

3. **About land reform in cities of the Latvian Republic**

According to the given law all persons can address with the request for purchase and realization of the right to use land of urban administrative territories of the Latvian Republic.

The given law stipulates duties of the subjects of legal usage of land during LR land reform. Being guided bt rules of the given law, private persons have the right to address about granting them the right to use land, having concluded the contract of rent, use of land or contract about use of land in another way, by conclusion of the appropriate contract between the responsible private person (both physical, and legal) and responsible self-management of city or state institution.

In item 20 of the given law are listed «subjects of the bargain», «which can receive the property right on the land of cities of the Latvian Republic:

a) Citizens of the Latvian Republic;

b) State and self-management, state enterprises and enterprises of self-managements (authorized companies);

c) registered in the LR Register of the enterprises authorized companies:

> if more than half of authorized capital belongs to the LR citizens, state or self-managements - each subject separately or in common to several subjects,
> if more than half of authorized capital belongs to the physical or legal persons of those states, with which LR had concluded international contracts, authorized by Saeima before 31.12.1996. The above mentioned concerns also physical and legal persons of the states, with which the international contracts were made after 31.12.1996, in a case if the given contracts provide the rights of physical and legal persons registered in LR, to get the rights on land of the appropriate state,
> if more than half of authorized capital belongs to several subjects described in items a) and в) together,
> which have the status of public (open) joint-stock company, in a case if their shares are quoted on a share stock exchange;

d) Religious organizations registered in Latvia till 21.07.1940 years.

Other physical and legal persons, which are not mentioned in the first item of the given clause, can get land in property with restrictions, which are determined in the given section.

In item 21 and 22 are determined restrictions in purchase of land in property and first priority of the right to purchase land by self-managements.

4. **About a privatization of land in a countryside**.

The given law regulates purchase in property of land in a countryside (villages etc.). It is important to note, that the given law names concrete subjects of the bargain / a circle of persons, which have the right to make the bargains with land:

The right of purchase land in property, according to the Civil Law and other laws working in territory of LR, have:

a) the citizens of the Latvian Republic;

b) the state and self-management, state enterprises and enterprises of self-managements (authorized companies);

c) authorized companies registered in the Register of the enterprises of LR:

> If more than half of authorized capital belongs to the citizens of LR, state or self-managements - each subject separately or in common to several subjects,
> if more than half of authorized capital belongs to physical or legal persons of those states, with which LR had concluded international contracts, authorized by Saeima before 31.12.1996.The above mentioned concerns also physical and legal persons of the states, with which the international contracts were made after 31.12.1996, in a case if the given contracts provide the rights of physical and legal persons registered in LR, to get the rights on land of the appropriate state,

if the more than a half of authorized capital belongs to several mentioned above in items a). and в). subjects;
which have the status of public (open) joint-stock company, in a case if their shares are quoted on a share stock exchange;

4) Religious societies registered in Latvia, term of work of which from the moment of their registration in the Latvian Republic, is not less than 3 years.

Other physical and legal persons who have not been mentioned in the first part of 1 given clause, have the right to purchase land in property with restrictions named in the given section.

Besides, it is necessary to consider, that according the given law the order of transfer of the property right on land is determined by the appropriate chiefs of self-managements, which are stated in an item 30 and say:

The chairman of self-management within 20 days agrees to purchase of land in property. The consent is made out as the statement, which is subscribed by the chairman of council of local self-management. In the statement are specified the purposes of use of land, got in the property also. The contract of purchase is considered valid for record in the Land book, only then, when the mentioned statement is enclosed. One copy of the statement the local self-management within 3 days after signing sends in a State Land service of the appropriate branch. Refusal to coordinate receptions of the property right on land can be appealed against by the parties of the contract in court.

Being guided by norms of the given law, both residents of LR, and non-residents of LR have the right for immovable property in village areas.

5. **Law on protection zones**.

The norms of the given law provide the order of use of land in protection zones of the Latvian Republic in the locations of coastal zone (zone of cemetaries, territory of a presence of natural riches etc.)

The norms of the given law provide also duties of the owners on use and management of land areas located in protection zone.

6. **Wood law**.

In the given law the definition of use of woods and land in a wood is given. The law stipulates the order of use, preservation and service of wood and land of a wood zone, as well as the rights and duties of the private and state owners of woods and land of woods.

The mentioned rules of law concern as to the owners and users of private land, and state.

7. **About transfer of the property to the lawful owners**.

The purpose of the given law is the settlement of restoration in the property rights of the persons or their successors, which owned property in territory of the Latvian Republic before 1940, and, which were deprived of the given right as a result of illegal actions as a result of occupation.

8. **About denationalized householderships of the Latvian Republic.**

The purpose of the given law is the restoration of the legal status of the owners on immovable property, which they were illegally deprived after 1940 as a result of institutions' nationalization by the Soviet authority.

According to the given law, persons or their successors, whose property was nationalized, in the order stipulated by the law can address to self-management with the request about denationalization and restoration of their rights on immovable property. Also the given law provides the rights of the employers on use of apartments in denationalized real estate, the maximal size of rent payment and restriction on time, during which the owner of the real estate should not interrupt the contract of hiring with the employer, having the right to live and to manage apartment in denationalized house.

9. **About record of immovable property in the Land book.**

The given law describes the order of entering of property, property rights for property, as well as burdening with law of estate in Public register of immovable property of the Latvian Republic - Land book, which is carried out by branches of the Land book of LR.

In the Land book, as a unique source of the Public register, the rights on property and property of Latvia are fixed. The property right on immovable property is considered completely confirmed only from the moment of entering record about it in the Land book. According the given law, as a result of fulfilment of any bargain with immovable property the property right to immovable property completely passes to the parties of the bargain, as well as to the third persons, only after registration of the bargain in the Land book.

10. **Law on self-managements (78 clauses).**

In the bargains with real estate the right of prime purchase of those objects of real estate which are in territory of the appropriate self-management, is given to self-managements.

Particularly about the given right - right of prime purchase is spoken in clause 78:

78 clause. The local self-management has right of prime purchase, if the immovable property is alienated in administrative territory of the given self-management and this real estate is necessary for performance of the functions, assigned to self-management by the law.

Right of prime purchase is not distributed on:

a) Real estate got by the State;

b) Real estate got for diplomatic and consular needs by other states;

c) Privatized by the State and self-management objects;

d) Industrial objects with all equipment;

e) The immovable property, which passes from one person to another gratuitously or by exchange;

f) The immovable property, from which the ideal share is alienated and which remains the joint property of the seller and buyer;

g) The immovable property, which is sold in voluntary or compulsory auction;

h) The immovable property, when the right of prime purchase or repayment have third persons, which is founded by the law, contract or will;

i) The room property, and also apartments, which are got in the property up to privatization of an apartment house.

Self-management, which have got the immovable property as a result of the right of prime purchase, within five years can sell it only on open auction.

The order of realization of the right of prime purchase is defined by Cabinet of the Ministers.

The rules of Cabinet of the Ministers № 110 define, that if the alienation of the immovable property occurs differently, than is determined in mentioned clause, it is necessary to the participants of the bargain to give the contract of purchase of the property in self-management and self-management, not later than 20 days, makes a decision on realization of the right of prime purchase or refusal of use of this right. If the self-management refuses to use the right of prime purchase, alienator have the right to alienate this property only according the contracts of purchase, which was concluded and given in self-management.

11. **About a privatization of apartment houses of the state and self-managements**

The given law defines the order of realization of a privatization in state houses and houses of self-managements (purchase of the real estate in the property for a payment, where as a payment means the privatization certificates are applied).

Each proprietor of privatization certificates who is registered or concluded the contract with appropriate house-management, has the right to privatize the given apartment, getting thus given apartment in the property. The norms of the given law concern persons, who have the right to privatize inhabited premises - proprietors of the privatization certificates.

12. **About renting inhabited premises**.

The law regulates legal attitude of the employer and the renter of inhabited premises, defines rights and duties of the parties of the rent contract. Exception is only stipulated by the law « About denationalization of the real estate in the Latvian Republic » the moratorium (7 years from the moment of denationalization and right of the employers of denationalized buildings, which meet the requirements of the Law «About denationalization of huseholderships in the Latvian Republic».

In Latvia conclude and admit as lawful contracts of renting of apartments and inhabited premises only adequate to the given law.

Rules of the Cabinet of Ministers to the present law and appropriate decisions of self managements define the size of the maximal payment for usage of inhabited premises in denationalized houses and houses of self-managements, for example in Riga the size of payment makes LVL 0,4865 for square meter.

The legal attitudes of the employer and the renter are regulated also by Civil law of the LR, but, as the norms of the Law «About renting inhabited premises» are special,, hence, they are applied first of all and only then the norms of the Civil law of the LR or norm of other legal certificates are applied.

13. **About the room property**.

The given law regulates the room property, as a separate kind of property which can be got in property by any person (is not dependent on that whether he is the resident of the LR or not).

The property rights to an apartment, up to a complete privatization of a house, are coroborated (fixed) in room cadastre of the Cadastral register of a State Land service of the Latvian Republic. The records in the given cadastral register are equated to records made in the Land book, thus, rights of the persons who have been written down in the cadastral register as of the proprietor of an apartment, can not be challenged, differently as on the basis of submission of the claim in court.

In cases, if together with an apartment ideal shares of immovable property are alienated also, the property rights of the purchaser - proprietor are fixed in the Land book. For fastening the property rights of the non-resident of the LR, the consent of the chief of local self-management (chairman of Dome) is necessary which is made out as statement and is given together with the documents confirming the property rights.

14. The law on the Land book.

In the given law the order in which records about the property rights to the real estate in the land books of the Latvian Republic are made is determined. The given law will help you to understand in what order and what judge accepts the decisions and make records about the property rights, burdenings, marks about restrictions of use of the real estate.

Besides in the given law there are norms, by which the sizes of the state and writing duties, order of their payment at submission of the documents in branches of the Land book for fastening the property right on property by are determined.

15. **About usage of land and arrangement**

The law defines the order of use and arrangement of land up to the moment of buying of the property on it. In the basis the Law adjusts the attitudes on usage and arrangement of land, which are established on the basis of rent contracts between the private persons (physical and legal) and state or self-management.

The norms of this law concern both land in cities, and agricultural land.

The purpose of the given law is definition of general duties of land users concerning environment, character of land's use and purposes of use, and also right of the users on use and improvement of land and on purchase it in the property.

16. **The tax to the real estate**

According to norms of the given law the proprietors, users, legal owners or the tenants of the real estate on territory of the Latvian Republic estimate and pay the tax to the immovable property.

In the second part of first clause of the given law the objects of the real estate which are not taxed with the given tax are defined.

The payers of the tax are both physical, and legal persons, in the property, management or usage of which is an immovable property.

The period of taxation of the given tax is a calendar year, thus, tax is necessary to pay annually, and the payment is made according to accounts of Financial department of a State service of the incomes (usually payment is broken quarterly).

The give tax will be not not paid by the persons in the property, legal government or usage of which is a real estate listed in the second part of first clause of the law, and also residents of the states, with which Latvia has made and ratificated international contracts and conventions on avoidance of the double taxation, if given contracts or conventions are included the tax to the immovable property. These persons can pay the given tax or similar one on the native land, giving in a State service of the incomes of Latvia statement of the appropriate sample on payment of the tax.

It is necessary to note also, that the given law has replaced the law «About the tax with land» and the given tax to the real estate concerns both land and buildings, which are on this land.

LAND OWNERSHIP AND HOUSING IN LATVIA

Latvia has gained significant success in transition process to market economy and democracy. Since 1996 there is observed further improvement of economy, financial sector in Latvia. Stable growth of economy has been achieved. Democratic institutions, which have put in action democratic principles in different areas, have more and more influence in the politics. In the social area activities to solve society development problems are taking place. Solving these problems is one of the main keystones for development of united society and increase of inhabitants' welfare.

There have been carried out activities to make improvements in the legal framework, central and local management and economics. Also "third counterpart" (NGO's) has become stronger. These organisations have more and more influence on processes of society importance. The role of mass media has risen in discussing different topics and raising information level, education etc. of inhabitants. A lot of activities have been carried out, but there is still need for additional effort to provide sustainable development of Latvia and effective solutions in all main areas, – economy, social affairs, environment, etc.

Priorities set by Action plan of National Report of Latvia (Habitat II) are implemented gradually: development of network of inhabited localities, provision of possibilities for inhabitants to get suitable settlement, activation of new construction and all building branch, harmonisation of environment in small Latvian towns, villages, etc.

In 1996 when National Report for conference Habitat II was worked out the main attention was paid to analysis of processes in housing sector and urban development. Attention was paid also to development of historically occupied areas according to Latvian traditions, habits and mentality. Therefore detailed analysis about different areas has been carried out in order to prepare National Report, – housing issues, social development, increasing of poverty, environment management, economic development, international co-operation. In the National Report there is included overview of present situation and development tendencies since 1996. Problems, achievements in state and municipal affairs, obstacles and solutions in legal framework, institutional capacity as well as several other topics are overlooked. The questions, which are at the prior level for Latvia at the moment, both at state and municipal level are described and analysed deeper.

The multi-institutional approach has been used in preparation of the National Report; there is included information about wide spectrum of questions. Some questions are not analysed deep enough because of the luck of information. In the future there will not be as much problems with getting information as now, because the EUROSTAT system for collecting, analysing and distributing of statistical information will be adopted from EU.

In preparation of the National Report specialists from Ministry of Environmental Protection and Regional Development, other ministries, municipalities, professional organisations and NGOs' have participated.

SHELTER

Increase of living standard has crucial impact on development of Latvia. One of the main criteria for increase of living standard is inhabitants' provision with housing. It is also main prediction to ensure welfare of inhabitants.

In Latvia reforms of the housing sector have started in the 1990s and are continued in fields of privatisation process, denationalisation, housing market, etc. The opinion, more and more significant in the society, is that there should be paid more attention to the process of provision with suitable housing for inhabitants. Therefore a lot of activities have been carried out to develop crediting system and improve the legal framework.

In the beginning of 1999 there was housing with a total area of 53.4 mill. m^2 (in cities 34.7 mill. m^2 or 69%, in rural areas 18.7 mill m^2 or 31%) in Latvia. In the capital of Latvia, Riga, where live approximately one third of all inhabitants, is housing with a total area of 16.2 mill. m^2 or 30.3% of all.

In the 1990s the average area of housing property per capita has increased from 21.3 m^2 in 1996 to 22.0 m^2 in 1999. Mainly this number was achieved because of decrease of population, not because of new construction, which is still very low. In 1990 there were built 5 new apartments per 1000 inhabitants, in 1996 – just 0.6 apartments and in 1999 – just 0.4 apartments.

The question about insulation and renovation of the buildings is priority at the moment as approximately one third of all buildings are built before 1940 and heat resistance and quality of building envelopes for prefabricated panel buildings built after 1958 (another third of all housing) are not according building codes.

SECURITY OF TENURE

Changes in housing fund ownership structure. Ownership structure of the housing fund has changed significant in Latvia because of denationalisation and privatisation processes, which are taking place. In 1996 47.8% of housing was state and municipal property and 46% was private property. In 1999 private property was already 69.9%, public property – just 30.1% (state – 4%, municipal – 26.1%). After prognosis of the Central Statistical Bureau by the end of privatisation process approximately 80% of Latvia housing will be private property and municipalities will maintain only 20% of the housing as rental or social houses.

Transition process from public to private sector in Latvia is rather complicated. In 1990 the Law "On Land Reform in the Republic of Latvia Rural Regions" was admitted, in 1991 the Law "On Land Reform in the Republic of Latvia Cities" was admitted and started process of real estate retrieve to previous owners. In 1995 according to the Law "On Privatisation of State and/ or Municipality Owned Dwelling Houses" privatisation process was started. According to above-mentioned law it was possible to privatise an apartment in dwelling house without privatisation of land under the building. Sometimes land under dwelling houses belongs to previous owner, sometimes it is even more complicated – land can be property of several owners. In these cases owner or owners of the land sign a long-term contract on rent of land.

According to the Law "On Real Estate Recording in Land Book" (1997) all rights concerning real estate (land, houses owned by private persons, houses owned by municipalities/state, housing property, etc.) should be written into land book.

The privatisation process (tenants of the municipal or state owned apartments become owners of these apartments) continues. The apartment can be privatised (bought from state or municipality) using privatisation certificates. In dwelling houses the apartments, which are not privatised, remain municipal property, therefore mixed ownership form of dwelling houses grows up and the questions about maintenance, administration of building and involvement of all inhabitants surface as well. Amendments in the laws and other legal acts, which will ensure that technical conditions in the housing do not become worse, are under preparation at the moment. Owners of the apartments should establish apartment owners association, which is responsible for maintenance and administration of the building. At the moment we are looking for financial sources to stimulate establishment of house owners associations and to ensure ability to pay for these associations.

At the moment municipal enterprises still are carrying out maintenance in major part of housing fund (including privatised part). Establishment process of house owners' associations is very slow. The main obstacles in house owners' association establishment process are difference among inhabitants' income levels, luck of information and education, low responsibility level of inhabitants for common property.

As the result of denationalisation process, 9995 houses are returned to the previous owners with more than 75 000 apartments with total area of 3.5 mill. m^2. In the cities the private rental housing has been established as the result of this process. It was determined by law that tenants, who lived in these buildings before denationalisation, are "protected" for 7 years. Within this "protection period" it is not possible to evict from apartment without provision of another apartment. Also rental fee should not exceed the "rent ceiling" determined by municipality. After "protection period" new contracts between tenants and owner of building can be signed and owner can have more profitable agreement. Therefore increase of this part of housing do not solve the housing problem for households that do not have enough financial recourses for rent and services payments.

Social housing. There is municipal housing fond and assistance system that are used as tools to provide social housing. Issues related to social housing in Latvia are described in Law "On the Assistance Rendered by the State and Municipalities in Order to Resolve Housing Issues" (1993) and Law "On Social Apartments and Social Houses" (1997).

One of the main housing problems in Latvia is high price level for services in comparison with income level. Government has delegated responsibility to set "rent ceiling" to municipalities, which are also responsible for social support, but prices for services usually are nominated by enterprise, which provides the service.

Municipalities are providing following assistance to poor people or people with low income:

- ✓ rent of social apartments (apartments with lower rent in ordinary house owned by municipality or in special social house),
- ✓ subsidies as part of payment for services and rent.

There were 703 social apartments in Latvia in 1998 and there lived 1409 inhabitants. In 1999 there were 38 social houses and 461 social apartments in Latvia and there lived 3026 inhabitants (including 1150 pensioners and 607 children).

There are 5 social dwelling houses with 400 apartments in Riga, the capital of Latvia. There are situated also social assistance and medical offices in these houses. The 75% of rent and 25% of services of these houses are subsidised by municipality of Riga.

In the maintenance and development concept of the Riga housing there is quit a lot attention paid to develop successful assistance and support system. There are several main objectives mentioned: by the year 2005 there should be 25 social houses and social support for social apartments should be developed (there should not be determined criteria such as ownership or location of building). It is planned that in 2001 the construction of new municipal apartment buildings for rent will be started and each year 2 – 5 new buildings will be constructed.

In spite of activities carried out – development of social housing sector, social assistance and municipal support –, there are groups of people whose rights to suitable housing are not satisfied. The houses for people, who have lost their homes, are established.

Eviction from apartment. One of the most essential problems, which are faced by inhabitants in last years, is possibility to be evicted from apartment. In the law "On the Rent for Dwelling" (1993) all aspects connected to renting, eviction, court procedure, etc. are defined. In all cases when somebody is evicted form an apartment, the ruling of the Court should be taken. Ruling of the Court on interruption of rental agreement with tenant, who has debts for rent and services is the legal basis to evict a tenant from apartment. Usually people, who are evicted from apartments, are without high enough income level: pensioners, unemployed people, sometimes even families with children.

In Riga, 860 people, who are evicted from apartments, have applied for social assistance in year 2000. Estimates of the specialists from Apartment Administrative Board show that approximately two thirds from evicted families apply for social assistance. Mainly people, who are evicted from apartment according the ruling of the Court, are transmitted to the rooms without convenience or hostels. It is planned to include regulations on protection of these people in the legal framework.

RIGHTS TO ADEQUATE HOUSING

Rights on dwelling. One of the main questions for inhabitants after regaining of independence of Latvia was to provide their families with housing.

In Law "On the Assistance Rendered by the State and Municipalities in Order to Resolve Housing Issues" (1993) it is determined that all persons (families) have rights to receive the state and/ or municipal support to solve question of housing and the types of this assistance is described as well.

In the law it is foreseen, that following assistance is provided:
- ✓ rent of apartments;
- ✓ support for rent and service payments;
- ✓ elimination of apartments where more than one family are living.

According to this law the priority of municipalities, state enterprises and institutions is their responsibility to rent apartments from their housing to persons (families) who are in prior status to get housing. Prior status to get housing is to several social groups, such as families with three or more children, disable persons or families with disable persons, pensioners without supporters, people with low income and families with necessity to improve living conditions (e.g. very bad technical conditions of apartment, not enough living area).

The Law sets the groups of people who should receive immediate support for housing as well. These groups are: persons left their apartments because of emergency (fire, flood), people living in emergency houses, motherless children, repatriates, persons returning from jail, persons evicted from apartment according the ruling of the Court and some other groups.

When this law became into force privatisation and denationalisation processes were not started, there did not exist housing market and the social problem was not so hard. At the moment the law does not fit the economic and social situation and real rental relations, therefore the development process of new law is initiated. It is planned that the new approach will be used in new law. Municipalities will be responsible for provision with housing persons disable to work, the poor or families with one or more under age children, pensioners with low income level and without support, motherless children, disable persons and persons returning from jail.

Prices of housing and their ratio to income level. Housing market in Latvia developed irregular and relations in market are still deformed because of the following reasons:

- low ability of inhabitants to pay;
- law rent prices that do not cover expenditures for maintenance and amortisation therefore owner can be in red;
- dependence of maintenance of houses on the rent for the area used for commercial purposes (e.g. workshops, shops, etc.);
- luck of demand for housing in economically low active regions, especially in rural areas;
- policy tendencies that do not support housing development.

Therefore there are very significant fluctuations in market value of housing property. In rural areas there can be situations when market value of the housing property is lower than the balance value, sometimes close to zero. In cities, especially in the capital price for equal housing property can be very high.

Main factors, which have impact on housing prices, are type of the housing property, technical conditions, place where housing property is situated, etc. Most expensive apartments are in the centre of Riga. In the end of 1999 average apartment price in this part of the city was 850 – 950 USD per m^2, sometimes even 1600 USD per m^2 (In Latvia prices for apartments in housing market usually are set in USD). In suburbs of Riga the price for apartment since 1993 has raised 2-3 times and in 1999 it was between 200 and 375 USD per m^2. Average apartment price at the moment in suburbs is 8 – 20 thousands USD.

If the tenant is privatising his/ her apartment he/ she "buys" it from state and "pays" with privatisation certificates. In this case price for m^2 is approximately 2 certificates (nominal value of certificate is LVL 28) or USD 33,6 per m^2.

Construction of new housings. In 1999 only 4% of all construction works was construction of housings and mainly inhabitants financed these works. Private investments for housing construction in 1996 were LVL 38.9 mill. In 1999 this number reached LVL 40.9 mill. Average costs for construction of single family houses since 1996 have not changed and are approximately 207 LVL per m^2.

Here and after calculations are carried out using currency exchange rate 1 USD = 0.60 LVL

Mostly construction of new housing and reconstruction of existing housing is carried out in Riga and Riga region (42%). In rural areas this process is very passive.

The description of situation in Riga is used to evaluate ratio between of inhabitants' average income level and market prices for housing. According investigation about household income in Riga carried out by the Central Statistical Bureau of Latvia, average disposable income per one person of household is LVL 78.2 what makes average income per one household per year LVL 2252. Ratio between average income and price of housing property is 1.5, which is rather good figure if compared to other Central and Eastern European countries; but it should be taken into account that real minimum for living is LVL 83.18 per months and only 8% of inhabitants announced that they are able to purchase better apartment.

In spite of positive tendencies in growth of inhabitants' income level, big part of inhabitants is not able to purchase housing. New families mostly are not able to get their first housing without credit or another support. Very good and remarkable is fact that in Latvian commercial banks in year 2000 long-term credits are offered and interest rate is lower – approximately 10 – 14%.

EQUAL ACCESS TO LAND

Rate of land prices compared to inhabitant income. In Latvia land market was established in 1991 when Laws "On Land Reform in Republic of Latvia Cities" and "On Land Privatisation in Rural Regions" became into force. In these laws free land market was not defined and only in 1996 the amendments to these laws became into force and the liberalisation of land market occurred.

In Latvia it is possible to trade land only in case if it is registered in Land Book. It is allowed to be an owner of the land for citizens of Latvia, state and municipal enterprises and some additional categories of enterprises registered in Enterprise Register of the Republic of Latvia. For other private persons and legal entities it is possible to get land with some restrictions and municipality is making decision in each separate case.

Land and real estate market similar to housing market is more developed in Riga, Riga region and Jurmala. Higher demand is for land for construction of single family houses with developed infrastructure, good transportation to city centre etc. In Riga average price for 1 m^2 of land is 5 – 25 USD.

Factors, which determine value of land, are level of economic development and density of inhabitants. Taking into account that there is rather low density of population, the value of land in rural areas and small cities is low in Latvia. It is difficult to evaluate average rate of land price compared to income level because of very big fluctuations of these two indicators.

EQUAL ACCESS TO CREDIT

One of the main circumstances for stimulation of new construction in Latvia, repairs and reconstruction in existing housing, development of housing and real estate market, provision with opportunity for inhabitants to get suitable housing is development of crediting system.

According to the Concept "On Latvian Housing Policy", which is accepted by the Cabinet of Ministers in 1996, the main objective is development of housing crediting system. In the end of 1997 several documents linked with each other were accepted: the Concept "On Development of Mortgage Crediting System", the Concept "On Long-term Crediting of Housing Construction, Reconstruction, Renovation and Modernisation", the law "On Commercial Mortgage" and the law "On Mortgaging Bonds".

"Suggestions for usage of fiscal policy in development of crediting system for construction, reconstruction, renovation and insulation of housing" were prepared and government in June 13, 2000 accepted "Crediting programme for housing development". At the moment the preparation of first stage of this programme is carried out.

According information provided by Latvia Central Bank, in the end of 1999 there were 23 banks, which offered possibility to get commercial credits for housing crediting. Of course conditions for getting credits, terms and interest rates in these banks are different, but there is a provision required in all cases – the repayment monthly should not be more than 30% of total income. In 1999 interest rate for purchasing or renovation of housing was approximately 12 – 16%. According investigations of housing specialists, the housing market in Latvia could become active if the interest rate would be 9 – 10%.

Obstacles to get credits are: not sufficient conditions (terms, interest rate), low ability of inhabitants to pay, it is not possible to get enough co-financing and offered gage do not fit criteria of commercial banks.

In 1998 crediting portfolio of Latvian banks reached amount of LVL 622.4 mill. In the year 1999 Latvian banks provided LVL 831 mill for credits and only LVL 59 mill. or 7.1% of those had real estate mortgage. Credits guaranteed with real estate mortgage in 1999 were only 1.6% compared to GDP. This indicator shows that real estate and housing market in Latvia is still at the development stage.

There is tendency for crediting portfolio of Latvian banks to increase slowly, but in real figures this amount is too low to secure improvements in housing of Latvia.

ACCESS TO BASIC SERVICES

Landscape of housing and availability of communications. It is not a problem for inhabitants, especially in cities, to get access to basic services. These services are usually included in housing landscape.

93.7% of apartments in Latvia in 1999 were connected to the water supply network and this density has not changed significantly in last years.

In Latvia cities major part of apartments are connected also to wastewater system (92.7%), electricity network (100%), telephone communications (59.8%), central heating (83.7%), gas supply network (85.4%) and hot water supply network (77.3%).

Landscape level of apartments in cities is higher than in rural areas.

In Latvia availability of communications is not a technical problem anymore. Sector of telephone communications is developing rapidly, there are provided both opportunities – fixed and mobile services. In the end of 1998 the total amount of fixed telephone connections was 482 thousands. 66% from this amount were connected to analogue network and 249 thousands (34%) to digital network. In the year 1999 digital connection was already for 412 thousands fixed telephone connections. In 1996 there was 28.5 thousands mobile connections and in 1999 number of mobile connections reached 278.9 thousands.

There are carried out a lot of activities in last years to develop ownership structure. Privatisation and denationalisation processes are in the final stage. Amendments in existing legal acts are worked out and the new are developed in order to develop social assistance system. More and more attention is paid to opportunities of housing provision to people from social groups. The income level increases slowly; housing crediting system becomes more active and available for inhabitants.

Nevertheless at the moment situation of inhabitants' provision with housing is not enough satisfactory both in quality and quantity sense. There are still a lot of things to be done in housing sector and housing financing sector both in state and municipal levels.

Macroeconomic and real estate market development will have significant impact on further development of housing sector in Latvia. Development of housing sector is close connected to development of economics. Big role in this game will play government plans and reforms in housing sector.

DIFFERENCES BETWEEN RIGHTS OF LATVIAN CITIZENS AND NON-CITIZENS - LATVIAN RESIDENTS

Before October 15, 1991 all residents of Latvia enjoyed equal legal status. On October 15, 1991, the Latvian Parliament passed the Resolution "On the Renewal of the Rights of Citizens of the Republic of Latvia and Fundamental Principles of Naturalization" which divided the residents of Latvia into two major categories: citizens (approximately two thirds), and non-citizens (approximately one third). According to the data of the Naturalization Department published in the newspaper "Diena" on August 6, 1997, there were 676,981 non-citizens in Latvia (27.7% of the population) in May 20, 1997. On January 1, 2001 the number of stateless "non-citizens" stood at 551,064 (Latvian Center for Human Rights and Ethnic Studies, June 2001).

The Resolution "On the Renewal of the Rights of Citizens of the Republic of Latvia and Fundamental Principles of Naturalization" provided the Latvian citizenship only to the pre-war citizens and their descendants. In the meantime, the non-citizen population was left in a legislative vacuum for almost four years, as no law clearly determined their legal status, rights and obligations.

In April 1995, under the pressure of European structures, a new law has been passed – "On the Status of the Former USSR Citizens, who are not Citizens of Latvia or any other State." This law, for the first time, determined the legal status of the majority of non-citizens.

However, this law did not become an effective cure against restrictions on the rights of Latvia's non-citizens. While some differences mentioned in the original list have been abolished, other legislative acts were a source of new ones.

In the year 2000 the list contained 57 differences between the rights of citizens and non-citizens.

a) State Institutions

Jobs reserved for Latvian citizens only:

1. STATE OFFICE

(Senior Public Service), (see Note 1) Constitutional Law "The Rights and Obligations of a Citizen and Person" adopted on December 10, 1991, Art.8 (abolished by amendments to the Satversme)

Amendments to the Satversme (Constitution), adopted on October 15, 1998, Art. 101

2. Civil Servants (1) The Law "On the State Civil Service," adopted on April 21, 1994, Art.6 (1)

Amendments to the Satversme (Constitution), adopted on October 15, 1998, Art. 101

3. Constitutional Court Judges Constitutional Court Law adopted on June 5, 1996, Art. 4(2)

4. Judges (1) The Law "On Judicial Power," adopted on December 15, 1992, Art.51 (1)

5. Court bailiffs The Law "On Judicial Power," adopted on December 15, 1992, Art. 109(1)

6. Public Prosecutors (1) The Law "On the Public Prosecutor's Office," adopted on May 19, 1994, Art.33 (1)

7. State Security Officers (1) The Law "On State Security Institutions," adopted on May 5, 1994, Art.18 (1)

8. Diplomatic and Consular Service (1) The Law "On Diplomatic and Consular Service," adopted on May 11 1993, Art.3 (2)

A new Law with the same title and restrictions was adopted on September 21, 1995

9. Sworn surveyors (1) The State Land Service Order "On the procedure for issuing licenses to sworn surveyor practices," adopted on July 21, 1993, p.7

10. Sworn evaluators (1) The Land service regulations "On special licenses to be obtained to value and fix the statute ore price of real estate according to categories of fixing the statutory price and valuation," adopted on December 27, 1995, Art. 15

11. Police Service (2) Amendments to the Law "On Police" adopted by the Cabinet of Ministers of the LR on January 11, 1994, Rules 19, and Art. 1.5

12. Access to information declared to be a state secret (3) Law "On State Secrets," adopted on October 17, 1996, Art. 9 (2)

b) Private Sector

Jobs reserved for Latvian citizens only:

13. Sworn Advocates and Advocate's Assistants (4) The Law "On Advocacy," adopted on April 27, 1993, Art.14 (1) and 83

14. Sworn Notaries and Notary's Assistants (1) Notary Law, adopted on June 1, 1993, Art.9 (1), 147(1)

15. Private Detectives (4) The Law "On Operative Activities" adopted on December 16, 1993, Transitional Regulations, Art. 4 Amendments to "The Regulations of Detective Activities

and Its Licensing in the Republic of Latvia," Order Nr 74 of the Ministry of the Interior on March 28, 1994

16. Security Service, use of fire arms (4) Ministry of the Interior, Order Nr 288, signed on November 17, 1993, Art. 8.2

17. Aircraft Captain (4) Law "On Aviation," adopted on February 23, 1993 Art.35. At present Law "On Aviation," adopted on October 5, 1994 Art.35

18. Captains on Latvian ships Maritime Regulations of Latvia (Maritime Code), Art. 137

(Regulations of Cabinet of Ministers No.168, adopted on August 16, 1994)

19. Head of undertaking having issued a license for guard activities Law "On Guard Activities," adopted on October 29, 1998, Art. 6

c) Public sector

Only citizens have the right:

20. To be elected as jurors (1) The Law "On Judicial Power" adopted on December 15, 1992, Art.56

21. To serve in the National Guard (1) The Law "On National Guard," adopted on April 6, 1993, Art. 5(1)

22. To be elected to religious organizations' governing bodies, excluding their ecclesiastical personnel (4) The Law "On Religious Organizations," Art.7 (1), adopted on September 7, 1995

23. To establish political parties The Law "In Public Organizations and Associations," adopted on December 15, 1992, Art. 43

24. Political parties are allowed to operate if at least 1/2 of the members are citizens The Law "In Public Organizations and Associations," adopted on December 15, 1992, Art. 45 with amendments adopted on April 5, 1995

25. To participate in local elections, (5) see also (1) The City Dome and Rural District Councils Election Law adopted on January 13, 1994, Art. 5

26. To elect and to be elected to the Council of Students' management at the University of Latvia (6) Statutes (Constitution) of the Students' Self - Government of the University of Latvia, 1998, Art.8, 10

27. Contacts with foreign citizens, access to cultural monuments and mass media are guaranteed to citizens only in some of the Agreements 5 Agreements, signed from August 7, 1992 to May 10, 1999

II. PROPERTY RIGHTS

Only citizens have the right to:

28. To transfer the right to use state and municipality owned land to their heirs (7)Amendments to the Law "On the Land Reform in the Cities of the Republic of Latvia" adopted on March 31, 1994, Art. 4

29. Acquire the land into ownership with building on it if the land was not owned by them before July 22, 1940 (7) The Law "On Amendments to LR," Law "On the Land Reform in the Cities of LR," adopted on March 31, 1994, Art.8: amendments to 12(1),(2) of the Law "On the Land Reform in the Cities of LR"

30. A judicial person has the right to acquire the land plot into ownership in the LR cities if more than a half of its statute capital belongs to LR citizens. Should this ratio be changed, the deprivation of the land plot is envisaged (7) The Law "On Amendments to LR," Law "On the Land Reform in the Cities of LR," adopted on November 24, 1994, Art.3: amendments to Art. 20, 26 of the "On the Land Reform in the Cities of LR"

31. Similar to No.30 limitation for judicial persons when buying land plots in rural areas (7) Amendments to the Law "On the Land Privatization in Rural Regions," adopted on December 8, 1994, Art. 14; Amendments to Art. 28 (4), 35, 36 of the Law "On the Land Privatization in Rural Regions"

32. The right to become a member of an Apartment Owners' Association (de facto to buy a privatized "cooperative" apartment in Riga) belongs to non-citizens too, but only having the permanent residence permit and residence time in Riga of 16 years (8) Riga City Council Regulations Nr 5 "For Persons wishing to acquire an apartments in a cooperative society of housing owners," adopted on October 4, 1994, Art.1

33. Every citizen of Latvia is allotted 15 certificates more then a non-citizen. A non-citizen born outside Latvia gets another 5 certificates less (9). One certificate is an equivalent of state property volume, created during 1 year of a person's life The Law "On Privatization Certificates," adopted on November 4, 1992, Art. 4, pp.2,4

The Law "On Privatization Certificates," adopted on March 16, 1995, Art. 5, pp.2, 4

34. Non-citizens who arrived in Latvia after the retirement age (60 for men, 55 for women) and who had less than 5 years of hired employment receive no privatization certificates (9) The Law "On Privatization Certificate," adopted on November 4, 1992, Art 4, p.4

The Law "On Privatization Certificates," adopted on March 16, 1995, Art 5, p.4

35. The Latvian citizen is allotted with certificates if he lived in Latvia before December 31, 1992 and at any time was registered as permanent inhabitant.

Non-citizen of Latvia is allotted with certificates since the last arrival to Latvia only and having purpose for the permanent living in Latvia (9)

The rules Nr. 179 "On Privatization Certificates" adopted by the Cabinet of Ministers on August 23, 1994, p.5

36. Only citizens and legal entities are guaranteed the protection of their investments abroad 25 Agreements with 26 states, adopted within the period August 26, 1991-June 17, 1998

37. Protection of intellectual property abroad is guaranteed by some bilateral Agreements to citizens only 2 Agreements with 5 states, adopted within the period November 21, 1995-December 7, 1995

III. PRIVATE ENTERPRISE

38. Licenses for air transportation abroad are guaranteed, by bilateral agreements to the companies controlled by Latvian citizens. If such control is lost, the license is revoked 17 Agreements, signed within the period July 1, 1992-March 4, 1999

39. Only companies controlled by Latvian citizens can make fishing at the territory under USA jurisdiction Fishery agreement with USA April 8, 1993, art. 1

40. Non-discrimination regarding double taxation is guaranteed to citizens only 6 Agreements, signed within the period November 17, 1993-October 16, 1998

IV. SOCIAL RIGHTS

41. Citizens only are registered in the line to receive aid from State and local authorities if they have lived for more than 40 years in an apartment without modern conveniences (central heating, water, hot water) or live in a 'communal' apartment (shared by several families) (9) 'On the Rules of Registering Residents (Families) to Receive State or Local Governments' Housing Support' Nr. 17, adopted by the Cabinet of Ministers on November 23, 1993, Art. 8.6

42. To receive assistance solving housing problems, the non-citizens require a permanent registration notice (s.c. "propiska") in their passports. Such a limitation has not been provided for the citizens The Law "On Housing Support, granted by the State and Local Governments" adopted on May 11, 1993, Art.3

43. Only citizens have the right to receive a loan for purchase the right to hire a flat (8) Resolution 83 of Riga City Council, adopted on March 7, 1997, p.2. Amendments to the Resolution 160 of Riga City Council "On Allotment of Loans for purchase of Apartments"

44. A possibility to hire flats for unlimited time in the 'hotels for employees' in Riga exists only for those non-citizens who have lived and worked in Latvia at least 10 years. Citizens have such right regardless of the length of their stay and work in Riga (8)Regulations of Riga Council No. 52 "On Use Service of Hotels for Employees" adopted on March 26, 1996, Art. 4

45. Years of employment outside Latvia are not included into the non-citizens' employment record when calculating pension rates (9, 10) Law "On State Pensions," adopted on November 2, 1995, transitional regulations, Art. 1

V. OTHER RIGHTS AND FREEDOMS

46. Only citizens have the right to study in certain higher education establishments Statute (Constitution) of the Academy of Police, adopted by the Cabinet of Ministers on June 17, 1998, Art. 69

Statute (Constitution) of the National Academy of Defense, adopted by the Cabinet of Ministers on June 30, 1998, Art. 22

47. Latvian citizens may enter 30 foreign countries without visas. Non-citizens may enter, without visas, only 4 of them The latest agreement was signed with Belgium, Netherlands, Luxembourg on June 9, 1999

48. The right on repatriation enjoyed by the citizens of Latvia or by the persons having one parent with Latvian or Liv nationality. Repatriation Law adopted on October 21, 1995, Art. 2

49. Exemption from the customs duty during transit is provided, in some cases, to citizens only 2 Agreements, signed on November 29, 1991 and December 7, 1991

50. Only Latvian citizens and (in some cases) legal entities are guaranteed legal assistance 9 Agreements, signed from November 11, 1992 to May 21, 1998

51. A citizen can be deprived of citizenship by court only.

A non-citizen can be deprived of his status administratively by decision of administrative authorities (11)

Citizenship Law adopted on July 22, 1994, Art. 24

52. Former Soviet military personnel, who left service after January 28, 1992, conscripted from outside Latvia, members of their families and relatives who arrived in Latvia with them, do not have a right to a legal status, if there are no Latvian citizens among them (12) Law "În the Status of the Former USSR Citizens Who Are Not Citizens of Latvia or Any Other State," adopted on March 12, 1995, Art. 1 (3)

53. Non-citizens who have received compensations when leaving Latvia (i.e. as compensation for apartments left behind) from any state institutions or from abroad, apart from losing their former legal status, also lose the right to enter Latvia for residency Ibid., with Amendment, adopted on June 18, 1997 Law "În the Entry and Stay of Foreign Citizens and Stateless Persons in the Republic of Latvia," adopted on June 9, 1992, Art.35 (p. 12), Art. 36 (p. 14) with amendment, adopted on December 16, 1996

54. Non-citizens can be acknowledged as politically repressed persons (by the Nazi regime), if they were repressed because of their national identity or who were minors and were confined in prisons and concentration camps in the territory of Latvia at that time (13) The Law "On Determining the Status of Politically Repressed Persons who are Victims of Communist and Nazi Regimes," adopted on April 12, 1995, Art.4, pp. 1-3

*The earlier similar Latvian Law of 13.05.92 did not contain limitations for non-citizens.

55. The possibility of obtaining residence permits by the family and relatives of non-citizens and aliens is connected with the capacity to provide for such persons. Such a requirement does not apply to citizensThe Law "În the Entry and Stay of Foreign Citizens and Stateless Persons in the Republic of Latvia", adopted on June 9, 1992, Art.35, p.2.

56. If the marriage which was the basis for receiving a temporary residence permit by a foreigner is dissolved, the temporary residence permit is annulled except in a cases when the court awards the child – a Latvian citizen – to the parent who isn't a citizen of Latvia, a non-citizen, foreign person or stateless person. If the child is a non-citizen, he is deported from the country with a

parent-foreignerThe Law "On the Entry and Stay of Foreign citizens and Stateless Persons in the Republic of Latvia" adopted on June 9, 1992, Art. 25

57. The right to self-defense: possession of firearms is allowed only to citizens [9)Law "On Firearms and Special Devices for Self – Defense," adopted February 23, 1993, Art. 11

PRACTICAL INFORMATION FOR BUSINESS ACTIVITY

POLITICAL AND BUSINESS ENVIRONMENT

Latvia- U.S. relations are excellent and our two countries maintain an active dialogue, including frequent exchange of high level visitors. Latvia is actively seeking to integrate into Western economic and political institutions including NATO, EU and OECD. It is an active participant in Partnership for Peace events. The leading political issue that could affect Latvia's business climate would be any serious downturn in relations with Russia.

Latvia is a parliamentary democracy. On September 30 -October 1, 1995, the country held its second parliamentary elections since regaining independence. The vote was split among right, leftist and centrist parties, which formed a coalition government. Under the leadership of a dynamic, business-indeed prime minister, the country has accelerated market-oriented reforms, despite a significant left -of- center presence in the coalition. However, in January 1997, the prime minister tendered his resignation, ostensibly over criticism of his choice for finance minister (a post which had been vacant since early in the autumn). At the request of the president, the prime minister formed a new government which received parliamentary approval in late February. In late July, the Prime Minister resigned. A new Prime Minister, Guntar Krasts, was formally voted into power. Krasts was formerly the Minister of Economy, and has said he would continue the strict monetary and budget policies of former Prime Minister Andris Skele. He also has pledged to accelerate economic reforms and to pursue Latvia's membership in the European Union and NATO.

Latvia is a relatively small nation with a dynamic, though recently troubled, economy and a stable political environment. Latvia is similar in size to North Carolina, but with a population of approximately 2.27 million inhabitants. The country provides a potentially attractive market for American IT equipment and services, capital machinery and equipment, medical and consumer products. Located at the center of the three Baltic States, Latvia is a member of the European Union (EU) and provides a strategic location as a commercial, financial, and transportation hub for the Nordic/Baltic region.

COMMERCIAL ENVIRONMENT

The commercial environment is generally friendly to foreign companies, and EU directives are implemented and observed. There are no controls on import, export, or the use and conversion of foreign currencies, which facilitates investment and repatriation of profits. The Latvian government has adopted modern laws establishing copyrights, patents and trademarks and the means for enforcing their protection. Telecommunication services are modern, and the real estate market provides both modern housing and business venues. English is the West European language of choice in government and business. Many U.S. companies doing business in Latvia rate the business environment among the best in Central and Eastern Europe. The legal system, tax structures, and trade and other regulations have been significantly modified to harmonize them with EU standards. Most EU directives have been incorporated into the Latvian legislative system. Latvia has been a member of the WTO since 1999. The country joined the EU and NATO in 2004.

ECONOMY

The Latvian economy is based on service industries including transportation, information technology, and financial services. At the same time the construction industry plays an important

role, as do wood, food, metalworking, and light industries (e.g., textiles). Tourism is growing rapidly.
Currently Latvia is experiencing serious economic difficulties and has received a 7.5 billion euro ($10.4 billion) assistance package from the International Monetary Fund (IMF) and the European Union. The IMF will provide 1.7 billion Euros, the Nordic countries - 1.8 billion Euros, the European Commission - 3.1 billion Euros, and the EBRD and other EU Member States – 0.9 billion Euros. The financial assistance program's terms do not call for monetary policy changes, thus allowing Latvia to maintain its currency's exchange rate peg to the euro. In order to achieve the goals of the program without devaluation, severe fiscal policy tightening is required. Key elements of the government's revised budget and economic restructuring program are the following: immediate measures to stem the loss of bank deposits and international reserves; steps to restore confidence in the banking system in the medium-term and to support private debt restructuring; fiscal measures to restrain inflation, limit government spending and reduce current account imbalances (while also avoiding a substantial widening of the budget deficit due to decreasing revenues and preparing for early fulfillment of Maastricht criteria); and social policy and structural reforms that will rebuild competitiveness and make government more efficient.

MARKET FOR U.S. PRODUCTS

American products face strong competition in the Latvian market from EU countries and the Commonwealth of Independent States (CIS). Due to historical trade relations, companies from Scandinavian countries and Germany approach the Latvian market with greater confidence. Government bureaucracy and corruption are seen by the U.S. government as the main impediments to U.S. trade and investment in Latvia. The U.S. hosts the largest Latvian immigrant community in the world, and several Latvian-Americans have returned to Latvia and assumed leading roles in the business community. Latvia became a member of WTO in 1999 and joined the EU and NATO in 2004. They have free trade agreements with 29 countries, including European Union, EFTA, several CEFTA countries and Ukraine. Latvia has also concluded bilateral investment agreements with the majority of European and CEE countries and the United States.

MARKETING PRODUCTS AND SERVICES

Marketing consumer products in Latvia has been inhibited by the lack of large distributors or wholesalers, but the situation has changed rapidly over the past few years. Food and grocery import, wholesale and retail operations are handled by private food wholesale companies, only a handful of which are considered reliable and strong enough to engage in foreign commercial activity. Interpegro, Prodimpex, Imanta, Mono Trading House, Interskonto, Laval and Hanzas Uznemums are among the larger Latvian companies having their own network of small food stores and groceries, or supplying the myriad of small retail outlets that characterize the Latvian commercial scene.. Meat processing enterprises also import meat or livestock directly. Seasonal agriculture and food products are still mainly sold to the public at farmers markets located in largest cities, although there is a growing network of small grocery and produce stores. Traditionally, most grocery shopping has been done in small specialized stores, such as a dairy store or a corner bakery. The first supermarkets have begun to open in the past years. The grocery/dry goods situation has been altered substantially with the entry on the scene of the Norwegian-Latvian joint venture Varner Baltija, which has brought the Norwegian retail chain "Rimi" to Latvia. The group has opened one modern supermarket and is in the process of transforming the Soviet style department store in the center of Riga into a modern grocery and department store. Variety in grocery stores is continually expanding, only a few product groups, such as fat-free or more exotic products from other parts of the world are not available.

At present, there are no laws that regulate the relationship between a foreign company and its distributors or agents in Latvia. A distributor relationship can be terminated according to the provisions stipulated in each specific distributor agreement. Franchising is not well known or understood in Latvia. There are no laws regulating it, therefore franchise agreements might be difficult to enforce.

A joint venture with a local partner can be a significant help for a US company that has no experience with the east European business practices. A good bet is a company that is already registered with the Latvian Chamber of Commerce and Industry. It is, however, highly advisable to find out as much as possible about potential partners. The basic data on a local company as well as its credit ratings can be obtained from Latvian mpaniey alat as t speights ed a juridical person. A joint stock company may be established with a minimum statutory capital of 5,000 lats (higher amounts are required to establish banks, insurance companies, currency exchanges and pawnshops). In five years, the minimum legal capital of a joint stock company will be increased to Ls 25,000. Establishment of a foreign bank branch is subject to the approval of the Bank of Latvia.

Representative offices of foreign companies may be established for an initial period of five years. The fee for opening a representative office is $800; extensions cost $100. Non-profit organizations and branch operations without an office in Latvia may be established for $50.

Representative offices of foreign companies are not allowed to carry out commercial activities (business for profit) in Latvia. Such offices should be registered with the Register of Enterprises. These representative offices do not have a status of a separate legal entity. At present, the Register of Enterprises also has a separate procedure for registration of permanent representative offices that have the right to engage in commercial activities. This option, however, is expected to be revoked in near future.

Market for consumer products in Latvia is fragmented. Consumer preferences differ significantly among var company also has the rights of a juridical person. A joint stock company may be established with a minimum statutory capital of 5,000 lats (higher amounts are required to establish banks, insurance companies, currency exchanges and pawnshops). In five years, the minimum legal capital of a joint stock company will be increased to Ls 25,000. Establishment of a foreign bank branch is subject to the approval of the Bank of Latvia.

Representative offices of foreign companies may be established for an initial period of five years. The fee for opening a representative office is $800; extensions cost $100. Non-profit organizations and branch operations without an office in Latvia may be established for $50.

Representative offices of foreign companies are not allowed to carry out commercial activities (business for profit) in Latvia. Such offices should be registered with the Register of Enterprises. These representative offices do not have a status of a separate legal entity. At present, the Register of Enterprises also has a separate procedure for registration of permanent representative offices that have the right to engage in commercial activities. This option, however, is expected to be revoked in near future. Market for consumer products in Latvia is fragmented. Consumer preferences differ significantly among various income, age and ethnic groups.

No reliable data on income distribution is available; according to the research conducted by the Statistics Committee, in the third quarter of 1996, 0.2% of the surveyed households characterized their living conditions as very good, 5% of respondents said that their living conditions are good, 50.2% answered that their living conditions are neither particularly bad nor good, 27.5% -- fairly bad and 17.1% -- very bad. Latvian Statistics also calculates the so-called Gini index. In 1996,

Gini index for Latvia was 32%, which means that 10% of the poorest Latvian residents receive 3.3% of the total income, while 10% of the richest earn 25% of the total income.

Advertising may be conducted freely in any printed or electronic media. The leading newspaper in Latvia is "Diena" (Day), which is published in both Latvian and Russian. The leading business newspapers are "Dienas Bizness" (Business of the Day), published in Latvian, and "Biznes i Baltiya" (Business and the Baltics), published in Russian. "Vakara Zinas" is a popular tabloid. "SM-Segodnia" is widely read by the Russian-speaking population.

Applications for the grant of a patent or registration of a trademark can be made in Latvian, English, Russian, or German to the Latvian patent office, either directly or through a legal representative. Any patent or trademark may be invalidated by a court if it does not meet the legal requirements for granting a patent or the substantive provisions for registering a trademark. Intellectual property rights may be enforced through Latvian court action.

Consultation with a Latvian attorney is recommended before establishing a business or an intellectual property right in Latvia. While an attorney must be a Latvian citizen to be admitted to the bar, a number of practicing attorneys in Riga are dual-national immigrants who have received their entire legal education in the United States or Canada. The U.S. Embassy can provide upon request a list of U.S. lawyers practicing in Latvia.

LEADING EXPORT-IMPORT PROSPECTS

The Latvian market appears to hold the most potential for American computer systems, office equipment, capital goods, building supplies and consumer products. U.S. products enjoy a particular cachet because they are American; companies frequently attempt to market products and services on the basis of their "American-ness," sometimes even for products that are essentially Latvian. Fed by flight capital from Russia and realization of pent-up demand, the market for imported consumer goods, particularly in Riga, is substantially richer than the country's per capital GDP level of $2016 (approximate 1996 data) would suggest.

The private sector is expanding very rapidly in Latvia. There is a high demand for office supplies and equipment, particularly computers, cellular telephones, copiers, and fax machines. During the Soviet years, houses and office buildings were allowed to deteriorate. The commercial boom sweeping Riga and, to a lesser degree, other Latvian cities has contributed to very wide-scale rehabilitation of commercial property. Virtually all products associated with building rehabilitation -- paint, doors, windows, locks, plumbing equipment, lighting and alarm systems -- are in high demand. Sheetrock, which was unknown during the Soviet period, is beginning to be used. Privatization of apartments that has just begun should contribute further to the demand for construction materials.

While Latvian heavy industry has never recovered from its collapse in the wake of the fall of the Soviet Union, there are signs of revival in light industry, particularly textiles and clothing manufacture, food processing, and in the timber and wood products industries. The best prospects for sales of capital goods are in these industries, and in the upgrading of plants producing electricity and supplying district heating. Good prospects also appear to exist for metering devices. Sales of capital equipment in the agribusiness area have been hampered by the lack of financing. As loans to agribusiness become available, a good potential market may be developing for food packaging and processing equipment. Water purification equipment for commercial and institutional users is another promising niche market. Frozen foods, another unknown during the Soviet era, are coming on the market in Latvia, creating a demand for commercial freezers and display cases.

The best opportunities for agricultural products are for items not produced in these latitudes, including cotton, tobacco, rice, fresh and dried tropical fruit, and seeds. The main agricultural imports in 2005 were wheat and feed grains $25.0 million, fish -- $24.8 million, alcoholic beverages -- $14.6 million and fruits and nuts -- $12.9 million. Latvia is also potentially a very good market for consumer-ready convenience foods, snacks and drinks. New entrants will have to be aggressive, as suppliers from European countries have established distributor networks for such products as beverages, coffee, cheese, tobacco, and yogurt.

Viewed strategically, Latvia is attractive as a gateway to larger regional markets, including northwestern Russia with a population of 44 million, Belarus (population 10.3 million) and other two Baltic countries (combined population 5.1 million). However, transit and customs problems, as well as weak economies in the East, have slowed the realization of this market potential. In this context, Latvia's capital, Riga, ranks with St. Petersburg and Moscow as one of three regional centers for commerce, finance and transportation.

BEST PROSPECTS FOR NON-AGRICULTURAL GOODS AND SERVICES

1. Telecommunications Equipment (TEL)
2. Computers & Peripheral Equipment (CPT)
3. Computer Services (CPS)
4. Drugs/Pharmaceuticals (DRG)
5. Sporting Goods/Recreational Eq. - (SPT)
6. Forestry/Woodworking equipment (FOR)
7. Pollution Control Equipment (POL)

Sector Rank: 1
Sector Name: Telecommunications Equipment
ITA Industry Code: TEL

The telecommunication sector has been growing rapidly in Latvia since the establishment of Lattelekom in 1994. Then 49% of the stake Latvian government sold to Danish Tilts Communications. This joint venture between the state and a consortium of European Telecom companies is still in the process of modernizing the fixed public telecommunications network. Its total capital investments in the country's telecommunications system at the end of 2000 were valued to be LVL 350 million (or around USD 560 million). Latvian government had granted exclusive rights on the wired telecommunication services to Lattelekom for a period up to year 2013. In 2002 Latvia as the EU aspirant country shortened this period to year 2003, in order to meet the EU requirements for open telecommunications market by the respective amendments adopted to the Law on Telecommunications. Tilts Communications, the strategic investor disagreed with it and requested a compensation through the Court of Arbitrage. Negotiations between the government and Tilts Communications about finding a way out of this magic circle are still in the process.

VITA, the Latvian State Information Network Agency is engaged in the development and maintenance of the country's State Significance Data Transmission Network. The project is planned to be completed in 2003, with a total cost of USD 10 million.

The best growing sub-sectors of telecommunications are digital lines and mobile telecommunications services. Latvia has one of the highest mobile phone penetration rates in CEE with 30% of the population using mobile telephony (including pre-paid phone). In years 1996-99, a number of subscribers has almost doubled every year, however, it slowed down in year 2000. Mobile operators are eager to keep in pace with the latest technology and network infrastructure. Prepaid mobile communication service was one of the most popular ones among customers in 1998 and 1999 and continues to be quite popular. Although its market share has decreased since mobile operators started to offer subsidized mobile phone offers. In May 1999 both operators introduced WAP service. In October 2000, Baltkom GSM, the second largest operator was taken over by Swedish Tele2. New management of the company came with aggressive marketing strategy that resulted in more rapid increase in the number of subscribers, thus also increasing mobile phone sales. Latvian GSM operators offer wide range of m-payment and e-payment services. Now their customers can do banking, pay their insurance payments, TV, internet, newspapers subscription and public utilities companies' invoices. In May 2002 the number of mobile phones exceeded the number of fixed phones. The current trend is the number of subscribers to fixed lines is decreasing while number of mobile phones is increasing. Latvia's largest mobile operator- LMT whose market share is above 60 per cent finished 2001 with USD 48 million profit and turnover of USD 170 million. Tele2 does not disclose its data about subscribers and finance in Latvia.

The paging era is over in Latvia. The last paging company finished its operations on May 15, 2002 by giving its customers over to the existing mobile operator Tele 2.

To further increase the competition and keep up with new technologies, in October 2002 there was completed a tender for the 3rd mobile communications operator to work in UMTS Standard in Latvia. Both current mobile operators obtained the license, however, no company interested in becoming the third mobile operator in Latvia.

Among Latvians the most popular cell phone brand is Nokia (approximately 50 per cent of all sold phones in 2000). It is followed long behind by such brand names as Siemens, Alcatel, Samsung, Motorola, Sony, a.o.

In 2001 the value added in the telecommunications industry reached 4 % of total GDP of Latvia. The number of Internet users during the 2002 according to the Latvian Internet Association has increased by 100 000, reaching 310 000 or 13,3% of total population. The popularity of internet has grown due to widely available services through cable TV operators, ISP using fixed wireless broadband connections and even mobile operators offering GPRS services.

Sector Rank: 2
Sector Name: Computers & Peripheral Equipment
ITA Industry Code: CPT

Information technology is the most dynamic and most rapidly developing industry in Latvia. The development of Western-style information society has been a vital part of Latvia's strategy prior joining the EU. Computer hardware segment covers approximately 50% of the Latvian IT market. In 2001 economic activities related to the IT sphere constituted 4.6 per cent of Latvia's GDP while in 1997 it was only at 3.2 per cent.

Sales were accelerated by implementation of the Latvian Education Informatisation System (LIIS). This program provides for that every school will have specialized computer classes with access to Internet, providing one computer per 10 students in grades 10-12, one computer per 25 students in grades 5-9, and one computer per 10 teachers.

In 2000 computer equipment market grew by 20 per cent from LVL 42 million in 1999 to LVL 50 million (excluding VAT). The market for computers, servers and portable computers totalled LVL 21.4 million that represents 43,000 units.

The best prospects for U.S. computer hardware exports to Latvia are new personal computers with the latest versions of processors, small and medium multi-processor servers and multimedia equipment, LAN accessories and relevant computer parts, IP related equipment. A very significant niche that recently opened is the second-hand and overstock personal computers market. Main customers there are private persons who obtain computers for use at home.

Sector Rank: 3
Sector Name: Computer Services
ITA Industry Code: CPS

During the past years the software development sector has significantly increased its role in country's economy and its exports. If according the Central Statistical Bureau in 1997, the added value in this sub-sector provided was USD 16 million or 0.3 per cent of GDP then its share in 2000 it reached 0.7 per cent of GDP. The Cabinet of Ministers of Latvia has adopted regulations that stipulate discounts on the corporate income tax of 30 per cent for enterprises where the supported products are established by regulations of, exceed 75% of net turnover in the taxation period and which are certified according to ISO 9001 or ISO 14001 standards which must further stimulate the sector.

One of Latvia's priorities since regaining independence has been to update the outdated tele- and data communications network, and large investment have been made both on telecommunication and high-speed data transmission networks.

Latvian government has adopted e-Latvia concept and program, which has a goal of country's and Nation's informatization. The most important element of the program is a mega-system -a logical unity of the information systems that have national importance: Population Register, Enterprise Register, Tax Payers Register, Cadastral Register, information system of the Road Traffic Safety Directorate. Besides there approximately 30 smaller branch information systems which address a specific sector, ministry or region. It is planned to integrate these systems in one united system. Several unified information systems programs' are under realization or in a project phase in order to establish a unified, interlinked database and data exchange system.

There was completed a pilot project for the Library Informational Network which linked first 8 libraries into a network. It was done with the assistance of The Andrew W. Mellon Foundation who donated USD 500,000. The next phase will be to connect to the network remaining 1400 public and school libraries and its estimated costs will be USD 20 million. This project is a part of the National library project and must be completed not later than December 31, 2008.

Government of Latvia and other institutions recognize that a system and network security issue becomes a top priority for further implementation of e-Latvia concept.

The majority of Latvian companies, government institutions and financial institutions have commenced the development of their IT systems, including back office systems, LANs, accounting and financial control systems. Most big to medium size enterprises are upgrading their IT systems with aim to take advantage of opportunities provided by e-business. Both electronic commerce and Internet are rapidly penetrating the Latvian market, increasing the need for IT related services and support. U.S. exports have very good prospects in the IT&T services sector are: Internet/intranet systems and networks implementation, education and training, and support services.

Sector Rank: 4
Sector Name: Drugs/Pharmaceuticals (DRG)
ITA Industry Code: DRG

There is a strong state influence on the medical services in Latvia. All the main hospitals and recreation centers are state owned and receive centralized financing from the state budget. Therefore the largest portion part of drugs and/pharmaceuticals procurement passes through as the state organized tenders.

In the same time retail and wholesale market of drugs and pharmaceuticals is completely in hands of private businesses.

Steady development of the economy (average 5-7 pct. Growth of GDP) have improved also the situation in the public welfare and have allowed for the state to increase procurement of drugs with highly added value. Pharmaceuticals totaled in 4.5 per cent of total Latvian imports or USD 182 million in 2002.

Some of prescribed drugs, like the ones used for diabetes, HIV, TB, are subsidized by the state and compensated to the pharmacies. Latvian state has indicated as priorities fight of the following diseases, such as Tuberculosis, Tick Encephalitis, HIV.

The way for the American pharmaceuticals company to enter the market would be either to open the branch or representative office in Latvia or to approach a Latvian wholesale company who have established its solid base and sound name there.

All the drugs sold in Latvia must be certified by the State Drugs Agency before entering the market. FDA certification is not enough for selling the drugs in Latvia, although FDA results will be helpful in certification process.

Sector Rank: 5
Sector Name: Sporting Goods/Recreational Eq. (SPT)
ITA Industry Code: SPT

There was significant visibility of development in sports recent years in Latvia. Latvians have "discovered" for themselves several kinds of sports unknown to the public earlier, like golf, bowling, pool a.o. Besides also old well known sports have received significant investments. In a few last years there were open several ice rinks all around in Latvia which in comparison with 1 and a half rinks before 1995 is a very important sign that Latvians have more time, money and interest in doing sports.
They are run on business for profit basis and have proved to be very popular, especially, the ones located outside the capital city Riga where entertainment possibilities are limited. The ice hockey teams are mushrooming which gives good opportunity for companies selling various ice-hockey equipment.
If before the turn of centuries fitness centers were booming offering just a place for work-out, and it was enough to attract customers, then now the competition requests to offer wide range of additional services, including café, professional trainers, pool, sauna etc. and at the high quality. However, there still is a room for new centers in a market as one could see from the price levels in Latvia, especially outside the capital city.
In 2002 there were open two new bowling centers in Riga and the first complete 18-hole golf course. As for the golf, then experts predict great future to it's development in Latvia taking into account largely unspoiled environment and location almost in the center of Europe next to Sweden, country with the largest per capita ratio of golf players.

General increase of wealth of the population also shows that there is very limited selection of good quality toys and games for kids in Latvia. None of the large companies have opened the store, yet. The first company who announced its intentions to open the amusement park there was Tivoli, Copenhagen. It will be the first try after Riga had to live with movable on-roads amusement parks who visited Riga for several years and had profitable business being the only such park offering entertainment for youth in the city with a population of 800'000.

Sector Rank: 6
Sector Name: Forestry/Woodworking equipment (FOR)
ITA Industry Code: FOR

Forestry and wood processing industry has a long tradition in Latvia. Some 45% of the land area is classified as forest out of which approximately 7 million acres are available for commercial forest operations. The approximate amount of annual timber harvest is 8.3 million cubic meters. Wood and Wood products count for 45 per cent of total Latvia's exports. The local saw mill industry has potential for expansion but the existing mills are in need of technology and machinery upgrades and the new establishments both managerial and marketing know-how. Timber and saw mill industries have potential for foreign investment. Both raw materials and labor are available at low cost. Since 1995 Latvia is trying to initiate recovery of pulp and paper industry. The Government of Latvia has "provided a green light" for a project to build cellulose plant in Latvia with a capacity of 600,000 t pulp per year. Swedish "Sodra group" and Finnish "Metsae-Serla" have been accepted as partners to Latvian Government in this project. According to the latest information the estimated costs of the plant will be around USD 960 million. The plant will be placed in Latgale (Latvia's Eastern region) near the Daugava river.
The annual allowable cut of pulpwood is 4 million m3 under bark annually which exceeds mill's demand (2.4 - 2.9 million m3 annually) for both softwood and hardwood. Currently, pulpwood is exported to Finland and Sweden. This is leaving plenty of room for developing smaller pulp and paper mills to Latvia.

Best prospects for U.S. exports are saw mill equipment, woodworking and furniture making machinery, plant technologies and training, pulp and paper mills (new and second hand).

Sector Rank: 7
Sector Name: Pollution Control Equipment
ITA Industry Code: POL

The Soviet era left behind heavy polluted large industrial areas, transportation crossroads and abandoned Russian army bases. Latvia is eager to invest funds and resources in environmental protection in order to meet the EU and other international convention requirements. Both Latvian Ministry of Environmental Protection and the municipal governments have implemented several environmental projects ranging from wastewater treatment to landfill.

Best prospects for U.S. exports in the environmental sector are counseling services, wastewater treatment technology, ozone-friendly technologies on industry level, pollution control equipment for oil and transportation industries and water supply and sewerage development. As a transit oriented country, Latvia also needs advanced technologies for various radiation pollution control at border crossing points, ports, railway hubs, etc. Latvia has allocated money in its budget for taking down the Salaspils Nuclear Reactor in 2003. This provides a good opportunity for companies who have relevant experience in similar operations or can offer special nuclear safety equipment like various detectors, containers etc.

TRADE REGULATIONS AND STANDARDS

The Latvian customs tariff system is still evolving. Under the tariff law that was adopted in December 1994, Latvian customs tariffs on raw materials, spare parts and capital goods are 0.5 to 1 percent. Latvia extends MFN treatment to U.S. products, with consumer product tariffs at about 15%. Tariffs on agricultural products are relatively higher, reflecting the attempt to protect the ailing farm sector. According to the Latvian -EU association agreement, tariffs on some agricultural and industrial goods of EU-origin will be gradually lowered starting in 1996. A new tariff law which enetered into force July 1, 1997 brings anti-dumping and counter-value measures and customs valuation in accord with WTO requirements. Valuation of agricultural products (reference prices) is based on EU import prices. Latvia currently licenses imports of sugar, grains, alcohol, fuel and arms. There are no other quantitative constraints on imports. Latvian tariff classifications are based on the Harmonized Commodity Description and Coding System (HCDC).

In addition to tariffs, imports are subject to excise taxes and the 18 percent VAT. Fixed investment goods imported into Latvia are not subject to VAT provided the importer is a registered VAT-payer and the imported asset does not threaten Latvian competitiveness. Zero percent tax rate is levied on export services, international transportation and services related to export of goods. Excise taxes are applied to alcoholic beverages, tobacco, jewelry, cars and gasoline, at rates varying from 10% (cars) to 100% (tobacco products). The excise tax on gasoline and diesel fuel is gradually being increased to European levels. Import documentation required by Latvian customs authorities are a copy of the contract, an invoice, a bill of lading indicating the amount, weight and value of goods, and an original copy of a certificate of origin (form EUR.1 or form A). At the border, an importer or his agent must complete a customs declaration and a customs freight delivery note.

For meat imports, the State Veterinary Department provides border inspection controls for bovine spongiform encephalopathy, classical swine fever, salmonella, etc. As of August 1996, imports of meat, milk and eggs are required to show that they at least meet Latvian quality standards. (Most countries' quality certificate are accepted.) A producer's declaration or a food conformity certificate is required for food imports, cosmetics and toys.

Transit freight (mainly to and from Russia) must take place in special customs convoys for shipments of non-ferrous metal or metal scrap or hazardous cargoes such as chemical, explosives, ammunition, or drugs, as well as alcohol or tobacco. The convoy fee is 100 lats per truck for non-ferrous metal shipments and Ls 50 for other types of cargoes. A high security deposit may be paid at the border in lieu of convoy. The security deposit is transferred to the customer's bank account two months after the shipment has left Latvian territory. Some Latvian exports (mainly raw materials, metals, antiques and art works) are subject to an export tax.

Latvia is pursuing foreign trade policies consistent with market reforms and the need to diversify country's trade partners beyond the former Soviet Union. On January 1, 1995, a phased implementation of the Free Trade Agreement with the European Union has begun. Latvia also has free trade agreements with EFTA countries, Ukraine, the Czech Republic, Slovakia and Slovenia. In April 1994, a trilateral free trade agreement between the three Baltic countries was implemented, abolishing all tariffs on industrial products. A separate agreement on agriculture, forestry and fishery products was concluded in mid-1996 and went into effect on January 1, 1997. In January 1997, Latvia and Poland initialed a free trade agreement, which is expected to go into force in July 1997 or January 1998. Latvia will probably concluded accession negotiations with the World Trade Organization later this year.

Latvia passed its current customs laws in October, 1994, with adjustments for the European Union requirements taking effect on July 1, 1997. Customs duties apply both to the import and export of goods. Latvia requires licenses for the import of grains, sugar, fuel, tobacco, alcohol and arms, and for the export of ferrous and non-ferrous metal scrap, ethyl alcohol, and spirits. Overall, there are 98 classes of goods which correspond to HS Codes. In case of disputes, the official European version of codification is used.

The transit of goods through Latvia is not a subject to import and export duties or Value Added Tax.

For goods to be declared as transit or for temporary import a non-resident may do the declaring by way of exception if approved by the State Revenue Service.

The applicable import rates vary depending on the origin and the type of the goods imported. Since Latvia is a member of WTO, rating practices required by this organization have been adopted in Latvia. The basic rate is from 0 to 55 percent. There are separate rates applicable to goods originating in countries with Most-Favored-Nation (MFN) status and with which Latvia has free-trade agreements. The basic 20% tariff rates are applied to the countries with which Latvia has no trade agreements however the basic tariff import rate is 15% for countries that have MFN status in trade with Latvia. These tariffs mainly are applied to goods deemed for the release for free circulation. Customs tariffs are lower or goods are completely exempt from tariffs for machinery/equipment, chemical products and metals. At the same time customs tariffs are higher for agricultural products: basic rate is 20%-55%, for the countries with MFN status - 15%-45%.

Export rates are not imposed on exports, except for art objects and antiquities (0-20%) and for goods with strategic value, namely minerals, metal and wood products.

The Customs Law provides for customs duty exemptions. Foreign investors most commonly exempt the temporary import of goods. Temporary import into Latvia may not exceed 24 months.

Besides customs duties, imports are also subject to excise, value-added-taxes (VAT) and tax on natural resources. VAT rates are either 0, 9 or 18 percent. However, as Latvia plans to join EU, VAT rates will have to change, as EU has requested to diminish 0 per cent VAT rate. This will influence such industries as press, medical services, pharmaceuticals and entertainment industry that currently are VAT exempt.

The following groups of supplies are subject to a zero percent VAT rate:

- Export of goods from Latvia
- Services which are related to the supply of goods outside Latvia
- Services and supply of goods not supplied within Latvia
- Supply of goods and services related to the maintenance and service of international transportation
- Tourism services in certain instances
- On the basis of reciprocity, services and goods related to diplomatic and consular officers enjoying immunity
- Certain services if the recipient is a non-resident

Foreign investors are Value Added Tax exempt on the foreign investment of fixed assets for manufacturing, provided that importer is a registered VAT-payer in Latvia.

VAT taxpayers are entitled to deduct the tax which they pay on supplies (input VAT) from the tax which they charge their customers (output VAT), provided that the input supplies relate to the activity of the taxpayer. Persons whose sales, excluding exempted sales, exceed 10,000 Lats (approx. USD 18,000) within a 12 month period must, within the following 30 days, be registered with the State Revenue Service for VAT payers.

Excise taxes are applied to soft drinks, coffee, tobacco products, alcoholic beverages (including beer and wine), gold/jewelry, and cars at various rates. Excise taxes for fuel and oil also apply, with the tax for petrol, oil, and diesel fuel ranging from USD 160 to USD 340 per 1000 litres. Oil gases are taxed at USD 85 per 1000 kilograms.

There are several exemptions from the excise tax in regard to vehicles, such as smaller cars and certain trucks. Since January 1, 2001, only cars that correspond to the EU technical requirements and standards can be registered in Latvia.

Excise tax for alcohol and tobacco products is generally paid by purchasing excise tax stamps.

Latvia has a TAX ON NATURAL RESOURCES that was adopted on 14 September 1995 and subsequently amended. The tax on natural resources also applies to **packaging of products.** The packaging tax is applied (at different rates) to glass, polymers, plastic, metal, paper, cardboard, laminates with metal or poly-metal components, pulp and other natural fibers raw materials and is payable on the border. For locally produced packaging, the tax should be paid by the 20th date of the month after the quarter during which the packaging was sold. In some occasions Government may grant a tax relief to a taxpayer that finances projects aimed at the reduction of environmental pollution, up to an amount of the financed sum.

Latvian customs authorities require the following documentation for imported goods/services: VAT payer certificate, an invoice, a bill of lading indicating the amount, weight and value of the goods, the original certificate of origin (from EUR.1 or form A), necessary licenses if such are applicable, and in case the deal includes multiple shipments, there also should be attached a copy of the contract. At the border, an importer or his agent must complete a customs declaration and a customs freight delivery note and show the documents confirming that all applicable duties had been paid. Document requirements for exports include a declaration, transport documentation, a contract, a certificate of origin, and a license. Transit enables the movement of Latvian goods, which are subject to the completion of the export procedure and the movement of non-Latvian goods from one customs office to another within the customs territory of the Republic of Latvia without any customs tariffs applied. The said movement is ensured by means of the following:
under the transit procedure;
under cover of a TIR carnet (TIR Convention);
under cover of an ATA carnet (ATA Convention) used as a transit document

State Revenue Service is planning to start to offer its customers the opportunity to submit all declarations in the electronic form via internet.

To obtain more detail information about the Latvian customs procedures and regulations you may at the Latvian Development Agency website: http://www.lda.gov.lv

There are over 60 customs warehouses in Latvia with storage terms that are unlimited in length. Products stationed there can be further processed in order to improve their appearance and prepare them for distribution or re-sale.

Latvia became a member of the World Trade Organization on February 10, 1999, and has free trade agreements with 26 countries, including all European Union and European Free-trade Association (EFTA) countries, the Czech Republic, Slovakia, Poland, Slovenia, Lithuania and

Estonia. The existing free-trade agreement with the Ukraine does not extend to food commodities. Latvia also has Most-Favored-Nation trade agreements with 21 other nations, including the United States, Canada, China, India, Australia, the CIS countries, and Hungary.

Latvia also has four special economic zones (SEZ) with eased tax regimes. They are the Ventspils Free Port (law "On the Ventspils Free Port", adopted on December 19, 1996), the Riga Free Port (law "On Riga Free Port", adopted March 9, 2000), the Liepaja Special Economic Zone (law "On the Liepaja Special Economic Zone," adopted on February 17, 1997) and the Rezekne Special Economic Zone (the law "On the Rezekne Special Economic Zone" adopted on October 1, 1997). More information on SEZ is available at the website: www.lda.gov.lv

There are several fields of businesses in Latvia, where a specific license is required **prior starting of business activities which can be obtained** from a relevant or local institution.

The following Latvian State institutions are responsible for issuing respective export/import or activities' licenses:

MINISTRY OF DEFENSE: import, export, transit through Latvia, sale of weaponry, ammunition, warfare technique, explosives and their parts.

FINANCIAL AND CAPITAL MARKET COMMISSION: issues special permits (licenses) or certificates authorizing operation in the financial and capital market in Latvia (such as banking, insurance, investment funds, brokerage activities etc.).

MUNICIPALITIES:
· services of shooting galleries shooting stands (after a permit is received from the relevant State police institution);
· cremation;
· commercial conveyance of passengers within the territory of the relevant municipality.

MINISTRY OF FINANCE and state institutions under its control and supervision:
· sale, manufacturing, services related to precious metals, precious stones and their articles as well as accepting the above as pledge objects;
· organizing and up-keeping of lotteries and gambling;
· investment companies activities;
· production, sale, import for free circulation and wholesales of tobacco products;
· production, import, wholesale and retail sale of alcohol;
· production, import, wholesale, retail sale and storage of fuel;
· repayment of value added tax to foreign physical persons for goods obtained in Latvia, which are taken out from Latvia;
· production of technical spirits.

MINISTRY OF WELLFARE and state institutions under its control and supervision:
· Training of employees in work protection, qualification of work protection specialists;
· Designing, processing, mantling, repairs, maintenance and modernizing of dangerous equipment;
· Blasting, pyrotechnics activities, as well as production and storing of articles and explosives used in blasting and pyrotechnics activities (after a permit is received from the relevant State police institution);
· Storage, sales and usage of dangerous substances for disinfection;
· Employment (except employment of sailors on ships);

MINISTRY OF HEALTH:

· Activities related to drugs and narcotics:
· Activities with radioactive substances and other ionizing irradiance used in medicine.

MINISTRY OF INTERIOR:
· Activities of detectives;
· Security activities;
· Import, export, processing, sales and repairs of hunting, sports, self defense weapons (inclusive small-arms, cold steel and airguns), ammunition, explosives and special means - gas revolvers and electroshock devices;
· Import, export and sales of pyrotechnics.

MINISTRY OF TRANSPORT and state institutions under its control and supervision license:
· Rail conveyance of passengers and freight;
· Airlifting;
· Special aviation activities;
· Commercial conveyance of passengers within the territory of Latvia and for international conveyance of passengers by bus;
· Commercial conveyance of freight within the territory of Latvia and for international conveyance of freight by truck;
· Retail trade of mechanical transport means, their units and sidecars;
· Conveyance of passengers and freight by sea transport;
· Underwater works related to exploitation of ports and ships;
· Post services;
· Mediation services for employment of sailors on ships;
· Wireless communication services.

MINISTRY OF ENVIRONMENT PROTECTION AND REGIONAL DEVELOPMENT and state institutions under its control and supervision:
· Entrepreneurship in construction (management, designing, consulting and execution of construction works);
· Activities with radioactive substances and other sources of ionizing irradiance (inclusive import and export);
· Aggregation of ship wastage and its utilization in ports;
· Liquidation of pollution consequences in aquatories.

MINISTRY OF AGRICULTURE and state institutions under its control and supervision:
· Import and export of grain;
· Veterinary pharmaceutical activities;
· Sales of plant protection means;
· Fishery and aqua-culture;
· Import of sugar, inclusive for inward processing;
· Wood servicing works.

STATE LAND SERVICE:
· Geodesy, topography, land surveying and servicing activities;
· Works on Photogrammetry and cartography;
· Depreciation and appreciation of real estate.

MINISTRY OF ECONOMY and state institutions under its control and supervision:
· Mediation services with privatization certificates;
· Obtaining and export of ferrous and non-ferrous metal's scrap;

· Activities with 1st and 2nd category precursors;
· Supply of heating and electrical energy, natural gas and liquid gas, if entrepreneurial activities are carried out in accordance with the law on energy.

MINISTRY OF EDUCATION AND SCIENCE issues licenses for opening of educational establishments.

NATIONAL BOARD OF RADIO AND TELEVISION issues broadcasting permits and re-translation permits and licenses activities of cable television and cable radio.

ELECTRO TECHNICAL COMISSION licenses for designing, processing, mantling and check-up of electrical equipment.

In general **fees for the licenses differ from LVL 5** (approx. USD 8.50) for the grains import or export license up **to LVL 20000** (approx. USD 34000) for commercial cross-border or national television broadcasting.
At the same time fees for licenses of the same activities **differ due to various factors**, for example:
activities with fuel:
import and wholesales LVL 200 (approx. USD 340);
retail sale LVL 30 (approx. USD 50).
opening of pharmacies:
in cities LVL 150 (approx. USD 250);
in rural areas LVL 70 (approx. USD 116).
commercial car transport conveyance:
if company has less then 5 transport units LVL 10 (approx. USD 16);
if company has more then 10 transport units LVL 50 (approx. USD 83).

CUSTOMS REGULATIONS

According to the Law on Customs Tarriffs of the Republic of Latvia every person is entitled to bring into the territory of Latvia goods up to 300 Ls (1 US $ is aproximately 0.52 Ls-Lats) worth without paying any duties.

There should be no more than three items per one kind of goods unless the total value of goods is equal to or less than 15 Ls.

The total value of food products should not exceed 15 Ls.

Every person at least 18 years old is entitled to bring in 1 liter or 1 unit (should not exceed 3 liters) of alcoholic drinks and 200 cigarettes or 20 cigars or 200 grams tobacco.

The total value of goods in each parcel sent by mail should not exceed 50 Ls.
Because of the veterinary or sanitary considerations the import of animals and food products can be restricted. It is suggested to check on these matters with the Veterinary Department of Latvia (Phone: +371 2 327474, 327473) or Sanitary Department of Latvia (+ 371 2 379287, 375928).

When importing cars into Latvia custom tax (according to current tariff scedule), VAT (18 %) and excise tax (10 %) have to be paid.

It is allowed to bring arms in Latvia only if special permission is obtained from the Department of Police of the Ministry of Interior Affairs of Latvia. Address: Stabu iela 89, Riga, LV-1009, Latvia , phone: + 371 7208618)

The import of medicine is also restricted. The amount of medicine should not exceed the amount necessary for the time of traveling. In case the medicine contains narcotics permission from the

Department of Pharmacy of the Ministry of Welfare of Latvia has to be obtained. (address: Skolas iela 28, Riga, LV-1331, Latvia , phone: +371 7273619, fax: + 371 7276445)

BASIC EXPORT REGULATION

Customs Valuation: What are the duties and taxes to be paid at Customs?

All tax payments must be paid at the border, unless cargo is forwarded to a bonded warehouse.

Duty

The Latvian customs tariff system is still evolving. Under the tariff law that was adopted in December 1994, Latvian customs tariffs on raw materials, spare parts, and capital goods are .5 to 1 percent. Latvia extends MFN treatment to U.S. products, with consumer product tariffs at about 15%. Tariffs on agricultural products are relatively higher.

Duties vary by the good that is exported. CEEBIC at Tel:(202)482-2645 can provide the duty rate if exporter supplies the Harmonized code for the good. Harmonized codes can be found on the internet by running a key word search on the Census Bureau web site at:

or by calling Customs Service at Tel:(202)301-457-3492.
*The duty is assessed on the CIF, or cost, insurance and freight.

Import Tax

There is no import tax in Latvia.

VAT

The Value Added Tax is a European type of sales tax that is applied at all stages of production of a good, and is also applied to export transactions. The VAT rate in Latvia is 18%. Fixed investment goods imported into Latvia are not subject to VAT provided the importer is a registered VAT-payer and the imported asset does not threaten Latvian competitiveness. Zero percent tax is levied on export services, international transportation, and services related to export of goods. *The VAT is assessed on the CIF plus the amount paid in duties.

Excise taxes, Consumption taxes and Luxury taxes

Excise taxes are applied to alcoholic beverages, tobacco, jewelry, cars, and gasoline at rates varying from 10 percent (cars) to 100 percent (tobacco). The excise tax on gasoline and diesel fuel is gradually being increased to European levels.

Exemptions from taxes and duties

The customs duty is not applied to:

- Latvian and foreign currency and securities

- Goods supplied within the framework of investment and credit agreements concluded by the Cabinet of Ministers to implement the projects included in the Public Investment Programme
- Transit cargo haulage
- Goods brought to or out of customs warehouses of Latvia or inland customs zones
- Property imported into the Republic of Latvia as a foreign investment not designated for sale
- Humanitarian aid consignments and gifts
- Inherited property and household articles of natural persons
- Goods for use or consumption at exhibitions
- Goods for the disabled
- Mass media
- Other goods in cases specified by law

Goods not for re-sale

According to the Law on Customs Tariffs of the Republic of Latvia, every person is permitted to bring into the territory of Latvia-DUTY FREE- goods not exceeding 300 Lats (approximately $575) in value. There should be no more than three items of one type of good unless the total value of said good is less than 15 Lats (approximately $28). The total value of food products should not exceed 15 Lats. Every person at least 18 years old is allowed to bring in 1 liter or 1 unit (not exceeding 3 liters) of alcoholic beverages, 200 cigarettes, 20 cigars, or 200 grams of tobacco duty free. The total value of each parcel (gift) sent by mail should not exceed 50 Lats (approximately $96) in order to enter duty free.

Import Documentation

Entrepreneurs and companies registered in the Republic of Latvia have the right to declare goods (this does not refer to transit cargo transporters). Goods are declared by submission of a filled-in standard declaration form and other documents to a customs institution. At the border, an importer or his agent must complete a customs declaration and a customs freight delivery note. The following documents are indispensable:

The contract of the deal or its copy, invoice, consignment note
Bill of lading indicating the amount, weight, and value of goods
Original copy of a certificate of origin (form EUR.1 or form A)
A notarized registration certificate of the entrepreneur or company
A license if transportation of the particular goods across the border of the Republic of Latvia is restricted
A warranty entitling the holder to act on behalf of the entrepreneur or business company
In specific cases, certificates verifying that the goods in transit are not hazardous to health or environment.

A Latvian language label with information on ingredients, producer, country, importer name, and consumption end-date is mandatory for food products. Such a label should be attached to each retail package, unless the original product package contains the required information.

Quotas.

Quotas of customs duties with a term up to one year are used to permit the import or export of a limited amount of goods at reduced rates of customs duties or a zero rate, thus distributing the volume of customs tariff quotas provided for by international agreements. The quotas are set in order of a competition for particular importers and exporters by the Consultative Council of Customs Tariffs. The decisions of which serve as the basis for the Ministries of Agriculture and Economy to issue licenses.

Import Licenses

Latvia currently licenses imports of alcohol, fuel, and arms. In 1997, Latvia lifted the licensing requirement for grains and sugar, however, a formal procedure for registering imports remains for statistical purposes.

For food imports, a producer's declaration or a food conformity certificate has been required for food products under HS code groups 2-4, 7-12, and 15-23 since July 1995. The conformity certificate should be issued by an accredited laboratory. Imported products have to be approved for sale in Latvia. Prior to issuing a retail sale permit, the National Food Center (NFC) tests and certifies all commodities. The procedure may include sampling and testing of product for conformity to Latvian regulations.

The Latvian veterinary department applies unified import certification of meat and meat products, dairy products, and fish. The veterinary certificates for U.S. poultry and beef imports were agreed in 1995. Currently, veterinary legislation is being adjusted to EU accession requirements. One should check on these matters with:

Veterinary Department of Latvia
tel: (371-2) 327-474; 327-473

Sanitary Department of Latvia
tel: (371-2) 379-287; 375-928

The importation of arms into Latvia is only permitted through special permission obtained from:
Department of Police of the Ministry of Interior Affairs of Latvia
Stabuiela 89
Riga, LV-1009, Latvia
tel: (371-7) 208-618

The import of medicine is restricted. In case the medicine contains narcotics permission must be obtained from:
Department of Pharmacy of the Ministry of Welfare of Latvia
Skolas iela 28
Riga, LV-1331, Latvia
tel: (371-7) 273-619
fax: (371-7) 276-445

EXPORT LICENSES

Most high-tech western technology can flow into Central and Eastern Europe without U.S. Export Licenses. However, the goods that need an export license are different for every individual country and are constantly changing. Generally, defense products and equipment such as optical equipment and software that may have a dual usage still require an export license. Export licenses can be obtained from the Bureau of Export Administration (Or BXA at the US

Department of Commerce). BXA coordinates the licensing process with the Departments of State and Defense.

If an exporter has a good that he/she believe may need a license, he/she must determine the Export Commodity Control Number (ECCN) from the manufacturer. He/she can also obtain this number form by filling out the BXA-748 Multipurpose Form. It can be obtained by calling BXA's form request line at (202)482-3332. This form also serves as the application for the export license itself. BXA's telephone number for specific questions about Export Licenses is: (202)482-4811.

STANDARDS AND QUALITY CONTROL

For meat imports, the State Veterinary Department provides border inspection controls for bovine spongiform encephalopathy, classical swine fever, salmonella, etc.

For Further Information Contact:

Latvian Customs Department
Normunds Niedols, Director
Kr. Valdemara Street
1 a, Riga LV-1841, Latvia
Tel: (371) 732-3858
Fax: (371) 732-2440

Latvian National Certification Center
H. Jurevica, Director
Klijanu Street 7
Tel: (371) 237-5667
Fax: (371) 237-5464

Company which prepares all customs documents and policies
Mr. Andris Spulis, Director
Komin Ltd.
Perses street 2
Riga, LV 1011
tel: (371-7) 228-647 or tel/fax: (371-7) 227-774

BANKING SYSTEM IN LATVIA

During the second half of 1997 and in 1998, a considerable improvement in the main macroeconomic indicators of the Latvian economy took place. In 1996, GDP growth was 2.8%, and a 4% growth is forecast for the current year. The end-of-year inflation in 1996 was 13.1%, and a further decline in the consumer price index continued in 1997, reaching 8.1% on a year-to-year basis by the end of September. These developments allow us to forecast single digit inflation for this year. Fiscal policy was tightened considerably in 1996, and the year was ended with a general government fiscal deficit of 1.3% of GDP. The central government budget for the current year is balanced.

Increasing confidence in Latvian economic policies has resulted in a noticeable decline in interest rates. The discount rates on government T-bills with maturity up to one year have come down to the level of 3.5%-5.5%. The first issue of government two-year bonds was sold at a discount rate of 9.5%. The Bank of Latvia reduced its refinancing rate to 4% in April 1997 and extended the duration of this facility to up to 3 months.

The interbank money market has responded to the economic developments by a considerable increase in volumes of operations and stabilisation of interest rates for transactions in the national currency at the level of 3.0%-3.5%.

The continuing macroeconomic stabilisation has provided a solid basis for the further development of the Latvian banking system. Already the results of 1996 showed that the banking sector had fully recovered from the problems experienced in 1995. During 1996, all major indicators of the banking sector - assets, equity, deposits and credits - increased by 30%-40% and exceeded the pre-crisis level. Banks finished the year with a net profit of 30 million lats (around 54 million US dollars), and, most notably, 90% of the profit was used to strengthen their capital base.

The first eight months of 1997 witnessed further strengthening of the Latvian banking sector. By the end of this period, total assets had reached 1.5 billion lats (around 2.6 billion US dollars), and total equity 187 million lats (320 million US dollars). During the eight months, the total assets of the banking sector increased by 34%, total equity by 26%, deposits by 27% and credits by 36%.

The profitability of banks has also grown: total net profit for the first 6 months of 1997 was 22 million lats. This shows a notable level of efficiency - a 4% return on assets, and a 24% return on equity for the whole banking industry.

The Bank of Latvia continued to improve its supervisory practices and the regulatory framework. New regulations on annual financial statements of commercial banks and a new format of monthly balance sheet statements have been introduced. To assist the management of commercial banks, the Bank of Latvia has established guidelines for internal control systems in credit institutions.

The positive macroeconomic developments have allowed the Bank of Latvia to eliminate reserve requirements on liabilities to foreign banks as of April this year.

The achieved stability and rapid development of the Latvian banking sector is evident. This gives a good reason for further and more rigorous evaluation of the domestic banking industry in conformity with international standards and criteria.

Latvia is strongly committed to become a full member of the European Union. This is our strategic objective. Therefore, we have to assess the readiness of the banking sector to follow the Community rules and to provide services at the same level of effectiveness and guarantees as in the European Union. And, especially, we have to assess our ability to withstand the increasing competition that the integration process will inevitably lead to.

Recently we have received that assessment from the European Commission itself. The "Agenda - 2000" document expresses the opinion of the Commission on Latvia's application for membership of the European Union. The evaluation of the financial services sector forms part of the report. We have to admit that the opinion of the Commission on the Latvian banking system is highly critical. Though we can question some data used in the report, and argue that the rapid pace of development has not been adequately assessed, we have to recognise the problems indicated by the Commission and concentrate on resolving them.

The main criticism of the European Commission is not directed towards the legal and regulatory framework for banking activities. It is recognised in the report that the banking regulations in Latvia are "well advanced" and would not form an obstacle for the country's integration into the

Union in a medium term. Indeed, the main requirements of the Community directives for banking activities have been incorporated into the Law "On Credit Institutions" and the Bank of Latvia's regulations.

Additional measures in the area of financial services are under way. Draft laws against money laundering and on deposit insurance have been prepared and are in the legislative process. The rapid advancement of the financial sector requires implementation of further Community requirements. Namely, directives on consolidated accounts, on investment services and on capital adequacy. The Bank of Latvia has started to work on these regulations for credit institutions.

It should be also admitted that the essentials for the development of the banking system, still non-existent in some of the transition economies, had been established in Latvia at an early stage. These include full liberalisation of financial services, abolition of foreign exchange restrictions both on current and capital accounts, opening the domestic markets for foreign competitors and changing the ownership structure of the banking sector from state-dominated to privately owned.

The early resolution of the mentioned issues in Latvia, as well as the introduction of Community requirements for banking activities, in our opinion, have created an environment for banking activities that is close to international standards.

However, the main concerns expressed in the Commission report apply to the functioning of banks themselves, despite the well-established regulatory framework.

I would like to comment on the three major problems indicated in the report: poor capitalisation of banks, rather weak bank lending and a significant amount of non-performing loans.

The report says that Latvian banks are "weak" and "undercapitalised". Obviously, the point is not capital adequacy, which is quite high in the Latvian banking sector. However, we cannot deny that Latvian banks are still rather small measured by international standards. Though capital is growing rapidly, the small size of most of our banks might become a serious obstacle for both competing successfully in the domestic and international markets and for undertaking large and important projects.

According to Latvian legislation, all commercial banks have to attain the minimum capital level of 2 million lats by April 1, 1998. A further increase to 5 million ECU must be completed by the end of 1999. Obviously, the vast majority of banks will be able to comply with these minimum requirements, but we would warn bankers against viewing the established "floor" as a comfortable resting-place in future.

As a rule, small banks can only exist if their high operating costs are covered by uncommonly high returns on certain types of investment. Though still available, such opportunities may soon disappear. It is rather clear that, in the long run, small banks with limited resources and narrow range of operations will not be competitive, even if they are viable in current circumstances.

Many of the small banks have focused on servicing non-resident customers, and this business so far has proved to be profitable. However, this type of activity requires skilful forecasting of economic developments in neighbouring countries, as well as full awareness of the risks involved. The risks are sometimes quite unpredictable, as some of our banks have recently experienced in St. Petersburg. In our opinion, these events should serve as a warning to the banking community that continuous success in the CIS markets must not be taken for granted.

In general, the concentration of the banking sector is continuing in Latvia, and the four biggest banks now hold more than a half of total assets. The Bank of Latvia cannot accelerate the consolidation process artificially; however, we would favour further developments in this direction.

Bank lending is another area of criticism in the Commission's report. It is stated, that bank lending in Latvia is weak and the intermediary role of the banking sector in supporting domestic investment is far from adequate. In addition, the maturity of loans is considered rather short, and the spread between deposit and lending rates much too high.

Nevertheless, the latest developments in the banking sector show positive signs. As already mentioned, bank lending capacity has considerably strengthened during the eight months of this year. An increase in lending to the private sector is particularly promising. From January to August, growth in credits to private enterprises was 52%, and to private persons 46%, compared to overall growth in lending by 36%.

Notable changes have also taken place in respect of the maturity of loans. By the end of August, loans with the maturity of one year and longer comprised around 44% of gross loans of the Latvian banking sector, compared to 32% at the beginning of the year. In eight months, total medium- and long-term loans increased by 89%, compared to only 7% growth in short-term lending. These figures clearly outline a gradual shift from short-term trade finance towards an increased focus on lending to the productive sector of economy.

As positive as these developments are, they do not allow us to question seriously the European Commission's criticism. Despite the rapid growth in volume, loans still comprise only around 25% of bank assets. This figure is below the international standards, and obviously does not correspond to the needs of the economy. Besides, the credit / asset ratio of the banking sector has even decreased slightly since the end of 1995. The other similar indicator, domestic credit / GDP ratio, also stands at a rather low level of 9.4%, though it has improved somewhat in 1997.

The spread between deposit and lending rates, though not 15% as mentioned in the Commission's report, is still between 7% and 10% on the average, and thus, without doubt, high.

What are the reasons for the insufficient progress in the described areas?

Regretfully, I have to mention the same impediments to bank lending that have been noted already at the previous conferences. Namely, slow progress in enterprise restructuring and privatisation, delay in apartment privatisation, insufficient speed of the titling and registration of land and movable property, and lack of proper accounting in the enterprise sector.

Although some progress has taken place in the mentioned areas during the previous year, the problem of collateral is still far from being resolved. As a result, banks still have to seriously consider how to extend standard quality loans in a sub-standard business environment. And the spread between deposit and lending rates is mostly the price for the excessive risks.

Until recently, due to loose fiscal policies, discount rates were high, and the state was crowding out private borrowers from the credit market and affecting the lending policies of banks. The situation has changed dramatically during the last year, but banks obviously need more time to forget the previous easy gains and shift over to a more sophisticated lending.

The markets to the east of Latvia still offer high returns on central and local government securities, as well as on some other types of investments. However, macroeconomic stabilisation in our neighbouring countries reduces opportunities for comparatively easy earnings, and banks should be aware of this when planning their future policies.

Another reason hampering progress in bank lending is lack of long-term resources. More than 80% of deposits in the Latvian banking sector are demand deposits. This results in excess short-term resources and a rather limited potential for medium- and long-term lending. There are no reasons to expect fast accumulation of domestic long-term resources in the near future. Therefore, this problem can be currently resolved only by attracting foreign financing, and several Latvian banks have started this quite successfully.

However, there are at least two obstacles for expanding this type of international co-operation. First, most of Latvian banks are too small to arouse substantial interest in foreign partners. And secondly, sufficient transparency is considered a necessary precondition for partnership. As frequently indicated by foreign bankers, there are Latvian banks that do not satisfy this requirement. Certainly, it depends on banks themselves whether they would become attractive enough partners for the international banking community.

The excessive amount of bad loans is another problem of the Latvian banking sector pointed out in the Commission's report. In our opinion, the large share of non-performing loans (large by western standards) in total lending reflects the contradictions between the high demand of new businesses for credits on the one hand, and high risks in lending to new customers on the other hand. No transition economy can avoid these contradictions, and they cannot be overcome in the short term.

However, the recent developments in the Latvian banking sector are quite promising also in this respect. Despite the considerable increase in lending, both the share of non-performing loans in overall lending and their total volume are declining.

Currently, 15% of gross loans are classified as non-performing, compared to 20% at the end of 1996. Of gross loans, 8% fall into the category of lost or bad. These figures are certainly far from western banking standards, but they reflect a realistic approach to loan classification in a transition economy.

Under such circumstances, loan loss provisioning is very important. In Latvia, the loan loss provisioning scheme is adequately developed and tight. All non-performing loans are fully covered by provisions. Thus the bad loans, though influencing bank profitability, do not pose a threat to the stability of the Latvian banking system.

The transition process itself, by its nature, generates problems and contradictions that western economies do not experience. Latvia, and the Latvian banking system in particular, is not an exception in this respect. In my opinion, it is important that we recognise the problems and challenges, and find the right way to master them, though not all problems can be eliminated instantly.

The recent developments show that Latvian banks are well on their way to meeting rigid international standards. We are fully confident that the current growth of the banking sector is of a very different nature than it was in the first years of the transition, as it goes hand in hand with the positive changes in the general economy. The adequate regulatory framework and supervisory practices established by the Bank of Latvia will provide for the further stability of the banking system which currently is in the process of rapid development.

SUPERVISION OF CREDIT INSTITUTIONS IN THE REPUBLIC OF LATVIA

Credit institutions form a significant sector in a national economy. They accumulate money resources of both individuals and legal entities, ensure functioning of a payment system in a state, and are the largest providers of loans in the market. Ensuring of these functions is a significant prerequisite in building up a sound system of economic relationships. The necessity to perform a centralized supervision of credit institutions has been recognized world-wide.

One of the main supervision aims is to provide for the stability, soundness and development of banks. Mere existence of the supervision system cannot guarantee the soundness of banks; moreover, giving of any strict guarantees would be an unacceptable interference into free market relationship. The aim of supervision is to pinpoint problems that are likely to arise and to assist banks in avoiding them, as well as to curb negative economic consequences. In order to attain this goal, the central bank elaborates various requirements to the activities of banks, which are aimed at reduction of risks. At the same time, freedom of the management of a credit institution in taking decisions is hindered as little as possible.

LEGAL FRAMEWORK FOR SUPERVISION

SUPERVISORY AUTHORITY

Pursuant to Article 10 of the Law "On the Bank of Latvia", the Bank of Latvia performs supervision as well as on-site and off-site examinations of credit institutions. To ensure this function, the Credit Institutions Supervision Department has been formed within the Bank of Latvia. The Department issues licences (Licensing and Legal Divisions), supervises credit institutions (Supervision Division), participates actively in elaborating legislative bills governing banks' activities, and works out the Bank of Latvia's regulations (Methodological and Analytical Division).

LEGAL FRAMEWORK FOR THE ACTIVITIES OF BANKS

1. Republic of Latvia laws:

- Law "On Entrepreneurial Activity" (adopted on September 26, 1990);
- Law "On Cooperative (Joint Activity) Companies" (adopted on August 6, 1991);
- Law "On the Bank of Latvia" (adopted on May 19, 1992);
- Law "On Bookkeeping" (adopted on October 14, 1992);
- Law "On Joint-Stock Companies" (adopted on May 18, 1993);
- Law "On Securities" (adopted on August 23, 1995);
- Law "On Credit Institutions" (adopted on October 5, 1995).

2. Bank of Latvia regulations:

- "On General Principles Regarding the Annual Report, Balance Sheet, and Profit and Loss Account of Credit Institutions" (approved on September 21, 1993);
- "Provisions on Accounting Income and Expenses of Credit Institutions" (approved on January 11, 1996);
- "Provisions on Estimation of Credit and Off-Balance-Sheet Liabilities" (approved on January 17, 1996);
- "Regulations on Issuing Licences (Permissions) to Credit Institutions" (approved on March 14, amended on July 11, 1996);
- "Regulations on Amending the Charter, Changing the Shareholders, the Initial Capital, the Management, the Chief Accountant, the Legal Address, the Name of Credit Institutions, and Undertaking Merger or Split-Up of Credit Institutions" (approved on March 15, 1996);

- "Regulations on Calculating the Indicators that Characterize Activities of Credit Institutions" (approved on May 17, 1996).

LICENSING OF CREDIT INSTITUTIONS

Credit institutions, their branches and representative offices may begin their activities only after they have received a licence (permit) from the Bank of Latvia. To receive the licence a bank has to submit the following documents:

1. Founding documents, the charter and documents regulating the activity of the credit institution that give a clear idea of its intended activity and organisational structure corresponding to this activity.
2. A document certifying that the minimum initial capital has been paid in.
3. References characterizing the candidates to the positions of the Chairperson of the Board, his/her first Deputy, and the Chief Accountant.
4. Documentation on the financial standing of the founders of a bank, which evidences the adequacy of the financial funds at their disposal.
4.1. If the founder is a legal entity
4.1.1. registered in the Republic of Latvia - a document issued by the Department of the State Revenue Service of the corresponding district, which certifies that this legal entity has been registered as a tax-payer and has paid all amounts payable to the budget, as well as audited financial statements for the two last operational years.
4.1.2. registered abroad - documents required by the legislation of its domicile.
4.2. If the founder is an individual
4.2.1. A resident, whose investment will exceed 14 000 lats - a copy of the declaration of annual income certified by the Department of the State Revenue Service in his/her district of residence.
4.2.2. A non-resident - a document issued by the bank with which he/she holds accounts, which states the average accounts' balances in the current year, and a copy of the income declaration.

There are several demands that a foreign bank has to fulfil in order to obtain a licence for opening of a branch or representative office in the Republic of Latvia. A foreign bank has to be at least in Category A (a low expectation of investment risk) if the bank's capacity to meet its obligations in long-term is evaluated and in Category B (a bank with a sound risks profile and without significant problems) if the bank is evaluated individually according to IBCA (International Bank Credit Agency) ratings. Moreover, the initial capital of a foreign bank may not be less than 100 million US dollars.

STANDARDS TO THE INITIAL CAPITAL OF A CREDIT INSTITUTION

The minimum initial capital of a bank is equivalent to 5 million ECU and is calculated in lats according to the exchange rate set by the Bank of Latvia. Those banks that have been registered before the Law "On Credit Institutions" came into effect have to observe the Transitional Provisions of the Law, which stipulate that the minimum initial capital of a bank is:

1. not less than 100 000 lats from the date the Law "On Credit Institutions" takes effect to March 31, 1996;
2. not less than 1 000 000 lats from April 1, 1996 to March 31, 1998;
3. not less than 2 000 000 lats from April 1, 1998 to December 31, 1999.

The minimum initial capital of a credit union is equivalent to 50 thousand ECU and is calculated in lats according to the exchange rate set by the Bank of Latvia. Credit unions that have been registered before the Law "On Credit Institutions" came into effect have to comply with these standards gradually by January 1, 2000.

REGULATIONS GOVERNING ACTIVITIES OF CREDIT INSTITUTIONS

Since the re-establishment of the Bank of Latvia in 1991, the Bank has tailored and developed the supervisory system in Latvia. The main EU directives, counsels of the International Monetary Fund (IMF), International Accounting Standards, as well as the experience in supervising credit institutions of other countries had to be introduced. The Bank of Latvia carried out the reforms in a relatively short period of time, and by 1995, when the banking crisis began, most of the new regulations had already been introduced. Prior to the Republic of Latvia's formal application for accession to the EU, the Bank of Latvia had started to introduce those most important EU directives concerning the banking sector, the observance of which is a prerequisite in becoming a full-fledged member state of the EU. The Bank of Latvia undertook these reforms not only to satisfy the requirements of EU directives, but also to create a strong and stable banking environment. With the adoption of the Law "On Credit Institutions", these requirements acquired legal force.

CAPITAL ADEQUACY RATIO

The proportion of a credit institution's own funds to risk-weighted assets and off-balance-sheet items may not be less than 10%. This requirement follows the Directive on solvency ratio for credit institutions (89/647/EEC) and the Directive on the own funds of credit institutions (89/299/EEC). The Bank of Latvia has fixed higher weighting applied to some categories of assets items and has defined a credit institution's own funds more strictly than it has been done in the above directives.

LARGE CREDIT EXPOSURES

A credit institution's exposure is considered to be large if its value exceeds 10% of a credit institution's own funds. The total of large exposures may not exceed a credit institution's own funds more than eight-fold. A credit institution has to report about a loan that exceeds 100 000 lats to the Bank of Latvia within a week after the loan has been extended. Exposure to a single customer or a group of connected customers may not exceed 25% of a credit institution's own funds. The total of a credit institution's exposures to persons related to the credit institution may not exceed 15% of its own funds.

LIQUIDITY RATIO

A credit institution must place its assets so that it is able to satisfy legally motivated claims of its creditors at any time. In order to ensure liquidity, a credit institution must:

1. assess and plan the term structure of its assets and liabilities;
2. keep liquid assets in the amount necessary to meet its liabilities, but not less than 30% of current total liabilities.

OPEN FOREIGN EXCHANGE POSITIONS

The open foreign exchange position in any single currency may not exceed 10% of a credit institution's own funds. The total open foreign exchange position may not exceed 20% of a credit institution's own funds.

PARTICIPATION IN UNDERTAKINGS

A credit institution's participation in an undertaking (other than a bank) may not exceed 15% of a credit institution's own funds. The total of such participations may not exceed 60% of a credit institution's own funds.

PROVISIONS FOR LOAN LOSSES

A credit institution has to assess its assets and off-balance-sheet liabilities. Credits are classified as standard, close-watch, substandard, doubtful and bad/lost credits. Off-balance-sheet liabilities are classified in the same manner, evaluating the borrower's financial standing and solvency. Provisions for credits and off-balance-sheet liabilities have to be made in the following amounts: 10% of credit institution's own funds for close-watch items, 30% for substandard, 60% for doubtful and 100% for bad/lost. Provisions for loan losses are expenses that decrease profit and even incur losses to a credit institution; this results in a reduction in a credit institution's own funds, bringing into foreground the necessity to attract additional shareholders' capital in order to replenish capital basis and to protect depositors' interests.

SUPERVISORY PRACTICE

REPORTING REQUIREMENTS ESTABLISHED BY THE BANK OF LATVIA

Pursuant to Article 39 of the Law "On the Bank of Latvia", the Bank of Latvia approves reporting forms of statistical reports for banks and other credit institutions, as well as the procedures of submitting such forms. A credit institution is required to submit to the Bank of Latvia the information that is necessary for the Bank in order to perform its functions. The following information is collected on a regular basis:

1. Monthly balance sheet statement (monthly)
2. Profit and loss statement (quarterly)
3. Report on classification of credits and off-balance-sheet liabilities (quarterly)
4. Report on indicators characterizing the activity of a credit institution (monthly): capital adequacy, the term structure of assets and liabilities, liquidity ratio, large exposures, exposures to persons related to the credit institution, open foreign exchange positions

ANNUAL FINANCIAL STATEMENTS AND AUDIT

A credit institution draws up annual financial statements that include a balance sheet, a profit and loss account with appendices, and a report of the Council and Board of the credit institution, for every year of its activity. The duty of a credit institution is to ensure that its annual financial statements are available at its premises not later than on April 1 of the year following the reporting year and that anyone interested in this information may receive the full text of the annual financial statements for the price not exceeding their administrative cost. The annual financial statements have to be submitted to the Bank of Latvia within ten days after they have been approved by the general meeting of a credit institution's shareholders but not later than three months after the end of the reporting year. After the annual financial statements have been submitted to the Bank of Latvia, a credit institution publishes its balance sheet and auditors' report in the newspaper *Latvijas Vestnesis*, indicating that the short version of the annual financial statements is being published and that these statements in full are available at the credit institution, not later than on May 1 of the year following the reporting year.

The audit of a credit institution's annual financial statements may be carried out by an auditor that is approved by the Bank of Latvia. The 1995 financial statements of banks were audited by internationally recognized auditing companies *Arthur Andersen, Coopers & Lybrand, Price Waterhouse, Deloitte Touche Tohmatsu International* and *KPMG*. The annual financial statements of a credit institution are audited in accordance with the Law "On Credit Institutions" and International Standards on Auditing.

Banks that are entitled to attract deposits from individuals also publish the balance sheet and profit (loss) account as at the end of the first, second and third quarters in the newspaper *Latvijas Vestnesis* not later than a month after the end of the quarter.

In 1996, by the request of the Bank of Latvia, the above auditor companies audited the quality of reviews submitted to the Bank of Latvia by the banks that were entitled to attract private person deposits in the respective period of time, as well as assessed semi-annual financial statements of such banks.

THE BANK OF LATVIA'S ON-SITE EXAMINATIONS OF CREDIT INSTITUTIONS

Pursuant to Article 106 of the Law "On Credit Institutions", the Bank of Latvia performs regular on-site examinations in credit institutions at least once a year. Lending, especially to shareholders, and other banking transactions are examined. Reports on the results of examinations are prepared and mailed together with a cover letter requiring that the credit institution eliminates the discovered deficiencies. Most often it is necessary to establish additional provisions for bad debts.

In accordance with the Law "On Credit Institutions", the Bank of Latvia is entitled to apply intensified supervision in the following cases:

1. The total amount of paid-up capital of a credit institution, retained capital or losses is less than the paid-up capital of a credit institution.
2. Capital adequacy of a credit institution is less than 10%.
3. A credit institution violates requirements to the activities of credit institutions, and the Board of a credit institution fails to ensure that these requirements are met on a regular basis.

If intensified supervision procedures are applied, the Bank of Latvia is entitled to:

1. issue a warning to a credit institution;
2. stop allowing the credit institution to utilize the Bank of Latvia's credit facility;
3. suspend servicing of foreign exchange transactions of the credit institution;
4. prohibit the credit institution to invest in assets of low liquidity;
5. restrict or prohibit the credit institution's activity in taking deposits;
6. restrict or prohibit the credit institution's activity in lending;
7. suspend the credit institution's transactions through correspondent accounts;
8. suspend partly or completely the authorisation to conduct other banking transactions.

In order to control the fulfilment of requirements set by intensified supervision procedures, the Bank of Latvia is entitled to appoint an authorised representative.

The Bank of Latvia is entitled to revoke the licence of a credit institution if:

1. the credit institution has failed to commence its activity within twelve months after it has been granted a licence;
2. it is established that the credit institution has submitted false information in order to receive the licence;
3. the credit institution performs banking operations that are not provided for in the licence;
4. the credit institution regularly fails to comply with the requirements of the Law "On Credit Institutions" and Bank of Latvia regulations;
5. the credit institution has been declared bankrupt.

When revoking the licence granted to a bank, the Bank of Latvia lodges a claim with the Court to liquidate the said credit institution.

The Law "On Credit Institutions" passed by the Saeima of the Republic of Latvia and amendments to the Code of Administrative Offences of Latvia and the Criminal Code of Latvia elaborated responsibilities of credit institutions, their shareholders, management, employees as well as customers. These laws provide for administrative and criminal liability for deliberate rendering of incorrect or incomplete information, for concealing information required by the law, for utilizing a credit for the purpose not stipulated in the credit agreement, and for non-observance of the law governing activities of credit institutions and of binding regulations established by the Bank of Latvia.

DEVELOPMENT OF THE BANKING SECTOR

The Bank of Latvia has granted licences to 67 banks (to 14 banks in 1991, to 36 in 1992, to 16 in 1993, to 1 in 1994).

From 1992 to 1994, total assets of the banking sector increased more than three-fold.

Out of 55 banks having licences at the end of 1994, 47 banks were able to submit their annual financial statements for 1994. Of these, only 16 had ended the year with profit.

The number of banks decreased drastically in 1995. The Bank of Latvia revoked licences of 15 banks, and at the end of the year, 38 banks were operating.

As a result of the banking crisis, the demand for foreign currencies increased in the Latvian foreign exchange market. The Bank of Latvia offset speculative pressures on the exchange rate of the lats, maintaining the stability in the foreign exchange market.

The main causes of the 1995 banking crisis were as follows.

- The banking sector developed more rapidly than the economic environment.
- The real estate and securities markets were weak; therefore, it was difficult to obtain secure and liquid collateral for loans.
- Both bankers and businessmen lacked experience how to work in a market economy.
- Lending and business plans were assessed incorrectly. Due to the incompetence of banks' managements, developments in the financial and foreign exchange markets were not forecast correctly.
- The influence of external conditions was aggravated by internal reasons.
- Shareholders tended to regard banks as an easily available source for financing their own businesses. Such activity can be qualified as misappropriation and abuse of shareholder's position, thus this is a criminal act.
- Falsification of bookkeeping entries and submitting of false information to the Bank of Latvia.

Latvian banking sector was comprised of 33 banks on October 1, 1996.

In 1996, assets of the banking sector have increased due to a growth in deposits (mainly enterprise deposits). When lending, banks are more careful in selecting borrowers. There are less instances of lending to persons connected with the bank. Previously, this was one of the most common transgressions. Lending by utilizing credit lines of the World Bank and the European Bank for Reconstruction and Development allows to extend credits for productive goals.

Latvian banks have placed considerable part of their financial resources with foreign credit institutions, especially those in OECD countries. Although claims to credit institutions of OECD countries have decreased if compared with January 1, 1996, the share of these claims in total claims is considerable. Concurrently, liabilities to credit institutions of OECD countries has increased. This indicates that confidence of foreign banks in Latvian banks has strengthened.

The tendencies in the development of the banking sector in the Republic of Latvia in 1996 indicate stabilization and gradual development of the financial system. A consolidation process is going on in the banking sector. The Bank of Latvia has elaborated additional requirements to weaker banks, thus controlling their problems and not allowing them to affect the activities of other banks.

INVESTMENT CLIMATE AND OPPORTUNITIES

Low inflation and stable and fully convertible currency
Europe Agreement with the EU signed in June 1995, with expected accession to the WTO in 1996/97
Free Trade Agreements in force with the EU, All EFTA countries, with other Baltic states and Ukraine
Capital market serves as a financial centre as there is no transaction based tax
Strong overall growth expected, especially in transport and communications

After starting the process of a transition to a market - oriented economy in the beginning of the 1990s Latvia has succeeded in conducting a programme of radical economic reforms and creating preconditions for further sustainable growth of the national economy. A wide programme of extensive liberalization, beginning with the exchange and trade system and ending with the price reform to realign domestic prices with world prices and with domestic production costs, has been rapidly implemented.

Macroeconomic stabilisation of the economy has been achieved as well. After a drop in gross domestic product (GDP) of around 50% in 1991-93, GDP began to stabilise in 1994 and has experienced only slight fluctuations since. Sustainable growth is expected to begin in 1996.

Successful introduction of the national currency, which is one of the most stable among all the economies in transition, and implementation of a tight monetary policy have led to a reduction in the inflation rate from around 1000% to 23%. The fall in real wages has been arrested and since 1993 they have started to increase. The unemployment rate is relatively low in comparison with many other Central and East European countries.

Rural and small-scale privatisation is already completed. As a result, most agricultural production, retail trade and public catering is now carried out by private companies.

All this progress could have not been achieved without consistent implementation of the programme of economic reforms or without political stability and agreement among all the major political forces with regard to Latvia`s transition to a market economy and its integration into European economical and political structures.The results of the parliamentary elections which took place in the autumn of 1995 have once again confirmed this. Further evidence of the gradual improvement in Latvia`s economic enviroment also exists in the form of a inflow of foreign direct investments.

Latvia has many advantages for foreign investors. As a result, more than 5,000 private companies have been established in Latvia with the participation of foreign capital. Companies from more than 80 countries have started joint ventures. Some large investment projects are being implemented, including a joint project involving Cable&Wireless and Finnish Telecom to establish the consortium Tilts Communications. This project is aimed at modernising the Latvian communications system.

Latvia is strategically located in the Baltic region, and well connected with many of its neighbouring countries. It has an inexpensive and well-qualified labour force as well as a relatively well-developed transport infrastructure. Under Latvian legislation foreign investors enjoy a certain number of privileges, such as having the same rights and taxes as Latvian citizens and businesses, not having to pay customs duties on long-term investments in fixed capital, free repatriation of profits after the payment of taxes, and the ability to found and enterprise with exclusively foreign investments.

However, Latvia needs a larger inflow of foreign investments in order to restructure and modernise its economy. This was the main reason for the relatively slow implementation of large - scale privatisation which cannot be successfully completed with domestic investments alone. The Latvian government believes that an increase in the inflow of foreign investments will give Latvia not only capital, but also new technology, know-how, business techniques and experience, which will help to open the doors to international markets.

LEGAL ENVIRONMENT FOR INVESTORS

Indirect investment, such as securities or investment funds, is not specifically regulated. Limited-liability partnerships and joint-stock companies or permanent establishments of non-residents may be wholly owned and managed by foreigners. Profits may be expatriated freely. Land may be owned or leased by foreigners or foreign-owned local companies. The transfer abroad of fully convertible currencies does not require government approval. Where private property is expropriated, compensation is required to be paid at the time of the expropriation being carried out.

LEGAL ENVIRONMENT FOR FOREIGN INVESTORS

Foreign Investment laws
Law on Goreign Investment (Nov.1991)
amended (March 1993, July 1994 and March 1995).

Restrictions on activities
Must be limited liability or joint stock, or permanent establishment.
Permission needed if gaining control of company with capital greater than US $ 1 million. Few industries prohibited, many others require licences.

Profit and capital repatriation
No restriction on profit or capitel repatriation

Property ownership
Land may be owned by foreign-owned companies established in Latvia from countries with which Latvia has concluded investment protection agreements, companies with foreign participation established in Latvia in which at least 51% of statutory capital belongs to the citizens of Latvia, and foreign individuals who are citizens of Latvia. Land may be leased by foreigners or foreign - owned local companies.

Tax treatment and incentives
Enterprise income tax rate is 25% for incorporated companies and permanent establishments of non-residents. Enterprise income tax on payments to non-residents, including natural persons, is:

1. on dividends-the tax shall be 10% of the total amount of dividends;
2. on fees for management and consultation services - the tax shall be 10% of the amount of the fee;
3. on interest payments (yield), if the payer and the recipient are associated enterprises or persons associated with enterprises - the tax shall be 10% of these payments , but no interest paid by commercial banks registered in the Republic of Latvia to their associated enterprises or persons - 5% of said payments;
4. on payment for intellectual property:

    a) royalty payments, or payments for the rights to use the copyright on a work od literature or art, including movies, videos and recordings. The tax shall be 15% of these payments;

    b) payments for other types of intellectual property. The tax shall be 5% of this consideration; 5, on consideration for the use of property located in Latvia - the tax shall be 25% of said gains. It is possible to claim tax relief provided under the provisions of current tax treaties for the avoidance of double taxation and certain other types of income.

Participation in privatisation
Participation in privatisation permitted with approval government - established Privatisation Agency.

MARKETS AND TRADES

PRICE LIBERALISATION

Price liberalisation began in early 1991 and was virtually completed by late 1992. Few formal price controls remain. Rents and public transport and heating prices are set by municipalities, often with inadequate allowance for capital costs. Electricity tariffs charged by the state-owned power utility are approved the central government. They cover about 60% of economic costs at present. An increase to full economic cost level is envisaged by the authorities only for the year 2005.

COMPETITION POLICY

An Anti-monopoly Law was passed in 1991, with subsequent amendments in 1993. Compliance with the law is monitored by the Anti-monopoly Committee. Competition policy is sceduled to be harmonised with EU legislation within four years. As in other small countries with a liberal trade regime, imports are the main competitive force in the economy.

WAGE LIBERALISATION

Wages are set freely by enterprise managers, with union influence remaining modest. The existing minimum wage legislation is without material impact on wage setting in the private sector.

INTEREST RATE LIBERALISATION

Banks have been free to set interest rates since 1992. The spread between lending and deposit rates has fallen recently but remains about 15-20%. Based on 1995 inflation of 23.1 %, deposit rates of all maturities are negative in real terms.

MAJOR FOREIGN TRADE AGREEMENTS

WTO (formerly GATT) observer status (Oct. 1992), working party on accession (1993).
EC Trade and Cooperation Agreement in force since February 1993. EU Free Trade Agreement entered into force in January 1995. Europe Agreement signed in June 1995 allowing for the free movement of goods, services and capital.
EFTA Multilateral Free Trade Agreement (Norway, Liechtenstein, Iceland and Switzerland), signed in December 1995 will replace bilateral agreements in force with Switzerland, Liechenstein and Norway.

All other OECD countries except New Zealand and Mexico have granted MFN and/or GSP.

Baltic FTA in force since April 1994, agricultural trade under negotiation.
FTA with Ukraine signed in November 1995.
Latvia and Slovenia have finalised negotiations on a Free Trade Agreement, November 1995.
Negotiations on FTA with Czech/Slovak customs union are in final stage, FTA negotiations with Poland, Hungary and Bulgaria proposed.

TRADE AND EXCHANGE RATE REGIME

Substantial trade liberalisation is under way. Quantitative restrictions on imports and exports have been virtually eliminated. Import tariffs are generally modest (0.5 % ad valorem most-favoured-nation rate on raw materials and component parts, and a 15% most-favoured-nation rate on finished products), except in the agricultural sector which remains protected by an average trade-weighted tariff of 23 %. Import licensing exists for tobacco, spirits, alcoholic beverages, sugar, cereals and military products.

Export duties apply to certain raw materials (timber, limestone, gypsum) ferrous and non-ferrous metals and antiques. Export duties, except those for antiques, are subject to gradual elimination. Quantitative restrictions are not applied to exports from Latvia. Latvian exports have been successfully redirected to Western markets, whose share in total exports outside the CIS countries reached 62.5 % in 1995 compared with 56.5% in 1993.

The Europe Agreement with the EU, signed in June 1995, together with expected accession to the WTO in 1996/97 will further the integration process.

FISCAL AND SOCIAL SAFETY NET REFORM

Taxation

Total tax revenues are expected to amount to about 36% of GDP in 1995. Personal income tax accounts for approximately 16% of total tax revenue, with indirect taxes, mainly VAT, and corporate profit tax accounting for another 27% and 6%, respectively. The rate of personal income tax is 25%. The standart VAT rate has been 18% since November 1993. Since mid-1994, the standart VAT rate has also applied to food.

Social security

The social security tax is 37% (of the wagesum) for employers, and 1% for employees. From July 1 1996 this will change to 33 % for employers and 5% for employees. Pensions and unemployment benefits are fianced from these revenues. A gradual transformation of the pay-as-you-go system to a funded system has been initiated. The number of pensioners per 1,000 employees has been projected to increase from 391 to 429.

FOREIGN INVESTMENTS IN LATVIA

Total foreign investments reached more than one billion US$ last year in Latvia. It is envisaged that the number will increase considerably this year, considering that the privatization of big companies is proceeding. Maris Elerts, the Director General of the Latvian Development agency (LDA) reviews in details the LDA achievements in attracting foreign investments and export promotion of products made in Latvia.

One of the main tasks of the LDA is to attract export orientated and import substituting foreign direct investments to Latvian economy thus increasing its potential and creating new jobs to provide stable and harmonic development of Latvian economy. It is clear that this priority will not loose its importance in the near future as well. Foreign investments obtained in privatization have rather big proportion. I believe the role of the LDA will increase in attraction of investments when privatization is concluded.

On the contrary to investments in objects under privatization, activities of the LDA are more orientated to identifying new investment projects in Latvia and looking for potential investors to specific projects, for example, pulp plant project and others. The work with such investment projects bears fruit only in certain period of time.

The creation of interest on investment opportunities in Latvia is an important precondition to attract investments. The LDA has obtained massive experience in organising seminars and business days with the participation of Latvian entrepreneurs abroad within the framework of governmental visits. The LDA has became one of leading organisations in the country to organise such events.

From the attraction of investment point of view last year is valued as successful part of work. 26.1 million US$ have been invested in the projects attracted by the LDA and the total investments (since the foundation of the LDA in 1994) reached 40 million US$. 1045 jobs were created or maintained during the span from 1994 - 1997 implementing investment projects.

The total investments in the near future will reach 465 million US$ considering the started projects approved by investors. Total foreign investments in 1997 were some one billion US$. It is expected to reach two billion US$ by the end of 1998 considering the privatization of big companies.

The LDA is ranked among the most successful development agencies in Central and Eastern Europe despite small human and financial resources of the LDA. Every US$ used to finance the LDA attracted 65 US$ in 1997, total investments per one employee of the LDA were 1.2 million US$. To compare with, Czech investment attraction agency "Czechinvest", which is one of the leading ones in Eastern Europe attracted investments of 115 US$ per each financially used US$ in 1996. The investments per employee totalled two million US$. The other priority of the LDA's activities is to promote exports of Latvian goods and services. The exports increased last year by 21 per cent.

Creation of business contacts between Latvian and foreign companies plays essentially important part in export promotion. The LDA has prepared 32 visit programmes and organised 5 visits of trade missions during 1997, where 50 representatives of foreign companies met with some 140 representatives of Latvian companies. 27 smaller visits of business partners' groups or individual businessman were organised. As a result 36 foreign entrepreneurs visited 54 Latvian companies to agree on production orders or purchase agreements.

Last year 382 specific requests of export products were sent from abroad to different Latvian companies. Considering the fact that local companies often tend not to disclose information on started contacts development into concrete deals it is hard to evaluate the efficiency of these requests. However, the total amount of six deals reaches nearly one million US$ out of concluded 15 export contracts, which were made public.

Joint stock company "Latvian Trade Centre" (LTC) was established in August last year consolidating more than 70 Latvian companies and organisations with a view to increase exports to Russia and other CIS countries. Shipments worth 1.3 million US$ were sent to Sankt Peterburg, Moscow and Kazahstan during the first five working months with the participation of the LTC.

The official opening of the LDA's European Information Centre (EICC) took place in September 17, 1997, where Latvian entrepreneurs now can obtain information on the EU legislation, statistics, potential co-operation partners and announced tenders. The employees of the EICC provide specific market analysis on requests, organise direct marketing campaigns to look for customers or potential investors.

With the assistance of the EICC Latvian companies have access to more than 240 similar centres, as well as to the services of a specially created ES assistance centre in Brussels. A possibility to distribute offers through specialised information networks Business support bureau BRE (Bureau de Rapprochement des Enterprises) and Global Trade Point Network (GTPN), which in Latvia are represented by EICC has created great interest.

Important source of information about our good in target markets are LDA representative offices abroad - in UK (London) and Germany (Frankfurt). LDA representatives in different forms are in the US, Australia, Italy, Ukraine and other countries. The representative offices of the LDA abroad have a very important function to provide information about Latvian exports and production possibilities. Last year around 1500 foreign companies received 200 such offers, on which we received almost 450 responses.

Export promotion is also very successfully done through international exhibitions. Last year the main event was the participation of Latvian enterprises in the Hanover Messe. The LDA prepared expositions of 21 Latvian company in this messe, where we presented our best achievements in machine building industry, electromechanical, automatisation, computer technologies and electronic industries. Seven Latvian food processing companies (dairy, meat, fish and beverage exporters) took part in the World Food '97 exhibition in Moscow. The LDA plans to organise the participation of Latvian companies in Hanover Messe and World Food '98 exhibitions also this year

With the financial support of the EU PHARE programme, the LDA hopes to launch an export support programme within which Latvian companies will receive financing for entering new markets.

ENCOURAGEMENT OF FOREIGN INVESTMENT

The government of Latvia has introduced a number of new provisions into the country`s business law to speed up privatisation and attract foreign investment. The documents have the force of law and determine changes in existing legislation. Enterprises can now be privatised along with the land on which they stand - which is the first measure towards creating a free land market in the country. Previosly, foreigners could only lease land for up to 99 years.

Foreign investors can now take control of companies developing natural resources, including those on the continental shelf, if they obtain permission from the government first.

Foreign investment accelerated in the third quarter of 1995. By the end of September, total FDI reached US$480 million, up from US$ 317 million at the end of 1994. The United Kingdom leads in terms of the value of the investments, with a massive 23.3 % stake. This is due to one investment of lats 43.1 million in telecommunications. These figures are followed by the US, Finland, Germany, Russia and Switzerland with 14%, 10%, 7%. and 6% respectively. Only 17% of all investments have been injected into industry. There are aproximately 5,200 firms with a foreign capital share. Russian investors dominate with 23% of companies established.

In August 1995 the Baltic Venture Fund was set up in association with EBRD as a limited partnership based in Jersey. The Fund, which has so far attracted US$10.5 million, undertakes equity investments primarily in medium-sized enterprises in Latvia and the other Baltic states.

INVESTMENT AND BUSINESS CLIMATE

OPENNESS TO FOREIGN INVESTMENT

The Latvian government is actively trying to encourage foreign direct investment.

Under the 1991 Investment Law, the laws of the Republic of Latvia apply equally to domestic and foreign investors. Amendments to the Investment Law passed in 1996 removed virtually all restrictions on foreign investment. However, foreigners are still prohibited from controlling basic timber industries. Latvia does not restrict the repatriation of profits. In January, 1995 the United States and Latvia signed an agreement on mutual protection of investments. The agreement was ratified by the U.S. Senate in summer 1996 and went into effect on December 26, 1996.

A foreign investor is allowed to lease land for up to 99 years. Companies that are owned by foreigners can purchase land if the foreign investors represent countries with which Latvia has entered into international agreements on mutual protection of foreign investments. Land can also be purchased by companies the controlling share of which is owned by citizens of Latvia. Though some liberalization of the land law has been made, some restrictions on the purchase of land by individual foreigners still exist. Foreign investors appear to have fair access to enterprises that are eligible for privatization. In the past, company managers or employees have an inside track for purchasing an enterprise from the state. For example, in privatization of milk processing enterprises, blocks of shares were reserved for enterprise employees and dairy farmers. There have been no reports of a serious foreign investor having been excluded from a privatization due to the reservation of blocks of shares. On the contrary, foreign investors frequently appear to have priority over domestic investors in a privatization when it appears that the foreign investor can bring more money to the table.

CONVERSION AND TRANSFER POLICIES

The exchange rate of the lat is determined by market forces with limited intervention by the Bank of Latvia. Starting in February 1993, Bank of Latvia policy has been aimed at stabilizing the lat at a value of 79.97 santims (one santim equals 1/100 of a lat) to one SDR. On June 1, 1997, the lat was worth roughly $1.70. Latvia does not restrict the import, export, exchange of or payment in foreign or domestic currencies inside the country. The Bank of Latvia has foreign reserves of Ls 231.5 million; based on these reserves, the Bank of Latvia guarantees full convertibility of the lat. The Bank of Latvia is exercising a policy of monetary restraint consistent with International Monetary Fund guidelines.

Latvia's laissez faire currency policies have drawn substantial amount of foreign currency to the country, apparently from the east. Given the success of its foreign exchange policies, the risk that the government would limit the convertibility of the lat appears to be very low. All embassy currency exchange transactions are conducted at free market exchange rate offered by private commercial banks. Though the banking crisis of summer 1995 put some pressure on the lat, it recovered strength by late August and has remained stable over the past year.

The larger commercial banks appear to have no problem converting and remitting funds out of Latvia.

EXPROPRIATION AND COMPENSATION

Since independence, the Latvian government has begun de-nationalizing private property seized by Soviet authorities during the occupation. The are no cases of arbitrary expropriation of private property by the Latvian government. Latvian law allows expropriation for compensation under the right of eminent domain.

DISPUTE SETTLEMENT

There are no investment disputes with the Latvian government involving either U.S. or other foreign investors in independent Latvia. (There have been some disputes involving claims by U.S. citizens for restitution of property.) Latvia is moving to re-organize its court system according to Western standards. In general, the Latvian judiciary is independent of improper government influences.

Latvia is in the process of updating and implementing the pre-war commercial code. A modern bankruptcy law was adopted in 1996. In October 1995, the new law on credit institutions was passed which also regulates bank bankruptcy and liquidation. Business activities are regulated by the Law on Entrepreneurial Activities and Business Operations, which serves as the legal framework for establishing, registering, operating and closing a business in Latvia.

Legally-transferable rights to private real property are slowly being reestablished as properties are registered in reconstituted land registers. A law on collaterialization of non-movables is expected to be introduced to the parliament in 1997.

PERFORMANCE REQUIREMENTS/INCENTIVES

There are no performance requirements for a foreign investor to establish, maintain or expand and investment in Latvia, or any incentives thereto.

PRIVATE OWNERSHIP AND ESTABLISHMENT

Under Latvian law, foreigners may conduct business activity under one of three forms of business organization: -- the limited liability company ("Sabiedriba ar Ierobezotu Atbildibu" or SIA);

-- the joint stock company ("Akciju Sabiedriba" or AS); and
-- the representative (branch) office of a foreign company.
Limited liability and joint stock companies are established upon registration with the Latvian Enterprise Register and have the rights of a juridical person. (See Section IV for a description of requirements for the formation of limited liability and joint stock companies). Other full liability forms of business organization are closed to foreigners, including sole proprietorships (individualie uznemumi), partnerships (ligumu sabiedribas, public and religious organization enterprises (sabiedrisko/religisko organizaciju uznemumi), companies with added liability (sabiedribas ar papildinatu atbildibu), and private farms (zemnieku saimniecibas).

Establishment of a foreign bank branch is subject to the approval of the Bank of Latvia. One French bank has already opened a branch bank in Riga; a German bank has opened a representative office and the Estonian Hansa Bank has purchased the shares of an existing bank, Deutsch-Lettisch bank. In April 1997, the German Veriens und Westbank together with the World Bank's International Finance Corporation opened the Vereinsbank in Riga. Private enterprises have competitive equality with public enterprises with respect to access to markets and business operations.

PROTECTION OF PROPERTY RIGHTS

Legal rights to property are in the process of being restored in Latvia. The government of Latvia is committed to attaining a level of protection for intellectual property rights comparable to that provided under international conventions. Pursuant to that commitment, the Latvian parliament in 1993 passed legislation to protect copyrights, trademarks and patents. Foreign owners may seek redress for violation of their intellectual property rights through the Appellation Council at the Latvian Patent Office; court action can also be sought in such cases. While the legal basis for intellectual property rights has been established and some of its enforcement mechanisms are in place, Latvian law has not defined penalties for violation of these rights.

In July 1994, President Clinton signed a Trade and Intellectual Property Rights agreement with Latvia. Latvia has been a member of the World Intellectual Property Organization since January 1993, a member of Paris Convention since September 1993, and a member of Bern Convention since August 1995. Latvia has also acceded to the following international treaties and agreements:

- Patent Cooperation Treaty (September 1993);
- Budapest Treaty on the International Recognition of the Deposit of Microorganisms for the Purposes of Patent Procedure (December 1994);
- Madrid Agreement on International Registration of Trade Marks (January 1995);
- Nice Agreement on International Classification of Goods and Services for the Purposes of Trade Mark Registration (January 1995).

Unauthorized reproductions of copyrighted video recordings imported from Russia are widely distributed in Latvia. To halt the use of pirated films imported from Russia by private Latvian television stations, the Latvian Radio and Television Board on October 27, 1992, adopted a ruling under which the license of any domestic television company would be revoked if it is unable to show that it has legally acquired the rights to the films it broadcasts.

Latvia's intellectual property practices have not had any serious impact on U.S. trade outside the film and video industry.

Regulatory System: Laws and Procedures

Latvia adopted laws on competition and restriction of monopolies in 1991 and 1993. Businesses are precluded from manipulating prices or quantities of goods offered for sale and may not create artificial shortages in order to boost prices. The Latvian Anti-Monopoly Control Committee overseas implementation of the laws. Companies proposing a merger that would result in concentration of more than twenty-five percent of the market for a particular good or service must have the approval of the Anti-Monopoly Committee. In June, 1997 the Parliament passed a new anti-monopoly law which is basically in accord with EU legislation. It will come into force January 1998. Latvian banking is regulated by the Bank of Latvia.

CAPITAL MARKETS AND PORTFOLIO INVESTMENT

Government policies do not interfere in the free flow of financial resources or the allocation of credit. In practice, the efficiency of credit and equity markets is hampered by the weak underlying legal and judicial system. Commercial credit is largely restricted to high-interest, short-term trade related loans which are in theory available to foreigners but in practice are totally unattractive to foreign investors with other sources of credit. Banks became more reluctant to lend domestically in the wake of the 1995 banking crisis, but have begun in recent months to more actively pursue project as well as trade financing

. The underlying weakness of the banking system became apparent in the spring and summer of 1995 when the largest commercial bank, Banka Baltija, as well as a number of smaller banks, collapsed. Risky lending practices, unsustainable deposit interest payments, insider trading, as well as inadequate banking laws and regulations led to the crisis. In an effort to prevent further losses to depositors, the Bank of Latvia has selected 12 banks as eligible to collect deposits. These banks should form the core of a future, stronger banking system.

As of June 30, 1997, the assets of Latvia's five largest commercial banks (Parekss-Banka, Latvijas Unibanka, Rigas Komercbanka, Latvijas Krajbanka, and Rietumu Banka) totaled 739.8 million lats ($1286.61 million).

The Riga Stock Exchange was re-established on July 25, 1995 with only four stocks quoted on the first trading day. Presently about 30 stocks are quoted. In the future, Riga Stock Exchange plans to quote securities of neighboring countries. France assisted Latvia in setting up the securities market based on a continental European model. In September 1997, The U.S. Agency for International Development will begin to provide technical assistance for strengthening the regulatory structure of the stock exchange and related institutions.

Political Violence

There have been no reports of political violence or politically-motivated damage to property since Latvia re-achieved independence in 1991. Civil disturbances are unlikely and there are no signs of any nascent insurrection movement.

BILATERAL INVESTMENT AGREEMENTS

Latvia has concluded bilateral investment agreements with Austria, Canada, the Czech Republic, Denmark, Estonia, Finland, France, Germany, Israel, Lithuania, the Netherlands, Norway, Poland, Sweden, Switzerland, the Republic of China (Taiwan), the United Kingdom and Vietnam. The agreement with the U.S. came into force in December 1996. Agreements with Benelux countries, Greece, Portugal, Spain and Uzbekistan are signed but have not taken effect yet.

OPIC AND OTHER INVESTMENT INSURANCE PROGRAMS

Overseas Private Investment Corporation (OPIC) coverage is available for U.S. investments in Latvia.

LABOR

The official unemployment rate is about 7.2 percent, but estimates by official sources are closer to 18 percent. Unemployment is significantly higher in rural areas, especially in the southeastern Latgale region. Skilled and unskilled labor are both available. With regard to labor management relations, labor unions with roots in the Soviet period are weak and politically discredited. Latvia has not seen any major industrial strikes since re-achieving independence. The Latvian government appears to be attempting to uphold ILO convention protecting worker rights. Labor is not a significant factor in choice of technology.

FOREIGN FREE-TRADE ZONES/FREE PORTS

Three laws are in various stages of adoption to establish free trade zones at Riga, Ventspils and Liepaja ports.

CAPITAL OUTFLOW POLICY

The Latvian government does not have any policies on the outflow of capital. Large amounts of funds flow freely through Latvia to the West from former Soviet countries.

MAJOR FOREIGN INVESTORS

Major foreign investors in Latvia include the consortium of Cable and Wireless (U.K.) and Finnish Telecom, which obtained a 49-percent share in the Latvian telecommunications company Lattelekom in return for a $160 million investment over 8 years; the 380-room Radisson-SAS Daugava Hotel owned by the U.S. BEK and the city of Riga ; Kellogg's, which opened a $22 million plant to produce breakfast cereals for the Baltic, Russian and Belarussian markets in November 1993; the Danish company "House of Prince", which has purchased 51 percent of the Riga Tobacco Factory and the U.S. based Metromedia which has joint ventures in cable TV, pager service, radio station and cellular phone network. In addition to the grocery stores mentioned above, the Norwegian Varner Baltija has privatized or purchased two hotels in Riga, including the large, Soviet-era, Hotel Latvia, and has plans to renovate the central rail station.

Other significant U.S. investors in Latvia include Coca-Cola Baltics, InterSource Inc., Jeld-Wen, LatHaag, McDonalds, Colgate Palmolive, and ProctSU and Gamble. The American Chamber of Commerce in Latvia currently has more than eighty members.

CORRUPTION

Corruption, ranging from small bribe taking by low level civil servants for completion of bureaucratic tasks, to high level officials involved in the award of government contracts, is widely believed to be a problem in Latvia. In the spring and summer of 1997, allegations of corruption have led to the sacking of several ministers, including the Minister of Defense.

Except for cases involving customs officials, no one to our knowledge has been prosecuted for corruption. Conflicts of interest among government officials are common. Despite the ministerial level resignations it is doubtful that the law on corruption which forbids elected officials from holding positions in private or state enterprises will have much real impact on the situation. Moreover, the law does not prohibit civil servants from holding jobs which might create conflicts of interest with their government responsibilities. The lack of transparency in government procurement has been an obstacle for U.S. companies on several recent occasions. The recently enacted law could help address the problem if implemented in practice.

TRADE AND PROJECT FINANCING

With the exception of the Mortgage and Land Bank, Latvia's commercial banking system is completely private. (The state Savings Bank (Krajbanka) system and Unibank are both being privatized). Since the first private commercial banks were established in the late 1980's, banking has grown exponentially in Latvia. However, established under very loose banking regulations, those banks were not viable. The banking system is still in the process of consolidation. On June 30, 1997, assets of Latvian commercial banks totaled 1314.5 million lats ($2286.1 million). At present, bank services are limited to short-term lending, international financial transfers, foreign currency exchange transactions, as well as credit and debit card operations.

The Latvian government maintains no controls over the import, export, use or exchange of foreign currencies in Latvia.

Medium-term Eximbank financing is available in Latvia for credits that are backed by the full faith and credit of the Latvian government, or guaranteed by a proven, reputable financial entity. In October 1996, EXIMbank extended its first loan not backed by a sovereign guarantee in Central and Eastern Europe to the Latvian railways. EBRD financing is also available for both private and public sector projects.

The Bank of Latvia reports that the following Latvian banks currently have correspondent arrangements with U.S. banks: Rigas Komercbanka, Parekss-Banka, Unibank, Zemes Banka, Baltijas Tranzitu Banka, Hansabank-Latvija, Rietumu Banka, Latvijas Krajbanka, Multibanka, Ogres Komercbanka, Baltijas Starptautiska Banka, Saules Banka, Latvijas Tirdzniecibas Banka, LAND Banka, Latvijas Kapitala Banka, Doma Banka, Lainbanka, Latvian Investment Bank, Viktorija Bank, Latvijas Biznesa Banka, LATEKO Banka, Rigas Naftas un Kimijas Banka, Trasta Komercbanka, United Baltic Bank of Riga, United Baltic Bank of Ventspils and VEF Banka.

FOREST INDUSTRIES

Well over 40% of Latvia`s territory is covered by woods, making it one of the most densely forested countries in Europe. Forest acreage has grown from the 24.7% existing in 1923. Wood is one of the country`s major national assets, while wood-processing ranks among its principal industries. The forestry sector, which is now the leading export industry in Latvia, receives 10 times as many requests for wood products from the West than present productioncapacity allows. The local timber industry has grown substantially and has the potential to increase still further.

The biggest development obstacle is the lack of cheap credit. Current interest rates on commercial credit are around 35%.

Jaako Poyry Consulting AB (Sweden), a subsidiary of Finland`s Jaako Poyry Group, has been doing a preliminary study for a new pulp plant in Jekabpils. It is being financed by the Latvian government and the Swedish International Development Authority (SIDA), which is providing SEK 2.5 million. The new plant will be capable of producing 350,000 tonnes of bleached softwood TCF kraft pulp a year. The construction of the plant will require an investment of up to US$ 1 billion. Investors are being sought for a US $ 700 million cellulose plant proposed by the Latvian Forestry Service and Jaako Poyry AB.

MAJOR INDUSTRIAL SECTORS

FOOD PROCESSING

Positive growth has been developing in this sector because of increased demand which is also presenting a number of investment opportunities for foreign companies in the form of joint ventures. A Chilean non-alcoholic beverage producer is considering investing up to US$ 6 million in a project to produce concentrates and powdered drinks, and a French firm plans to open a company which will produce foofstuffs for both domestic consumption and for export. One of the largest and most successful foreign investments has been made by the US company, Kellogg, which invested US $ 21 million in a joint venture in 1991. Raisiio (Finland) has acquired a 20% stake in the Dzirnavnieks grain mill for US $ 2.39 million. The mill is the largest in the Baltic area and supplies nearly half of all wheat and rye flour in Latvia. Its net sales will amount to about Fmk 65 million in 1995. Cultor Oy, also from Finland, bought 51% of shares in Rigas Maiznieks, a company with three bakeries and one flour mill. Another Finnish company, Ab Chips has acquired a 75% stake in Latfood, which makes potato chips and frozen potato products. Latfood has a 60% share of the local market and supplies the McDonald`s (US) restaurant in Riga. Ab Chips plans to expand production and export to Lithuania, Estonia and parts of Russia.

Baltic Brewery Holding, a JV between Pripps Bryggerier (Sweden), Ringnes (Sweden) and Hartwell (Finland) , has acquired another 25% of shares in Latvia`s biggest brewery, Aldaris. The JV now has an 85% holding in Aldaris, which controls most of Latvia`s beer market. The rest of the shares belong to the brewery`s employees.

AGRICULTURE AND FISHING

Now that there is associate membership of the EU there are opportunities for expanding the export sector of the industries which are in need of more investment and cheaper short-term credits. Production has been slowed due to a number of factors ranging from poor husbandry and crop rotation to fewer livestock and lack of modern farm machinery. There has also been a fall-off in demand for some farm products. Development of the agricultural sector has also been hampered by the existence of large numbers of small autonomous farm units.

The fishing industry will receive a boost when the Free Trade Agreement between Slovenia and Latvia, already initialled, takes effect, as Slovenia is an important market for Latvia`s fish products. Furthermore, an investment of US $ 133,000 will be made in a fish industry enterprise by the Norwegian-Latvian Bussiness Development Fund.

MANUFACTURING

There have been significant structural changes in both domestic and foreign markets which have had a negative effect on many sectors. There is an extensive and diverse manufacturing base much of which is in need of investment and new technology as market demand changes. On the engineering side, minibus output has been falling. However, there has been an incease in the production of transport vehicles and passanger rail cars. Base chemical production narrowed slightly and has been mainly influenced by a fall in demand for household detergants, natural and artifical fibres. In some areas there have been build-ups of inventories for such consumer items as radios, television sets and telephone equipment.

A US $ 500,000 investment was made by Varner Oegland (Norway) to establish a network of knitwear outlets throughout the country.

CONSTRUCTION

Since 1994 there has been a general improvement in this sector which has been growing faster than any other sector of the economy by 20.7%. There were 24.900 persons employed in 545 companies in the industry at the beginning of the year but by the end of the year the number of companies had jumped to 800. There were also another 4,000 workers in the industry. National companies are also becoming more involved in projects abroad.

LIYEPAYA FREE ECONOMIC ZONE

The Saeima (the Parliament of the Republic of Latvia) has passed the Law "On Liepaja Special Economic Zone" proving for the establishment of the Special Economic Zone in the city of Liepaja and Liepaja district (the territory of the airport).

Establishment of Liepaja Special Economic Zone is aimed at the development and promotion of commerce, industry, shipping and air transport, as well as international exchange of goods via Latvia. Its task is to attract the investments for the development of production and infrastructure and creation of new job places in Liepaja.

Liepaja Special Economic Zone shall promote development of the region of Liepaja.

Liepaja Special Economic Zone shall be constituted by the territory of Liepaja Special Economic Zone, where entrepreneurial activity is carried out by the entrepreneurial associations of Liepaja Special Economic Zone, and which is managed and supervised by the management of Liepaja Special Economic Zone.

Land may be alienated into the ownership of the entrepreneurial associations of Liepaja Special Economic Zone if the amount of no less than 100 000 Lats has been invested per hectare.

The entrepreneurial associations of Liepaja Special Economic Zone may receive the following tax allowances:

exemption from the customs tax, the excise tax and the value added tax;
discount of 80% from the property tax and the land tax which can be supplemented with a discount of 20% upon the decision of the local government;
discount of 80% from the calculated enterprise income tax;
for purposes of calculating the enterprise income tax the deprecation rate up to 100% may be applied.

The Law provides that Liepaja Special Economic Zone is established for twenty years - from March 1, 1997 till March 1, 2017. Its term of operation may be extended under the procedure established by law.

SELECTED INVESTMENT AND BUSINESS OPPORTUNITIES

ENVIRONMENT & BUSINESS OPPORTUNITIES

During the last 50 years when Latvia was under Soviet occupation, industrial development was often made at the expense of the environment. Large industrial areas, transportation crossroads and abandoned Russian army bases now are heavily polluted. However, the rest of the territory of Latvia has acceptable inland water quality, as well as comparatively low pollution levels and high biological diversity compared to many European countries.

Since re-achieving independence in 1991, Latvia has made striking progress toward restoring a market economy. However, most of the industry developed under the Soviet system was not viable in the capitalist world. Therefore, industrial output declined considerably during the first few years of independence. Accordingly, environmental pressures were reduced. Industrial consumption of water and energy fell significantly, along with the volume of municipal waste, toxic waste, wastewater and use of pesticides and fertilizers. Thus, reduction of emissions in the first years of independence did not result from cleaner technologies, but from a reduction in the volume of industrial production. As the Latvian economy grows, the increased consumption of natural resources, the growing number of cars and the replacement of relatively clean fuels by heavy oil, wood and peat may cause deterioration of environment quality.

Even though the Latvian economy has recovered considerably in 1997 (by the end of the year, GDP is expected to reach 4.5%-5%), government investment in environment is still low because of Latvia's tight fiscal policy.

AIR POLLUTION

Air quality monitoring on the national level is mainly performed by the Environmental Pollution Observation Center (EPOC). Generally speaking the current air quality in the Latvian cities is not alarmingly bad. Due to the presence of central heating systems and the mix of energy sources the pollution level of SO_2 is quite low and does not exceed the European precaution standards. This might change with the trends in quality of fuels. Especially those heating facilities not being registered in the emission data base up to now should be observed very carefully.

The emission of sulphur dioxide from point sources decreased from 58,5 thousand tons in 1991 to 45 thousand tons in 1996. About 98% of this is emitted from heat and power production in boiler houses. Compared to the emission trend,the primary energy supply has fallen by 50 % during the same time. The comparably small reduction of sulphur emission is due to a shift in the primary energy sources. While the consumption of natural gas and coal has decreased significantly, the consumption of heavy fuels has remained nearly unchanged, and the combustion of wood has increased. Transport is main source of nitrogen oxide emission. In 1995, emissions of NOX have been calculated to be about 21 thousand tones, but this is a very crude estimate based on fuel consumption, total transport kilometers vehicle type and standard emission factors. The number of private passenger cars has increased during the last two years by about 50%; truck traffic activity is increasing as well. However the technical standards of the vehicle fleet have been improving step by step at the same time. Both trends will influence the nitrogen emission balance in the coming years. Small heating plants are another common source of air pollution because of their short stacks and use of low grade oil. Industrial facilities, such as Riga power plant, Broceni asbestos cement and construction materials plant, as well as Liepaja ferrous metallurgical plant are among the most significant stationary pollution sources. In addition, there is some transboundary air pollution from Lithuanian enterprises.

The average level of ozone and nitrogen oxide clearly exceeds the Western European precaution standards but does not reach limit or alarm values. This will probably change with increasing traffic in the future. The most intensive air pollution caused by traffic is in Jurmala and Riga city. Due to long range transport the ozone concentration in rural areas can be elevated without local sources of ozone precursors. The current ozone and nitrogen oxide level in Latvia probably affects the health of forest ecosystems and other plants. This impact can only be controlled by limitation of individual car traffic, technical improvement of light hydrocarbon storage and substitution of solvents in paints and varnishes. Latvia has joined the Vienna Convention On Ozone Layer Protection and signed the Montreal protocol on substances that are harmful to the ozone layer. Latvian Ministry of Environmental Protection hopes that Latvian businesses will stop using such substances by 1998.

The average level of dust and lead in urban air is quite high compared with the situation in Western European cities and compared with the precaution standards.

Concerning the concentration of formaldehyde in ambient air all cities show a normal urban level.

WATER POLLUTION

There is a large river network in Latvia due to uneven moraine relief, wet climate and peculiarities of geographical structures. Four large rivers -- the Daugava, the Lielupe, the Gauja and the Venta -- account for 88 % of total Latvian river discharge. The annual Latvian river discharge is 34.7 km3 which amounts to almost 8% of the total river discharge into the Baltic Sea. There are about 12,400 rivers and brooks in Latvia with a total length of over 37 thousand km. About 35% of Latvian rivers, exceeding 10 km in length, are partly or fully regulated.

According to World Bank data, about 35% of discharged wastewater in Latvia is untreated. The volume of the wastewater has decreased significantly over the last 5 years, partly due to overall decrease in industrial and agricultural production. Major Latvian cities discharge wastewater either directly into the Baltic sea or into two rivers -- Daugava and Lielupe that, in turn, discharge in the Gulf of Riga. The Baltic sea waters of the Latvian economic zone are moderately polluted, mostly with organic material and nutrients. The bacteriological pollution near the popular resort town Jurmala often leads to swimming prohibition in summer. High levels of heavy metals and hydrocarbons have been registered in the ports of Riga, Liepaja and Ventspils.

At present most of the sludge produced in wastewater treatment plants is dried in facilities that cover large areas of land and are poorly lined and monitored. The current way of disposal and reuse of sludge also needs to be improved.

Agriculture run-off created by application and storage of fertilizers as well as livestock and poultry farms contribute 40%-50% of river and Gulf of Riga nutrient pollution.

The major sources of groundwater pollution are leakage from municipal and industrial waste disposal sites, sludge disposal sites contaminated with heavy metals, oil storage sites, as well as fertilizer and pesticide application and storage. Excessive exploitation of groundwater has resulted in salt water intrusion into one of the coastal city's (Liepaja) groundwater.

The municipal economy discharge of biogenous substances, the nutrient run-off from agriculture and heavy metal containing waste water from Riga's electroplating industry are the main waste water problems in Latvia. Furthermore, permanent or accidental pollution of the river Daugava may have a serious impact on the quality of drinking water in Riga and Daugavpils.

The National Environmental Policy Plan lists the improvement of potable water quality as a priority goal, along with measures for improvement and modernization of water supply systems and optimization of water tariffs.

With an assistance of PHARE Funds a comprehensive strategy for water supply and sewerage has been elaborated in Latvia. The required amount for infrastructure development up to year 2010 is USD 200 million of which USD 33 million has been secured. Investors for the rest USD 167 million are sought to fully implement the project.

WASTE

Most of the waste is generated by the largest Latvian cities. Riga's waste consists of paper, cardboard and food wastes (about 65% in total), followed by textiles, plastics, ferrous metals and glass (3%-4% each). Latvia generates about 200 kilograms of household waste per capita a year, but this number is expected to rise as poorly packaged local consumer goods are replaced by Western imports and domestic producers shift to Western style packaging. Latvia lacks a good household waste management system and comprehensive statistics.

Most of the waste is deposited in landfills, most of them in a bad shape and are not equipped for such purpose. There are more than 400 small, active dump sites and landfills for non hazardous waste. The landfills have been created without proper groundwater protection measures or monitoring system. Medical and hazardous industrial waste are often combined with the household waste in the landfills, causing significant groundwater contamination.

In Latvia, there are no facilities for incineration of hazardous waste, nor an adequate hazardous waste storage site. As large amounts of hazardous waste are stored on the grounds of agricultural enterprises and factories, establishment of an ecologically safe temporary storage site is planned. The volume of hazardous waste has decreased due to the decrease in industrial production. According to Latvian Environment Consulting and Monitoring Center, data calculation on the 70 largest hazardous waste generating entities show that the total amount of hazardous waste fell from 220,000 in 1990 to about 60,000 in 1995 (however, this is a conservative estimate; since various agencies have different definitions of hazardous waste, the numbers vary dramatically). Now Latvia annually produces approximately 60-70 thousand tons of hazardous wastes of which 9 tons has to be incinerated.

The Latvian Ministry of Environmental Protection and Regional Development is looking for cooperation with companies involved in the production and exploitation of mobile and semi-mobile hazardous waste incineration facilities.

During the last two years, Latvia with assistance of EU and Danish government has worked out the National Hazardous Waste Management Strategy (NHWMS) and now has started the implementation stage of this strategy the key parts of which include the following:

- incineration and treatment of hazardous wastes;
- establishment of secure landfill for final disposal of hazardous wastes;
- physical/chemical treatment of inorganic wastes

- preparation of Guidelines for pollution assessment and remediation of former storage sites of unwanted pesticides and other kinds of hazardous wastes.

BEST BUSINESS PROSPECTS

The market for environmental services and technologies can be divided into private market, and publicly or donor-financed projects.

The private market, besides being very small (approximately 2.5 million inhabitants) currently offers only a few good business opportunities. The current environmental legislation has little economic incentives for manufacturers to implement environment protection measures. In addition, most Latvian enterprises simply have no money to invest in such measures. However, the Law on Natural Resources Tax that came into force in January of 1996 has introduced more stringent requirements to polluters. As the result, at least some of the manufacturers would consider new technologies; there might also be an increase in demand for water metering devices and analytical equipment. Consulting services to the manufacturers, such as optimal production planning and cost-minimization could be of interest to Latvian manufacturers.

Another business prospect is environmental audits. Completion of environmental due diligence procedures before start-up of a project is required by many creditors. Foreign companies usually go through this procedure to ensure there are no unpleasant surprises for them in the future. Since more and more Western companies are entering the Latvian market, the demand for environmental assessment of property is growing.

More successful Latvian industries can afford to install pollution control equipment. Such niches are in the oil industry -- transportation, gas stations -- and fish processing plants. Small dairies often need better pollution control mechanisms, but their financial situation varies from good to close bankruptcy.

Aerosol manufacturers, refrigerator manufacturing and maintenance companies as well as other users of the substances that deplete the ozone layer are required to switch to environmentally friendly production processes or stop the production by 1998. Latvia has prepared a national program on ozone layer protection, which includes six projects that deal with restructuring of such businesses. The state will support Latvian companies that participate in the projects and thus create a potential market for "ozone-friendly" technologies.

State projects go through several stages: identification of a project, pre-feasibility study, feasibility study, design and construction work, analysis and follow-up. A tender is most often used to find consultants/contractors at any project phase. The tender is usually evaluated by the Project Department of the Latvian Environment Protection Ministry; the evaluation is carried out according to the requirements set by financing institutions (EBRD, EU PHARE, the World Bank or donor countries) or the Ministry (if financing comes from Latvian State Budget). A company can also identify a project that is in line with the government environmental priorities and get financing, but good personal contacts in Latvian government are necessary to do so.

The World Bank, EBRD, Latvian Ministry of Environmental Protection and other institutions use various environmental consultancies in the projects they finance. Latvian government prefers to work with local consulting companies or joint ventures.

At present, most of the foreign environmental companies operating in Latvia are consultancies. Among the European firms currently present in the Latvian market are: Danish -- Carl Bro Latvia, KowiConsult, Krueger, Dutch -- EDON, Tebodin, Belgian -- Ecolas, DHV, European Dredging

Company and English -- Parkman, Halcrow, Dynamco. There are virtually no US environmental companies in Latvia. An exception is Baltec Associates, Inc. with headquarters in Bedford, NY. The company is involved in environmental consulting and contaminated site remediation. Despite many problems common to Eastern Europe, good local contacts and an extremely proactive policy has made Baltec operations in Latvia successful. At present, the Ministry of Environmental Protection is working on the following major projects:

- water supply and waste water treatment, - waste management, including hazardous waste treatment, - nature protection, - air protection (energy and transport)

The national Program for Protection of the Baltic Sea Environment has materialized in the following investment programs:

- water supply and sewerage in Latvian small and medium size towns -- Program 800+, - national solid waste management system in Latvia -- Program 500-, - hazardous waste management system of Latvia - integrated coastal zone management planning

CONTACTS

Peter Frederick
Senior Commercial Officer
(resident in Stockholm)
U.S. Embassy
Strandvagen 101, 11589 Stockholm
tel: 46-8-783-5346; fax: 46-8-660-9181

Anna Zisser
Commercial Assistant
US Embassy
7 Raina Blvd, Riga, LV 1510, Latvia
Tel. (371) 782 0046; fax (371) 782 0047

TRANSPORTATION

The country is particularly well placed to act as a transit country for trade to and from Russia. Aside from the good land links, the only oil pipeline from the Siberian steppes to the Baltic ends at Ventspils, the main oil port, which has a 46 million tonne annual capacity and a 14 metre draught. A recent agreement with Russia looks set to increase traffic through Ventspils, now working at 66% capacity.

Riga, and Liepaja) eastwards (to Russia and Belarus) as well as along the Via Baltica route (which runs north-south). To provide financing for repair, maintenance and development of the state road network, the State Road Fund was established in 1994. As local financial resources are insufficient to cover maintenance expenses, a government-guaranteed loan of US $ 20.8 million) was borrowed from the EBRD and JEXIM. Negotiations have recently begun between the Ministry of Transport , the World Bank and the Kuwait Fund on a loan of US $ 40 million for the maintenance and development of the state road network.

The total length of the Latvian railway network is 2,413 kilometres, including 12 border crossings, which is sufficient for transportation of all transit cargo. As transit cargo accounts for 75% of the total, maintenance and development of rairoads and infrastructure is very important, especially on the routes to Russia and Belarus. Analysis of further development of the North-South corridor os presently under way in cooperation with the neighbouring countries. The "Balt Rail 2000" project will play a significant part. Investments will also be needed to improve the Jelgava-Liepaja railway line and the Ventspils and Liepaja port railway junctions, and to develop port access roads and infrastructure. Air Baltic replaces Latvian Airlines and Baltic International Airlines as the national carrier of Latvia. Major shareholders include the Latvian state, Baltic International USA, SAS (Sweden), Swedfund and the Investment Fund for Central and Eastern Europe. The Latvian national carrier has signed a protocol of intent with Britain`s Avro International Aerospace, part of British Aerospace, for the lease of three RJ70 aircraft for seven yers. This makes Latvia the first country in Eastern Europe to make use of the short-range RJ70 transports (70-seater aircraft).

A plan exists for the establishment of free economic zones at the ports of Riga, Ventspils and Liepaja.

ENERGY

Energy is intensively used and almost fully imported. In February 1996 debts for gas owed to Russia`s Gazprom stood at US $ 20 million, with Gazprom threatening to reduce supplies unless some of the debt were settled. Latvijas Gaze, the Latvian gas utility, is in its turn owed money by its consumers, including large concerns such as the state energy utility, Latvenergo, and the Liepajas Metalurgs metallurgical plant. Action is being taken to reduce reliance on imports. For example Latvenergo is seeking loans totalling US $76.2 million to rebuid the Daugava hydroelectric plant, including a US $ 34.1 million from the EBRD which is arranging the remeining financing . Latvenergo otself is being privatised.

A recent energy generating initiative by Latvenergo involved construction of a 2*600-KWh windmill near Ainazi in the north of the country at a cost of about US $ 2 million. Equipment was supplied by Germany`s Tacke Windtechnik. The windmill will generate about 2.5 million KWh of electricity per year and is expected to pay for itself within six years. The project was carried out with the German Federal Ministry`s financial support and Preussen Electra`s technical support.

In December 1995 a privatisation scheme was approved for Latvijas Gaze. The first stage of privatisation planned to sell off 24% of the company, and to raise its charter capital from lats 270 million (US $ 50 million) to lats 40 million (US $ 75 million), primarily through state contributions. In the second phase strategic investors are being slected and offered 25% of the shares. Gazprom aims to acquire a 16.25% stake in the company. Seven other firms which have shown interest in buying into Latvijas Gaze are all Western: Ruhrgas (Germany), Gaz de France, Norsk Hydro (Norway), BASF AG`s Wintershall AG (Germany), Edon (Dutch) and Enron Corp. (USA). In the third stage 2% of shares are being sold to Latvian residents in exchange for privatisation certificates at open auctions. The Latvijas Gaze personnel has already been allocated 0.75% of that portion. About 7% of the shares are to be distributed among private Latvian businesses.

A preliminary project for the construction of an oil terminal at the port of Riga has been completed. The new terminal, which must still be approved by the Riga city council, will reload Western fuel and crude oil from ships. The project`s work includes representatives of Initrade Petroleum, Man-Tess, Visbija, Neste Oy, Statoil, and Hansa Bunkering. Statoil, Neste and Visbija have already agreed to invest into the project. Construction could begin in 1996. It should cost around US $ 100 million and have an initial capacity of 1.5 million tonnes a year, rising to 2.5 million tonnes by the year 2000. The firms will share a jetty and port facilities. Neste`s oil operations division`s terminal will handle 500,000 tonnes a year to import Western gasoline, diesel and jet fuel products into the Latvian and other Baltic state markets. There is already an important oil terminal at Ventspils, which is supplied by pipeline from Russia. Exports of oil and oil products passing through Ventspils port in 1995 were 1.2 million tonnes up on 1994 and the highest for five years, reaching 21 million tonnes.

Amoco (USA) signed an agreement in January 1995 with the Latvian government to explore for oil in the Baltic Sea. Partnered by Oljeprospektering AB (OPAB) (Sweden), the project, which has been named Dalders, will involve an initial exploration well, probably to be dug in the second half of 1996, estimated to cost US $ 709 million. Amoco and OPAB each have a 45% interest in the project, with Latvia holding 10% and an option to increase its interest to 20%. Total investment in the oil exploration project may be up to US $1 billion. The first drilling, planned for the end of 1996 will cost between US& and 9 million, the second stage - calculation of the deposit`s size US $ 15-20 million, and the third stage, extraction , US $ 500 million.

U.S. COMPANIES IN LATVIA -

3M
A.L. & D. International
American Airlines
American Trans Air
American Fried Chicken
American Express
AMERILAT
Amoco Latvia Petroleum Co.
Architectural Invesments
Arthur Andersen
Asea, Brown & Boveri
Atwood Richards, Inc.
Avis
Baker & McKenzie
BALTA Travel Agency
Baltcom Ltd.
Baltec Associates, Inc.
Baltic American Enterprise Fund
Baltic Business Report
Baltic Forestry Products, Inc.
Baltic Fruit
Baltic Industries, Inc.
Baltic International Airlines
Baltic International Airlines Cargo
Baltic Technology Group
Baltic Trade International
Baltic Ventures, Inc.
Baltic World Air Freight
Big Sky Foods Trading, Inc.
Biosfera Ltd.
Carroll, Burdick & McDonough
Coca-Cola
Colgate-Palmolive
Computer Land Riga
Consensus Ltd.
Controlled Demolition, Inc.
Coopers & Lybrand
Costa Ltd.
Copley Pharmaceutical

Daytona Fastener Works
Dechert Price & Rhoads
Deloitte & Touche SIA
Digital Equipment
Digital Equipment Corporation
DigLat
DHL International
East-West Consulting and Management
Eli-Lilly
Enron Corporation
Ernst & Young
Firebird Transport, Latvia SIA
Ford Motor Company
Gateway International
Global Trade Group
Globex International, Inc.
Haag Industries
Hagler Bailly Consulting, Inc.
Hansa Investments
Hertz
Hewlett-Packard
ICT Latvia Ltd.
Inter Source, Inc.
International Business Machines (IBM)
International School of Latvia
International Trendsetters
Isod International Ltd.
Johnson & Johnson
Junior Achievement of Latvia
Kelloggs
Klavins and Slaidins
Klimas, Kurajevs, Marsans & Hough
Kliners
KPMG Peat Marwick - Policy
LAK International
Lanier
Latnet Services SIA
Latvian-American Eye Center
Latvian-American Shipping
Latvian Management Partners
Letton International
Logistics Baltic
Maersk, Inc.
Maija Blauberga Law Offices
McDonald's Latvia

Metromedia International Telecommunications
Motorola
NCH Advisors
Office USA
PepsiCola General Bottlers
PepsiCo-Latvian Snacks
Philip Morris
Poik-AB Trading Agency, Inc.
Polar Bek International
Price Waterhouse
Proctor and Gamble
Progress Projekts SIA
Radisson Daugava Hotel
Rank Xerox
Riga-American Ltd.
Riga Business School
Riga in Your Pocket
Rigas TV Ltd.
RigAm Impex Ltd.
Riga Stock Exchange
Sea-Land Service
SHELDAHL, Inc.
Spectrum Aviation, Inc.
Squire, Sanders & Dempsey
Stanislavska, Malouf, Lepins and Luhaar
SteelcaseTaLat SIA
T.I.T.A. International
Trade Holdings
UNIONTOURS
United Parcel Service
Verdins Bakery
Verdins Company
VIAMERIKA SIA
Watson International Ltd.
WEDCO Ltd.
Western Consulting
Westinghouse Electric
York Latvia

IMPORTANT BUSINESS AND GOVERNMENT CONTACTS

LATVIAN GOVERNMENT

LATVIA GOVERNMENT SITES & OFFICIAL SITES

Name	Email	Web Site
Ministry of Interior Affairs	iveta.kancena@iem.gov.lv	www.iem.gov.lv
Ministry of Finance	info@fm.gov.lv	www.fm.gov.lv
Ministry of Foreign Affairs	mfa.cha@mfa.gov.lv	www.mfa.gov.lv
Ministry of Justice	tm.kanceleja@tm.gov.lv	www.tm.gov.lv
Ministry of Agriculture		www.zm.gov.lv
Ministry of Culture	webmaster@km.gov.lv	www.km.gov.lv
Ministry of Defence	webmaster@mod.gov.lv	www.mod.gov.lv
Ministry of Education and Science	izm@izm.gov.lv	www.izm.lv
Ministry of Environment Protection and Regional Development		www.varam.gov.lv
Ministry of Transport	sarma.kocane@sam.gov.lv	www.sam.gov.lv
Latvian Development Agency	invest@lda.gov.lv	www.lda.gov.lv
Latvian Privatization Agency	info@mail.lpa.bkc.lv	www.lpa.bkc.lv
State Real Estate Agency	vnia@mail.vnia.lv	www.vnia.lv
Vidzeme Development Agency	vidzemes.aa@valm.lv	www.vidzemes-regions.lv
Cabinet of Ministers	vk@mk.gov.lv	www.mk.gov.lv
Republic of Latvia Cancellery of the President	chancery@president.lv	www.president.lv
Latvian Naval Forces		www.navy.lv
Latvian Navy Fast patrol boat LVNS Linga	petersala@navigator.lv	www.lvnslinga.lv
Saeima (Parliament) of the Republic of Latvia	web@saeima.lv	www.saeima.lv
CSBL	csb@csb.lv	www.csb.lv
Centre for the Study of Public Policy	o.j.robertson@strath.ac.uk	www.cspp.strath.ac.uk
Civil Aviation Administration of Latvia		www.caa.lv
Deparment of the State Land Service in Southern Curland		www.dkurzeme.vzd.gov.lv
Department of the Land Registers		www.zemgram.lv

European Integration Bureau		www.eib.lv
Land Cadastre Centre of Latvia	vzd@vzd.gov.lv	www.lzkc.org.lv

Latvian Embassy: Normunds Popens, Attach,, 4325 17th Street NW, Washington DC 20011, tel: (202) 726-8213 or (202) 726-6757, fax: (202) 726-6785

Latvian Development Agency: Maira Vesmane, Head, Investment Department, Perses Street 2, Riga LV-1442, Latvia, tel: (371) 728 8842, fax: (371) 728 2524

Latvian Development Agency Business Information Center, Perses Street 2, Riga LV-1442, tel: (371) 728 7995, (371) 728 3425, fax: (371) 782 0458, e-mail: invest@lda.gov.lv, http://www.lda.gov.lv

Latvian Privatization Agency: Selga Laizane, Assistant for Foreign Relations, Kr. Valdemara Street 31, Riga LV-1010, Latvia, tel: (371) 732 2281; fax: (371) 783 0363

Latvian Customs Department: Normunds Niedols, Director, Kr. Valdemara Street 1a, Riga LV-1841, Latvia, tel: (371) 732 3858; fax: (371) 732 2440

Ministry of Agriculture: Maris Sprindzuks, Director for Foreign Relations, Republic Square 2, Riga LV-1981, Latvia, tel: (371) 732 0162 or (371) 732 7894; fax: (371) 783 0272

Latvian National Certification Center: H. Jurevica, Director, Klijanu Street 7, tel: (371) 237 5667, (371) 237 5464

GOVERNMENT INSTITUTIONS IN THE REPUBLIC OF LATVIA

Chancery of the President Address: Riga, Pils laukums 3 LV-1900 Tel. +371 7377548 Fax. +371 7325800 Press Secretary Tel. +371 7092121	Saeima (Parliament) Address: Riga, Jekaba iela 11 LV 1811 Tel. +371 7087111 Fax.+371 7087100 Press Secretary Tel. +371 7027218
Cabinet of Ministers Address: Riga, Brivibas blvd 36 LV-1050 Tel. +371 7332232 Fax. +371 7286598 Press Secretary Tel. +371 7289505	Bank of Latvia Address: Riga, K. Valdemara iela 2a LV-1050 Tel. +371 7022300 Fax. +371 7022420 Press Secretary Tel. +371 7022300
The Ministry of Defence Address: Riga, K.Valdemara 10/12 LV-1473	The Ministry of Foreign Affairs Address: Riga, Brivibas blvd 36 LV-1395

Tel. +371 7210124 Fax. +371 7830236 Press Secretary Tel. +371 7211564	Tel. +371 7016101 Fax. +371 7282121 Press Secretary Tel. +371 7016117
The Ministry of Economy Address: Riga, Brivibas 55 LV-1519 Tel. +371 7013101 Fax. +371 7280882 Press Secretary Tel. +371 7013113	The Ministry of Finance Address: Riga, Smilsu 1 LV-1919 Tel. +371 7226672 Fax. +371 7095503 Press Secretary Tel. +371 7095405
The Ministry of Interior Address: Riga, Raina blvd. 6 LV-1050 Tel. +371 7219210 Fax. +371 7212255 Press Secretary Tel. +371 7219963	The Ministry of Education and Science Address: Riga, Valnu 2 LV-1098 Tel. +371 7222415 Fax. +371 7213992 Press Secretary Tel. +371 7216423
The Ministry of Culture Address: Riga, K.Valdemara 11a LV-1364 Tel. +371 7224772 Fax. +371 7224916 Press Secretary Tel. +371 7229737	The Ministry of Welfare Address: Riga, Skolas 28 LV-1331 Tel. +371 7021600 Fax. +371 2276445 Press Secretary Tel. +371 7021618
The Ministry of Transport and Communications Address: Riga, Gogola 3 LV-1544 Tel. +371 7226922 Fax. +371 7217180 Press Secretary Tel. +371 7028260	The Ministry of Justice Address: Riga, Brivibas blvd. 36 LV-1536 Tel. +371 7088220 Fax. +371 7285575 Press Secretary Tel. +371 7286364
The Ministry of Environmental Protection and Regional Development Address: Riga, Peldu 25 LV-1494 Tel. +371 7026400 Fax. +371 7820442 Press Secretary Tel. +371 7026418	The Ministry of Agriculture Address: Riga, Republikas laukums 2 LV-1981 Tel. +371 7027107 Fax. +371 7027250 Press Secretary Tel. +371 7027070

LARGEST LATVIAN COMMERCIAL BANKS

Name	Address	Tel	Fax	Email	Web Site
Baltic International	43, Kaleju str. Riga, LV-1050,	371 7222789	371 7216870	office@bib.lv	www.bib.lv

Bank					
Baltic Transit Bank	3, 13 Janvara st. Riga LV 1050	371 7024747	371 7211985	btb@btb.lv	www.btb.lv
LATEKO bank	E.Birznieka-Upisha street 21 Riga, LV-1011	371 7041100	371 7041111	welcome@lateko.lv	www.lateko.lv
NORD/LB	Smilshu 6, Riga - 50, LV-1803		371 7323449	info@nordlb.lv	www.nordlb.lv
Rietumu Banka	54 Brivibas St., Riga	371-7025202	371-7025202		www.rietumu.com
Trasta komercbanka	9 Miesnieku street, Riga, LV-1050	371 7027777	371 7027700	info@tkb.lv	www.tkb.lv
Unibank	Pils iela 23, Riga LV-1050	371 7215555	371 7215566	atsauksmes@unibanka.lv	www.unibanka.lv
Vereinsbank	Elizabetes iela 63 Riga, LV-1050	371 7085 500	371 7085 507	info@vereinsbank.lv	www.vuw.de

Parex Bank (Parekss Banka): Aleksandrs Gnedovskis, Smilsu street 3, Riga LV-1050, Latvia, tel: (371) 733 1970, (371) 701 0224, fax: (371) 701 0001

Unibank: Dainis Senbergs, Head of Board for International Operations, L. Pils street 23, Riga LV-1050, Latvia, tel: (371-7) 215-585, (371) 721 2808, fax: (371) 721 0775

Riga Bank (Rigas Kommercbanka): Viola Tribis, Head of Board for International Operations, Smilsu St. 6, Riga LV-1050, Latvia, tel: (371) 732 3892, fax: (371) 732 3449

Rietumu Bank: Olga Karbovnichaya, Director, 7 Vesetas St, Riga LV-1013, tel.: (371) 237 5205, fax: (371) 237 2897, (371) 782 8069

Latvian Savings Bank (Latvijas Krajbanka): Andris Ozolins, Investment and Foreign Technical Assistance Department, Palasta street 1, Riga LV-1050, tel: (371) 722 8601, (371) 782 0167

LATVIA CPA'S ACCOUNTANTS ACCOUNTING FIRMS AND COMPANIES

NAMA	Address	Tel	Fax	Email	Web Site
AUDIT auditing company	36-1 Blaumana St. Riga LV 1011	371 7284 125	371 7284109	audit@auditbirojs.lv	www.auditbirojs.lv

Rödl & Partner	K. Valdemara iela 33 1010 Riga	371 733 4280	371 733 4620	riga@roedl.lv	www.roedlusa.com
IBC Consulting Ltd	Antonijas str. 22-4 Riga, LV-1010	371 7333957	371 7333956	info@ibc.lv	www.ibc.lv
BDO	Pulkveža Brieža iela 19/1 Riga	371 7220320	371 7320180	invest.riga@bkc.lv	www.bdo.investriga.lv
Deloitte Touche	Biskapa gate 2 Riga, LV 1050	371 781 4160	371 722 3007		www.deloitte.com
Ernst & Young	11.novembra krastmala 23 LV 1050 Riga	371 704 3801	371 704 3802	Riga@lv.ey.com	www.ey.com
Sacco Ltd	Pulkveža Brieža 8-1, Riga LV1010	371 7505 000	371 7505 001	gramatvediba@sacco.lv	www.sacco.lv

LATVIA AIRLINES AND OTHER AIRLINES IN LATVIA

AeroSvit Airlines		371) 7207502	371 7207902	aerosvit@neonet.lv	www.aerosvit.ua
Air Baltic	15 Kalku str. Riga, LV-1050	371 7207777	371 7224282	reservations@airbaltic.lv	www.airbaltic.com
Austrian Airlines	Lidosta "Riga" LV-1053 Riga	371 7507700	371 7507701	office.rix@aua.com	www.aua.com
British Airways	Torna 4, Section 3A Riga, LV1010	371 7326 737	371 7326 747	retailsales.1.riga@britishairways.com	www.britishairways.com
CSA - Czech Airlines	Riga International Airport, Main Terminal - 3rd level, LV-1053 Riga	371 7207 636	371 7207 337	rix@czechairlines.com	www.czech-airlines.cz
Estonian Air	22 Aspazijas blv. Riga LV-1050	371 7224323	371 7212720	riga@estonian-air.ee	www.estonian-air.ee
FINNAIR	Riga International Airport, 2nd floor	371 720 7010		feedback@finnair.fi	www.finnair.com

LOT	St. Maza Pils 5 Riga LV-1050	371 722 7234	371 724 2869		www.lot.com

LATVIA CAR RENTAL COMPANIES

Name	Address	Tel	Fax	Email	Web Site
Avis	Krasta Strasse 3, Riga, LV 1003	371 7225876			www.avis.com
AGG	86, Ieriku st. Riga LV 1084	371 7597298	371 7549485	agg@riga.mail.telia.com	www.carrental-agg.lv
Sixt	Kalku 28 (Hotel De Rome, entrance from Aspazijas blv.)	371 7224 022	371) 7224 036	rent@sixt.lv	www.sixt.lv
Car4rent	52-14 A.Caka St. Riga, LV 1011	371-7316185	371-7316086		www.car4rent.lv
Europcar	REVAL HOTEL LATVIA Elizabetes st. 55 Riga LV 1010	371 7772214	371 7772214		www.europcar.com

LATVIA FINANCIAL CONSULTING

Name	Address	Tel	Fax	Email	Web Site
Development Project Institute (DPI)	32-7 Kr. Barona str. Riga, LV-1011	371 724 0042	371 728 1191	info@projects.lv	www.projekti.lv
Biznesa Konsultantu Grupa (BKG)	Tirgonu iela 10-7, Riga LV-1050	371 7224305	371 7224306	bkg@bkgriga.lv	www.bkgriga.lv
KPF	Biekensalas iela 6 - 301, Riga, LV-1004	7808553	7808552	future@kpf.lv	www.kpf.lv
Ars-inteks	118, K.Valdemara St. #407, Riga, LV-1013	371 7370588	371 7517378	arsint@mailbox.neonet.lv	www.arsinteks.lv
BBG Financial				r@balticbankingg	www.balticbankin

Services				roup.com	ggroup.com
Belokon Holdings	21 Valdemara str., Riga, LV-1010	371 7505866	371 7812065	secretary@belokonholding.com	www.belokonholding.com
Olio	Volguntes 32 Riga LV 1024			olio@olio.lv	www.olio.lv
Perfekta Consulting	Ganibu dambi 26-415 Riga, LV-1005	371 738 3810	371 738 2050	info@perfekta.lv	www.perfekta.lv
SACCO Enterprise Group	8 Pulkveza Brieza St. Suite 1 Riga, LV 1010	371 7 505 000	371 7 505 001	sacco@sacco.lv	www.sacco.lv
Observer Latvia	Brivibas iela 40-38 Riga, LV 1055	371 750 4408	371 724 0350	help@observer.lv	www.observer.lv

LATVIA INSURANCE FIRMS AND COMPANIES

Name	Address	Tel	Fax	Email	Web Site
SALAMANDRA-BALTIK	E. Birznieka - Upisa st. 12, Riga, LV-1050	371 7282225	371 7016586	lifeins@salbalt.riga.lv	www.salamandra-baltik.lv
BAN	Antonijas str. 23, Riga, LV-1010	7080408	7080407	office@ban.lv	www.ban.lv
Riga Re				rigare@rigare.as.lv	www.riga-re.com
RSK					www.rsk.lv

LATVIA LAWYERS LAW FIRMS AND COMPANIES

Name	Address	Tel	Fax	Email	Web Site
Lejins, Torgans & Vonsovics	Zverinatu advokatu birojs "Lejinš, Torgans un Vonsovics" Kr. Valdemara iela 20, Riga, LV-1010,	371 7821-525	371 7821-524	lt-v@lt-v.lv	www.lt-v.lv
LAW OFFICES OF VALTERS GENCS	3rd fl, Valdemara Center, 21 KR. Valdemara st., RIGA 1010	371 724 00 90	371 724 00 91	valters.gencs@gencs.lv	www.gencs.lv
Sorainen Law Offices	Kr. Valdemara iela 21 LV1010 Riga	371 7332 449	371 7332 450	sorainen@sorainen.lv	www.sorainen.com
BUMBIERIS Andis	Kr.Valdemara St. 51 Riga, LV	371-9211046	371-7334042	advokats@parks.lv	www.findlaw.com

	1384				
Blukis & Partners					www.blukislegal.lv
BRIZE, EGLITIS & PARTNERI	Brivibas iela 40-22 Riga, LV-1050	7240270	7224494	latvia@balticlaw.com	www.brize-eglitis.lv
Grunte&Cers	40 Brivibas street, 2nd fl. Riga, LV 1050	371 7 240022	371 7 821231	gc@grunte-cers.lv	www.grunte-cers.lv
IBC Consulting Ltd.	Antonijas str. 22-4 Riga, LV-1010	371 733 3957	371 733 3956	info@ibc.lv	www.ibc.lv
KPMG Latvia					www.kpmg.lv
Klavins & Slaidins	21 Kr. Valdemara St. Riga, LV-1010	371 7 035222	371 7 035252	advokati@klavinsslaidins.lv	www.klavinsslaidins.lv
Germane & Lizums		371 - 7273241		vlizums@rsp.lv	www.rsp.lv
Imeko	Engures street 11-50, Jurmala, LV-2016	371) 9113939		imeko@imeko.lv	www.imeko.lv

LATVIA REAL ESTATE FIRMS AND AGENTS, RIGA

Name	Address	Tel	Fax	Email	Web Site
Object.lv		371 9676867		info@object.lv	www.object.lv
ANNO	Brivibas iela 68, 5th floor, Riga, Latvia, LV-1011	7842333	7842360	anno@anno.lv	www.parks.lv
NZ agentura	Brivibas st. 37, 2 fl. office - 2a Riga	371 7240386	371 7243132	nz@nz-agency.lv	www.nz-agency.lv
ARCO REAL ESTATE	Skolas street 12a–3, Riga, LV–1010	7365555	7284423	riga@arcoreal.lv	www.arcoreal.lv
Arkada	12, Tomsona St. 17, LV-1013, Riga	371-7376916	371-7339211	arkada@apollo.lv	www.arkada.apollo.lv
Averts Ltd.					www.averts.lv
BKI NAMI	3, 8 Kalku str, Riga, Latvia, LV-1050	371)7509709	371)7509719	INFO@lv-bki.lv	http://www.bkinami.lv/
B.L. Property Agents	Gertrudes street 33/35 (2nd floor), Riga, LV -	371 7506170	371 7506162	info@blpa.lv	www.blpa.lv

	1011				

BEST RESTAURANTS TRADITIONAL AND INTERNATIONAL RIGA

Name	Address	Tel	Fax	Email	Web Site
Columbine	Aspazijas blv.,36/38 Riga, LV1050	371-7225411	371-7216140	metropole@brovi.lv	www.metropole.lv
Kaku Varti	Kalku iela 11a, Riga	371 7224 576			www.kalkuvarti.lv
Zagra		7211026	7211026		www.zagars.lv
Otto Schwarz	Kaleju str. 9/11, Riga, LV 1050	371 7087501	371 7087515	reservation@konventa.lv	www.derome.lv

LATVIA TRANSLATING & INTERPRETING SERVICES

Name	Address	Tel	Fax	Email	Web Site
Baltic Media	S-181 24 Lidingö Stockholm Sweden	46(0)8767-6024	46(0)8767-3693	info@balticmedia.net	www.baltikumspecialisten.se
Idea Media	Elizabetes iela 18 – 5, LV 1050 Riga	371) 7502047	371) 7502048	im@idea-media.lv	www.ideamedia.lv
Karina Livmane's Translation Bureau	Zakusalas krastmala 3-904 (Latvian TV building, 9th floor), Riga, LV-1509	371 7226052	371 7226051	info@tulkojumi.lv	www.tulkojumi.lv
STROMBUS	Tomsona iela 13-3, Riga	371 7501741		strombus@strombus.net	www.ltn.lv
Kaspars Melkis	Ernestines 41-8, Riga LV-1046	371 972-98-60		kaspar@latvianforyou.com	www.latvianforyou.com
Latvian Translators					www.world.lv
Adverbum	Stabu Street 27, block 2, No. 7 Riga	371 7299886	371 7299878	info@adverbum.lv	www.adverbum.lv
Tatjana Judina and Partners	47 Stabu St., 3rd Floor, Office # 3, LV-1011, Riga	371 731-2848	371 731-2848	vt@vide.lv	www.translations.lv

LATVIA DIRECTORIES AND SEARCH ENGINES IN ENGLISH

Name	Web Site
City Paper	www.balticsww.com
Hot Line	www.117.lv
Kontakti	www.kontakti.lv
TV Net	www.tvnet.lv
Virtual Riga	www.virtualriga.com

TRADE ASSOCIATIONS, CHAMBERS OF COMMERCE

American Chamber of Commerce in Latvia: J.C. Cole, President, Jauniela 24, Riga LV-1050, Latvia, tel: (371) 721 5205, fax: (371) 782-0090

Latvian Chamber of Commerce and Industry: Henriks Silenieks, Head, Business Promotion Department, Brivibas Bulvaris 21, 4th floor, Riga LV-1849, Latvia, tel: (371) 733 2205, fax: (371) 733 2276, e-mail: chamber@sun.lcc.org.lv

Latvian Bankers' Association: Teodoras Tverijonas, President, Stabu St.18, Riga LV-1001, Latvia, tel: (371) 727 1640, fax: (371) 782 8170

U.S. EMBASSY TRADE PERSONNEL

Constance Phlipot, Economic/ Officer
Iveta Aizbalte, Economic Assistant
Jolante Andersone, Agricultural Assistan
t Anna Zisser, Assistant
7 Raina Blvd, Riga LV-1510, tel: (371) 721 0005 or (371) 782-0046; fax: (371) 782-0047

U.S. GOVERNMENT CONTACTS

U.S. Department of Commerce: Amy Serrill, Deputy Director, Central/Eastern Europe Business Information Center, Washington D.C. 20230, tel: (202) 482-2645, fax: (202) 482-4473, web site: http://www.itaiep.doc.gov/eebic/ceebic.html

Export-Import Bank of the U.S.: Cheryl Conlin, Senior Loan Officer, International Business Development, 811 Vermont Ave, N.W., Washington, D.C. 20527-0001, tel: (202) 565-3900; fax: (202) 565-3931, e-mail: bdg@exim.gov http://www.exim.gov

Overseas Private Investment Corporation (OPIC): Joan J. Edwards, Managing Director,Business Development, 1100 New York Avenue, N.W., Washington D.C. 20527, tel: (202) 336-8617, fax: (202) 408-5145 OPIC web site: http://www.opic.gov

U.S. Trade and Development Agency: Geoffrey Jackson, Regional Director, Central, Eastern & Southern Europe, Room 309 SA-16, Washington D.C. 20523-1602, tel: (703) 875-4357, fax: (703) 875-4009

LATVIAN TRADE FAIRS AND EXHIBITIONS

U.S. companies interested in participating in the shows should contact trade shows organizers (contact information follows below) or Arturs Dombrovskis, director of exhibition department, Latvian Chamber of Commerce and Industry, 21 Brivibas Blvd., Riga, LV 1849, Latvia, tel: (371) 722-5595; 733-3228, tel/fax: (371) 782-0092; fax: (371) 733-2276; E-mail: chamber@sun.lcc.org.LV. www:http:/sun.lcc.org.LV/trade97.html

STATE ENVIRONMENT PROTECTION INSTITUTIONS

Ministry of Environmental
Protection and Regional Development
25 Peldu St, Riga, LV-1494
tel: 371-702-6402; fax: 371-782-0442

State Ecological Expertise Board
25 Rupniecibas St., Riga, LV 1045
Chairman: Dr. Magnus Vircavs,
Tel: 371-732-1209; tel/fax: 371-732-1049

ENVIRONMENTAL NGO'S

Environmental Protection
Fund Of Latvia
. Pils 17, Riga, LV 1046
Mr. Janis Bruninieks, Executive Director
tel. 371-722-2427; fax 371-722-1729

Environmental Consulting and Monitoring Center
Rupniecibas 25, Riga, LV 1045
Mr. Edgars Bojars
tel: 371-782-0263; 7323-595; 7323-665; fax: 371-783-0503

EU Phare PIU
Peldu 25, Riga, LV 1494
Mr. Michael Lavelle
tel: 371-722-6528; fax: 371-782-0442

Environmental Projects
800+PIU, 500-PIU, ICZMP
Mr. Andris Kiskurno
Pils 17, Riga, LV 1047
tel: 371-722-7331; tel/fax: 371-7229-553

US EPA Cooperation
Peldu 25, Riga, LV 1494
Ms. Inguna Grinsteine
tel: 371-702-6551; fax: 371-702-6558

Hazardous Waste Management
Organization BAO
Pils 17, Riga, LV 1047
Mr. Augusts Dzerkals
tel: 371-7211-321; fax:371-7215-272

Latvian Pollution Prevention Center
Gertrudes 33/35 - 514, Riga, LV 1011
Ms. Natalia Ladutko
tel/fax:371-229-3683

Coalition Clean Baltic
Raina 19, Riga, LV 1586
Mr. Girts Strazdins
tel: 371-722-0669; 722-1314; fax: 371-721-3566

Latvia Fund For Nature
Kronvalda 4, Riga, LV 1842
Mr. Maris Kreilis
tel: 371-732-2852; fax: 371-783-0291

World Wide Fund for Nature
Kristapa 30, Riga, LV 1046
Mr. Ugis Rotbergs
tel: 371-7619-015; fax: 371-722-0716; 722-0715

FOREIGN EMBASSIES IN LATVIA

Australia (honorary consulate)	**Austria (consulate)**	**Belarus**
17 Peterbaznicas tel/fax 7225908	21 Brivibas bulv tel: 7334231 fax: 7820364	12 Jezus Baznicas iela tel: 7322550 fax: 7322891 Consular section tel 7325361
Canada	China	Korea (honorary consulate)
4 Doma laukums tel: 7830141, 7821161 fax: 7830140	41 Mukusalas iela tel: 7212623 mob.fax: 9350502	9 Teatra iela tel: 7213243 fax: 7216093
Cuba	Czech Republic	Denmark
14 Vairoga iela tel: 7828414 fax: 561389	29 Elizabetes iela tel: 7217814, 7287306 fax: 7217821	11 L. Pils iela tel: 7226210, 7210433 fax: 7229218, 7820234
Estonia	Finland	France
13 Skolas iela tel: 7820460, 7334861 fax: 7820461 Consular section tel 7226845	1 Kalpaka bulvaris iela tel: 7332005, 7333596 fax: 7229549	9 Raina bulv tel: 7213972, 7213972, 7212878 fax: 7820131
Germany	Great Britain	Iceland (consulate)
14 Basteja bulv tel: 7229096, 7229764	5 Alunana iela tel: 7338126-31	45/47 Elizabetes iela tel: 7228370

fax: 7820223	fax: 7338132	fax: 7820013
Israel	Italy	Jakutia (representation)
2 Elizabetes iela tel: 7320739, 7320980, 7320849 fax: 7830170	9 Teatra iela tel/fax: 7216084	2 Elizabetes iela tel: 7321247 fax: 7321770
Lithuania	Moldova (consulate)	Norway
2 Elizabetes iela tel: 7321519, 7320919, 7320849 fax: 7321589 Consular section tel 7320919	99 K.Barona tel: 271521 fax: 274258	14 Zirgu iela tel: 7216744, 7216746 fax: 7820195
Philippines (consulate)	Poland	Russia
1 Raina bulv tel: 7325128 fax: 7830108	2 Elizabetes iela tel: 7321617, 7321593, 7320622 fax: 7338196 Consular section tel: 7322233	2 Antonijas iela tel: 7332151, 7220693 fax: 7830209 Consular section tel 7212579, fax 7210123
Sweden	Switzerland	Taiwan (commercial represent.)
13 Lacplesa iela tel: 7286276, 7286759, 7286469 fax: 7288501 8 Pumpura iela tel: 7828032 fax: 7828031	2 Elizabetes iela tel: 7338351, 7338352 fax: 7338354 Visa section tel 7338353	2 Elizabetes iela tel: 7321204
The United States of America	Ukraine	Uzbekistan
7 Raina bulv tel: 7210005, 7220367, 7229709 fax: 7226530	3 Kalpaka bulv tel: 7243082, 7332956 fax: 7325583 Consular section tel 7332956	3/5 Jekaba iela tel: 7222686, 9206739 fax: 7222686

LATVIA EMBASSIES

REPUBLIC OF AUSTRIA H.E. Mr. Martins Virsis Ambassador Extraordinary and Plenipotentiary, Vienna	Chancery: Währinger Str. 3/8, A-1090 Vienna, Austria Telephone: 43 1 403 31 12 43 1 403 31 13 Fax: 43 1 403 31 12/27 E-mail: lettbot@netway.at
REPUBLIC OF BELARUS Mrs. Ingrida Levrence Chargé d' Affaires a.i., Minsk	Chancery: 6a Doroshevica Str., Minsk 220013, Belarus Telephone: 375 172 849 393

	375 172 847 277 375 172 847 288 375 172 847 475 (Consular Section) Fax: 375 172 847 334 E-mail: daile@belsonet.net
KINGDOM OF BELGIUM H.E. Mr. Imants Liegis Ambassador Extraordinary and Plenipotentiary, Brussels	Chancery: 158 av. Molière, 1050 Brussels, Belgium Telephone: 32 2 344 16 82 Fax: 32 2 344 74 78 E-mail: lvembassybenelux@arcadis.be
REPUBLIC OF BULGARIA H.E. Mr. Aivars Vovers Ambassador Extraordinary and Plenipotentiary, Warsaw	See Warsaw, Poland
CANADA H.E. Mr. Janis Lusis Ambassador Extraordinary and Plenipotentiary, Ottawa	Chancery: 112 Kent Street, Place de Ville, Tower B, Suite 208, Ottawa, Ontario K1P 5P2, Canada Telephone: 1 613 238 60 14 1 613 238 68 68 (Consular Section) Fax: 1 613 238 70 44 E-mail: latvia-embassy@magmacom.com URL: http://www2.magmacom.com/~latemb/
PEOPLE'S REPUBLIC OF CHINA Mr. Peteris Pildegovics Chargé d' Affaires a. i., Beijing	Chancery: 3-2-21 San Li Tun Diplomatic Compound, Beijing 100600, China Telephone: 86 10 653 201 06 E-mail: kina@public.bta.net.cn
CZECH REPUBLIC H.E. Mrs. Aija Odina Ambassador Extraordinary and Plenipotentiary, Prague	Chancery: 3 Hradeshinska Str., P.O. Box 54, 10100 Prague, Czech Republic Telephone: 420 2 242 524 54 420 2 242 506 54 Fax:

	420 2 242 550 99 E-mail: zibens@lrvpraga.anet.cz
KINGDOM OF DENMARK H.E. Mr. Aivars Baumanis Ambassador Extraordinary and Plenipotentiary, Copenhagen	Chancery: 17 Rosbaeksvej Str., 2100 Copenhagen, Denmark Telephone: 45 39 276 000 45 39 276 168 Fax: 45 39 276 173 E-mail: letambas@pip.dknet.dk latembdk@mfa.gov.lv
REPUBLIC OF ESTONIA H.E. Mr. Gints Jegermanis Ambassador Extraordinary and Plenipotentiary, Tallinn	Chancery: 10 Tõnismägi Str., Tallinn EE 00001, Estonia Telephone: 372 646 13 13 372 646 13 10 (Consular Section) Telefax: 372 631 13 66 E-mail: gints@latvia.ee
REPUBLIC OF FINLAND H.E. Mr. Alberts Sarkanis Ambassador Extraordinary and Plenipotentiary, Helsinki	Chancery: 10 Armfeltintie, 00150 Helsinki, Finland Telephone: 358 9 476 472 44 358 9 476 472 33 (Consular Section) Fax: 358 9 476 472 88 E-mail: latemb.fin@latemb.inet.fi
REPUBLIC OF FRANCE H.E. Mrs. Sandra Kalniete Ambassador Extraordinary and Plenipotentiary, Paris	Chancery: 6, Villa Said, 75116 Paris, France Telephone: 331 536 458 10 331 536 458 16 (Consular Section) Fax: 331 536 458 19 E-mail: ambleton@easynet.fr
FEDERAL REPUBLIC OF GERMANY H.E. Mr. Andris Teikmanis Ambassador Extraordinary and Plenipotentiary, Bonn	Chancery: 110 Adenauerallee, 53113 Bonn, Germany Telephone: 49 228 264 242 49 228 264 437 (Consular Section) Fax: 49 228 265 840

	E-mail: lbger@lbger.bn.eunet.de latembger@mfa.gov.lv
GREECE /HELLENIC REPUBLIC/ H.E. Mr. Martins Perts Ambassador Extraordinary and Plenipotentiary, Rome, Italy Mr. Martins Lacis Chargé d' Affaires a.i., Athens	Chancery: 9 Irodotou Str., Kolonaki, 10674 Athens, Greece Telephone: 30 1 729 44 83 Fax: 30 1 729 44 79 E-mail: latvia@otenet.gr
THE HOLY SEE H.E. Mr. Atis Sjanits Ambassador Extraordinary and Plenipotentiary, Vilnius	See Vilnius, Lithuania
REPUBLIC OF HUNGARY H.E. Mr. Martins Virsis Ambassador Extraordinary and Plenipotentiary, Vienna	See Vienna, Austria
REPUBLIC OF ICELAND H.E. Mr. Aivars Baumanis Ambassador Extraordinary and Plenipotentiary, Copenhagen	See Copenhagen, Denmark
IRELAND H.E. Mr. Normans Penke Ambassador Extraordinary and Plenipotentiary, London	See London, UK
STATE OF ISRAEL H.E. Mr. Ivars Silars Ambassador Extraordinary and Plenipotentiary, Tel Aviv	Chancery: 52 Pinkas Str., Apt. 51, Tel Aviv 62261, Israel Telephone: 972 3 546 24 38 Fax: 972 3 544 43 72 E-mail:

	latvembi@netvision.net.il
ITALIAN REPUBLIC H.E. Mr. Martins Perts Ambassador Extraordinary and Plenipotentiary, Rome	Chancery: Viale Liegi, 42, 00189 Rome, Italy Telephone: 39 6 8841 229 Fax: 39 6 8841 239 E-mail: embrom@micanet.it
KYRGYZ REPUBLIC H.E. Mr. Andris Vilcans Ambassador Extraordinary and Plenipotentiary, Tashkent	See Tashkent, Uzbekistan
PRINCIPALLITY OF LIECHTENSTEIN H.E. Mr. Martins Virsis Ambassador Extraordinary and Plenipotentiary, Vienna	See Vienna, Austria
REPUBLIC OF LITHUANIA H.E. Mr. Atis Sjanits Ambassador Extraordinary and Plenipotentiary, Vilnius	Chancery: 76 M.K.Chiurlionio Str., 2009 Vilnius, Lithuania Telephone: 370 2 231 260 370 2 231 125 370 2 231 220 (Consular Section) Fax: 370 2 231 130 E-mail: lietuva@latvia.balt.net URL: http://www.parks.lv/home/latvijos-ambasada/
LUXEMBOURG H.E. Mr. Imants Liegis Ambassador Extraordinary and Plenipotentiary, Brussels	See Brussels, Belgium
UNITED MEXICAN STATES H.E. Mr. Ojars Kalnins Ambassador Extraordinary and Plenipotentiary, Washington	See Washington, U.S.A.

KINGDOM OF THE NETHERLANDS H.E. Mr. Imants Liegis Ambassador Extraordinary and Plenipotentiary, Brussels Mr. Karlis Eihenbaums Chargé d' Affaires a. i., Haag	Chancery: Balistrat 88, 2585 XX's-Gravenhage, The Netherlands Telephone: 31 70 306 39 34 Fax: 31 70 306 28 58 E-mail: amb.letland@cornnet.nl
KINGDOM OF NORWAY H.E. Mr. Valdis Krastins Ambassador Extraordinary and Plenipotentiary, Oslo	Chancery: Bygdøy Alle 76, Post Box 3163 Elisenberg, 0268 Oslo, Norway Telephone: 47 22 54 22 80 47 22 54 22 81 Fax: 47 22 54 64 26 E-mail: latve@newmedia.no
REPUBLIC OF POLAND H.E. Mr. Aivars Vovers Ambassador Extraordinary and Plenipotentiary, Warsaw	Chancery: 15-19 Tadeusza Rejtana, 02516 Warsaw, Poland Telephone: 48 22 84 81 947 48 22 84 89 805 48 22 84 95 706 Fax: 48 22 84 80 201 E-mail: amlotew1@warman.com.pl
REPUBLIC OF PORTUGAL H.E. Mrs. Sandra Kalniete Ambassador Extraordinary and Plenipotentiary (agréé), Paris Mr. Rolands Lappuke Chargé d' Affaires a.i., Lisbon	Chancery: Avenida Miguel Bombarda 36, 5C, 1050-165 Lisbon, Portugal Telephone: 351 1 781 51 20 Fax: 351 1 796 32 42 E-mail: np95im@mail.telepac.pt

ROMANIA H.E. Mr. Peteris Vaivars Ambassador Extraordinary and Plenipotentiary, Kyiv	See Kyiv, Ukraine
RUSSIAN FEDERATION H.E. Mr. Imants Daudiss Ambassador Extraordinary and Plenipotentiary, Moscow	Chancery: 3 Chapligina Str., 103062 Moscow, Russian Federation Telephone: 7 095 925 27 07 7 095 925 00 52 7 095 925 51 82 (Consular Section) Fax: 7 095 923 92 95 7 095 923 72 25 (Consular Section) E-mail: latemb@co.ru latembru@mfa.gov.lv
SLOVAK REPUBLIC H.E. Mr. Martins Virsis Ambassador Extraordinary and Plenipotentiary, Vienna	See Vienna, Austria
REPUBLIC OF SLOVENIA H.E. Mr. Martins Virsis Ambassador Extraordinary and Plenipotentiary, Vienna	See Vienna, Austria
SPAIN H.E. Mr. Olgerts Pavlovskis Ambassador Extraordinary and Plenipotentiary, Madrid	Chancery: c/Diego de León 36-4°, 28006 Madrid, Spain Telephone: 34 91 563 17 45 Fax: 34 91 411 04 18 E-mail: letspan@lite.eunet.es
KINGDOM OF SWEDEN	Chancery: Odengatan 5, Box 19167, 104 32 Stockholm, Sweden

H.E. Mr. Janis Dripe Ambassador Extraordinary and Plenipotentiary, Stockholm	Telephone: 46 8 700 63 00 Fax: 46 8 140 151 E-mail: lettlands.ambassad@swipnet.se URL: http://www.lettland.nu/ambassad/
SWITZERLAND /SWISS CONFEDERATION/ H.E. Mr. Martins Virsis Ambassador Extraordinary and Plenipotentiary, Vienna	See Vienna, Austria
REPUBLIC OF TURKEY H.E. Mr. Aivis Ronis Ambassador Extraordinary and Plenipotentiary, Riga	Chancery: Brivibas bulvaris 36, 1395 Riga, Latvia Telephone: 371 72 85 918 Fax: 371 78 28 121 E-mail: ARonis@mfa.gov.lv
UKRAINE H.E. Mr. Peteris Vaivars Ambassador Extraordinary and Plenipotentiary, Kyiv	Chancery: 4/6 Desiatinna Str., 252025 Kyiv, Ukraine Telephone: 38 044 462 07 08 38 044 229 38 80 (Consular Section) Fax: 38 044 229 27 45 38 044 462 07 19 (Consular Section) E-mail: latemb@public.ua.net
UNITED KINGDOM OF GREAT BRITAIN AND NORTHERN IRELAND H.E. Mr. Normans Penke Ambassador Extraordinary and Plenipotentiary, London	Chancery: 45 Nottingham Place, London W1M 3FE, UK Telephone: 44 171 312 00 40 Fax: 44 171 312 00 42 E-mail: latemb@dircon.co.uk
UNITED STATES OF AMERICA H.E. Mr. Ojars Kalnins Ambassador Extraordinary and Plenipotentiary, Washington	Chancery: 4325 Seventeenth Str., N.W. Washington, D.C. 20011, U.S.A. Telephone: 1 202 726 82 13 1 202 726 82 14 Fax: 1 202 726 67 85

	E-mail: latvia@ambergateway.com URL: http://www.latvia-usa.org/
REPUBLIC OF UZBEKISTAN H.E. Mr. Andris Vilcans Ambassador Extraordinary and Plenipotentiary, Tashkent	Chancery: 6 Murtozaeva Str., Tashkent, Uzbekistan Telephone: 7 371 2 349 213 7 371 2 342 489 (Consular Section) Fax: 7 371 2 349 213 E-mail: latvemb@bcc.com.uz

LATVIAN PRIVATIZATION AGENCY - KEY CONTACTS

(+371)

Information bureau	7332082
Director General Mr Janis Naglis	7321084
Privatization Process Director Mr Andrejs Tiknuss	7321338
Legal Affairs Director Mr Viktors Sadinovs	7321262
Finance Director Mr Ilmars Razumovskis	7322401
Technical Director Mr Arvis Freibergs	7321929
Barents Group Mr John Noble	7334236
Public Relations Unit Mr Edgars Zellis	7322281
Advisors Mr Agnar Johanson	7021372
TOB	7021359
Secretariat Ms Ludmila Ozolina	7021348
Privatization Regulations Development and Execution Unit Ms Inga Piterniece	7021376
Privatization Process Division Ms Daina Pruse	7021374
Enterprise Liquidation Division	7021318

Ms Ilona Skadina	
Land Privatization Ms Zinta Grutkovska	7021301
Legal Affairs for Statutory Company Privatization Ms Inta Abakuka	7021366
Lease Buy-out Division Ms Zigrida Gorodnicina	7021362
Legal Affairs for Privatization Ms Maija Laksevica	7021368
Privatization Vouchers Accounting Mr Agris Aldis Rudzitis	7021338
Payment Accounting Division Ms Valda Apele	7021316
Accounting Division Ms Smaida Elerte	7021361

USEFUL GOVERNMENT & BUSINESS CONTACTS

GOVERNMENT	Saeima (Parliament)	Ministry of Foreign Affairs
36 Brivibas iela tel: 7332232 fax: 7286598	16 Jekaba iela tel: 7322938 fax: 7211611	36 Brivibas iela tel: 7223307 fax: 7227755
Ministry of Economy	Ministry of Agriculture	Statistical Committee
55 Brivibas iela tel: 7285304, 7280882	2 Republikas lauk tel: 7327010 fax: 7324512	1 Lacplesa iela tel: 270126 fax: 7830137
Latvian Information Institute	The Latvian Chamber of Commerce and Industry	Latvian Foreign Trade Centre
2 Perses iela tel: 7223540	21 Brivibas iela tel: 7332205 fax: 7820092, 7332276	2 Elizabetes iela tel: 7320619, 7321818, 7322816 fax: 7830035, 7323313
Latvian Development Agency	Latvian Stock Exchange	Dept. of Citizenship and Immigration
2 Perses iela tel: 7283425 fax: 7820458, 7282524	6 Doma lauk tel: 7229449 fax: 7224515	5 Raina bulv tel: 7219181 fax: 7820156
Customs Department	Riga City Council	
1a Valdemara iela	3 Valdemara iela	

tel: 7323858 fax: 7322440	tel: 7320680 fax: 7325439	

LATVIA HOTELS, RIGA

RIGA ACCOMMODATION TIPS

When choosing good accommodation in Riga, please read the following tourist info:
The list of Riga hotels & accommodation in this site includes mainly luxury four stars & five stars hotels in Riga.
An important factor when choosing a good hotel in Riga is hotel location. Many Riga hotels are located near Metro stations in Riga, enabling a very quick and easy travel in Riga.
Before choosing your Riga hotel try checking that your stay in Riga does not cross a national holiday when many tourist attractions are closed. Another point, try avoiding visiting Riga in periods of big Congresses in Riga, in this time it is quite difficult to get a good hotel in Riga at reasonable prices.
Before arrival to Riga please visit Riga hotels web sites, you may sometimes find a cheaper price for your hotel.
Certain hotels in Riga offer a cheaper rate when you stay in Riga in a weekend.
Most good hotels in Riga have an impressing tourist information material, maps and free travel information in various languages for your stay in Riga.
Most of the good hotels in Riga have internet facilities helping you be updated from Riga.

Name	Address	Tel	Fax	Email	Web Site
Ainavas	Peldu St. 23, Riga LV - 1050	371 7814316	371 7814317	reservations@ainavas.lv	www.ainavas.lv
Grand Palace Hotel	Pils 12 Riga, LV-1050	371 704 4000	371 704 4001	grandpalace.reservations@schlossle-hotels.com	www.schlossle-hotels.com
Gutenbergs	Doma laukums 1 Riga, LV-1050	371 7814090	371 7503326	hotel@gutenbergs.lv	www.gutenbergs.lv
Bergs	83/85, Elizabetes Street, Riga, LV-1050	371 777 0900	371 777 0940	hotelbergs@hotelbergs.lv	www.hotelbergs.lv
MAN-TESS	Teatra St. 6 Riga LV-1050	7-216-056	7-821-249	info@mantess.lv	www.mantess.lv
Maritim		706-9000	706-9001	info.rig@maritim.lv	www.maritim.lv
Radisson SAS Daugava Hotel	24 Kugu st. Riga LV-1048	371 706 1111	371 706 1100	Info.Riga@RadissonSAS.com	www.radissonsas.com
Reval Hotel	Elizabetes 55, LV-1010 Riga	371 777 2222	371 777 2221	latvija.sales@revalhotels.com	www.revalhotels.com
Hotel de Rome	Kalku str. 28, Riga, LV 1050	371 7087600	371 7087606	reservation@derome.lv	www.derome.lv
Hotel Centra	1 Audeju St, Riga, LV-1050	371 7226441	371 7503281	hotel@centra.lv	www.centra.lv

SUPPLEMENTS

BUSINESS TRAVEL TO LATVIA

Latvia presents some inconveniences, but few real difficulties for the seasoned business traveler. U.S. citizens do not require visas for stays of up to 90 days in a calendar year. Multiple entry visas agreements exists among Riga and the capital of the other two Baltic states.

There are now numerous restaurants in Riga with first class cuisine and service. Outside Riga, selection and quality of food is much more limited. Supply and diversity of imported food, household supplies, common medications and personal items are exjor hotels, a few quality restaurants and some stores accept credit cards, but it is still mainly a cash economy. Mastercard and Visa are the most widely accepted; Diners Club and American Express are also accepted at the de Rome, Eurolink, Metropole and Radisson hotels and some restaurants and service stations. Budget accommodations, fast-food restaurants, smaller retail establishments and outdoor markets are on a cash-only basis.

A few commercial banks cash traveler's checks or provide cash advances against credit cards; service charges are high. Latvian currency, the lat, may be easily bought or sold at numerous currency exchanges. Outside Riga, travelers should be prepared to pay cash for all expenses. Travelers should also be aware that exchange bureaus will not accept or will charge a fee f o tattelter dirater ilsrecommended for drinking. Imported spring water is widely available at reasonable prices. Food contamination can be a problem in the summer months.

Latvian statutory holidays are New Year's Day (January 1), Good Friday, Easteratvia and between Riga and the capital of the other two Baltic states.

There are now numerous restaurants in Riga with first class cuisine and service. Outside Riga, selection and quality of food is much more limited. Supply and diversity of imported food, household supplies, common medications and personal items are excellent. Unleaded gas is available in Riga and at a number of service stations in the countryside; gasoline contamination is still a problem.

The availability of modern housing is growing, but still quite limited. Securing housing up to Western standards entails leasing and renovating an apartment to suite tenant needs. Despite recent improvement, hot water may not always be available through municipal district heating systems; major apartment renovations should include installation of hot water heaters.

Street crime is relatively high in Riga; travelers should take the same precautions they would visiting an unfamiliar urban center in the U.S. Although drinking water is now free of viruses, it is frequently contaminated by heavy metals from old pipes. Bottled or filtered water is recommended for drinking. Imported spring water is widely available at reasonable prices. Food contamination can be a problem in the summer months.

Latvian statutory holidays are New Year's Day (January 1), Good Friday, Easter Monday, Constitution Day (May 1), Midsummer (June 23-24), Proclamation Day (November 18), Christmas (December 25-26), and New Year's Eve (December 31).

Latvian is the official language; most Latvians speak Russian. English is widely used in government and business and is the most popular West European language. German is also encountered, particularly in establishments catering to the tourist trade.

IMPORTANT FACTS FOR BUSINESS TRAVELER

General Information		Tourists Information		Geography
Area: 64.589 (24.938 sq miles) Population: 2.566.352 (Jan.1,1994) Capital: Riga, Population 889,500 (1992) Major cities: ▪ Daugavpils (127,000) ▪ Liepaja (108,000) ▪ Jelgava (72,000) ▪ Jurmala (60.000) People: 52% Latvians, 34% Russians, 4,5% Byelorussians, 3,5% Ukrainians, 2,3 % Poles. Cultural and historical division: Kurzeme (western part of Latvia), Zemgale (southern part), Vidzeme (middle and northern part), Latgale (eastern part) Highest point: 'Gaizins' - 311.5 metres. Largest lake: Lubans - 82 sq km. Largest river: Daugava - 1020 km (within Latvia 367 km). Woodland: 40% Northern Kurzeme and Northern Vidzeme are most forested areas. Nature preserve areas: Gauja National Park, 5 natural reserves, 11 landscape parks, 189 restricted areas. Average		Can be obtained trough the Latvian Tourists Information Offices: ▪ RIGA 22 Skarnu, LV-1615,tel 371-7-221731, fax 371-7-227680 ▪ JURMALA 42 Jomas, LV-2015, tel 371-2-764493 ▪ SAULKRASTI 12 Ainazu, Riga distr., LV-2160, tel/fax 371-2-951141 ▪ SALACGRIVA 2 Sila, Limbazi distr., LV-4033,tel 371-40-41254 ▪ SIGULDA 15 Raina, Riga distr., LV-2150, tel 371-2-971345 ▪ JEKABPILS 116a Brivibas, LV-5200, tel 371-52-31391, fax 371-52-33335 ▪ TUKUMS 15a Pils, LV-3100, tel 371-31-24451 ▪ LIEPAJA 3 Rigas, LV-3400, tel 371-34-22113 ▪ KULDIGA 5 Pils, LV-3300, tel 371-33-22364 ▪ CESIS 3 Uzvaras ,LV-4100, tel 371-41-22248 ▪ SALDUS 12 Avotu, LV-3800, tel-371-38-		Latvia is situated on the Baltic coast and borders Estonia in the North, Lithuania in the South, the Russian Republic in the East and Byelorussia in the Southeast. The coastal plain is mostly flat, but inland to the east the land is hilly with forests and lakes. A total of 43%of the country is covered by forests, 10% consist of peat bogs, 2-3% of fresh water reservoirs, 40% is used for agriculture and 4% consist of towns, villages and roads. Raznas Lake is the largest in Latvia, total number is 2.300. There are about 12.000 rivers in Latvia, but only 17 are longer than 100 km, the biggest being the River Daugava (1.020 km-the part that flows through the territory of Latvia is 365 km in length). The ports of Riga,Liepaja and Ventspils are ice free during winter. **Holidays and Celebration Days** 1st of January - New Year Day 1st of May - Labor Day,the convocation day of the Constituent Assembly of the Republic of Latvia 1nd Sunday of May - Mother's Day 23rd of June - Ligo Day 24th of June - St.John's Day,the summer solstice 18th of November - The day of proclamation of the

temperature: July +16.9 C, February -4.9 C. Time: GMT +2 (GMT + 3 in summer). Language: Latvian is the official language. It is an Indo-European, non-Slavic and non-Germanic language and is similar only to Lithuanian. Russian, English and German are widely spoken. Religion: Predominantly Protestant (Lutheran) with Roman Catholic in the East of the country. There is also a Russian Orthodox minority. Electricity: 220 volts AC, 50 Hz. European-style 2-pin plugs are in use.		22184 ▪ VENTSPILS 13a Annas, LV-3600, tel 371-36-24777 ▪ LIMBAZI 5 Burtnieku, LV-4000, tel 371-40-23108 ▪ DAUGAVPILS, 46 Gimnazijas, LV-5400, tel 371-54-20950 Student and Youth Travel Information: ▪ Latvian University Tourist Club: 19 Raina bulv., Riga, tel 7223114		Republic of Latvia 25th and 26th of December - New Year Eve **Remembrance Days** 25th of March - Commemoration Day of victims of the communism terror 4th of May - The proclamation day of the Independence Declaration of the Republic of Latvia 9th of May - Memorial Day of victims of the World War 2 14th of June - Commemoration Day of victims of the communism terror 4th of July - Commemoration Day of genocide against Jews 11th of November - Lacplesis Day

SELECTED FINANCIAL INDICATORS

	(in thousands of lats)
ASSETS	683 403
Foreign assets	562 194
Gold and convertible currencies	560 830
Non-convertible currencies	1 364
Domestic credits	107 943
incl. Government	100 392
Other assets	13 266
L I A B I L I T I E S	683 403
Foreign liabilities	124 622
Convertible currencies	124 140
Non-convertible currencies	231

Deposits in lats	251
Lats in circulation	359 353
Domestic deposits	152 077
incl. Government	69 482
incl. bank deposits with the central bank in lats	80 408
Capital and reserves	36 600
Other liabilities	10 751

RIGA STOCK EXCHANGE: KEY INDICATORS

Market capitalisation (at the end of the period, m LVL)	233.01	201.83
Number of sessions (per period)	62	59
Number of listed shares	53	65
Official list	8	10
Second list	24	28
Free list	21	27
Central Market (total turnover, m LVL)	11.83	9.50
Continuous Trading at Variable Prices (turnover, m LVL)	11.21	9.31
Block Trading (turnover, m LVL)	2.02	6.01
Public Offers for Cash (turnover, m LVL)	0.03	-

BASIC TITLES ON LATVIA[2]

Title
Latvia A "Spy" Guide - Strategic Information and Developments
Latvia A Spy" Guide"
Latvia Air Force Handbook
Latvia Air Force Handbook
Latvia Army Weapon Systems Handbook
Latvia Army Weapon Systems Handbook
Latvia Army Weapon Systems Handbook
Latvia Army, National Security and Defense Policy Handbook
Latvia Army, National Security and Defense Policy Handbook
Latvia Banking & Financial Market Handbook
Latvia Banking & Financial Market Handbook

[2] Titles updated annually. Please contact Intl Business Publications, Inc. at ibpusa32gmail.com for the latest ISBN numbers and additional information.

Title
Latvia Business and Investment Opportunities Yearbook
Latvia Business and Investment Opportunities Yearbook
Latvia Business and Investment Opportunities Yearbook Volume 1 Strategic Information and Opportunities
Latvia Business and Investment Opportunities Yearbook Volume 2 Leading Export-Import, Business, Investment Opportunities and Projects
Latvia Business Intelligence Report - Practical Information, Opportunities, Contacts
Latvia Business Intelligence Report - Practical Information, Opportunities, Contacts
Latvia Business Law Handbook - Strategic Information and Basic Laws
Latvia Business Law Handbook - Strategic Information and Basic Laws
Latvia Business Law Handbook - Strategic Information and Basic Laws
Latvia Business Law Handbook - Strategic Information and Basic Laws
Latvia Business Law Handbook Volume 2 Investment and Trade Laws Volume 2 Investment and Trade Laws
Latvia Clothing & Textile Industry Handbook
Latvia Clothing & Textile Industry Handbook
Latvia Company Laws and Regulations Handbook
Latvia Constitution and Citizenship Laws Handbook - Strategic Information and Basic Laws
Latvia Country Study Guide - Strategic Information and Developments
Latvia Country Study Guide - Strategic Information and Developments
Latvia Country Study Guide - Strategic Information and Developments Volume 1 Strategic Information and Developments
Latvia Customs, Trade Regulations and Procedures Handbook
Latvia Customs, Trade Regulations and Procedures Handbook
Latvia Diplomatic Handbook - Strategic Information and Developments
Latvia Diplomatic Handbook - Strategic Information and Developments
Latvia Ecology & Nature Protection Handbook
Latvia Ecology & Nature Protection Handbook
Latvia Ecology & Nature Protection Laws and Regulation Handbook
Latvia Economic & Development Strategy Handbook
Latvia Economic & Development Strategy Handbook
Latvia Education System and Policy Handbook
Latvia Energy Policy, Laws and Regulation Handbook
Latvia Export-Import Trade and Business Directory
Latvia Export-Import Trade and Business Directory
Latvia Foreign Policy and Government Guide
Latvia Foreign Policy and Government Guide
Latvia Government and Business Contacts Handbook
Latvia Government and Business Contacts Handbook
Latvia Immigration Laws and Regulations Handbook - Strategic Information and Basic Laws
Latvia Industrial and Business Directory
Latvia Industrial and Business Directory
Latvia Insolvency (Bankruptcy) Laws and Regulations Handbook - Strategic Information and Basic Laws

Title
Latvia Internet and E-Commerce Investment and Business Guide - Strategic and Practical Information: Regulations and Opportunities
Latvia Internet and E-Commerce Investment and Business Guide - Strategic and Practical Information: Regulations and Opportunities
Latvia Investment & Business Guide
Latvia Investment & Business Guide
Latvia Investment and Business Guide - Strategic and Practical Information
Latvia Investment and Business Guide - Strategic and Practical Information
Latvia Investment and Business Guide Volume 2 Business, Investment Opportunities and Incentives
Latvia Investment and Trade Laws and Regulations Handbook
Latvia Justice System and National Police Handbook
Latvia Justice System and National Police Handbook
Latvia Labor Laws and Regulations Handbook - Strategic Information and Basic Laws
Latvia Land Ownership and Agriculture Laws Handbook
Latvia Medical & Pharmaceutical Industry Handbook
Latvia Medical & Pharmaceutical Industry Handbook
Latvia Mineral & Mining Sector Investment and Business Guide - Strategic and Practical Information
Latvia Mineral & Mining Sector Investment and Business Guide - Strategic and Practical Information
Latvia Mining Laws and Regulations Handbook
Latvia Privatization Programs and Regulations Handbook
Latvia Privatization Programs and Regulations Handbook
Latvia Recent Economic and Political Developments Yearbook
Latvia Recent Economic and Political Developments Yearbook
Latvia Recent Economic and Political Developments Yearbook
Latvia Research & Development Policy Handbook
Latvia Research & Development Policy Handbook
Latvia Research & Development Policy Handbook
Latvia Starting Business (Incorporating) in Latvia Guide
Latvia Starting Business (Incorporating) in....Guide
Latvia Tax Guide
Latvia Tax Guide
Latvia Taxation Laws and Regulations Handbook
Latvia Telecom Laws and Regulations Handbook
Latvia Telecommunication Industry Business Opportunities Handbook
Latvia Telecommunication Industry Business Opportunities Handbook
Latvia Transportation Policy and Regulations Handbook
Latvia: How to Invest, Start and Run Profitable Business in Latvia Guide - Practical Information, Opportunities, Contacts

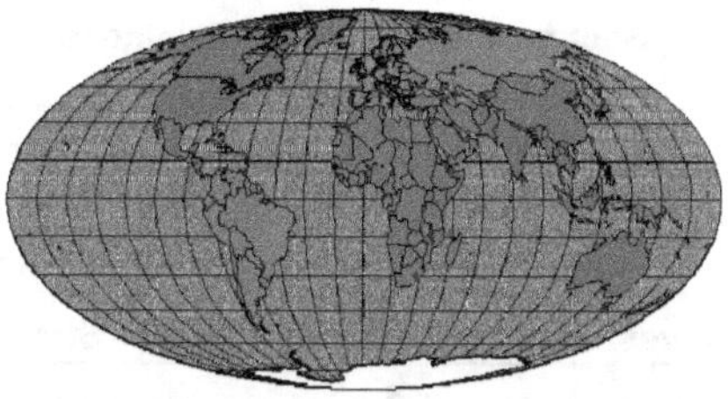

WORLD MINERAL AND MINING SECTOR INVESTMENT AND BUSINESS GUIDES LIBRARY

Price: $149.95 Each

1. Afghanistan Mineral and Mining Sector Investment and Business Guide - Strategic Information and Regulations
2. Albania Mineral and Mining Sector Investment and Business Guide - Strategic Information and Regulations
3. Algeria Mineral and Mining Sector Investment and Business Guide - Strategic Information and Regulations
4. Angola Mineral and Mining Sector Investment and Business Guide - Strategic Information and Regulations
5. Argentina Mineral and Mining Sector Investment and Business Guide - Strategic Information and Regulations
6. Armenia Mineral and Mining Sector Investment and Business Guide - Strategic Information and Regulations
7. Australia Mineral and Mining Sector Investment and Business Guide - Strategic Information and Regulations
8. Austria Mineral and Mining Sector Investment and Business Guide - Strategic Information and Regulations
9. Azerbaijan Mineral and Mining Sector Investment and Business Guide - Strategic Information and Regulations
10. Bahrain Mineral and Mining Sector Investment and Business Guide - Strategic Information and Regulations
11. Bangladesh Mineral and Mining Sector Investment and Business Guide - Strategic Information and Regulations
12. Belarus Mineral and Mining Sector Investment and Business Guide - Strategic Information and Regulations
13. Belgium Mineral and Mining Sector Investment and Business Guide - Strategic Information and Regulations
14. Benin Mineral and Mining Sector Investment and Business Guide - Strategic Information and Regulations
15. Bolivia Mineral and Mining Sector Investment and Business Guide - Strategic Information and Regulations
16. Bosnia and Herzegovina Mineral and Mining Sector Investment and Business Guide - Strategic Information and Regulations
17. Botswana Mineral and Mining Sector Investment and Business Guide - Strategic Information and Regulations
18. Brazil Mineral and Mining Sector Investment and Business Guide - Strategic Information and Regulations
19. Brunei Mineral and Mining Sector Investment and Business Guide - Strategic Information and Regulations
20. Bulgaria Mineral and Mining Sector Investment and Business Guide - Strategic Information and Regulations
21. Burkina Faso Mineral and Mining Sector Investment and Business Guide - Strategic Information and Regulations
22. Burundi Mineral and Mining Sector Investment and Business Guide - Strategic Information and Regulations
23. Cambodia Mineral and Mining Sector Investment and Business Guide - Strategic Information and Regulations
24. Cameroon Mineral and Mining Sector Investment and Business Guide - Strategic Information and Regulations
25. Canada Mineral and Mining Sector Investment and Business Guide - Strategic Information and Regulations
26. Cape Verde Mineral and Mining Sector Investment and Business Guide - Strategic Information and

Regulations
27. Cayman Islands Mineral and Mining Sector Investment and Business Guide - Strategic Information and Regulations
28. Central African Republic Mineral and Mining Sector Investment and Business Guide - Strategic Information and Regulations
29. Chad Mineral and Mining Sector Investment and Business Guide - Strategic Information and Regulations
30. Chile Mineral and Mining Sector Investment and Business Guide - Strategic Information and Regulations
31. China Mineral and Mining Sector Investment and Business Guide - Strategic Information and Regulations
32. Colombia Mineral and Mining Sector Investment and Business Guide - Strategic Information and Regulations
33. Comoros Mineral and Mining Sector Investment and Business Guide - Strategic Information and Regulations
34. Congo Mineral and Mining Sector Investment and Business Guide - Strategic Information and Regulations
35. Congo, Dem. Republic Mineral and Mining Sector Investment and Business Guide - Strategic Information and Regulations
36. Cook Islands Mineral and Mining Sector Investment and Business Guide - Strategic Information and Regulations
37. Costa Rica Mineral and Mining Sector Investment and Business Guide - Strategic Information and Regulations
38. Cote d'Ivoire Mineral and Mining Sector Investment and Business Guide - Strategic Information and Regulations
39. Croatia Mineral and Mining Sector Investment and Business Guide - Strategic Information and Regulations
40. Cuba Mineral and Mining Sector Investment and Business Guide - Strategic Information and Regulations
41. Czech Republic Mineral and Mining Sector Investment and Business Guide - Strategic Information and Regulations
42. Denmark Mineral and Mining Sector Investment and Business Guide - Strategic Information and Regulations
43. Djibouti Mineral and Mining Sector Investment and Business Guide - Strategic Information and Regulations
44. Dominican Republic Mineral and Mining Sector Investment and Business Guide - Strategic Information and Regulations
45. Dubai Mineral and Mining Sector Investment and Business Guide - Strategic Information and Regulations
46. Ecuador Mineral and Mining Sector Investment and Business Guide - Strategic Information and Regulations
47. Egypt Mineral and Mining Sector Investment and Business Guide - Strategic Information and Regulations
48. El Salvador Mineral and Mining Sector Investment and Business Guide - Strategic Information and Regulations
49. Equatorial Guinea Mineral and Mining Sector Investment and Business Guide - Strategic Information and Regulations
50. Eritrea Mineral and Mining Sector Investment and Business Guide - Strategic Information and Regulations
51. Estonia Mineral and Mining Sector Investment and Business Guide - Strategic Information and Regulations
52. Ethiopia Mineral and Mining Sector Investment and Business Guide - Strategic Information and Regulations
53. Fiji Mineral and Mining Sector Investment and Business Guide - Strategic Information and Regulations
54. Finland Mineral and Mining Sector Investment and Business Guide - Strategic Information and Regulations
55. France Mineral and Mining Sector Investment and Business Guide - Strategic Information and Regulations
56. Gabon Mineral and Mining Sector Investment and Business Guide - Strategic Information and Regulations
57. Gambia Mineral and Mining Sector Investment and Business Guide - Strategic Information and Regulations
58. Georgia Mineral and Mining Sector Investment and Business Guide - Strategic Information and Regulations
59. Germany Mineral and Mining Sector Investment and Business Guide - Strategic Information and Regulations
60. Ghana Mineral and Mining Sector Investment and Business Guide - Strategic Information and Regulations
61. Greece Mineral and Mining Sector Investment and Business Guide - Strategic Information and Regulations
62. Greenland Mineral and Mining Sector Investment and Business Guide - Strategic Information and Regulations

63. Guatemala Mineral and Mining Sector Investment and Business Guide - Strategic Information and Regulations
64. Guinea Mineral and Mining Sector Investment and Business Guide - Strategic Information and Regulations
65. Guinea-Bissau Mineral and Mining Sector Investment and Business Guide - Strategic Information and Regulations
66. Guyana Mineral and Mining Sector Investment and Business Guide - Strategic Information and Regulations
67. Haiti Mineral and Mining Sector Investment and Business Guide - Strategic Information and Regulations
68. Honduras Mineral and Mining Sector Investment and Business Guide - Strategic Information and Regulations
69. Hungary Mineral and Mining Sector Investment and Business Guide - Strategic Information and Regulations
70. Iceland Mineral and Mining Sector Investment and Business Guide - Strategic Information and Regulations
71. India Mineral and Mining Sector Investment and Business Guide - Strategic Information and Regulations
72. Indonesia Mineral and Mining Sector Investment and Business Guide - Strategic Information and Regulations
73. Iran Mineral and Mining Sector Investment and Business Guide - Strategic Information and Regulations
74. Iraq Mineral and Mining Sector Investment and Business Guide - Strategic Information and Regulations
75. Ireland Mineral and Mining Sector Investment and Business Guide - Strategic Information and Regulations
76. Israel Mineral and Mining Sector Investment and Business Guide - Strategic Information and Regulations
77. Italy Mineral and Mining Sector Investment and Business Guide - Strategic Information and Regulations
78. Jamaica Mineral and Mining Sector Investment and Business Guide - Strategic Information and Regulations
79. Japan Mineral and Mining Sector Investment and Business Guide - Strategic Information and Regulations
80. Jordan Mineral and Mining Sector Investment and Business Guide - Strategic Information and Regulations
81. Kazakhstan Mineral and Mining Sector Investment and Business Guide - Strategic Information and Regulations
82. Kenya Mineral and Mining Sector Investment and Business Guide - Strategic Information and Regulations
83. Korea, South Mineral and Mining Sector Investment and Business Guide - Strategic Information and Regulations
84. Kuwait Mineral and Mining Sector Investment and Business Guide - Strategic Information and Regulations
85. Kyrgyzstan Mineral and Mining Sector Investment and Business Guide - Strategic Information and Regulations
86. Laos Mineral and Mining Sector Investment and Business Guide - Strategic Information and Regulations
87. Latvia Mineral and Mining Sector Investment and Business Guide - Strategic Information and Regulations
88. Lesotho Mineral and Mining Sector Investment and Business Guide - Strategic Information and Regulations
89. Liberia Mineral and Mining Sector Investment and Business Guide - Strategic Information and Regulations
90. Libya Mineral and Mining Sector Investment and Business Guide - Strategic Information and Regulations
91. Lithuania Mineral and Mining Sector Investment and Business Guide - Strategic Information and Regulations
92. Macedonia Republic Mineral and Mining Sector Investment and Business Guide - Strategic Information and Regulations
93. Madagascar Mineral and Mining Sector Investment and Business Guide - Strategic Information and Regulations
94. Malawi Mineral and Mining Sector Investment and Business Guide - Strategic Information and Regulations
95. Malaysia Mineral and Mining Sector Investment and Business Guide - Strategic Information and Regulations
96. Mali Mineral and Mining Sector Investment and Business Guide - Strategic Information and Regulations
97. Mauritania Mineral and Mining Sector Investment and Business Guide - Strategic Information and Regulations
98. Mauritius Mineral and Mining Sector Investment and Business Guide - Strategic Information and Regulations
99. Mexico Mineral and Mining Sector Investment and Business Guide - Strategic Information and Regulations

100. Moldova Mineral and Mining Sector Investment and Business Guide - Strategic Information and Regulations

101. Mongolia Mineral and Mining Sector Investment and Business Guide - Strategic Information and Regulations

102. Morocco Mineral and Mining Sector Investment and Business Guide - Strategic Information and Regulations

103. Mozambique Mineral and Mining Sector Investment and Business Guide - Strategic Information and Regulations

104. Myanmar Mineral and Mining Sector Investment and Business Guide - Strategic Information and Regulations

105. Namibia Mineral and Mining Sector Investment and Business Guide - Strategic Information and Regulations

106. Nepal Mineral and Mining Sector Investment and Business Guide - Strategic Information and Regulations

107. Netherlands Mineral and Mining Sector Investment and Business Guide - Strategic Information and Regulations

108. New Zealand Mineral and Mining Sector Investment and Business Guide - Strategic Information and Regulations

109. Nicaragua Mineral and Mining Sector Investment and Business Guide - Strategic Information and Regulations

110. Niger Mineral and Mining Sector Investment and Business Guide - Strategic Information and Regulations

111. Nigeria Mineral and Mining Sector Investment and Business Guide - Strategic Information and Regulations

112. Norway Mineral and Mining Sector Investment and Business Guide - Strategic Information and Regulations

113. Oman Mineral and Mining Sector Investment and Business Guide - Strategic Information and Regulations

114. Pakistan Mineral and Mining Sector Investment and Business Guide - Strategic Information and Regulations

115. Papua New Guinea Mineral and Mining Sector Investment and Business Guide - Strategic Information and Regulations

116. Paraguay Mineral and Mining Sector Investment and Business Guide - Strategic Information and Regulations

117. Peru Mineral and Mining Sector Investment and Business Guide - Strategic Information and Regulations

118. Philippines Mineral and Mining Sector Investment and Business Guide - Strategic Information and Regulations

119. Poland Mineral and Mining Sector Investment and Business Guide - Strategic Information and Regulations

120. Portugal Mineral and Mining Sector Investment and Business Guide - Strategic Information and Regulations

121. Qatar Mineral and Mining Sector Investment and Business Guide - Strategic Information and Regulations

122. Romania Mineral and Mining Sector Investment and Business Guide - Strategic Information and Regulations

123. Russia Mineral and Mining Sector Investment and Business Guide - Strategic Information and Regulations

124. Rwanda Mineral and Mining Sector Investment and Business Guide - Strategic Information and Regulations

125. Sao Tome and Principe Mineral and Mining Sector Investment and Business Guide - Strategic Information and Regulations

126. Saudi Arabia Mineral and Mining Sector Investment and Business Guide - Strategic Information and Regulations

127. Senegal Mineral and Mining Sector Investment and Business Guide - Strategic Information and Regulations

128. Serbia Mineral and Mining Sector Investment and Business Guide - Strategic Information and Regulations

129. Sierra Leone Mineral and Mining Sector Investment and Business Guide - Strategic Information and Regulations

130. Slovakia Mineral and Mining Sector Investment and Business Guide - Strategic Information and Regulations

131. Slovenia Mineral and Mining Sector Investment and Business Guide - Strategic Information and Regulations

132. Somalia Mineral and Mining Sector Investment and Business Guide - Strategic Information and Regulations

133. South Africa Mineral and Mining Sector Investment and Business Guide - Strategic Information and Regulations

134. Spain Mineral and Mining Sector Investment and Business Guide - Strategic Information and Regulations

135. Sri Lanka Mineral and Mining Sector Investment and Business Guide - Strategic Information and Regulations

136. Sudan Mineral and Mining Sector Investment and Business Guide - Strategic Information and Regulations

137. Suriname Mineral and Mining Sector Investment and Business Guide - Strategic Information and Regulations
138. Swaziland Mineral and Mining Sector Investment and Business Guide - Strategic Information and Regulations
139. Sweden Mineral and Mining Sector Investment and Business Guide - Strategic Information and Regulations
140. Syria Mineral and Mining Sector Investment and Business Guide - Strategic Information and Regulations
141. Taiwan Mineral and Mining Sector Investment and Business Guide - Strategic Information and Regulations
142. Tajikistan Mineral and Mining Sector Investment and Business Guide - Strategic Information and Regulations
143. Tanzania Mineral and Mining Sector Investment and Business Guide - Strategic Information and Regulations
144. Thailand Mineral and Mining Sector Investment and Business Guide - Strategic Information and Regulations
145. Togo Mineral and Mining Sector Investment and Business Guide - Strategic Information and Regulations
146. Trinidad and Tobago Mineral and Mining Sector Investment and Business Guide - Strategic Information and Regulations
147. Tunisia Mineral and Mining Sector Investment and Business Guide - Strategic Information and Regulations
148. Turkey Mineral and Mining Sector Investment and Business Guide - Strategic Information and Regulations
149. Turkmenistan Mineral and Mining Sector Investment and Business Guide - Strategic Information and Regulations
150. Uganda Mineral and Mining Sector Investment and Business Guide - Strategic Information and Regulations
151. Ukraine Mineral and Mining Sector Investment and Business Guide - Strategic Information and Regulations
152. United Arab Emirates Mineral and Mining Sector Investment and Business Guide - Strategic Information and Regulations
153. United Kingdom Mineral and Mining Sector Investment and Business Guide - Strategic Information and Regulations
154. United States Mineral and Mining Sector Investment and Business Guide - Strategic Information and Regulations
155. Uruguay Mineral and Mining Sector Investment and Business Guide - Strategic Information and Regulations
156. Uzbekistan Mineral and Mining Sector Investment and Business Guide - Strategic Information and Regulations
157. Venezuela Mineral and Mining Sector Investment and Business Guide - Strategic Information and Regulations
158. Vietnam Mineral and Mining Sector Investment and Business Guide - Strategic Information and Regulations
159. Yemen Mineral and Mining Sector Investment and Business Guide - Strategic Information and Regulations
160. Zambia Mineral and Mining Sector Investment and Business Guide - Strategic Information and Regulations
161. Zimbabwe Mineral and Mining Sector Investment and Business Guide - Strategic Information and Regulations

WORLD INVESTMENT AND BUSINESS GUIDE LIBRARY

Ultimate guides for business and investment operations in the country.

Price: $99 each

1. Afghanistan Investment and Business Guide
2. Aland Investment and Business Guide
3. Albania Investment and Business Guide
4. Algeria Investment and Business Guide
5. Andorra Investment and Business Guide
6. Angola Investment and Business Guide
7. Anguilla Investment and Business Guide
8. Antigua and Barbuda Investment and Business Guide
9. Antilles (Netherlands) Investment and Business Guide
10. Argentina Investment and Business Guide
11. Armenia Investment and Business Guide
12. Aruba Investment and Business Guide
13. Australia Investment and Business Guide
14. Austria Investment and Business Guide
15. Azerbaijan Investment and Business Guide
16. Bahamas Investment and Business Guide
17. Bahrain Investment and Business Guide
18. Bangladesh Investment and Business Guide
19. Barbados Investment and Business Guide
20. Belarus Investment and Business Guide
21. Belgium Investment and Business Guide
22. Belize Investment and Business Guide
23. Benin Investment and Business Guide
24. Bermuda Investment and Business Guide
25. Bhutan Investment and Business Guide
26. Bolivia Investment and Business Guide
27. Bosnia and Herzegovina Investment and Business Guide
28. Botswana Investment and Business Guide
29. Brazil Investment and Business Guide
30. Brunei Investment and Business Guide
31. Bulgaria Investment and Business Guide
32. Burkina Faso Investment and Business Guide
33. Burundi Investment and Business Guide
34. Cambodia Investment and Business Guide
35. Cameroon Investment and Business Guide
36. Canada Investment and Business Guide
37. Cape Verde Investment and Business Guide

38.	Cayman Islands Investment and Business Guide
39.	Central African Republic Investment and Business Guide
40.	Chad Investment and Business Guide
41.	Chile Investment and Business Guide
42.	China Investment and Business Guide
43.	Colombia Investment and Business Guide
44.	Comoros Investment and Business Guide
45.	Congo Investment and Business Guide
46.	Congo, Democratic Republic Investment and Business Guide
47.	Cook Islands Investment and Business Guide
48.	Costa Rica Investment and Business Guide
49.	Cote d'Ivoire Investment and Business Guide
50.	Croatia Investment and Business Guide
51.	Cuba Investment and Business Guide
52.	Cyprus Investment and Business Guide
53.	Czech Republic Investment and Business Guide
54.	Denmark Investment and Business Guide
55.	Djibouti Investment and Business Guide
56.	Dominica Investment and Business Guide
57.	Dominican Republic Investment and Business Guide
58.	Ecuador Investment and Business Guide
59.	Egypt Investment and Business Guide
60.	El Salvador Investment and Business Guide
61.	Equatorial Guinea Investment and Business Guide
62.	Eritrea Investment and Business Guide
63.	Estonia Investment and Business Guide
64.	Ethiopia Investment and Business Guide
65.	Falkland Islands Investment and Business Guide
66.	Faroes Islands Investment and Business Guide
67.	Fiji Investment and Business Guide
68.	Finland Investment and Business Guide
69.	France Investment and Business Guide
70.	Gabon Investment and Business Guide
71.	Gambia Investment and Business Guide
72.	Georgia Investment and Business Guide
73.	Germany Investment and Business Guide
74.	Ghana Investment and Business Guide
75.	Gibraltar Investment and Business Guide
76.	Greece Investment and Business Guide
77.	Greenland Investment and Business Guide
78.	Grenada Investment and Business Guide
79.	Guam Investment and Business Guide
80.	Guatemala Investment and Business Guide
81.	Guernsey Investment and Business Guide
82.	Guinea Investment and Business Guide
83.	Guinea-Bissau Investment and Business Guide
84.	Guyana Investment and Business Guide
85.	Haiti Investment and Business Guide
86.	Honduras Investment and Business Guide
87.	Hungary Investment and Business Guide
88.	Iceland Investment and Business Guide

89. India Investment and Business Guide
90. Indonesia Investment and Business Guide
91. Iran Investment and Business Guide
92. Iraq Investment and Business Guide
93. Ireland Investment and Business Guide
94. Israel Investment and Business Guide
95. Italy Investment and Business Guide
96. Jamaica Investment and Business Guide
97. Japan Investment and Business Guide
98. Jersey Investment and Business Guide
99. Jordan Investment and Business Guide
100. Kazakhstan Investment and Business Guide
101. Kenya Investment and Business Guide
102. Kiribati Investment and Business Guide
103. Korea, North Investment and Business Guide
104. Korea, South Investment and Business Guide
105. Kosovo Investment and Business Guide
106. Kurdistan Investment and Business Guide
107. Kuwait Investment and Business Guide
108. Kyrgyzstan Investment and Business Guide
109. Laos Investment and Business Guide
110. Latvia Investment and Business Guide
111. Lebanon Investment and Business Guide
112. Lesotho Investment and Business Guide
113. Liberia Investment and Business Guide
114. Libya Investment and Business Guide
115. Liechtenstein Investment and Business Guide
116. Lithuania Investment and Business Guide
117. Luxembourg Investment and Business Guide
118. Macao Investment and Business Guide
119. Macedonia Investment and Business Guide
120. Madagascar Investment and Business Guide
121. Madeira Investment and Business Guide
122. Malawi Investment and Business Guide
123. Malaysia Investment and Business Guide
124. Maldives Investment and Business Guide
125. Mali Investment and Business Guide
126. Malta Investment and Business Guide
127. Man Investment and Business Guide
128. Marshall Islands Investment and Business Guide
129. Mauritania Investment and Business Guide
130. Mauritius Investment and Business Guide
131. Mayotte Investment and Business Guide
132. Mexico Investment and Business Guide
133. Micronesia Investment and Business Guide
134. Moldova Investment and Business Guide
135. Monaco Investment and Business Guide
136. Mongolia Investment and Business Guide
137. Monserrat Investment and Business Guide
138. Morocco Investment and Business Guide
139. Mozambique Investment and Business Guide

140. Myanmar Investment and Business Guide
141. Namibia Investment and Business Guide
142. Nauru Investment and Business Guide
143. Nepal Investment and Business Guide
144. Netherlands Investment and Business Guide
145. New Caledonia Investment and Business Guide
146. New Zealand Investment and Business Guide
147. Nicaragua Investment and Business Guide
148. Niger Investment and Business Guide
149. Nigeria Investment and Business Guide
150. Niue Investment and Business Guide
151. Northern Mariana Islands Investment and Business Guide
152. Norway Investment and Business Guide
153. Oman Investment and Business Guide
154. Pakistan Investment and Business Guide
155. Palau Investment and Business Guide
156. Palestine (West Bank & Gaza) Investment and Business Guide
157. Panama Investment and Business Guide
158. Papua New Guinea Investment and Business Guide
159. Paraguay Investment and Business Guide
160. Peru Investment and Business Guide
161. Philippines Investment and Business Guide
162. Pitcairn Islands Investment and Business Guide
163. Poland Investment and Business Guide
164. Polynesia French Investment and Business Guide
165. Portugal Investment and Business Guide
166. Qatar Investment and Business Guide
167. Romania Investment and Business Guide
168. Russia Investment and Business Guide
169. Rwanda Investment and Business Guide
170. Saint Kitts and Nevis Investment and Business Guide
171. Saint Lucia Investment and Business Guide
172. Saint Vincent and The Grenadines Investment and Business Guide
173. Samoa (American) A Investment and Business Guide
174. Samoa (Western) Investment and Business Guide
175. San Marino Investment and Business Guide
176. Sao Tome and Principe Investment and Business Guide
177. Saudi Arabia Investment and Business Guide
178. Scotland Investment and Business Guide
179. Senegal Investment and Business Guide
180. Serbia Investment and Business Guide
181. Seychelles Investment and Business Guide
182. Sierra Leone Investment and Business Guide
183. Singapore Investment and Business Guide
184. Slovakia Investment and Business Guide
185. Slovenia Investment and Business Guide
186. Solomon Islands Investment and Business Guide
187. Somalia Investment and Business Guide
188. South Africa Investment and Business Guide
189. Spain Investment and Business Guide
190. Sri Lanka Investment and Business Guide

191. St. Helena Investment and Business Guide
192. St. Pierre & Miquelon Investment and Business Guide
193. Sudan Investment and Business Guide
194. Sudan South Investment and Business Guide
195. Suriname Investment and Business Guide
196. Swaziland Investment and Business Guide
197. Sweden Investment and Business Guide
198. Switzerland Investment and Business Guide
199. Syria Investment and Business Guide
200. Taiwan Investment and Business Guide
201. Tajikistan Investment and Business Guide
202. Tanzania Investment and Business Guide
203. Thailand Investment and Business Guide
204. Togo Investment and Business Guide
205. Tonga Investment and Business Guide
206. Trinidad and Tobago Investment and Business Guide
207. Tunisia Investment and Business Guide
208. Turkey Investment and Business Guide
209. Turkmenistan Investment and Business Guide
210. Turks & Caicos Investment and Business Guide
211. Tuvalu Investment and Business Guide
212. Uganda Investment and Business Guide
213. Ukraine Investment and Business Guide
214. United Arab Emirates Investment and Business Guide
215. United Kingdom Investment and Business Guide
216. United States Investment and Business Guide
217. Uruguay Investment and Business Guide
218. Uzbekistan Investment and Business Guide
219. Vanuatu Investment and Business Guide
220. Vatican City Investment and Business Guide
221. Venezuela Investment and Business Guide
222. Vietnam Investment and Business Guide
223. Virgin Islands, British Investment and Business Guide
224. Wake Atoll Investment and Business Guide
225. Wallis & Futuna Investment and Business Guide
226. Western Sahara Investment and Business Guide
227. Yemen Investment and Business Guide
228. Zambia Investment and Business Guide
229. Zimbabwe Investment and Business Guide

www.ingramcontent.com/pod-product-compliance
Lightning Source LLC
LaVergne TN
LVHW080036210926
848481LV00011B/3207
* 9 7 8 1 4 3 3 0 2 9 3 2 5 *